Federalism and Democracy
in Latin America

Federalism

AND

Democracy

IN

Latin America

Edited by Edward L. Gibson

The Johns Hopkins University Press

Baltimore and London

The Johns Hopkins University Press

2715 North Charles Street

Baltimore, Maryland 21218-4363

www.press.jhu.edu

Library of Congress Cataloging-in-Publication Data

Federalism and democracy in Latin America / edited by Edward L. Gibson.

  p. cm.

Includes bibliographical references and index.

  ISBN 0-8018-7423-8 (cloth)—ISBN 0-8018-7424-6 (pbk)

  1. Federal government—Latin America.   2. Democracy—Latin America.

  3. Latin America—Politics and government—1980–   I. Gibson, Edward L.

JL956 S8F43 2004

320.4′049′098—dc21

2003006217

A catalog record for this book is available from the British Library.

For Judy

Pasaron volando nuestros primeros veinte años

Contents

Preface and Acknowledgments

This edited volume is an exploration into the dynamics of federalism and its impact on politics and the practice of democracy. Through comparative essays and theoretically framed studies of Latin American cases, the book casts new light on old debates and proposes new agendas for the comparative study of federalism. It also provides a rare comparative examination of the operation of federalism in Latin America, and of the complex relationships between federal institutions and democratic change in the region.

The decision to collaborate on an edited volume was made at a June 1999 conference in Mexico City at the Centro de Investigación y Docencia Económicas (CIDE). The conference participants were brought together by common interests in the causal effects of federalism on Latin American politics and by the insights these could provide for general theories about federalism. Several of us at the Mexico conference had come together earlier at a June 1997 conference on "Democracy, Nationalism, and Federalism" organized by Alfred Stepan at All Souls College, Oxford University, and have since organized collaborative projects and conference panels in other venues. It is my hope that the conversations that link the chapters of this volume provide our readers with a taste of the many discussions that enriched and enlivened our professional interactions over the years.

Beyond the volume's contributors, I am indebted to several individuals and institutions that provided intellectual and material support during the years of writing, editing, and discussion. My heartfelt thanks go to Teri L. Caraway, today an assistant professor of political science at the University of Minnesota. As my research assistant, Teri piloted the project into safe harbor during the final year of editing and compilation of the book's chapters. I became utterly dependent on her for her lucid editing skills, her analytical mind, and her constant reminders to an overwhelmed and vacillating editor to gain perspective and complete the project "one task at a time." I am also indebted to Blanca Heredia and Carlos Elizondo, Academic Dean and President of CIDE, respectively, for graciously offering financial and logistical support for the 1999 Mexico City conference at CIDE's pleasant campus, and for their hospitality during my year at CIDE as visiting professor. At Northwestern I was the fortunate recipient of comments and advice from such colleagues as Kathleen Thelen, Peter Swenson, Ben Ross Schneider, Kenneth Janda, Michael Hanchard, Jeffrey Winters, and Tyler Colman. I am also thankful to Al Montero, Juan Linz, Hector Schamis, Gerardo Munck, Kent Eaton, Ignacio Marván, Nancy Bermeo, Steven Solnick, Allyson Lucinda Benton, María Amparo Casar, Joy Langston, Benito Nacif, Enrique Zuleta Puceiro, Natalio Botana, and Jorge Domínguez for help and comments along the way. This project would not have been possible without the financial support of the National Science Foundation, which through its "Faculty Early Career Development Program (CAREER)" allowed me to finance numerous activities associated with this project over a five-year period. Northwestern University's Weinberg College of Arts and Sciences and the Center for International and Comparative Studies also provided vital financial and logistical support. Finally, I would like to thank my wife, Judith S. Gibson, for the inspiration, love, and support that sustained me through this and so many other endeavors.

Federalism and Democracy
in Latin America

CHAPTER 1

Federalism and Democracy

Theoretical Connections and Cautionary Insights

—EDWARD L. GIBSON

"This is the age of federalism." So wrote William Riker (1964) in his landmark book on the origins and evolution of federal systems. At one level he was right. In the 1950s and 1960s most of the large and important countries of the world were governed by federal constitutions. Both superpowers locked in their struggle for global hegemony were federal republics. India, the world's largest democracy, was a federal republic. In Latin America the "ABRAMEX" triad of regional hegemons—Argentina, Brazil, and Mexico—were federal republics as well. Thus, federalism was indeed a constitutional order that belonged to governments controlling the largest share of the planet's populations and resources. And it was, as Riker well remarked, the most important political formula for bringing heterogeneous populations spread across large landmasses under a single form of government.

However, from the perspective of the early twenty-first century, Riker's proclamation seems premature. On paper, Riker's age may well have been one of federal

1

constitutions, but in the realms of political action and political power, the world was far less "federalized" than it is today. The United States, which served as model to Riker's theory, was a federal country in name and in practice, but to most people living in the developing world the middle of the twentieth century was still an age of centralization, in which leaders and revolutionaries built national states that sought to bring wide-scale social, political, and economic change to their countries. In many cases, from Mexico and Venezuela to the Soviet Union, the existence of federal constitutions were mere formalities, or at best institutional devices that effectively linked territories together under a formal federal structure whose constituent units were overawed by the centralizing national state. In others, from Brazil to Yugoslavia, central and subnational authorities were locked in permanently unresolved struggles for hegemony. To much of the federal world, therefore, the formal jurisdictional divisions, territorially determined identities, and subnational political structures that embodied the federal political order coexisted with practices and institutions that tended to keep the spheres of independence of the federations' constituent units to a minimum.

Today we may not have a significantly larger number of federal countries in the world, but there is little question that the institutional features of federalism have a greater impact on the daily lives of people living in federal countries in the early years of the twenty-first century than they did in the middle years of the twentieth century. Today *federalization* has meant a process of political decentralization that has given greater protagonism to subnational governments and political actors, has often heightened the importance of territorial representation (as opposed to population representation) in national political institutions, and has redistributed power and resources between levels of government. In federal countries this has led to the activation of institutional features, particularly those related to the empowerment and representation of territorially based actors, that were less visible under centralization. This has meant that the formal existence of dual levels of government characteristic of federal systems has become increasingly a matter of actual practice in many of the world's federal systems. If the mid–twentieth century was indeed the "age of federalism," then it might be said that in the early twenty-first century we find ourselves in an epoch of federal practice.

The revival of federalism has generated considerable interest in how federal institutions shape politics, policy making, and the quality of life of those living in federal systems. These are concerns that brought the present volume's authors together in this collaborative endeavor. The chapters that follow make a number of theoretical and empirical contributions. Theoretically, they explore the extent to which federal institutions matter for politics, policy making, and democratic practice. They also offer conceptual approaches for studying federal systems, their origins, and their internal dynamics.

The volume's contributors have also sought to shed light on the internal dynamics of a constitutional order that governs a majority of Latin America's population. Only four countries in Latin America are formally federal, but they comprise 65 percent of the region's population. The region's three largest countries, Brazil, Mexico, and Argentina, have federal constitutions, as does Venezuela. Substantively, therefore, federalism is an important topic of study, and this volume aims to provide a better understanding of the internal political dynamics of its federally organized polities.

The volume also advances research agendas toward relatively unexplored dimensions of the politics of democratization in the region. The manifold political processes we tend to lump under the "democratization" label have involved well-analyzed struggles along different dimensions of conflict. These have included struggles between social classes, partisan forces, social movements, and economic interests. Less well analyzed have been the geographic dimensions of conflict—conflict between center and periphery, conflict between levels of government, and conflict between regionally organized collective actors. These dimensions of conflict, until now seen as hopelessly old-fashioned topics of study, have now been cast back into the limelight, as new realities emerge that defy prior explanatory frameworks and push politics in unexpected directions.

The rediscovery in recent years of the "subnational" in comparative politics, and of the "politics of decentralization" in the field of political economy, represent important new scholarly agendas in the comparative study of Latin American politics.[1] Noticeably absent, however, have been parallel agendas on the comparative study of federalism in the region and the interactions between federalism and democratization.[2] Recent political developments make a compelling case for such agendas, for federalism has become an important strand in the unfolding story of democratization in the region.

As a collection of separately authored essays, this book develops a variety of themes and perspectives on federalism and territorial politics more broadly. It is also not without debate and disagreement between the authors. However, the volume is a collaborative effort in which the authors have met with one another in various opportunities and forums and have converged around a number of overarching questions. Their theoretically driven explorations into the dynamics of federalism in Latin America shed light on questions about federalism that go beyond the specificities of the Latin American cases. Before outlining the contours of the debate and insights of the volume's chapters, it might be useful to list some of the overarching questions linking the contributions to this volume:

- How do we define and measure federalism, and how do we study it comparatively?
- Does federalism matter for politics and public policy?
- What explains the origins of federal systems, and why should this matter?
- What is the relationship between federalism and democracy (especially in regard to political representation, democratic transition processes, and the operation of democratic government)?
- What is the relationship between federalism and party politics?
- Does federalism have an impact on public policy and the flow of economic resources within the federation?
- What are the determinants of change in federal systems?
- How can we understand Latin American federalism in a broader global perspective?

Federalism: Definitions

Before continuing with a discussion of the issues addressed by this book, it might be helpful to clarify the concept of "federalism" that is employed by the authors in this volume. Definitions and usages of "federalism" abound in the social sciences and policy-oriented fields, and there is thus an understandable confusion about what, in fact, the term "federalism" denotes in the real world. Two general conceptualizations have dominated the literature. These can be labeled as the "federalism as decentralization" school and the "federalism as alliance" school. Under the first conceptualization, "federalism" can be understood as a set of practices in which the distribution of political and economic activities is spatially decentralized in any given national territory. Thus, the literatures on "fiscal federalism" or "market-preserving federalism" stress the decentralization of political and economic authority in their conceptualizations, regardless of whether these are constitutionally determined. In this approach, "federalism" is more a synonym for decentralization than a term that denotes a particular political or constitutional order.

The "federalism as alliance" school stays true to the Latin meaning of the term *foedus,* which signifies "league, covenant, or alliance" (Elazar 1991, 115; Glassner 1996, xv). This conceptualization encompasses a wide variety of political organization forms. As Daniel Elazar (1991, xv) writes, "federal principles are concerned with the combination of self-rule and shared rule. In the broadest sense, federalism involves the linkage of individuals, groups, and polities in lasting but limited union, in such a way as to provide for the energetic pursuit of common ends while maintaining the respective integrities of all parties. . . . In the twentieth century it has come to be particularly useful for its flexibility when it comes to translating principles into political systems." What links all these possible forms of political organization, then, is the combination of the principles of unity and internal autonomy. The twentieth-century "federal idea" has thus found expression in a variety of political organizations, ranging from confederal arrangements between sovereign countries (the European Union, for example), to federations (e.g., the United States of America, Russia, or Brazil), or to condominia, where small relatively autonomous territories are ruled jointly by larger powers.[3]

The "federalism as alliance" definition thus captures an important common element in political systems involving shared rule between constituent governments. However, its broad denotative scope still leaves problems of operationalization. While some may be interested in the entire genus of federalisms, the contributors to this volume are focused on a particular species that is national, rather than international, and is also constitutionally specified. This species of federalism, whether it is labeled "federation" (Watts, Elazar), "centralized federalism" (Riker), or just plain "federalism," can be defined as *a national polity with dual (or multiple) levels of government, each exercising exclusive authority over constitutionally determined policy areas, but in which only one level of government—the central government—is internationally sovereign.* This definition builds upon various definitions in the literature that stress the fact of two governments ruling over the same territory as the defining characteristic. The stress on international sovereignty for the national level of government sharpens the distinction between federalism as a constitutional order for the nation-state and other political forms often grouped under the term "federalism."

The levels of government of a federal system are territorially defined and are always divided between a central government with national jurisdiction and subnational governments (e.g., "states" or "provinces") with jurisdiction over delimited areas of the union.[4] The division of powers between levels of government varies by constitutional design or political practice. However, as Robert Dahl puts it, it results in a political arrangement in which "some matters are exclusively within the competence of certain local units—cantons, states, provinces—and are constitutionally beyond the scope of the authority of the national government; and where certain other matters are constitutionally outside the scope and authority of the smaller units" (Dahl 1986, 114). This form of government, first created by the founders of the United States of America and subsequently adopted in Latin America and elsewhere, "makes two sovereignties abide in the same body politic" (Finer 1997, 1515). However, the sovereignty of the subnational units exists not in relation to the international system, but in relation to the central government and the other constituent units of the federation. Thus it is possible to distinguish such polities from such other political arrangements as confederacies, leagues, or condominia.

Does Federalism Matter?

One of the overarching questions linking the contributions to this volume is whether federalism "matters" for politics and policy making. There is little question that, in theory and in practice, federalism has retained enormous importance as a formula for overcoming problems of national unification and integration over the centuries, and its luster has seldom been brighter than in the contemporary period. However, its impact on the day-to-day workings of politics is more ambiguous than its popularity as a political formula would suggest. Put simply, when we examine a range of political outcomes commonly associated with federalism, such as the decentralization of the political system, the power of particular political actors and institutions, or patterns of policy making, it is difficult to tell whether these are being caused by the specific institutions of federalism or by other factors in the political system. William Riker, one of the earliest contemporary theorists (and proponents) of federalism, was also one of the most famous skeptics on this question. In different writings on the subject he suggested that, in order to understand the actual operation of federal systems, we should look not to constitutional structure, but to such "real forces in the political system" as national party systems, entrenched political practices, and political and economic power structures (Riker 1969, 1975; Stepan: references to Stepan's contribution to this volume refer to chapter 2).

Today, in a period of rediscovery of the causal importance of institutions, Riker's arguments provide a tempting target for the obvious rejoinder that federal institutions *do indeed* matter. However, the proponents of this argument must still shoulder the burden of proof, for the skeptics' position is based not only on Riker's early doubts about the enduring impact of institutional forms and constitutional design, but also on the fact that federal systems seem to vary widely in their internal practices, centralization, and power relationships regardless of similarities in constitutional design. This alone provides evidence that much more is at work in shaping the internal power dynamics of federalism than the institutional features of federalism per se.

Federalism as an "independent variable" is indeed a moving target, one whose causal impact eludes parsimonious theorization. However, a consensus that emerges in the following chapters of this volume is that there is an intrinsic power to constitutional design, and the fact that a constitution is federal shapes probabilities for the distribution of power, both between levels of government and between regionally based actors.[5] Federalism is a system with a built-in presumption that powers will be divided between a central government and subnational governments, and that political representation will balance representation of territories against representation of people. Nevertheless, empirical evidence and the cases analyzed in this volume show considerable variation in practice, and this variation often exceeds what might be predicted from institutional design. Constitutional structure alone does not predict the causal impact of federal institutions or the internal political dynamics of federal countries. Understanding these dynamics requires systematic attention not only to the institutions of federalism themselves, but to how they relate to the broader political system in which they are embedded.

The book's chapters suggest that there is an interactive effect between the endogenous institutional features of federalism and the characteristics of the broader political system. This raises important issues for measurement and explanation. If measures or theories of federalism are to be useful, they must identify those features and effects that are clearly attributable to federal institutions and those that are not. Similarly, explanations focusing on the interaction between federal institutions and the broader political system must be able to separate the two clusters of variables and specify the mechanisms whereby they jointly affect political outcomes.

Unpacking this interaction thus requires that we proceed analytically in two steps. First, we need to look at the constitutional features of the federal system. These will spell out the attributions of authority, the limitations of power, the policy scope of different governmental bodies and levels of government, etc. They express a *presumptive* division of power between actors and institutions at different points in the federal system. Second, we must look to the relationship between federal institutions and characteristics of the broader political system. This includes such variables as regime type (i.e., whether a regime is democratic or authoritarian), party system characteristics, electoral laws and legal frameworks, and key aspects of fiscal politics and political economy. The cases analyzed in this book show that in varying ways and in different contexts these systemic factors affect the centralization of federal systems and the distribution of power between institutions and political actors— shaping and reshaping arrangements codified in federal constitutions. However, our cases also show that causality works in both directions. Federal institutions also shape the scope and pace of centralization and decentralization, fragmenting party systems, creating multiple arenas for political mobilization, empowering political actors, and limiting the prerogatives of others.

What Does Federalism Actually Do When It Matters?

The effects of federalism on politics can theoretically be felt in any type of federal system and at any level of centralization. It may make a significant difference to national unity or integration, for example, if a system is federal rather than unitary, even if that federal system is highly centralized and grants few prerogatives to its constituent units. Here the "fiction" of federalism (to quote Riker) in preserving collective identities through the constitutional legitimation of self-government and shared rule can provide important solutions to collective dilemmas of state and nation building (Riker 1969, 146). However, regarding the day-to-day practice of politics and government, it is fair to say that the theoretical importance of federalism increases with its degree of decentralization. In quotidian political life, a centralized federal system is hardly distinguishable from a centralized unitary state. A federal system matters most for politics and public policy when it is decentralized, or when its decentralizing characteristics, once dormant, have been activated.[6]

If emerging from a period of dormancy, federal institutions are likely to have been activated by an exogenous change from the system at large, whether via regime change (as the Samuels and Mainwaring chapter on Brazil shows), by changes in electoral laws (as seen in the Mexico chapter by Ochoa-Reza), or other external "shocks."[7] However, as several of our authors show, once activated, federal institutions often take on a life of their own, accelerating the decentralization process beyond the original policy makers' intent, or shifting the arenas and resources for political competition and mobilization. This dynamic is consistent with a general pattern of institutional change observed by Kathleen Thelen and Sven Steinmo (1992, 16), who write that "changes in the socioeconomic or political context can produce a situation in which previously latent institutions suddenly become salient, with implications for political outcomes."[8] In this sense, the "dormancy" of federal institutions can lull would-be reformers into a complacency they will in time regret, for these can become catalysts for unexpected (and unwelcome) change.

In what ways does a decentralized or activated federal system structure politics and shape political outcomes? At the risk of overlooking important examples, a review of the evidence presented in the book's chapters suggests that federalism affects politics in the following ways:

- It establishes de jure limits to the scope of governmental action
- It increases the number of veto players in the political system
- It creates multiple arenas for political organization and mobilization
- It shapes patterns of democratic representation, generally expanding the scope of territorial representation over population representation (representation by "state" or "province" rather than by numbers of people)
- It distributes power between regions and regionally based political actors
- It affects the flow of material resources (fiscal or economic) between populations living in the federal union.

Federalism and Democratization: Conventional Wisdoms and New Questions

The exogenous "shocks" that sparked federalism's late-twentieth-century revival in Latin America are little understood, but they were undoubtedly linked to the two macrolevel shifts of the time: regionwide market-oriented reforms and democratization. The turn toward market reforms and economic stabilization policies brought about a significant reorientation of the roles and functions of the central (national) government and led to a decentralizing trend in many countries, regardless of whether they were federal or unitary. Democratization altered the context of party competition and political contestation.

The new economic models adopted throughout the region after the economic crises of the 1980s unleashed a search for alternatives to the central state as agent of national economic development and fiscal management. In economic investment and production, private enterprise increasingly replaced state-owned enterprise. In the management of public affairs, attention was shifted to other levels of government, namely, the province and municipality, as national policy makers sought to relieve the central government of fiscal burdens and administrative responsibilities. The political structures of federalism provided obvious built-in alternatives to the national government, as well as constitutional mechanisms to enhance the empowerment of subnational actors once the process of decentralization was initiated. As several chapters point out, the dusting-off of institutional provisions empowering subnational authorities, and the transfer of political and fiscal resources to governors with formal (but previously unmobilized) constitutional powers, set in motion a real redistribution of power in Mexico and Venezuela, which were federal systems in name only. In Brazil, it swung the proverbial federal pendulum back toward the empowerment of subnational authorities.

Democratization had a similar activating effect on federal institutions, but this was not due to any inherent compatibility or teleological relationship between federalism and democratization.[9] Rather, it was due to the effects of democratization on party system dynamics in federal systems. Dramatic shifts in patterns of political contestation (e.g., the devolution of power from military authorities to civilian party politicians, as in Brazil, or electoral reforms, as in Mexico and Venezuela) led in varying ways to the activation of federal institutions and the empowerment of subnational political actors. This, in turn, structured the incentives, institutional arrangements, and power dynamics governing political life, reshaping relations between center and periphery, altering policy-making patterns, and redistributing power within the political system.

The power shifts that resulted from these developments drive many of the questions in this volume and make an understanding of the actual relationship between federalism and democracy all the more pressing. The decentralization of federalism has indeed been a consequence of the myriad economic and political developments of the current "wave" of democratization, but what expectations should we have about how the decentralization of federalism will affect the operation, efficacy, and fairness of these democracies?

The conventional wisdom about federalism is strikingly celebratory in general scholarly and policy-oriented work, and the expansion of federal practices and institutions in Latin America has thus been greeted with enthusiasm. Among the celebrators it is possible to distinguish between two schools, one stressing the connections between federalism and efficiency, the other stressing the connections between federalism and democracy.

The "efficiency" school of federalism draws its insights from economic and fiscal theories of federalism, principally the work of Charles Tiebout (1956), the French social scientist who forty years ago argued for the importance of competition between different levels of government for the efficient provision and distribution of goods and resources. Tiebout's insights have had a major influence on various recent publications, from those of the World Bank to the recent work by Barry Weingast (1995) on "market-preserving federalism," all of which see federal arrangements, particularly those promoting subnational autonomy, fiscal decentralization, and economic accountability as conducive to economic growth.[10] This is a generally prescriptive school, and the analytical boundaries it provides between federalism per se and decentralization are blurry at best. Nevertheless, it has been highly influential, particularly in the domains of fiscal federalism and decentralization studies.

The "democracy" school of federalism similarly has its exponents in theoretical and policy-oriented work and is deeply ingrained as well in popular conceptions of politics and political institutions. Elementary and high school civics and social studies texts in the United States routinely extol the democratic aspects of federalism, and it is not unusual to find this in other federal countries as well.[11]

Among proponents of the "democracy" school, federalism is seen as intimately connected to democratic practice, whether from a perspective that sees local governments as more responsive to individual citizens than national governments, or from one that sees such governments as democratic bulwarks against the encroachments of a central state. Federalism, or the decentralization of federal systems, is thus seen as a natural institutional consequence of the contemporary wave of democratization that is sweeping much of the developing world. Daniel J. Elazar, the author of some of the most widely cited texts on contemporary federal systems, sees federalism as a liberating global movement that follows from centuries of centralizing state-building and authoritarian rule.[12] Regarding Latin America, he writes, "The strengthening of federalism has been a significant item on the agendas of Argentina and Brazil in their turn from authoritarianism to liberal democracy. Brazil's new constitution increases the formal powers of the states vis-à-vis the federal government in the name of democracy. The formal and rather weak federal system of Mexico is becoming a vehicle for the emergence of an effective and competitive political opposition there through the Mexican states. Venezuela has elected to strengthen its existing federal system by providing for the popular election of state and local chief executives to strengthen its democratic regime" (1991, x).

This book offers cautionary insights into these celebratory schools of federalism. The authors of the following chapters see federalism not as arrangements for enhancing the efficiency of policy making, but as a constitutional order that structures power relationships between regionally organized actors and levels of government. As several authors suggest, the "federalization" of politics bears no predictable relationship to increases in economic efficiency or the efficacy of economic policy making.[13] Similarly, the contributing authors see federalism not as an outcome or end of the democratizing process, but as a variable that interacts with democratization—strengthening democratization at some levels and inhibiting the operation of democratic government at others. Federalism and democracy are linked not ontologically, but via institutional mechanisms. Uncovering and specifying these mechanisms is one of the challenges assumed by the authors of many of the following chapters.

The Origins of Federalism: Theoretical Understandings and Significance

In considering the origins of modern federalism, we turn once again to William Riker, whose notion of a "federal bargain" between sovereign or potentially sovereign entities dominates our theoretical understanding of the genesis of federal systems. Riker suggested that political entities with actual or presumptive claims to sovereignty agree to join together in a federation to meet a joint security threat or foreign military opportunity that they are unable to meet on their own.[14] The constituent units of the federation thus willingly trade sovereignty for security and military power in a "federal bargain" (Riker 1975, 11–14). Drawing from the experience of the late-eighteenth-century North American colonies, Riker proposed this as a general model for the formation of federal systems.

Two essays in this book explore this issue, and they offer substantial amendments to Riker's theoretical understanding of the origins of federal systems. The chapter by Stepan and the chapter by Gibson and Falleti both question the generalizability of the United States model to other parts of the world. Conceptually, Stepan views Riker's model of federalist formation as only one possible model, one that Stepan labels "coming together" federalism. However, the paths to federalism, as Stepan notes in this volume, are many, and "some of the most important federations in the world emerged from a completely different historical and political logic." One such logic, Stepan suggests, is the preservation of a preexisting union, such as a multi-ethnic unitary state that adopts federal arrangements in order to prevent the union's dissolution or to manage ethnic tensions more effectively. Stepan labels such cases, whose more notable members include India, Spain, and Belgium, as examples of "holding together federalism." Another "logic" driving federal formation is coercion, and Stepan, building on the example of the Soviet Union, proposes "putting together" federalism an additional ideal type of federal formation to incorporate this and similar historical examples.

Gibson and Falleti's case study of the origins of Argentine federalism also suggests the need for a more fine-grained view of the processes by which federal systems form. Theoretically, the authors question the generalizability of two key elements in Riker's model: the consensual connotations of the notion of a federal "bargain," as well as the precondition of an external military threat or opportunity for federal formation. The adoption of federalism in Argentina, the authors suggest, was a result of civil war, political conflict, and institutional gamesmanship. The drive toward unification between mutually antagonistic provinces was based on economic need in a geopolitical context void of common external military threats or opportunities at the time of federal unification.

Methodologically, Gibson and Falleti draw attention to the need to distinguish between the concepts of state formation (e.g., "the United States" or "Argentina") and regime formation (federal or unitary), two concepts that are conflated in Riker's theory. In the cases of Argentina and other countries, state formation preceded regime formation, and the first several decades of statehood were consumed by often bloody conflict over the choice of federal or unitary regimes.

Gaining a theoretical understanding of the genesis of federal systems has much more to it than historical interest. It reveals much about the continuing internal dynamics of federal systems. To Stepan, the distinctions between "holding together" or "coming together" federalism reveal a great deal about dynamics of change, whether in federal systems themselves, or in the transformation of unitary states into federal or quasi-federal systems. It also reveals much about the dynamic relationship between federalism and ethnic differentiation—in a path-dependent sense, the origins indeed shape the subsequent trajectories of federal systems. To Gibson and Falleti, the exploration of the origins of federalism provides a way of understanding not only the eventual balance of power between the central government and provincial government (commonly referred to as "centralization" or "decentralization"), but also the balance of power *between the provinces themselves*. To a great extent, federalism is an institutional solution to the problem of power asymmetries between the constituent units of a federation, a fact that is startlingly overlooked in theoretical treatments of federal systems. To the bulk of the literature on federalism, the main line of conflict identified is intergovernmental—between the central government and the subnational governments as a whole. The origins of federal systems, where the distribution of power between the members of the federation is crystallized institutionally (either by bloodshed, deliberation, or both), provides an opportunity for understanding the regional power dynamics and the institutional compensatory mechanisms that continue to shape the operation of federal countries well beyond their initial period of unification.

As David Samuels and Scott Mainwaring note in their contribution to this volume, federalism often pushes democracies in the direction of what Arend Lijphart labeled "consensus" democracies, which place checks on democratically elected majorities and give minorities virtual veto power over major policy decisions. To Lijphart (1977), such majority-constraining devices were characteristic of highly divided societies, and in his work on "consociationalism" he listed federalism as one of several arrangements for multiethnic societies where language and ethnicity coincide with territorial cleavages. In such "multinational" societies the constraints on majoritarian rule under federalism had their origins and justifications in the protection of territorially organized national minorities. In Latin America, however, the absence of such territorially defined societal cleavages renders the driving forces behind the adoption of federalism, as well as the normative justifications for violating the "one person, one vote" norm, less clear. The origins of federalism in Latin America (just as in the United States) had little to do with multinationalism or linguistic cleavages drawn along territorial lines.

The Iberian colonization experience had a culturally and religiously homogenizing effect on the dominant strata of the region, so that territorial divisions and ethnicity did not coincide in any significant way.[15] The political division of Brazil and

Spanish-speaking Latin America into separate nation-states resolved the dominant linguistic divide in the region, between Spanish speakers and Portuguese speakers. Thus, in Latin America, as in the United States, it was not cultural or ethnic diversity between regions, but size, economic differentiation, strong traditions of local elite rule, and military stalemate that were the driving forces behind the adoption of federal forms of government.

These nineteenth-century "bargains" between regionally organized elites thus bequeathed a legacy of federalism to their twentieth- and twenty-first-century descendants. In many cases the causes and conditions that justified these federal arrangements have withered away in the modern age. In others, federal institutions continue to mediate the economic power disparities that exist between the constituent units of the federations. But whether the underlying conditions of the nineteenth-century nation-building phase of Latin American countries persist or not, federal institutions, forged in the cauldrons of a distant century's conflicts, continue to "structure" politics in the present day.

Federalism and Representation in Democratic Regimes

The norm of "one person, one vote" is the most invoked and exalted norm of democratic theory, and the most violated norm of democratic practice. This is due not only to illegal manipulations by nefarious authoritarians, but to constitutional design by revered democratic "founding fathers" wary of potential excesses from majority rule as well. Federalism poses potential limits to the "one person, one vote" principle by combining two norms of political representation in its institutions: representation by population, where the unit of representation is the individual citizen (one person, one vote), and representation by territory, where the unit of representation is the subnational territorial entity (e.g., each state receives a fixed standard of representation regardless of its population). All federal systems reflect internally the tensions between these two representational norms, and the balance between the two is often a permanent subject of controversy, reform, and manipulation in federal systems.

In his first contribution to this volume Alfred Stepan explores the theoretical links between federalism and democracy and proposes a scheme for comparing federal systems according to how such systems "constrain" democratically elected majorities at the center. His proposed "demos-constraining–demos-enabling" continuum highlights the fact that federalism divides nations not only into multiple and overlapping governments, but also into multiple and overlapping electorates—a national *demos* and various subnational *demoi*. The continuum measures the extent to which the institutional structure of federal systems constrains or enables leaders representing the national *demos* and pursuing policies supported by a unionwide majority. All federal systems, Stepan notes, constrain elected governments at the center. However, they vary considerably in the extent to which representation departs from the "one person, one vote" norm in favor of a territorial concept of representation. They also vary in the extent to which the distribution of powers in the federal system permits regional minorities to check policy making by governments representing the national *demos*. Stepan's scheme pushes us beyond a centralization-decentralization continuum—which measures how federalism structures relations between governments—toward a continuum that captures how federalism structures democratic representation. Theories of federalism are thus joined to theories of democracy in the conceptualization and comparison of federal systems.

One of the most significant devices for structuring the balance between population and territorial representation in federal systems is the apportionment of seats to national legislative bodies. Few issues in federal systems are more subject to controversy and political manipulation than apportionment. Even the United States, the world's oldest federation, is not exempt from continuous controversies regarding the balance between population and territorial forms of representation. Battles over legislative apportionment reflect the ongoing tension in U.S. federalism between these competing norms at all levels of the system.[16] In one of the more recent twists in the evolving balance, the U.S. Supreme Court weighed in on behalf of the "one person, one vote" norm in a series of decisions regarding the apportionment of seats for state legislatures. In a 1964 decision it asserted that, at least at the state level, "legislators represent people, not trees or acres."[17] Nevertheless, as we shall see below, the representation of "trees and acres" at the national level is secure in the U.S. Senate's equal allocation of two seats to all of the union's disparately populated states.

As several of the chapters in this volume show, patterns of legislative apportionment vary considerably across federal systems. In bicameral federal systems territorial and population representation are usually divided between the upper houses of the legislature (or "senates," as they are usually called), which are based on territorial representation, and the lower houses, where seats tend to be apportioned according to population. Malapportionment is thus built in to senates by definition, and it is here where the greatest disparities in representation tend to be found in federal systems.[18] Thus, in the U.S. Senate, the granting of an equal number of seats to all states regardless of population produces a high level of overrepresentation of small states. As a result, it takes sixty-seven times more voters to elect a senator in the state of California than it does in the state of Wyoming. In Brazil and Argentina, whose federal systems were modeled on that of the United States, the gaps are even larger. In Brazil one vote in the state of Roraima is in effect worth 144 votes in the state of São Paulo. In Argentina, one vote in Tierra del Fuego province is worth 180 votes in Buenos Aires province.[19]

One of the most striking findings in chapters in this volume, however, is that malapportionment is also very present in the lower houses of several Latin American countries, in spite of their theoretical embodiment of the one person, one vote norm. As the articles by Samuels and Mainwaring, Snyder and Samuels, and Gibson, Calvo, and Falleti demonstrate, malapportionment in Latin American lower houses is widespread, and apportionment formulas have been subject to repeated manipulation in response to political conflicts, power shifts, and regime changes over the years.

Richard Snyder and David Samuels take aim at legislative malapportionment in Latin America in their contribution to this volume. The authors provide methodological innovations for measuring malapportionment, as well as original insights into the practice of malapportionment in the region, and show that, although a prevalent and constitutionally sanctioned aspect of federal systems, legislative malapportionment is widespread in nonfederal systems as well. Snyder and Samuels provide striking evidence to suggest that malapportionment has worked historically as a powerful and evolving "political weapon" for political elites of varying stripes to structure the political system to their advantage. This has resulted, among other things, in a marked rural-conservative bias to representation in national lower chambers. In federal systems this enhances the territorial bias of legislative representation already provided by the upper chambers.[20] Thus, just as in their origins federal systems provided institutional protections for regionally based elites against the growing populations and influence of metropolitan areas, so have the institutions of federalism provided continuing opportunities to structure the outcomes and procedures of contemporary democratic politics.

The questions voiced by Snyder and Samuels raise concerns about the potential for the "darker" sides of Latin American politics to be reinforced by the expansion of federalism. Just as subnational politics can harbor sources of economic dynamism and democratic change (Montero 2001b), so can the subnational act as a bulwark for authoritarian enclaves in nationally democratizing polities.[21] Where changes in Latin American federalism empower subnational actors, therefore, their impact on the quality of democratic politics will have as much to do with the specific institutional features of federalism as with the sociopolitical characteristics of subnational politics in the region.

Party Politics and Change in Federal Systems

These insights shed interesting light on some of the political determinants of change in federal systems. However, before coming to any conclusions about an inherent bias to the evolution of federal systems (whether conservative, centralizing, peripheralizing, or democratizing), we should also bear in mind that institutional change in federal systems is, as with any political system, a contingent outcome of conflict and interaction between federalism proper and the political system as a whole. There is therefore an important element of indeterminacy to this process, even at its broadest levels. William Riker (1964, 7) assumed that in the "centralized federalisms" of the modern day the long-term tendency would be for the central government gradually to "overawe" the subnational governments. The evidence of the 1980s and 1990s, in which centralized federal systems experienced decentralization, contradicts that expectation.

Similarly, while the cases considered in this volume show that the scope of that decentralization, and the evolution of patterns of representation and policy making, varied significantly from country to country, a critical determinant of these variations was the relationship between federalism and party politics. To William Riker the nature of the party system was the most important determinant of the centralization of federal systems, and there is considerable empirical evidence to support his claim.[22] Stepan, while criticizing Riker's dismissal of the causal importance of other institutional variables, includes party systems (whether they are politywide or subnational in scope) alongside institutional variables proper to federalism in his list of factors shaping the "demos-constraining" dynamics of federal systems. In fact, the party system is the only variable exogenous to the federal institutional structure that Stepan includes in his list. To Stepan, therefore, change in federal systems can be understood fundamentally as a result of the interaction of federalism's institutional features and the party system.

This view is echoed in varying ways by most authors in the volume, although not without debate and qualifications. In his chapter on Mexico, Alberto Diaz-Cayeros adopts a Rikerian skepticism about the causal importance of federal institutions. Analyzing the shifting roles of governors and senators in the Mexican political system over time, as well as patterns of regional resource allocation by the federal government, Diaz-Cayeros concludes that party system dynamics, rather than federal institutions, play the preponderant role in conditioning the behaviors and institutional interactions of a federal system. "Although federal institutional arrangements might be similar in two countries," he writes, "the binding constraints are created by political practices, as expressed in political parties, not by the [federal] institutions themselves." As Diaz-Cayeros notes, in spite of continuity in constitutional structure in Mexico (whose federal constitution was promulgated in 1917), the practice of federalism has undergone major change since the 1980s. Diaz-Cayeros suggests that this is due to the dramatically changing context of party politics and to shifting coalitional imperatives stemming from electoral competition. The heightened protagonism of governors in the Mexican political system, the decentralization of policy making, and patterns of federal resource allocations between states are outgrowths of party system change and resulting political practices rather than the constitutional forms of federalism.

Enrique Ochoa-Reza's analysis of the Mexican democratic transition provides a contrasting view. While placing considerable weight on party system dynamics, Ochoa-Reza's chapter also suggests that there is an intricate and mutually determinative relationship between federal constitutions and party systems over time. Ochoa-Reza explores two phenomena: the impact of federalism on the democratic transition process in Mexico, and the impact of the transition process on the evolution of the federal system. Federalism structured the transition process by providing "multiple arenas" for political contestation. The transition process, in turn, decentralized the federal system but mitigated its more peripheralizing features. The dynamic connections between these two processes lay in the party system.

The "exogenous shock" that started the Mexican process of change was a series of national electoral reforms that pluralized party competition. Once these reforms were introduced, the federal structure channeled the pluralization of party politics into myriad local arenas where national parties could mobilize to challenge the ruling party. The pluralization of party competition was not only a national phenomenon but was reproduced over and over at the state level. State victories for the opposition provided power bases for new political actors invested with federal constitutional powers that, in turn, gave opposition parties leverage to advance their competition and bargaining with the ruling PRI at the national level. A "virtuous cycle" thus developed whereby intensified state-level competition sparked additional rounds of national negotiations and reforms by party leaders. However, the national orientation of the country's main political parties nationalized party competition and reduced the territorial nature of representation in both houses of the national legislature. Political reforms by national party leaders eager to bolster their own positions introduced, among other things, greater proportionality in the apportionment of seats to both houses of the Mexican Congress. Governors became empowered, and legislators developed deeper ties to regional support networks during this period, but political reforms by national party leaders also mitigated the peripheralizing tendencies of these dynamics.

In contrast, Samuels and Mainwaring's chapter shows how the Brazilian political system's evolution during the democratic transition of the 1970s and 1980s was shaped by the profoundly localist orientation of political parties in Brazil. Regime change (in the form of the political liberalization of military rule) took place first through local elections, which empowered party leaders in a regionally fragmented party system. This, in turn, fortified the decentralizing features of federalism and enhanced the sway of the states over national political life. As the once-centralist military government sought to bolster its civilian support, the civilian buttress of the military regime became effective in state-level conservative politicians that reconsolidated their bases of political support and gained new protagonism during the transition from authoritarian rule.[23] Once subservient allies of a national military regime, governors and senators regained political power vested in them by the very federal institutions the military government had temporarily deactivated. Similarly, during the first decades of democratic rule the party system provided powerful incentives to politicians to prioritize local politics over national politics, to strengthen the decentralization of federalism through constitutional reforms, and to utilize empowered local arenas to challenge the center's hegemony over national politics.

This latter dynamic is taken up by Michael Penfold-Becerra who, in his chapter on Venezuela, details how activated federal institutions can transform a centralized party system. Penfold-Becerra describes how a change in a fundamental institutional feature of Venezuelan federalism, a law approving the direct election of state governors and municipal mayors, set in motion a series of events that culminated in the unraveling of a centralized party system that had dominated Venezuelan politics for over four decades. The legislative reforms took place against a backdrop of widespread public disaffection with the country's two dominant parties, Acción Democrática (AD) and COPEI, and the centralized monopoly of power they exercised over political life. Direct elections of governors and mayors altered key incentives in the political system and empowered a new set of actors, primarily governors and local party leaders. These empowered actors seized upon their newfound constitutional powers to push for additional powers, most notably in the fiscal domains, eroding further the traditional party leaders' sway over day-to-day governance, party structures, and partisan competition. Penfold-Becerra thus draws our attention not only to some of the mechanisms through which federalism can shape change in party systems, but also to a little-known strand in the complex process of dissolution of Venezuela's centralized party system. As he tells us, "the activation of federal institutions was a primary cause of the demise of the AD-COPEI duopoly in Venezuelan politics and paved the way for the rise of Hugo Chávez Frías."

In varying ways, therefore, the volume's authors draw attention to the bidirectional nature of causality between party systems and federal institutions. Party systems, through the incentives they provide to political actors and the institutional mechanisms they set in motion, can exert centralizing or decentralizing influences on federal systems. However, federal systems, through the powers and political resources they impart to political actors located at different points in the federal structure, can also shape the nature of party competition, the structures of incentives for politicians, and the decentralization of parties and party systems.[24] Among the many lessons reforming politicians could draw from these complex interactions, two might be mentioned here. If you want to shape the internal operation of federal systems, pay attention to the design of your parties and party systems. On the other hand, if you wish to undermine hegemonic parties or party systems, activate federalism.

Federalism, Politics, and Policy Making

How do federal institutions shape the policy-making process? Several of the volume's contributors address this question. The chapters by Stepan and Samuels and Mainwaring address how federal institutions, particularly in decentralized federal systems, potentially constrain policy making by central governments. Stepan notes how under the given institutional arrangements that he labels "demos-constraining," federalism creates potential minority "win sets" that can block policy making by national executive branches and legislation from national legislatures.

Echoing Stepan's concern, Samuels and Mainwaring borrow from George Tsebelis's notion of "veto players" and suggest that federalism adds veto players to the politics of policy reform that can constrain central government initiatives. These veto players are generally located in the upper chambers of national legislatures and in state governorships. Other things equal, the authors note, "in federal systems there should be more constraints on central government initiatives." However, Samuels and Mainwaring also provide a dynamic picture of the policy-making process under federalism by suggesting that a continuous "bargaining game between presidents and states" shifts power between presidents and subnational actors in the struggle over national economic policy making. Their comparisons of economic policy making across several presidential administrations show that although regional minorities repeatedly availed themselves of federal institutions to block central government policy reforms over the years, presidential leadership and coalition building during the 1995–2003 Cardoso presidency neutralized subnational veto players and expanded the central government's control over the policy-making process. Thus, in addition to formal and informal structures of federalism, Samuels and Mainwaring draw our attention to such agency-based variables as presidential leadership, presidential performance and popularity, and coalition building between the national executive and the congress that directly affect the central government's leverage over subnational actors.

Gibson, Calvo, and Falleti explore the political impact of a particular feature of many federal systems: territorial overrepresentation of states and provinces that results from malapportionments of seats to national legislatures. The authors are concerned specifically with how overrepresentation can be utilized as a political tool in the processes of policy making and coalition building by overrepresented states and by central governments that seek the political support of such states. The comparative evidence they provide indicates that overrepresented states tend to attract disproportionate per capita shares of central government spending. The authors label cases in which overrepresentation has a diversionary effect on the territorial distribution of public spending as examples of "reallocative federalism." Their subsequent case study of Argentina details some of the political mechanisms at work in reallocative federalism, and suggests that, although overrepresentation does empower small provinces vis-à-vis large provinces and the central government, it also provides opportunities for central governments to manipulate spending for cross-regional coalitions in support of national policy-making initiatives. Federalism in Argentina, in contrast to the Brazilian case, actually enabled central government policy making in a context of major economic reform, and the success of economic reform in Argentina was intimately tied to the dynamics of the country's federal system.

In his chapter on Mexico, Alberto Diaz-Cayeros also measures the impact of territorial overrepresentation on spending patterns and finds a similarly positive relationship. However, he also suggests that other institutional dynamics in the political system may be better predictors of regional resource allocation than territorial overrepresentation per se (or, for that matter, other features of the federal system). He suggests the need to explore more closely the links between malapportionment and such variables as "conditions of party discipline and congressional committee structures" before seeing malapportionment as a measure of the power of individual legislators or legislative delegations.[25]

The contrasting evidence from these cases suggests, once again, the need to go beyond institutional design in order to understand federalism's varying effects on politics and policy making. Just as the design of federal institutions is often an outcome of conflicts between political actors, the impact of federalism on politics is an outcome of the interaction between federal institutions and partisan alignments, party system characteristics, political economy, and economic geography. Whether the empowerment of subnational units by institutional features of federalism constrains or enables central governments depends much on the political linkages or partisan alignments that exist between those controlling the central government and those controlling the subnational governments. Similarly, whether the formal constitutional attributions of governors empowers them vis-à-vis presidents depends much upon such factors as the fiscal independence of the governors, party system incentives, or presidential leadership.

These possible combinations and variations also have important implications for democratization. Some authors in this volume note an irony: federalism can play a supportive role in the transition to democracy and an obstructive role in the democratic consolidation period. When it comes to democratization, federalism is a decidedly double-edged sword. In the Brazilian and Mexican cases, federalism aided the transition from authoritarian rule by providing local arenas and power bases from which to challenge centralized authoritarian rule. However, during the Brazilian democratic consolidation period, federalism empowered local actors to hinder the efficacy of democratically elected governments at the center. The same institutional structures that empowered subnational challenges to national authoritarian rule also empowered subnational challenges to democratically elected governments in the consolidation period. In Argentina the effect was somewhat different. Federalism gave the authoritarian regime ready-made bases of regional support during the transition from authoritarianism, while enhancing the policy-making effectiveness of a democratically elected government during a difficult period of economic policy making (Gibson 1996; Gibson, Calvo, and Falleti, this volume). In the Mexican case, federalism may well play a supportive role for nationally elected democratic governments in the future. As Enrique Ochoa-Reza suggests in his contribution to this volume, the centralizing (or "demos-enabling") features incorporated into Mexico's federal system by the leaders of a nationally oriented party system, while empowering new political actors at all levels of the federal system, may provide important institutional counterweights to subnational challenges to democratic governments following the national defeat of the PRI.

Conclusion

The contributions to this volume reveal an array of theoretical and empirical relationships between federalism and politics. The following chapters address, in varying ways, how federalism affects the nature and quality of political representation, the efficacy of democratic governments, the implementation of public policy, and the balance of power between levels of government and subnational territorial units. We offer conceptual innovations for the study of federalism as well as cautionary insights about how federalism affects political conflict, policy making, and the functioning of democratizing regimes. In this way we hope to move scholarly agendas away from a democratic teleology of federalism, and toward a scientific understanding of federalism and its varying effects on politics.

NOTES

1. For an important theoretical statement on the study of the subnational in comparative politics, see Snyder (2001). For a recent work on the causes of decentralization, see Garman, Haggard,

and Willis (2001). For a suggestive work on the consequences of decentralization, see Montero (2001a); see also Falleti (2001). Remmer and Wibbels (2000) provide a discussion of a number of important issues and debates.

2. Notable exceptions are a small number of country studies, such as Abrucio (1998), Samuels and Abrucio (2000), and Gibson and Calvo (2000). For a rare full-book-length study of the politics of federalism in Latin America, see Samuels (2002).

3. For an extensive listing of such institutional possibilities, see Watts (1996, 8). Watts's listing, which is a slightly expanded version of that found in Elazar's *Federal Systems of the World,* offers the following "spectrum of Federal Political Systems": unions; constitutionally decentralized unions; federations; confederations; federacies; associated states; condominiums; leagues; joint functional authorities; hybrids.

4. The civil divisions of federal countries can vary, however. First-order civil divisions are usually states or provinces, and these are subdivided into lower-order civil divisions ranging from counties to municipalities, each with varying levels of autonomy across federal systems.

5. This "consensus" is not unquestioned by contributors to this volume. See, for example, Diaz-Cayeros's general support of the Rikerian position in his chapter on Mexico, as well as Snyder and Samuels's article on malapportionment and its effects, which they see as transcending federalism itself.

6. This emphasis on the importance of decentralization for the relevance of federal institutions to politics and public policy would be questioned by Stepan, who argues forcefully in this volume that "federal institutions matter for policy at *all* points on the demos-constraining / demos-enabling continuum."

7. As Michael Penfold-Becerra's chapter in this volume demonstrates, a change *within* the federal system—an endogenous shock—is also a possible catalyst for further change in the federal system (and the political system at large). In the Venezuelan case, the enactment of a law permitting the direct election of state governors (they had previously been appointed by the president), unleashed a series of events leading, first, to the decentralization of the federal system, and then to the fragmentation of the centralized party system.

8. See also Pierson (2000) for a related theoretical discussion of the potential for institutional structures to form additional complementary institutional structures in processes of change.

9. As many proponents of federalism would argue (see the discussion below).

10. The World Bank's *World Development Report, 1999 / 2000* devoted a major section of the report to the topic of federalism and decentralization. Similarly, the American Political Science Association's Comparative Politics Newsletter published a symposium on "The New Political Economy of Decentralization and Federalism," which focused primarily on the topic of fiscal federalism and economic theories of federalism. See APSA-CP (2000). See also Barry Weingast's (2000) contribution to that symposium.

11. The following excerpt from a seventh-grade Mexican civics textbook provides a nice illustration: in a table listing the "differences between federalism and centralism," we see the following distinctions: "*Federalism:* The republic is divided in free and sovereign states. *Centralism:* the republic is divided in departments subject to the Central Government. *Federalism:* Promotes greater citizen

participation. *Centralism:* Citizen participation is nonexistent. *Federalism:* Local laws are adapted to the needs of local inhabitants. *Centralism:* Laws are made without taking local conditions into account" (Castro and Vazquez Reyna 1998, 40).

12. In the introduction to his text, Elazar (1991, x) writes, "For well over 300 years, the major political efforts of European civilization as well as peoples and countries influenced by that civilization have been directed toward building such politically sovereign states, and all too often reifing them so that the states take on an existence separate from the peoples they are designed to serve. . . . While state-building and even statism has been the common denominator of the modern age and its immediate aftermath, parallel to it there has developed a second system of polity-building, one in which the benefits of statehood, namely liberty and autonomy, or, in contemporary terminology, self-determination and self-government, are gained through what generally may be denominated federal arrangements."

13. Or, as other authors have shown, it has no necessary relationship to improved governance or other valued goals of economic policy making. See Treisman (2000) and Linz and Stepan (2000).

14. For a theoretical critique of Riker's theories of federalism see Stepan in this volume.

15. These were, of course, multiethnic regions, but the indigenous populations were subjugated by the dominant Spanish or Portuguese nation-states, and federal systems were not structured according to the territorial organization of ethnic groups or nationalities.

16. Apportionment battles are also over partisan advantage (e.g., the notorious practice of "gerrymandering" to ensure a party's majority in a congressional district). Although not unrelated to the conflict over population representation and territorial representation, this is a separate analytical issue.

17. U.S. Supreme Court, *Wesberry v. Sanders,* 1964.

18. As the chapter by Michael Penfold-Becerra shows, Venezuela became a unicameral federal system after the constitutional reforms enacted by Hugo Chávez Frías, making it the only unicameral federal country in the world. However, the principle of territorial representation is represented in deliberate malapportionment of the legislative chamber, which grants a minimum of three deputies to all states, regardless of their population size.

19. See the chapters by the following authors for discussions of malapportionment and its impact on federalism and democratic politics: Stepan, Samuels and Mainwaring, Snyder and Samuels, Gibson, Calvo, and Falleti, and Diaz-Cayeros.

20. It also enhances the territorial bias introduced by electoral college systems to elect presidents, as in the United States or Argentina prior to the constitutional reform of 1994.

21. This is the normative concern and research agenda of the collection of essays in Cornelius (1999).

22. See David Samuels's (2000) suggestive essay in the APSA / CP Newsletter.

23. So did the democratic opposition, which availed itself of local elections and party mobilization to establish arenas of opposition to military rule.

24. For other works that analyze the impact of federalism on party systems, see Colomer (1999) and Geddes and Benton (1997).

25. Just as importantly, Diaz-Cayeros also raises questions about the reliability of independent

measures of overrepresentation, noting the difficulty in distinguishing them from other indicators of "size" for territorial units.

BIBLIOGRAPHY

Abrucio, Fernando Luiz. 1998. *Os Barões da Federação: Os Governadores e a Redemocratização Brasileira*. São Paulo: Editora Hucitec.

APSA-CP. 2000. The New Political Economy of Decentralization and Federalism. American Political Science Association, Comparative Politics Section Newsletter 11 (1): 1–32.

Castro, Gloria Currola, and Jose Lucio Vazquez Reyna. 1998. *Educación Cívica*. Mexico City: Editorial Patria.

Colomer, Joseph. 1999. *Las Instituciones del Federalismo*. México D.F.: Cuadernos de la Facultad Latinoamericana de Ciencias Sociales.

Cornelius, Wayne, ed. 1999. *Subnational Politics and Democratization in Mexico*. La Jolla, Calif.: Center for U.S.-Mexican Studies, University of California–San Diego.

Dahl, Robert A. 1986. Federalism and the Democratic Process. In *Democracy, Identity, and Equality*. Oslo: Norwegian University Press.

Elazar, Daniel. 1991. *Federal Systems of the World: A Handbook of Federal, Confederal, and Autonomy Arrangements*. Essex: Longman Group.

Falleti, Tulia. 2001. Federalismo y Descentralización Educativa en Argentina: Consecuencias (no Queridas) de la Descentralización del Gasto en un País Federal. In *El Federalismo Electoral Argentino: Sobrerrepresentación, Reforma Política y Gobierno Dividido en Argentina*, edited by E. Calvo and M. A. Medina. Buenos Aires: EUDEBA.

Finer, S. E. 1997. *The History of Government*, vol. 3: *Empires, Monarchies and the Modern State*. Oxford: Oxford University Press.

Garman, Christopher, Stephan Haggard, and Eliza Willis. 2001. Fiscal Decentralization: A Political Theory with Latin American Cases. *World Politics* 53 (2): 205–37.

Geddes, Barbara, and Allyson Benton. 1997. Federalism and Party System. Paper prepared for the conference "The Transformation of Argentina: Democratic Consolidation, Economic Reforms and Institutional Design," Universidad de San Andrés.

Gibson, Edward L. 1996. *Class and Conservative Parties: Argentina in Comparative Perspective*. Baltimore: Johns Hopkins University Press.

Gibson, Edward L., and Ernesto Calvo. 2000. Federalism and Low-Maintenance Constituencies: Territorial Dimensions of Economic Reform in Argentina. *Studies in Comparative International Development* 35 (3): 32–55.

Glassner, Martin Ira. 1996. *Political Geography*. New York: John Wiley and Sons.

Lijphart, Arend. 1977. *Democracy in Plural Societies: A Comparative Exploration*. New Haven: Yale University Press.

Linz, Juan J., and Alfred Stepan. 2000. Inequality Inducing and Inequality Reducing Federalism:

With Special Reference to the "Classic Outlier" the USA. Paper presented at the XVIII World Congress of the International Political Science Association, August 1–5, Quebec City.

Montero, Al. 2001a. After Decentralization: Patterns of Intergovernmental Conflict in Argentina, Brazil, Spain, and Mexico. *Publius* 31 (4): 43–64.

———. 2001b. Decentralizing Democracy: Spain and Brazil in Comparative Perspective. *Comparative Politics* 33 (2): 149–70.

Pierson, Paul. 2000. Increasing Returns, Path Dependence, and the Study of Politics. *American Political Science Review* 94 (2): 251–68.

Remmer, Karen L., and Erik Wibbels. 2000. The Political Economy of Decentralization in Latin America. American Political Science Association, Comparative Politics Section Newsletter 11 (1): 23–31.

Riker, William H. 1964. *Federalism: Origin, Operation, Significance.* Boston: Little Brown.

———. 1969. Six Books in Search of a Subject or Does Federalism Exist and Does It Matter? *Comparative Politics* (October): 135–46.

———. 1975. Federalism. In *Handbook of Political Science,* edited by F. Greenstein and N. W. Polsby. Reading, Mass.: Addison-Wesley.

Samuels, David. 2000. To Paraphrase Riker, "Six Articles in Search of a Subject": On the Political Economy of Decentralization and Federalism. American Political Science Association, Comparative Politics Section Newsletter 11 (2): 22–24.

———. 2002. *Federalism, Ambition, and Congressional Politics in Brazil.* New York: Cambridge University Press.

Samuels, David, and Fernando Luis Abrucio. 2000. Federalism and Democratic Transitions: The "New" Politics of the Governors in Brazil. *Publius* 30 (2): 43–61.

Snyder, Richard. 2001. Scaling Down: The Subnational Comparative Method. *Studies in Comparative International Development* 36(1): 93–110.

Thelen, Kathleen, and Sven Steinmo. 1992. Historical Institutionalism in Comparative Politics. In *Structuring Politics: Historical Institutionalism in Comparative Analysis,* edited by S. Steinmo, K. Thelen, and F. Longstreth. New York: Cambridge University Press.

Tiebout, Charles. 1956. A Pure Theory of Local Expenditures. *Journal of Political Economy* 64 (5): 416–24.

Treisman, Daniel. 2000. Why Are Federal Countries Perceived to Be More Corrupt? Paper prepared for the Annual Meeting of the American Political Science Association, Atlanta.

Watts, Ronald. 1996. *Comparing Federal Systems in the 1990s.* Kingston, Ontario: Queen's University Institute of Intergovernmental Relations.

Weingast, Barry R. 1995. The Economic Role of Political Institutions: Market-Preserving Federalism and Economic Development. *Journal of Law, Economics, and Organization* 11 (1): 1–31.

———. 2000. A Comparative Theory of Federal Economic Performance. American Political Science Association, Comparative Politics Section Newsletter 11 (1): 5–10.

CHAPTER 2

Toward a New Comparative Politics of Federalism, Multinationalism, and Democracy

Beyond Rikerian Federalism

—ALFRED STEPAN

The subject of this chapter is the role of federalism in the functioning, and occasionally even the making or breaking, of democracies. Federalism has never been more crucial for the study of democracy and comparative politics. If our unit of analysis is the total number of people who live in long-standing democracies, the majority of them live in federal systems.[1] If our unit of analysis is relatively long-standing (if often troubled) multinational and multilingual democracies, *all* the polities that fall most clearly into this category are federal.[2] However, *all* the territorial fragmentation of postcommunist Europe occurred in three multinational, formally federal, systems. It is crucial that we analyze and explain these two sharply different patterns. Finally, if we turn our attention to two major, recent democratizing efforts, in Brazil and Russia, any serious analysis of their democratic prospects involves an analysis of the difficulties presented by their distinctive federal systems (Stepan 2000a, b).

Yet despite the centrality of federalism to a very large number of polities in the world, the existing political science literature on federalism does not, in my judgment, help us sufficiently in the tasks of comparative analysis.

In this chapter I endeavor to show how we might begin to make federalism a more powerful conceptual and empirical category for a truly comparative analysis of politics by developing three themes. First, I show that the democracy, federalism, and nationalism literatures have been developed in relatively mutual isolation and that we can make more meaningful and powerful statements about comparative federalism only if we relate the three literatures to each other. Second, I demonstrate that all federal systems constrain the law-making capacity of the democratically elected legislators at the center. However, I argue that it is analytically and politically fruitful to study democratic federal systems as existing along a "demos-constraining" to "demos-enabling" continuum.[3] I also make a strong case that at *all* points in the continuum federal institutions can have a great impact on policy. I cannot develop these arguments without addressing the most influential political scientist who has written on federalism, the late William H. Riker. Riker's classic and still influential arguments about federalism stand in fundamental opposition to those I advance in this chapter. Third, I construct and operationalize the analytic framework of the demos-constraining / demos-enabling continuum by evaluating four propositions about federalism, using data from India, Germany, Spain, the United States, and Brazil.

Riker, Federalism, and Political Science

There are a number of major analysts of federalism. Two of the most prominent are K. C. Wheare (1946), an influential constitutionalist, and Daniel J. Elazar, the founder of the journal devoted to federalism, *Publius*.[4] But the analyst who has most affected political science approaches to federalism is William H. Riker, and we cannot progress too far without either building upon his arguments or showing good reasons to refine or even reject his arguments. Riker, of course, is one of the intellectual founders of rational choice theory in political science; he made enduring contributions to coalition theory, most notably in his seminal work on "minimum winning coalitions," and contributed to many other areas of political science. Indeed, according to a recent attempt to construct criteria for a political science "Hall of Fame" for the 1954–94 period, Riker emerged at the top of two important indices.[5]

One of the central themes in Riker's work was federalism. For thirty years, he was probably the major figure in the subfield. In 1964 he wrote *Federalism: Origin, Operation, Significance,* which discussed the United States and, briefly, every contemporary federal system in the world. In 1975, as the leading political scientist in the area of federalism, he contributed a very boldly argued, long article on the subject for the classic, eight-volume *Handbook of Political Science,* edited by Fred Greenstein and Nelson Polsby. In 1987 he brought together most of his writings on U.S. federalism in his book *The Development of American Federalism.* In 1995, just before his death, he was invited as the leading comparativist in the subfield to write the theoretical introduction to a volume written by European scholars on the federal future of the European Union (Riker 1996). Riker's thoughts on federalism were directly related to his normative and empirical concerns about how to avoid the dangers of democratic populism. Indeed, Riker's theory of individual choice and theory of democracy are brought together in his *Liberalism against Populism: A Confrontation between the Theory of Democracy and the Theory of Social Choice.*

My goal in this chapter is not to provide a systematic review of the entire Rikerian federalist framework but rather to argue that the building blocks of a more powerful approach to the comparative study of federalism, multinationalism, and democracy necessarily require serious consideration of some key analytic, historical, normative, and policy dimensions that either are not found, or are misleading, in the Rikerian framework.

In a book-length project, Juan Linz and I shall develop (and integrate) our thoughts on the interrelationship of democratization, federalism, and nationalism in much greater detail.[6] Here, in this brief introduction to my chapter, I indicate some of the most crucial distinctions that I believe must be made.

Federalism in Democratic and Nondemocratic Systems

A fundamental distinction should be made between a democratic system that is federal and a nondemocratic system with federal features. In a strict sense, only a system that is a constitutional democracy can provide *credible guarantees* and the institutionally embedded mechanisms that help ensure that the law-making prerogatives of the subunits will be respected. In a democracy the specificities of the federal formula that has been constitutionally adopted will routinely structure many political processes, such as how the most important laws are adopted at the center and in the subunits, and how the jurisdictional boundaries between the center and the subunits will be adjudicated and maintained. However, in a nondemocratic system, federalism may or may not structure significantly such political processes.

If one accepts, as Linz and I do, Robert A. Dahl's definition of a federal system, then in a very strict sense only a democracy can be a federal system.[7] This is so because, for Dahl, federalism is "a system in which some matters are exclusively *within* the competence of certain local units—cantons, states, provinces—and are constitutionally *beyond* the scope of the authority of the national government; and where certain other matters are constitutionally outside the scope of the authority of the smaller units" (1986, 114). Only a system that is a democracy can build the relatively autonomous constitutional, legislative, and judicial systems necessary to meet the Dahlian requirements for a federation. My focus here, then, is on federalism *in a democracy,* and all that this entails.

This is not, of course, to deny that in some circumstances the federal features of some nondemocratic polities may become extremely important. For example, during the period of high Stalinism in the Soviet Union, the party-state under Stalin's direction determined policy. This was so, notwithstanding the extensive range of sovereign rights that were given in the constitution to the Soviet republics. However, when the party-state began to weaken in the late 1980s, and a decree of electoral competitiveness was introduced into the federal subunits at the republican level, the same Soviet federal features, in the *new* political context, provided great "resource mobilization" opportunities for republican-level elites to reconstitute their power bases by emphasizing the sovereignty claims of their republics (Linz and Stepan 1996a).[8]

If we are to make progress as comparativists, we need to analyze the difference in how democratic and nondemocratic federal political systems function politically. Some of the most important works on federalism do not make this distinction. For example, Riker, in his much-cited 1975 article on federalism, lists Canada, the United States, Yugoslavia, and the Soviet Union as meeting his criteria for federal systems. Indeed, Riker (1975) classifies the United States and Yugoslavia as the same subtype, "centralized federalism." Binding together Yugoslavia and the United States into the same analytic category obfuscated, of course, the much more meaningful way in which the power structures and political dynamics of the two polities were fundamentally different. For example, precisely because Yugoslavia was not a democracy, its "quasi-federal system" could function peacefully as long as the party-state played the key steering role. Once elections began to breathe some life into the inert and incomplete federal system, it fragmented.

This point is of wider significance for the comparative analysis of federalism. If one excludes the German case as being "one nation in two states," then there were eight nondemocratic states in communist Europe in 1989. Five were unitary, and three had some quasi-federal features. The five unitary states are still five unitary states. However, the three quasi-federal states are now twenty-three independent countries, many of them nondemocratic majoritarian ethnocracies.

"Coming Together," "Holding Together," and "Putting Together" Federations: Origins, Purposes, and Structures

Another major distinction that must be made is between federations whose initial purpose is to "come together" versus those whose purpose is to "hold together." The idea of a "coming together" federation of course is that based on the U.S. model. In Philadelphia, in 1787, previously sovereign units made what Riker calls a "federal bargain." For Riker, the two necessary conditions for a federal bargain, which he asserts *all* long-standing federations have actually met (and he included the USSR and India as long-standing federations), are (1) that there exists a group of individual polities, all of which have strong identities and substantial sovereignty, and (2) as a group they perceive that they face external threats, which can be lessened if they agree to pool their sovereignty and make a federation (Riker 1975). The nature of the bargain is that even the least powerful members of the new federation, given their strong identity and their strong sovereignty, will attempt to keep as much of their identity and sovereignty as possible. The strongest members of the new federation, as part of the bargain, agree to accept a continuing high degree of political autonomy among the smaller or less powerful members as the price they pay for improving their own security by creating the federation. For the classic confederations that agreed to become federations, the United States of America and Switzerland, Riker's argument is powerful.

However, as comparativists, we must recognize that some of the most important federations in the world emerged from a completely different historical and political logic. India in late 1948, Belgium in 1969, and Spain in 1975 were all political systems with strong *unitary* features. Nevertheless, political leaders in all these three multinational polities came to the constitutional decision that the best way to "hold together" in a democracy would be to *devolve power* and to turn their threatened polities into federations. The 1950 Indian constitution, the 1976 Spanish constitution, and the 1993 Belgian constitution are all federal.[9]

To supplement Riker's version of federation formation, which I will call a "coming together" ideal type, I therefore suggest that we create a supplementary ideal type of federation formation that I will call "holding together."

The origins of "holding together" federation formation, and consequently the characteristic political structures that are crafted in a "holding together" federation, are quite different than those found in Riker's "coming together" federations.

A good example is the creation of federalism in India. The chairman of the drafting committee of the Indian constitution, B. R. Ambedkar, when he presented the draft constitution for the consideration of the members of the Constituent Assembly, was very explicit that the Indian constitution was designed to maintain the unity of India. He argued that the Indian constitution was guided by principles and mechanisms that were thus fundamentally different from those found in the U.S. constitution. In his address to the Constituent Assembly Ambedkar assumed that India was already a diverse polity with substantial unity, but that to maintain this unity, under democratic conditions, a federation would be useful. Ambedkar told the members of the Assembly that "[t]he use of the word Union is deliberate. . . . The Drafting Committee wanted to make it clear that though India was to be a federation, *the Federation was not the result of an agreement by the States to join in a Federation* and that the Federation not being the result of an agreement no State has the right to secede from it. . . . Though the country and the people may be divided into different States for convenience of administration the country is one integral whole, its people a single people living under a single imperium derived from a single source" (Government of India 1951, emphasis added).

Mohit Bhattacharya in a careful review of the mind-set of the Indian founding fathers points out that by the time Ambedkar presented the draft to the Constituent Assembly in November 1948, both the partition between Pakistan and India and the somewhat reluctant and occasionally even coerced integration of virtually all the 568 princely states had already occurred. Therefore, the strong bargaining power of units with a great deal of sovereignty, crucial to Rikerian views of "coming together" federalism, in essence no longer existed when Ambedkar presented his draft constitution.[10] Bhattacharya's reading of the Constituent Assembly papers is that the central motivation in the minds of the constitution drafters was to hold the center together: "What ultimately emerged was a 'devolutionary federation' as a fundamentally unitary state devolved powers on the units through a long process of evolution. . . . [Once] the problem of integration of the Princely States had disappeared after partition, the 'federal situation' itself had virtually evaporated with it. . . . The bargaining situation disappeared. . . . The architects of the Constitution were sensitive pragmatists. Their attention was focused on . . . the central authority that would hold the nation together" (Bhattacharya 1992, 101–2).

If we include nonvoluntary, nondemocratic federation formation (a category that Riker does not contemplate), we would need to supplement "coming together" and "holding together" federation formation with a third ideal type, which I will call "putting together." Let us see why this would be useful.

Riker famously argued that the Soviet Union in 1921–22 had the same two fundamental bargaining conditions (a felt need for security in a larger unit but a continuing sense of strong regional identities) as that found in the thirteen American states or the Swiss cantons. In his section on the formation of Soviet federalism in 1922, Riker wrote, "If one looks at the circumstances of its origin it is just like all the other federations here discussed, in that both bargaining conditions are clearly present. . . . There is a universally feared threat and there is a sense of provincial loyalty owing to differences of ideology, so that both the bargaining conditions were satisfied at the time that the Union of Soviet Socialist Republics was planned" (1975, 122). However, the fact is that some of the units, such as Georgia, Armenia, Azerbaijan, and Ukraine, did not receive much international support for their independence and were integrated by a significant degree of military force into the Soviet Union in the 1920s (to say nothing of Latvia, Estonia, and Lithuania, which were militarily "integrated" in 1940). All these countries were experiencing substantial popular pressures to become mononational "nation-states" when they were integrated into the Soviet Union as "union republics." It distorts history, theory, and language to say that in 1921–22 Georgian, Armenian, Azerbaijan, and Ukrainian bargaining preferences and bargaining capabilities were "just like" the states of the United States in 1787 or the cantons of Switzerland in 1848.[11] We need the ideal type of "putting together."

Riker suggests that all long-standing federations, including the Soviet Union and India, were in his "coming together" pattern. I suggest it is analytically more useful

Table 2.1

"Coming Together," "Holding Together," and "Putting Together" Ideal Types of Federation Formation

"Coming Together"	"Holding Together"	"Putting Together"
Largely voluntary bargain by relatively autonomous units to come together so that by pooling sovereignty but retaining their identity they can increase their security.	Largely a consensual parliamentary decision to attempt to hold together a unitary state by creating a multinational federal system.	Heavily coercive effort by a centralizing power to put together a multinational state, some units of which had been independent states.
Close to ideal type:	India 1948	USSR 1922
United States 1787	Spain 1978	
Switzerland 1848	Belgium 1993	
Australia 1901		
Farther from ideal type:		
Canada[a] 1867		
Germany[b] 1870, 1919, 1949		
Brazil[c] 1891		
Austria[d] 1918		

[a]Most English speaking provinces followed a "coming together" pattern. But, British conquest of French Canada in 1759 had elements of "putting together" federalism. Furthermore, in 1867 the British government told the English Canadians that the best way to "hold together" Canada would be to create an asymmetrical federation, which gave French-speaking Canada a variety of constitutionally embedded prerogatives.

[b]In 1870 Prussia was the hegemonic power in the empire, but all units were tied together by the German language and growing spirit of German nationalism. Federation formed in 1870 mainly by nonelected hereditary rulers. In 1949 most traditional boundaries had been changed by the Allied occupational powers.

[c]Most Brazilian states were not unhappy about the Brazilian Federal Republic being created in 1889. However, Brazil was an independent state and unitary empire from 1822 to 1889, and the military, after the coup overthrowing the emperor, unilaterally announced in their "Proclamation of the Republic" that the federation was formed and that the military would use force to ensure the unity of the federation. When the first federal constitution was constructed in 1891, the state of São Paulo was the hegemonic political and economic force at the Constituent Assembly.

[d]In 1918 Austria voted to join Germany in federation, but the post–World War I Treaty of Saint-Germain forbade Austrian unification with Germany. In 1946 occupied by the Allied powers.

to use at least three ideal types of federation formation. The actual historical analysis of the process of federation formation in a particular country, such as Canada, might even require simultaneous attention to all three ideal types (see Table 2.1).

Democratic Federalism in Multinational and Mononational Contexts: Questions of Identity and Asymmetry

The third fundamental concern of the new research agenda on democratic federalism should be nationalism, and especially federalism in multicultural and multinational polities. Just as we comparativists have to work on the relationship of federalism to democracy, we have to work on the relationship of nationalism (and multinationalism) to democracy. By 1986, three years before the Berlin wall came down, two new important bodies of literature were in place that should have helped us to think carefully about the difficult relationship between democratization and (multi-) nationalism. Ernest Gellner published his magisterial *Nations and Nationalism* in 1983, the same year that saw the publication of another modern classic on nationalism, Benedict Anderson's *Imagined Communities: Reflections on the Origin and Spread of Nationalism*. By 1986 the four-volume work edited by Guillermo O'Donnell, Philippe C. Schmitter, and Laurence Whitehead, *Transitions from Authoritarian Rule*, was released and immediately created the field of "transitology."

What strikes me now as amazing is that these two bodies of literature, which in retrospect should have learned so much from each other, were virtually separate and noncommunicating discourses. In the four volumes on democratic transitions, nationalism is never thematized as a major issue or even given one separate chapter. Indeed, the word "nationalism" appears only in the index of one of the four volumes, that on southern Europe, and the reader is referred to only one page on Spain, one page on Portugal, and two pages on Greece. The name of Ernest Gellner does not appear in the index of any of the four volumes, nor does the name of Benedict Anderson. As the author of one of the comparative articles in this series, I, of course, must share responsibility for this omission.

For their part, on the other hand, neither Gellner in *Nations and Nationalism* nor Anderson in *Imagined Communities* in any way thematized democracy, and indeed the word did not enter into the index of either book.

In my judgment, one of the most urgent problems facing modern democratic theorists and practitioners is how to reconcile nationalism and democracy, especially in multinational settings. Federalism (along with some consociational practices) is often one of the potentially attractive (but also potentially dangerous) political formulas those wishing to craft democracy in multinational polities must consider. Obviously, the two previously noncommunicating discourses of democratization and nationalism must come into constant dialogue with each other, especially if we are to address systematically the possibilities of multinational democratic federalism.[12]

Now that we have shown how, for comparative analysis, our three key political and conceptual concerns—democracy, federalism, and nationalism—stand in necessary relationship to each other, let me briefly illustrate two of the many questions about democratic federalism that can best be approached by using all three concepts in a closely connected framework.

Let us look first at the need in democratic federalism, especially if the demos is multinational, for multiple and complementary identities. If federalism is to be a useful concept to employ in the comparative analysis of democracy, we will have to develop the implications of the minimal Dahlian requirements of democratic federalism for political identities and loyalties. Democratic political systems probably should not be called federal systems unless they meet two criteria. First, within the state there must exist some territorial political subunits whose electorate is exclusively drawn from citizens of the subunit *and* that have areas of legal and policy-making autonomy and sovereignty that are constitutionally guaranteed. Second, there must be a statewide political unit, which contains a legislature elected by the statewide population, and which has some law and policy-making areas that are constitutionally guaranteed to fall within the sovereignty of this statewide body.

If one accepts these arguments, it also follows that in a robust democratic federal political system, the more citizens feel a sense of allegiance to both of the democratically legitimated sovereignties, each with its constitutionally guaranteed scope of action, the more democratically secure the federation. Ideally, therefore, citizens within a democratic federation should have *dual* but *complementary* political identities. This is so because, as members of a territorial subunit, if they and the elected leaders of the subunit do not feel that the center provides some goods, security, or identities that they consider valuable, and that are *not* available from the subunit alone, then their loyalty to the center will be weak. Potentially they will provide a constituency for the politics of secession. At the very least, they might provide a constituency for a politics of alienation, or a sense of exploitation, neither of which will help democratic consolidation. Likewise, if many citizens of the federal state and leaders of the center feel that the federal system entails few benefits but imposes many political and economic costs *and* that the costs of intervention (or encouraged exit) are relatively low, the democratic federation will be endangered.

Federalism is a potentially attractive formula for some types of multinational polities, but the politics of building and maintaining dual and complementary identities needs more thought and research. Public opinion surveys are a particularly promising tool in exploring the political circumstances in which loyalty to a "state nation" at the center can grow, while loyalty to a nonsecessionist but nonetheless nationalist subunit also grows.[13]

Another area where it is crucial to simultaneously employ concepts of democracy, multinationalism, and federalism is when we analyze the question of symmetrical federalism and asymmetrical federalism. There are two legitimate uses of the word "asymmetrical" in the study of federalism. The first refers largely to socioeconomic asymmetry and its implications for bargaining within the federation. Steven L. Solnick (1996) is doing important work in this area. The second legitimate use of the word "asymmetrical" in the study of federalism refers to constitutionally embedded differences between the legal status and prerogatives of different subunits within the same federation. In this section I am mainly concerned with *constitutional* asymmetry, but I will also discuss *aconstitutional* asymmetry, and *anticonstitutional* asymmetry.

Let us first try to make a distinction between multinational and nonmultinational states. I call a state multinational if (1) it has territorially based differences (often compounding) based on linguistic, religious, cultural, and ethnic identities and (2) there are significant political groups that would like to build political sovereignties, or an independent state or states, around these territorially based differences. If we use this definition of multinational states, of the eleven federal states with at least ten years of democratic rule at the moment, Canada, Spain, Belgium, and India are multinational. Democratic federations that may be multicultural, and that may have significant indigenous populations, but that are not multinational as I have defined the term, are Austria, Australia, the United States, Germany, Argentina, and Brazil. Paradoxically, the country that is the most difficult to classify as to whether it is actually multinational or not is Switzerland. Many analysts refer, of course, to Switzerland as multinational, because most of the cantons are (exclusively) French, German, or Italian speaking. However, part of the argument against calling Switzerland multinational is that Protestant and Catholic differences are linguistically cross-cutting rather than compounding. Most importantly, none of the parties that have been in the "magic formula" four-party power-sharing coalition that has ruled Switzerland since 1958 is built around a single language, and no significant party advocates secession from what Linz and I prefer to call the "state-nation" (rather than the "multinational state") of Switzerland.

If we employ the definitions I have just advanced, we can create, for analytic purposes, a dichotomy between multinational states and mononational states. We can also divide these states into (largely) constitutionally symmetrical federal states and (largely) constitutionally asymmetrical federal states. This gives us the standard foursquare table depicted in Table 2.2.

Regardless of how one classifies Switzerland, a powerful pattern is clear. *All* (or all but one) of the long-standing multinational federal democracies are constitutionally asymmetrical. *All* (or all but one) of the long-standing mononational federal democracies are constitutionally symmetrical. Therefore, in itself, the fact that Russia, as a multinational federal state, is asymmetrical does not make it a democratic exception. In this respect Russia conforms to the democratic norm.

Table 2.2
Constitutional / Legal Arrangements of Entire Universe of Federal Systems That Have Been Democracies since 1988

| | | Constitution | |
		Symmetrical	Asymmetrical
Demos	Mononational	Argentina Australia Austria Brazil Germany Switzerland (State-Nation?) United States	
	Multinational	Switzerland (Multinational?)	Belgium Canada India Spain (Russia: but not a democracy)

What is an exception to democracy, however, is the fact that Russia has forty-six aconstitutional, bilateral treaties that were negotiated and signed by the chief executive of Russia and the chief executive of one of the eighty-nine constituent members of the Russian Federation, without being signed, or even shown, to the Russian parliament. This is procedurally exceptional in a democratic federation. A further unconformity (indeed, gross incompatibility) with democracy is that many of the bilateral treaties were also substantively exceptional for a democratic federation because they contained passages or agreements that were in violation of the federal constitution (and sometimes even of the constitutions of the signatory republics). This compounded further the already profoundly anticonstitutional quality of Russian politics because of the fact that many of the eighty-nine members of the Russian Federation wrote and passed their own constitutions, or statutes, which contradicted parts of the federal constitution.[14] For what is not, and what is, exceptional about Russia's asymmetrical federalism, see Table 2.3.

If we had not made a distinction between democratic and nondemocratic federations, and between mononational and multinational federations, we would not have been able to identify the powerful and significant patterns revealed in Tables 2.2 and 2.3. Once these patterns are established, a new research agenda emerges for comparativists, especially the question of whether Spain, India, Belgium, and Canada could "hold together" as democratic polities if they were either unitary states or symmetrical federal states.

Rethinking the Normative Basis in Favor of Majority-Limiting Federalism: The Multiple Values Required for Consolidating Democratic Federalism

The distinction between "coming together federalism" and "holding together federalism" opens the way for a reexamination of a major normative issue. An implicit, and often explicit, normative argument for federalism is that it protects individual rights against a too powerful center or even a "tyranny of the majority." William Riker is explicit about the fact that, for him, one of the most attractive aspects of federalism is that it contributes to a limited government that is a check on populist majorities: "The populist ideal requires that rulers move swiftly and surely to embody in law the popular decision on an electoral platform" (1982, 247). Riker espoused normatively a multicameral legislature precisely because he believes it helps to limit populist majorities. Riker was happy to draw attention to the fact, that in the United

Table 2.3

Range of Symmetrical and Asymmetrical Federal Systems

Constitutionally Largely Symmetrical	Some Asymmetrical Differences Constitutionally Embedded and Implemented	Major Asymmetrical Differences Constitutionally Embedded, Extraconstitutionally Negotiated, or Anticonstitutionally Exercised
Australia Austria Brazil Germany Switzerland United States	Belgium: Extensive constitutional provisions for different linguistic communities and use of consociational and nonterritorial representation arrangements. Special status of Brussels and the small German-speaking territory. Canada: French-speaking Quebec has a number of prerogatives that the English-speaking provinces do not have in such areas as education, law, and immigration policy. India: Federacy relationship with Jammu Kashmir and numerous special linguistic and tribal arrangements. Spain: Different autonomies have different prerogatives that are constitutionally embedded. All new arrangements must be public and be approved by both chambers of parliament. Both center and autonomies subject to binding decisions by Constitutional Court.	Russia: Constitutionally, republics have higher status as members of Russian Federation than do "territories," "regions," "federal cities," "autonomous regions," and "autonomous areas." All these classifications stem from Soviet federalism. Extra-constitutionally, private treaties are negotiated between the executive of the center and the executives of the subunits, often with special prerogatives or dispensations, that were not voted upon by the Parliament or even widely known before they were signed. Anticonstitutionally, numerous provisions of the constitutions or statutes of the 89 subjects of the Federation are in contradiction with the 1993 Russian constitution. Constitutional Court often does not make a ruling, and when it does make a ruling, it often is not implemented. No "common legal space" in Russia.

States, the multicameral legislature is "really three houses: the president, Senate and House of Representatives based on different divisions of the people into constituencies. The different constituencies have typically kept the interests of rulers separate" (1982, 250). For Riker, the second great contribution of U.S.-style federalism to limited government is the division of authority between national and local governments and especially its fragmenting effect on parties: "This is the famous American federalism; copied over half the world. The constitutional restraint is not, however, the legal division of duties between central and local governments but rather the resultant localization of political parties that renders national leadership of them impossible" (1982, 250). For Riker, the beneficial constraints that U.S. federalism promotes is that "multi-cameralism and federalism have enforced localism in parties, and this in turn has forced rulers to persuade rather than to control. The total effect is that policy does not change either rapidly or sharply enough to hurt anyone very badly" (1982, 253).

But in multinational federations, especially in fragile new democracies, is it always normatively desirable or politically useful to have such a "localization of political parties" that it renders politywide leadership impossible? It is by no means clear. Consider, for example, the role of statewide parties in "founding elections" in multinational federal polities. In the founding elections in Nigeria in 1959, the polis was divided into a Northern Region, a Western Region, and an Eastern Region. In each of these regions an ethnically based regional party won control of its regional legislature. In the federal legislature there were virtually no elected representatives of statewide parties. This situation directly contributed to intense political conflict emerging out of the compounding cleavages of ethnoterritorial regionalism and eventually to the civil war over the Biafran secessionist attempt. In Yugoslavia the first competitive elections were at the republican level and were all won by regional and ethnic nationalist parties. The Yugoslav civil wars occurred before a single statewide election was held. In contrast, in Spain statewide and provincial elections were held simultaneously. Statewide parties formed the central government *and* twelve of the fourteen subunit governments. In India, after the simultaneous elections for the center and the subunits, the statewide Congress Party formed the government at the center *and* in all of the states. Clearly, if the goal is the consolidation of democracy in a multicultural or multinational polity, a strong case can be made that the existence of statewide parties is useful.

The role of statewide parties would seem to be especially important if the primary purpose is to "hold together" a federation in a form that reconciles cultural diversity with policy-making efficacy. Such a reconciliation is, of course, precisely what the Indian Constituent Assembly was striving to create. To quote Ambedkar again: "The . . . Constitution has sought to forge means and methods whereby India will have Federation and at the same time will have uniformity in all basic matters which are essential to maintain the unity of the country. The means adopted by the Constitution are three: (1) a single judiciary, (2) uniformity in fundamental laws, civil and criminal, and (3) a common All-India Civil Service to man important posts" (Government of India 1951).

Let us now directly address some critical normative and conceptual issues about democracy and my use of the phrases "demos constraining" and "demos enabling."[15] If one takes democratic consolidation as a desired normative goal, and if one recognizes the empirical reality that such consolidation is often not achieved, then it is useful to think deeply about what mix of values might, in a probabilistic sense, be associated with promoting, or inhibiting, democratic consolidation. In my judgment, democratic consolidation is helped if three core values—liberty, equality, and efficacy—are all addressed in such a way that none are neglected, and all reinforce one another.

Liberty of individual citizens is clearly a positive value. In a democracy this implies that the majority, however constituted, should not impose policies on minorities that violate individual rights. Constitutionalism and the rule of law are major democratic institutions that help to preserve liberty and individual rights. For many liberal thinkers, especially in the U.S. tradition, federalism is often presented as playing a key role, for some thinkers *the* key role, in constraining the "tyranny of the majority."

Another value in modern democracies is the *equality* of the citizens in a polity, the equality of the members of the demos. In a minimal sense this means "one citizen one vote." In a more expanded sense equality could also mean that the demos assumes some commitment to raise all individual citizens to a shared core of basic rights and well-being.

Finally, if a democracy is to persist, and if new democracies are to be consolidated, the institutions of governance should be crafted in such a way as to enable the demos of the overall polity and the demoi of the subunits to be governed with an acceptable degree of *efficacy*. Efficacy as a value (unlike liberty) is not uniquely related to democracy. Nondemocratic regimes can aspire to efficacy. But, if we understand democracy as a set of lived, valued, and historically precarious institutions, there are reasons to believe that a democratic polity with very low efficacy is *less* likely to endure than a democracy with moderate or high efficacy. Principled democrats should not, therefore, if possible, craft institutions of governance for the demos and the demoi that make efficacy especially difficult.

If one accepts that "liberty," "equality," and "efficacy" are *all* important for a high-quality democracy, how should these three values relate to each other in democratic federalism? A strong tradition in U.S. liberal thought gives a privileged place to federalism's contribution to liberty. As we have seen, Riker is a member of this tradition. Some theorists who are particularly interested in preventing "the tyranny of the majority" entertain ideas not only of "supermajorities" but even of legislative unanimity in multiple legislatures.[16] This, of course, in theory would help preclude a tyranny of the majority.

For some fundamental and controversial constitutional issues it is a great advantage if consensual, near unanimous, agreements can be achieved. However, theoretically and empirically, a "unanimity rule," or even a strict supermajority requirement for routine governmental decision making, is in strong tension with the values of efficacy and equality. The requirement of supermajorities makes legislation much more difficult to pass and gives minorities great blocking power.[17] Indeed, in an extreme demos-constraining form of federalism, legislators possibly representing less than 10 percent of the electorate might constitute what I would call a "blocking win-set." That is, they control sufficient votes to stop the status quo from being changed if they do not want it changed. In such circumstances these legislators, even if they were programmatically in favor of legislation, might be structurally tempted to exploit their blocking win-set position to get rent-seeking rewards. Clearly, small blocking win-sets that are constitutionally embedded in a democratic federal system also raise serious questions about the equality of one citizen one vote.

Politically, therefore, constitutionally embedded blocking win-sets can potentially raise acute questions about the efficacious and legitimate functioning of democracy. For example, there might be a prolonged period in a country during which a strong majority of the political leaders, and a strong majority of the electorate in the country, believe that major changes are necessary. But, if the federation has been crafted to facilitate "win-sets" of blocking vetoes by small minorities, the efficacy and legitimacy of that democracy could be eroded by such demos-constraining federal features. If many citizens believe that a popular government with popular policies is being blocked via the very institutions of democracy itself (such as in an extreme variety of demos-constraining federalism), it is possible that this situation could create a context whereby most of the legislation is not actually stopped, but is passed, with diffuse public support, by executive decree. Such a situation may be good or bad for efficacy. However, it is certainly not conducive to democratic consolidation, which is best advanced if the passage of major rules is done inside, not outside, democratic legislative processes.[18]

Federalism as a Demos-Constraining/Demos-Enabling Continuum

Riker argues that the fundamental structure of modern federalism is what he calls "centralized federalism." Riker sees the United States not only as the origin of this model, but as the modal form of federalism. I argue that it is much more empirically useful for a comparativist to approach democratic federalism as a continuum from least demos constraining to most demos constraining. In this alternative conceptual approach, the United States emerges, not as the modal type of modern federalism, but as an extreme outlier at the demos-constraining end of the continuum. Let me develop my argument.

Until 1787 the only form of federalism in the world, according to Riker, was "decentralized federalism." Riker argues that in 1787 the founding fathers "invented centralized federalism" (1987, 17–42). Throughout his writings Riker stresses the theme that "it is the centralized form of federation that the world finds attractive" (1975, 10). For Riker, all modern federal systems are derived from the U.S. model, and he often presents the U.S. model as the norm.

Riker urges the reader to accept the implicit dichotomy "decentralized federalism" versus "centralized federalism." But I urge the reader to see what Riker calls decentralized federalism as a variety of "alliances" or "confederations" in which the fundamental characteristic was that the sovereignty of the members of an alliance or a confederation was not constitutionally constrained. Members were situationally constrained, but only as long as each sovereign member judged it was in their interest to act collectively. In some cases before Philadelphia in 1787, what Riker calls "decentralized federalism" did require a unanimous vote. But, analytically, a decision rule requiring unanimity is, of course, consistent with the absolute sovereignty of the individual members, because no decision can be made against their interest.

Riker is right that something new emerged in Philadelphia. What emerged was a formula to *constrain constitutionally* all units of the federation in such a way that exit would be constitutionally impossible or extremely difficult. Also, unanimity was not required for compulsory decisions. If there is a dichotomy, therefore, it is between alliances and confederations on the one hand, and federations on the other. If the reader accepts this revision of the Rikerian dichotomy, then we are ready for the next step.

All democratic federations, qua federations, are *center-constraining*. Instead of "centralized federalism" being conceived of as standing in dichotomous opposition to "decentralized federalism," I suggest that it is analytically more fruitful to conceive of democratic federalism as forming a *continuum that runs from high demos-constraining to demos-enabling.* The framework of a continuum opens up the analytic and historical category of federalism to a range of empirical and conceptual distinctions that are not possible if we simply lump all federal systems into the single category of "centralized federalism." For example, I will show that, far from the U.S. version of "centralized federalism" being the federal norm, it is an extreme "outlier" on the demos-constraining end of the continuum that I will construct. In fact, as I shall demonstrate later, of the main federal systems in the world, only Brazil has a potential to block the democratic majority at the center comparable to the majority-blocking potential of the United States. Germany, rather than being ruled out of the category of federal systems because it deviates from the U.S. norm, as K. C. Wheare suggested, is actually much closer to the center (the norm) on the federal continuum. India, the survival of whose democratic political system cannot be understood without analyzing its federal component, but which Wheare called only "quasi-federal" because it deviated so much from the United States, is at the least demos-constraining end of the continuum, extremely far from the United States. In the conceptual terms of our discussion, India in the 1980s and 1990s shared only two characteristics with the United States: it was federal and democratic.

Why are *all* democratic federations inherently center constraining? There are four reasons. The first reason is conceptual and constitutional with empirical consequences. Robert A. Dahl's definition succinctly captured the dual sovereignty dimension of federalism that constitutionally constrains the demos at the center (1986, 114). If we accept Dahl's definition, we must accept that all democratic federations, qua federations, are center and, even to some extent, demos constraining. Consider federalism's impact on agendas. Democracies normally have an open agenda. That is, within the formulas prescribed by the constitution, there are no policy areas where the democratic majority in the polis cannot make laws. This is one of the reasons why Adam Prezworski (1986, 47–63, esp. 58–60) talks of democracy as a form of "institutionalized uncertainty." However, unlike a unitary democratic system, in all federal systems the demos at the center must accept a *closed agenda* in that some issue areas are constitutionally beyond their law-making powers (Dahl 1989, 135–52 and 193–212).

The second way in which all democratic federations constrain the demos is that the demos is diffused, not only into many demoi, but also into various authority structures. The demos is constrained vertically, as Dahl's argument makes clear. In addition the demos is also constrained horizontally. At the center there are two law-making legislatures. One legislature, the lower chamber, represents the principle of the population and can come close to the pure democratic equality of one person, one vote. But the upper chamber represents the principle of territory. The ideological discourse of territorial equality (one unit one vote) can mask *massive inequality* (a citizen's vote in a small state can count for more than a hundred votes in a large state).

The third way in which all democratic federations constrain the demos relates to the constitution. All democratic constitutions should be "self-binding," in that they should be (optimally) difficult to change (Elster and Slagstad 1988, 8–14). In an extreme case of a constitution that is extremely difficult to change, a democratic question could be raised about whether one generation of democrats should bind forever future generations of democrats. The more areas that are stipulated as being constitutionally *beyond* the democratic center in a federal system, the broader the range of policy areas in which future generations at the center must produce supermajorities in order to be able to legislate. Hypothetically, it is possible that at some time in the future the overwhelming majority of people in *all* the subunits might want to become a unitary state. However, the constitution's framing generation may have explicitly precluded any amendment that would change the fundamental nature of the federal system. In that case the only option would be to write a new constitution.[19]

Most political changes are not as extreme as the hypothetical case just referred to, but changing the rules of the game of a federation are exceptionally difficult. From the perspective of either game theory or legislative behavior, the hardest rules to change are decision rules that structurally favor a group whose positive vote is nevertheless needed to change those rules. A vote in the upper chamber to make a highly unequal federal system less demos constraining is such a vote.[20]

The fourth reason why all democratic federations are demos constraining follows from the previous three. Constitutions in democratic federations are necessarily more complex than constitutions in unitary democracies. Potential policy issues in areas such as the environment, welfare, legislation, health, and research are constantly being socially and economically reconstructed. The boundaries of what is consensually a subunit government concern, or a central government concern, are in continual flux. Boundary adjudication is therefore more essential, and more difficult, in a federal than in a unitary system. Thus, another major political actor that does not owe its law-making authority to periodic checks by the demos, or even the demoi—the judiciary—is normally empowered to play a bigger role in a federal system than it does in a unitary system.

For all the reasons I have just analyzed, all democratic federations are thus inherently demos constraining. However, as I shall document later, democratic federations can and do vary immensely in the degree to which they are demos constraining. In fact, some federations are constructed in such a way as to be, within the limits of federalism, demos enabling. The analytical weakness of Riker's concept of the fundamental dichotomy between "decentralized federalism" and "centralized federalism" is that it makes it difficult to see and evaluate the great variation within what he calls "centralized federalism." Later in this article I operationalize my concept of a federalist continuum and demonstrate how it opens up a more fruitful approach to the empirical, and even the normative, comparative analysis of federalism.

Federalism and the Potential for a Structurally Induced Policy Status Quo

The last major Rikerian thesis I want to examine concerns policy. The argument Riker makes appears paradoxical. Despite his normative argument in favor of federalism because of its majority-blocking tendency to fragment parties, he argues that federal institutions, by themselves, have *no* policy impact. I argue, on the contrary, that federal institutions matter—matter a lot. What is the structure of Riker's argument?

Riker sees individual preferences as being the driving force behind social choice. From this premise Riker argues that, if an aggregate of individuals believe that any particular set of institutions such as federal institutions contribute to policy outcomes they do not like, it is relatively easy for them to change those institutions, and to change policy. This line of argumentation is what leads Riker to the seemingly peculiar position of being the world's most prestigious academic authority on federalism *and* asserting that the object of his scientific observation is actually a powerless chimera. Let me quote at some length Riker's words on why federal institutions do not matter:

> It is difficult to escape the conclusion that the accidents of federalism (i.e. the constitutional and administrative details) do not make any difference at all. They simply provide a standard of style for federal countries that differ somewhat from the standard for unitary ones. In federal countries, it is often necessary to go through the form of showing that a government has legal authority to do what it wants to do. But of course, if it really wants to do it, the authority is always there. Lawyers, especially constitutional lawyers, have a little more work in a federation than in a unitary system; otherwise there is not much difference. (1975, 144)

> No matter how useful the fiction of federalism is in creating new government, one should not overlook the fact that it is a fiction. In the study of federal governments, therefore, it is always appropriate to go behind the fiction to study the real forces in a political system. (1969)

> What counts is not the rather trivial constitutional structure but rather the political and economic culture. . . . Federalism is at most an intervening and relatively unimportant variable. (1969, 144–45)

> Federalism makes no particular difference for public policy. (1975, 143, n23)

One of the reasons for the strange death of federalism in modern democratic theory is that the major theorist of federalism killed it. The reasoning behind such Rikerian judgments are that he sees collective decisions and policies as being fundamentally derived from an aggregate of individual preferences. In a stylized manner, we can say that Riker sees aggregated tastes as inherently unstable and as essentially incoherent. Democracy entails a "preference-induced disequilibrium." Tastes make demands. Institutions ultimately translate tastes into policies. Thus tastes are the fundamental explanation of policy outcomes. It is from the context of this logic that Riker asserts that federal institutions are "at most an intervening and relatively unimportant variable."

In some of his writings, to be sure, Riker acknowledges that institutions might matter, but the central thrust of his argument is that tastes matter more than institutions. For Riker, "institutions are probably best seen as *congealed tastes*. . . . If institutions are congealed tastes and if tastes lack equilibria, then also do institutions except for short-run events" (1980, 445, emphasis added).

Tastes do matter, but so do institutions. In some instances a democracy can break down or slide into civil war in the short term. In U.S. history a case could possibly be made that "in the short term" (say, in the twenty years leading up to the first shot being fired) the highly demos-constraining quality of U.S. federal institutions contributed to the Civil War.

As Kenneth Shepsle and Barry Weingast (1981, 1987) convincingly argue, part of the force of Riker's argument comes from the dual assumption that individuals do not have fixed tastes or agendas and that the institutions they are in do not have bounded contexts that structure incentives. If these two assumptions hold, then if the aggregate of individuals in a legislature actually have a preference for a policy measure, they can easily pass relevant legislation. But, as Shepsle and Weingast go on to demonstrate, *neither* of these assumptions is warranted in the study of legislatures. They show how, for example, even in the U.S. House of Representatives, institutional issues such as bureaucratic routines, decision rules, seniority on important committees, and the rule that any law passed must be superior, in the judgment of the gatekeepers, to the status quo often produce a "structurally induced equilibrium." Shepsle and Weingast show how such institutionally structured decision systems can have a strong impact on policy. The status quo often prevails, not because of individual tastes, but because of the specific institutional structures of the Congress, and because congressmen come into this institutional setting not from completely unbounded but from bounded contexts. The overall context within which individual congressmen actually function has something to do with the regional interest groups that send them, and that will help defeat or reelect them, in less than two years. Correctly understood, the vectors of new institutionalism, and the vectors of individual rational choice, may actually point in the same direction in the case of many federal systems, namely, the status quo.

If this can happen in the U.S. House of Representatives, which has close to proportional representation in terms of one person one vote, one does not have to be "a new institutionalist" to be sensitive to the policy implications of federalism in a country like Brazil, where the Senate's prerogatives place it at the extreme end of the demos-constraining continuum, and where the constituencies and governors that help send members to the Senate have their own agendas and control resources that the senators value.[21] Brazil is a struggling new democracy with one of the world's worst income distributions. In 1996 the majority of the population continually expressed strong preferences for reforms, and President Cardoso, who also backed reforms, ended the year with extremely high approval ratings. Nevertheless, neither the "tastes" of the citizens nor the preferences of the president were able to produce many reforms. In the Brazilian upper chamber, a group of senators who represent less than 9 percent of the electorate can produce a "win-set" to block major legislative reform. If the institutions of the equally apportioned U.S. House of Representatives can produce structurally induced equilibria, Brazilian federalism, which has an extremely malapportioned upper house *and* an extremely malapportioned lower house, can certainly help contribute to the continuation of a structurally induced status quo. No serious analyst of Brazil, after carefully studying the consequences of the decision rules and the prerogatives of the Senate, the states, and the governors, could sustain an argument that federalism is a relatively unimportant intervening variable.

Operationalizing the Demos-Constraining/Demos-Enabling Continuum

If I have raised empirical and normative questions about the Rikerian framework, it is now incumbent upon me to attempt to operationalize my concept of a demos-constraining continuum and to use it for the comparative analysis of politics in democratic federal systems.

Democratic federal systems can vary significantly on a number of constitutionally embedded practices and decision-making formulae that go against the general democratic principle of "one person, one vote." There can also be extremely important paraconstitutional patterns of political behavior that mitigate or exacerbate limits on the ability of a politywide majority to make policy. Although each of the above individual factors has some impact on the rule-making capacity of the demos, what is of most importance is how these factors interact with one another in such a way as to impede systematically a potential majority's capacity to alter the status quo or to facilitate (within the limits of the constitutionally guaranteed areas of subunit rights) the capacity of a majority to create politywide decisions they deem necessary for the quality of democracy and efficacious policy making. Here I give special attention to four variables, three of them constitutionally embedded and one, among the most important, a paraconstitutional practice of political parties. The four variables, and the associated propositions concerning their demos-constraining potential in federal systems, are the following:

Variable 1:	The degree of overrepresentation in the territorial chamber.
Proposition:	The greater the overrepresentation of the less populous states (and thus the underrepresentation of the more populous states) the greater the demos-constraining potential of the Senate.
Variable 2:	The "policy scope" of the territorial chamber.
Proposition:	The greater the "policy scope" of the chamber that represents the principle of territory, the greater the potential to limit the law-making powers of the chamber that represents the principle of population.
Variable 3:	The degree to which policy making is constitutionally allocated to subunits of the federation.
Proposition:	The greater the amount of policy-making competencies that are constitutionally prescribed as being beyond the law-making powers of the central government, the greater the demos is constrained.
Variable 4:	The degree to which the party-system is politywide in its orientation and incentive systems.
Proposition:	The more political parties are disciplined parties whose incentive systems, especially concerning nominations, privileges politywide interests over provincial and local interests, the more politywide parties can mitigate the inherent demos-limiting characteristics of federalism.

Variable 1: The Degree of Overrepresentation in the Territorial Chamber

All federations have a legislative chamber that represents the specific territories of the subunits that constitute the federation (hereafter called the Senate, the territorial chamber, or "the upper house") and one legislative chamber that represents the people as a whole (hereafter called the "lower house"). As measured by the democratic principle of "one person, one vote," all upper houses to some degree violate the democratic principle of equality. However, what is not often recognized is that there can be, and is, enormous variation in the degree of inequality in which small states are overrepresented in federal upper houses.

The most widely known example and emulated model of democratic federalism is that drafted in 1787 in Philadelphia. But the U.S. model has a number of characteristics that are not essential to democratic federalism. Indeed, a case can be made that the U.S. model, qua model, should be open to debate, negotiation, and challenge. One problematic characteristic of the U.S. model relates to the composition of the upper federal chamber.

The rationale of second chambers in federations is that they pay particular attention to issues of special relevance to the subunits of the federation. Not as a point of principle, but rather as part of the historical "grand compromise" between the big and small states, the representatives of the big states in 1787–88 made two major concessions that violated formal democratic equality.[22] First, they gave the small states equal representation or, more accurately, *massive overrepresentation* in the upper chamber. Second, with less awareness of the implications, they made the *policy scope* of both houses basically the same. These two decisions, which I call "disproportionate representation" and "symmetrical policy scope," are a fundamental part of the U.S. federal formula. But should they necessarily be a part of modern democratic federalism? Let us first restrict our attention to variable 1, the composition of the upper chamber.

Within existing democratic federal systems some states are overrepresented by more than a factor of one hundred. Such massive overrepresentation is not a necessary feature of democratic federalism. If an ethnic or cultural minority in a federation were overrepresented by such a drastic number in the upper chamber, and if the chamber had a policy scope equal to that of the more democratically elected house, this would almost certainly create problems of allegiance to the federation by some leaders at the center, especially in a multinational federation.

How great is the variation of overrepresentation in modern democratic federal systems? The democratic federal system with the least overrepresentation is Belgium, with a Gini coefficient of overrepresentation of only 0.015.[23] India is 0.10,

Germany is 0.32. But the United States has a Gini coefficient of overrepresentation in the second chamber of 0.49, while Brazil is close at 0.52.

What are the actual empirical patterns behind such differences in the Gini co-efficient of inequality of representation in the upper chamber? In Austria, for example, which is only slightly less proportional than Belgium, there are nine states (*Länder*). Each state is represented in the federal chamber, but the total number of representatives is allocated almost according to population as follows: Vienna: 12 seats, Lower Austria: 12, Upper Austria: 10, Carinthia: 4, Tyrol: 5, Burgenland and Vorarlberg: 3 each (*Europa World Year Book* 1990, 405).

In Germany the 1949 Basic Law (Bonn constitution) stipulates that the subunits (or *Länder*) of the federation will get between three and six votes in the upper chamber (*Bundesrat*): "Each *Land* shall have at least three votes; *Länder* with more than two million inhabitants shall have four, *Länder* with more than six million inhabitants five, and *Länder* with more than seven million inhabitants six votes" (Finer, Bogdanor, and Rudden 1995, 150). The smallest *Land*, Bremen, in 1993 had a population of 686,000 and was allocated three votes in the upper house. The largest *Land*, North Rhine–Westphalia, had a population of 17,679,000 and was allocated six votes in the upper house (*Europa World Year Book* 1995b, 1293). Thus, one vote in Bremen was worth thirteen votes in North Rhine–Westphalia.

The United States and Brazil have the same decision rule concerning votes in the upper chamber; each state, no matter the population, receives an equal amount of Senate seats (two in the United States and three in Brazil). In the United States the state with the smallest population in 1990 was Wyoming with 453,588 people, and the state with the largest population was California with 29,760,021 (*Whitaker's Almanac* 1997). Thus, one vote in Wyoming was worth sixty-six votes in California.

Brazil is even more demos constraining than the United States. The smallest state in Brazil in 1991 was Roraima, with a population of 215,790, and the largest state was São Paulo, with a population of 31,192,818 (Elazar 1994, 44; *Europa World Year Book* 1995a, 618). Thus, one vote cast in Roraima has 144 times as much weight as a vote cast in São Paulo.

The demos-constraining nature of Brazil's federalism is in fact even more extreme if we consider the lower house. For purposes of brevity I will not treat representation in the lower house as a separate variable. However, I should note that the rhetorical and political power of the need to represent territory (as opposed to pop-

Table 2.4

A Continuum of the Degree of Overrepresentation in the Upper Houses of Twelve Modern Federal Democracies[a]

Gini index of inequality[b]	Belgium	Austria	India	Spain	Germany	Canada	Australia	Russia	Switzerland	U.S.	Brazil	Argentina
	0.015	0.05	0.10	0.31	0.32	0.34	0.36	0.43	0.45	0.49	0.52	0.61

Ratio of best represented to worst represented federal unit (on basis of population)	Austria	Belgium	Spain	India	Germany	Australia	Canada	Switzerland	United States	Argentina	Brazil	Russia
	1.5/1	2/1	10/1	11/1	13/1	13/1	21/1	40/1	66/1	85/1	144/1	370/1

Percentage of seats of best represented decile	Belgium	Austria	India	Spain	Germany	Australia	Canada	Russia	Switzerland	U.S.	Brazil	Argentina
	10.8	11.9	15.4	23.7	24.0	28.7	33.4	35.0	38.4	39.7	41.3	44.8

[a]The status of Russia as a democracy is the most questionable of the twelve countries in the table. The Russian data are included for comparative purposes. This table was prepared with the help of Wilfried Swenden, as part of the Stepan-Swenden federal databank. We are grateful to Cindy Skach and Jeff Kahn for providing us with the data on India and Russia, respectively. Other data were taken from *Whitaker's Almanac* (1997); *Europa World Year Book* (1995a); and Elazar (1994). For the constitutional provisions on second chambers see S. E. Finer, Vernon Bogdanor, and Bernard Rudden (1995), and Blaustein and Flanz, (1991–).

[b]The formula is: $G = 1 + 1/n - 2n\,y\,(y_1 + 2y_2 + 3y_3 + \cdots + ny_n)$, with n = number of units, y = mean percentage of seats. In case one uses deciles as units, y is automatically 10; so is n. $y_1, y_2, y_3, \ldots, y_n$ stands for the percentage of seats that corresponds to each of the deciles. The Gini coefficient equals zero if the composition of the upper chamber is fully proportional and equals one if one subunit has all the votes in the second chamber. The Gini coefficient was among the first authors to use the Gini coefficient as a measure of inequality for the composition of second chambers. See Lijphart (1984, 174).

ulation, i.e., "one person, one vote") is so strong in Brazil that every state, no matter how small, receives a "floor" of eight deputies in the House of Representatives, and no state, no matter how populous, can receive more than the "ceiling" of 70 deputies. If there were perfect proportionality in Brazil, Roraima would receive one deputy and São Paulo close to 115 deputies. As it is, Roraima receives eight deputies and São Paulo only seventy.[24]

On our demos-constraining continuum, therefore, it is clear that on variable 1 Belgium, Austria, and India are at the low end. Germany is near the center, and the United States, Brazil, and Argentina are the most demos constraining (see Table 2.4).

Variable 2: The Policy Scope of the Territorial Chamber

There is no sense in having a federation unless the subunits can play some role in making, or at the very least reviewing, laws that directly affect how the federation works. This is particularly true for multinational or multicultural federations. Lawmaking powers concerning cultural issues such as language, religion, or education are among the more important reasons for the very existence of such multinational federations.

However, federal legislative systems differ greatly as to what politywide competencies are accorded to the upper house. The U.S. House of Representatives has greater prerogatives than the Senate in originating money bills, and thus some analysts believe its powers are greater than the Senate's. However, a case could be made that in some important respects the unrepresentative Senate has even greater powers than the House of Representatives (which is reapportioned every decade to reflect population changes). In the creation of Supreme Court justices, for instance, the president nominates, the Senate denies or confirms the nominations, and the House of Representatives is constitutionally marginalized. The same holds true for all major posts in the executive branch. The secretary, deputy secretary, and all assistant secretaries of all cabinet-rank departments must be confirmed by the Senate, and likewise for such positions as the directors of the Central Intelligence Agency, National Security Council, Federal Bureau of Investigation, and many other major government agencies.

Brazil in theory follows the U.S. constitutional formula of power symmetry between the two houses. The lower house, as in the United States, has greater authority in originating money bills. Also, unless the Senate votes against an entire bill, the House of Representatives can alter any changes the Senate makes to a bill without a conference. However, the Senate has twelve areas where it has exclusive competence. For example, the Senate directly appoints two-thirds of the judges that review federal expenditures, and it has the right to deny or confirm the other third. The Senate has exclusive competence to authorize state borrowing and can override a negative opinion of the Central Bank. The Senate has exclusive competence to approve the central administration's foreign borrowing levels. In Brazil, there is *no* policy area that is beyond the policy-making competence of the Senate, but there are many key policy areas that are the exclusive law-making prerogatives of the Senate.

In Brazil the interaction of variables 1 and 2 means that states that represent only 13 percent of the total electorate have 51 percent of the votes in the Senate. This small group of Senators thus has to be treated with deference, patronage, and logrolling because it is a group that can, theoretically, block policies supported by Senators representing 87 percent of the population.

The U.S. model of "symmetry of policy scope" is not, of course, the only model. Indeed, the U.S. model is once again at the extreme end of the demos-constraining continuum. It is important to emphasize that neither democratic theory nor modern democratic practice requires that a chamber with massive disproportionality be given policy-making powers equal to that of the proportional chamber. For example, I have not seen a serious charge that the second chamber in Germany, the Bundesrat, is treated unfairly or undemocratically because of its limited scope. The close-to-proportional first chamber, the Bundestag, which represents all the voters of Germany, has the *exclusive* power to elect and dismiss the chancellor. Germany's famous "constructive vote of no confidence" is only voted upon in the lower chamber.[25] Likewise, originally, the second chamber's consent was not needed for approximately 60 percent of the statutes passed by the lower chamber.[26] The upper chamber's right to cast a "suspensive veto," and thus to force a proposed statute to be considered by a joint committee, is of growing importance due to divided majorities in the lower and upper chambers. However, in the thirteen legislative periods between 1949 and 1998, the highest refusal rate on consent bills was only 2.5 percent. During the 1953–58 session and the 1983–87 session, the upper chamber did not effectively veto a single bill.[27]

This difference in policy scope between the U.S. model and what eventually became the German federal model was absolutely understood—and resisted—by the American Occupation authorities during the drafting of the Bonn constitution. According to the eminent scholar of political institutions Herman Finer, the Americans were "convinced of the desirability of a weak federal authority. They were persuaded by the kind of arguments for federalism and the separation of powers needed in the nascent United States in 1788, namely, to keep government weak for the sake of a durable and democratic (that is, atomized) system. This caused the SPD (the German Social Democratic Party) to go into opposition." Eventually the SPD prevailed over American objections and "secured that, broadly speaking, the second chamber should not be of the dominant state-powerful type over the lower chamber" (1956, 690).

So German federalism is less disproportionate than U.S. federalism, and less symmetrical in policy scope than U.S. federalism. On both dimensions, therefore, a case can be made that German federalism is more formally (and I believe substantively) democratic.[28]

Spain is less demos constraining than Germany. As in Germany, the lower chamber, the Cortes, has exclusive competence over the two most important politywide issues: the power to authorize the formation of the government and to vote a "constructive motion of no confidence." However, the upper chamber has even less scope than in Germany to veto legislation passed by the lower chamber.

The most important power the Spanish upper chamber has is the capacity to block an armed intervention of the central government in one of the autonomous provinces. Since such intervention is of direct relevance for the nature of the federation, it is correct that the territorial chamber has special powers in this respect. The constitution is very carefully crafted in this respect, as we will see when we discuss variable 3.

At the lowest end of the demos-constraining scale of territorial chambers are countries such as India, Spain, and Belgium. They are so low, indeed, that some analysts might even argue that the territorial chambers are too weak for these countries to be considered federations. However, if one accepts the fundamental Dahlian definition of a federation as involving powers of the subunits that are constitutionally *beyond* the power of the center, Spain and Belgium are clearly federal, because of variable 3 (to be discussed shortly), concerning the power of the subunits, which in Spain and Belgium are quite substantial. As a paper by the Belgian political scientist Wilfried Swenden makes clear, one of the most distinctive aspects about Belgian federalism is that it is a multinational and multicultural polity that combines substantial federal and consociational characteristics. On the Gini index, Belgium's upper house is the closest to pure proportional representation in the Stepan-Swenden database. However, the Belgian Senate has to consent to constitutional amendments and international treaties and to all legislation affecting the structure of federal institutions and the judicial organization of the country. But amendments to the constitution or all legislation that substantially affects the federal structure or the linguistic statute of the Communities require special majorities. All constitutional amendments require a two-thirds majority in both houses. Significantly, all legislation or constitutional amendments relating to linguistic matters not only require an overall two-thirds parliamentary majority, but also a majority within each linguistic group in parliament. It should be noted that on such occasions both houses are split according to linguistic lines. Critics have therefore argued that there is no need for a strong federal bicameral system, since this technique of so-called special majorities likewise applies to the lower house (Swenden 1997).

Constitutionally, the Spanish and Indian upper houses, like Germany's, play no role in votes of confidence or no confidence. However, unlike Germany, the Spanish and Indian upper chambers have no significant law-making role in the federation.[29] In fact, they are close to a revisionary chamber, like the House of Lords in the United Kingdom. In one important area, however, the Spanish upper chamber plays a crucial role in preserving the autonomy of the subunits. This area concerns the right of the center to use armed force to impose "order" on a subunit. All democracies have some provisions for emergency laws. The key question is whether the emergency provisions are written in an explicit enough manner that such powers actually can only be implemented with the consent of the legislature, for specific purposes agreed to by the legislature, and only for finite periods determined by the legislature. In a federation this is an area where it is absolutely appropriate for the upper chamber to play a central role, because armed interventions by the center in the subunits involve a fundamental aspect of the federation qua federation.

Federal interventions are discussed in Article 155 of the Spanish constitution. Interventions can only occur after four conditions are satisfied. First, the government must come to a legal determination that some subunit has violated the constitution, or is not upholding the constitution. Second, the central government must convey this legal determination in writing to the subunit and ask for a response. Third, if the government considers the response of the subunit to be inadequate, it can ask the upper chamber to vote for federal intervention. Fourth, no intervention can occur unless the upper chamber approves by an absolute majority. Given this clear set of guidelines, time for mutual adjustments and bargaining is built into the process. In the first nineteen years of the Spanish constitution, *no* intervention under Article 155 ever occurred. In my judgment it is probably correct to say that the upper house plays an appropriate demos-constraining role vis-à-vis federal interventions.

It is probably also correct to say that in India the constitutional formula concerning federal interventions does not sufficiently constrain a government in possession of a majority. The relevant constitutional article is Article 356, which simply says that the Council of Ministers (the cabinet) can instruct the president to ask for an intervention (called "president's rule") that would dissolve a provincial legislature and government and put the province under the direct rule of the center. The only requirement for such an intervention is that the governor (a nonelected official appointed by the center) indicates that the government of the province "cannot be carried on in accordance with the provisions of the constitution." No vote authorizing federal intervention is needed in either the upper or the lower house for the first sixty days of intervention. After two months the upper house and the lower house must formally vote a renewal for six months, or the intervention must cease. Thus the upper chamber does have the constitutional power to curtail a federal intervention. But the constitutional provisions on intervention are so loose, and the Congress Party in the past so often had such politywide party majorities and discipline (variable 5), that "president's rule" happened frequently, even under the democratic and consociational rule of Nehru. In fact, between 1947 and 1997 president's rule was implemented over one hundred times and affected every state.

However, a combination of factors, including recent court decisions that have begun to insist that the central government at least publish the explicit grounds for intervention, the increasing frequency of minority governments at the center, and the growing coalitional weight of provincial parties, has made the employment of president's rule more difficult and controversial.[30] If we restrict our analysis only to the majority-constraining features of the upper house, a case could be made that the federal dimension of Indian democracy might be enhanced if an absolute majority of the upper house were required *before* president's rule could be implemented. The recent court decisions are also probably right to insist that the central government explicitly document why an intervention is called for.

Unlike variable 1, namely, the principle of representation of the upper house, variable 2, concerning the legislative competencies of the upper house, does not lend itself to quantification. However, I believe sufficient qualitative evidence has

Table 2.5

Continuum of the Upper Chamber's Constitutional Prerogatives to Constrain a Majority at the Center

Least Constraining					Most Constraining
India	Spain	Germany	United States	Brazil
Upper chamber has no constitutional powers to protect subunit autonomy against a sixty-day central intervention. Upper chamber has capacity to review or deny president's rule only after sixty days. Virtually only a revisionary chamber.	Major power is Article 155 of the constitution, which precludes intervention by the center unless it has received the absolute majority approval of the upper house. Plays no role in constructive vote of no confidence or normal legislation. Largely a revisionary chamber.	Upper chamber plays no role in constructive vote of no confidence. This is the exclusive competence of the lower chamber. Only can play a potential veto role in the approximately 65 percent of the total legislative agenda that directly relates to center-subunit issues. Relatively slight capacity to block a potential majority	Extensive capacity to block a democratic majority. The unrepresentative chamber has the same voting rights on all legislation as the "one person–one vote" chamber. Senate has exclusive competence to confirm or deny all major judicial and administrative appointments. A chair of a committee can at times be a "win-set" of one. A "win-set" of senators representing only 15 percent	Excessive for the efficacious and legitimate functioning of democratic government. The extremely disproportional upper chamber must approve all legislation. The Senate has twelve areas where they have exclusive law-making prerogatives. A "win-set" of senators representing 13 percent of the total electorate can block ordinary legislation supported by senators representing 87 percent of the population.

of the lower chamber. Even in the years when the upper chamber was controlled by a different majority than the majority of the lower chamber, the upper chamber sustained less than 3 percent of its vetoes.

Upper chamber plays almost no role in confirming or denying major administrative appointments.

of the total electorate can block ordinary legislation.

been given to allow us to place the five countries I have discussed along a demos-constraining continuum for the variable (see Table 2.5).

Variable 3: The Degree to Which Policy Making Is Constitutionally Allocated to Subunits of the Federation

This is a complex variable that contains three closely related but analytically distinct components. The first component concerns the amount of potential legislative is-sues that are embedded in the constitution and that require exceptional law-making majorities. The second component concerns which powers are constitutionally given to the subunits and which to the center. The third component concerns whether, if the constitution is silent on an issue, the presumption is that residual law-making power resides with the center or with the subunits.

If the constitution is relatively parsimonious, or even when detailed is devoted to principles, most laws can be passed with simple majorities. Depending on variable 2, these votes may or may not involve the upper house. However, the above three components may interrelate in such a way that senators, representing less than 8 per-cent of the total electorate, might have a blocking veto over an extensive degree of legislation and could conceivably thwart a majority again and again. This is not only a question of democratic theory but of democratic practice. If a minority can use its blocking power to defend a status quo that democratic theorists, constitutional analysts, public opinion, and the majority of politicians believe should be changed, then this is dangerous for democracy. Such a situation could either create a climate of widespread "semiloyalty" to democracy itself and/or lead to a context support-ive of what Guillermo O'Donnell calls "delegative democracy," in which presidents rule via exceptional measures in the name of efficacy, but to the harm of the full democratic process (Linz 1978; O'Donnell 1994).

This variable also concerns the amount of policy-making authority reserved for the center and that reserved for the subunits. Democratic federations vary greatly concerning how much law-making authority is permanently given to the subunits, and how much is reserved for the center. Here an important distinction must be made. A polity can *decentralize administration* and *transfer most of the budget* to the sub-units in areas such as health, law enforcement, and welfare but *reserve for the central legislators the right to pass basic legislation and carry out authoritative oversight in these ar-eas.* Or the polity could give the subunits exclusive law-making and taxing powers in these areas, whether or not they contribute to overall citizen equality and well-being in the federation.

Once again, Brazilian federalism is the most demos constraining in all these matters. A frustrated former Minister of Planning, Dr. José Serra, the distinguished economist and a senator who received more votes than any senator in Brazil's history, says of the Brazilian constitution of 1988 that "it is not really a constitution, but a social, political, and economic law."[31] An extraordinary number of issues, such as the exact details of retirement plans, foreign and state ownership, special tax schemes for regional development projects, fixed percentages of tax allocations to the center, states, and municipalities, and numerous other items, are embedded in the 1988 constitution.[32] They are thus beyond the scope of ordinary majority legislation. To pass an amendment in any of these areas requires a 60 percent positive vote of *all* members, whether they are present or not, two times, in both houses. In a context of a country the size of a continent, where average nonattendance even at the Constituent Assembly was over 30 percent, this is an extremely arduous task. To be sure, this is an easier constitutional amendment process than in the United States, but the U.S. constitution is much more parsimonious than that of Brazil.

Even if we assume 100 percent legislative attendance—which would cost the government an extraordinary amount of lobbying and costly side payments—the minimum "win-set" for blocking any law that is constitutionally embedded is simply the negative vote of senators who represent 8 percent of Brazil's total electorate.[33] The influence of what Carl Friedrich called the "law of anticipated response" comes into play in such a situation. The Brazilian situation is thus a clear instance of what Shepsle and Weingast call "structurally induced equilibrium." Since all players are aware of the blocking potential of a small minority, many potential policy initiatives, even if they are backed by a majority of Congress and by public opinion, are taken off the agenda.[34] Even when the issue is not taken off the policy agenda, the cost of passing reform legislation is often extremely high in terms of logrolling and special regional payments. For a country like Brazil, which as late as 1993 had an inflation rate of over 2,000 percent per annum, such a pattern of "structurally induced" nonactions, and/or highly costly actions, puts enormous constraints on the central government's capacity to carry out coherent fiscal planning and to implement needed reform.

The other component of what is constitutionally embedded in Brazil concerns the powers of the states and municipalities. Until recently twenty-four of Brazil's twenty-seven states had their own state banks and frequently issued loans to themselves. The only federal body that had to approve outside bonds was the territorial chamber, the Senate. Until November 1996 states also had the power to tax exports. The cost of getting the Congress to approve a law abolishing state taxes on exports is estimated as one-half percent of Brazil's G.N.P. in 1997.

The final component of subunit authority concerns residual law-making authority. The presumption in Brazil is that if the constitution is silent on an issue, residual law-making authority rests with the subunits.[35] In Brazil the interaction of variables 1, 2, and 3 creates an extremely high majority-blocking potential and places Brazil, once again, on the extreme of the continuum we are examining.

The United States shares with Brazil the presumption that, for those areas that are not defined in the constitution, residual sovereignty resides with the states, a presumption that is, in itself, demos constraining. However, the political impact of what is in the constitution is substantially less constraining in the United States than in Brazil, because the U.S. constitution is more parsimonious, and among other things no banks are owned by the states.

Germany's constitution is much less demos constraining than that of the United States. A very large area of law-making authority is explicitly given to the federal center. Much legislation is also concurrent and thus shared by the center and the subunits. Moreover, the constitution is explicit and therefore reduces the power of courts to make law by the eight words contained in Article 31: "federal law shall take precedence over *Land* law." Articles 72–74 also make clear the wide range of areas in which the federal law can, if the lower house so wants, prevail.

One of the innovations in the practice of German federalism is that, while the majority in the lower chamber at the center retains the constitutional right to pass laws and to exercise oversight, a greater percentage of the total taxes that are collected are *actually* spent by the *Länder* than are spent by the states in the United States. Also, most of the federal programs are directly administered by *Länder* officials, whereas in the United States many federal programs are administered by federal employees. In conceptual and political terms, therefore, we can say that in Germany the lower chamber at the center retains more law-making power than in the United States but decentralizes more administration. The key point is that a polity can decentralize, without the demos at the center constitutionally yielding law-making and oversight authority.

The most significant part of Spain's federalism is the vertical dimension. Spain's system of *Autonomías* is an "asymmetrical federalism," in the sense that some provinces such as Catalonia and the Basque country negotiated, via the statutes of autonomy arrangements, greater prerogatives than other autonomous provinces. These prerogatives are embedded in statutes with constitutional standing. From the perspective of game theory, Spain's asymmetrical federalism has created an iterative bargaining game. For example, a nationalist political leader may control a nationalist party based in one province whose votes are needed to put together a governmental majority at the center. This situation would therefore give the province the bargaining power, de facto, to renegotiate the terms of the Statutes of Autonomy. Spanish asymmetrical federal bargaining games so far have been constructed *within* the constitution.

Russian federalism is also asymmetrical; however, many of the iterative bargaining games are *outside* the constitution. Russia's federal bargaining games are therefore often harmful to democratic consolidation because subunits unilaterally redraft their own constitutions, often in ways that violate the constitution of the Russian Federation.

The Indian constitution retains residual power at the center, but it is a constitution that in many respects helps India's multinational federalism. For example, the constitution allows the majority at the center, and clusters of linguistic minorities in the subunits, to work together to create, under parliamentary authority, new linguistic states with great facility.[36] This capacity has been extremely important in "holding together" India's polity in a democratic way. Precisely because the members of the Constituent Assembly knew that the most controversial issue surrounding Indian unity was language policy, and that there was a desire on the part of many delegates to reorganize the states along more linguistic lines eventually, the language of the constitution was extremely *demos enabling*. Future parliaments were given rights to redraw state boundaries completely. Article 3 of the constitution was categorical. With a simple majority "Parliament may by law (a) form a state by separation of territory from any state or by uniting two or more states . . . , (b) diminish the area of any state . . . , (c) alter the name of any state." In a true "coming together" federation the sovereign states would obviously have been able to bargain successfully for a much more demos-constraining constitution to protect states' rights.

The 1991 census indicated that India has more than three thousand mother tongues that are legally recognized. There are thirty-three different languages, each

Table 2.6
The Constitutional Allocation of Policy Making to Subunits of the Federation

Least   Most

India	Germany	Spain	United States	Brazil
Does not constrain majorities.	Slightly majority constraining.	Major constraints on majority at the center derive from the statutes of autonomy.	Strongly majority constraining. Constitution is extremely difficult to amend but is parsimonious, so vast majority of legislation can be passed as ordinary legislation.	Extremely majority constraining. 1988 constitution so extensive that much ordinary legislation can only be passed by the exceptional majorities required for constitutional amendments.
Capacity to respond to minority desires to redraw the linguistic boundaries of states.	Federal law explicitly given precedent over *Land* law.	Occasional iterative, within constitution, bargaining process if center needs votes of provincial party during process of government formation.	Power is horizontally shared at the center among three branches.	States and municipalities had such extreme control over export taxes and banking that central government's fiscal and trade policy in 1989–96 was impeded. Some centralization of tax and bank policies in 1995–96 but extremely costly to the center.
Probably should constrain the ease by which the majority can intervene in states.	Wide areas where law-making powers are either explicitly given to the center or are concurrent responsibilities.	Any asymmetrical provincial powers must be voted upon and approved by parliament at the center.	Power is vertically devolved and shared in "marble cake" federalism between the federal and the state governments.	Residual power with states.
Since 1994 Supreme Court decisions give somewhat more protection to subunits from the imposition of "president's rule" from the center.	More tax money is spent by the *Länder* than by the center. Many federal programs are decentralized so as to be administered by the *Länder*, while law-making and policy oversight remain the prerogative of the center.	Residual power with center.	Residual power with states.	
Residual power with center.	Most powers are concurrent, but residual powers are with the *Länder*.			

of which is spoken by at least one million people. In a relatively consensual manner, most of the boundaries of the states in India were redrawn between 1956 and 1966, and later a process of creating new tribal states in the North-East was begun.

In political terms, it is probably fair to say that the survival of India as the world's largest multicultural, multinational democracy was greatly facilitated by the constitutional structure of the federal system. India's demos-enabling federal structure allowed the majority at the center to respond to minority demands from states for greater linguistic and cultural autonomy. If India had been a unitary state (or had a U.S.-style demos-constraining federal structure), neither the demos nor the regional demoi would have had this constitutional flexibility available to them. The continuum concerning variable 3 can be presented as shown in Table 2.6.

Variable 4: The Degree to Which the Party System Is Politywide in Its Orientation and Incentive Systems

A federal system by definition has executives and legislatures elected in each of the constituent units. These executives and legislatures necessarily have some control over budgets and laws. Structurally and empirically, therefore, federalism per se is a system of patronage, power, and prestige that can challenge the power and authority of politywide parties. Such challenges are present in a systematically lesser degree in a unitary than in a federal political system. Some analysts infer from this that the relative absence of ideology and strong disciplined parties in the United States is produced fundamentally by the federal system (Truman 1955). This happens to be true for the United States, but it is *not* true of all federal systems. Let us see why.

Some federal party systems, for a variety of reasons, often produce a majority (coalitional or single party) at the center. Such a coalition may also have politywide discipline and a strong politywide organizational infrastructure that creates incentives for disciplined allegiance to politywide parties. In such cases the party system in itself can act as a centralizing, majority-producing force inside a mononational federation, as in Germany since 1949, or even in a multicultural, multilingual federation, as in India from 1947 until 1967.

There are many countervailing factors, including ideology, that can contribute to such politywide unity despite the inherent fragmenting pressures found in all federations. For example, if there are no primary elections; if there is either a closed-list proportional representation (in which parties rank the candidates), or a single-member district in which the politywide party selects the party nominees; if the politywide party provides the vast majority of campaign funding for its nominees; and if the system is parliamentary, there will be a strong set of structural and rational choice incentives—despite federalism—to produce disciplined politywide parties.

In sharp contrast, if the political system has either an open-list PR system or a single-member district with primaries; if the candidates must raise almost all their money independently of the politywide parties; and if the system is presidential, then there are very few structural or rational choice incentives to produce politywide party unity. The United States, and even more so Brazil, are systems of this latter sort (Mainwaring 1999).[37]

But Brazil and the United States are "state-nations." The situation is potentially more complicated (and democratically dangerous) if the polity is a multinational state and there are no disciplined statewide parties. In Russia, for example, 103 of the 171 members of the Federal Council in 1997 belonged to no party at all (Barber 1997). In the Yugoslavian and Soviet multinational polities, the first competitive elections for executive power were held not in the center, but in the provinces. The fact that there were virtually no politywide parties in the Soviet Union or Yugoslavia contributed to state disintegration in both countries (Linz and Stepan 2001). In contrast, in the federal "state-nation" of Brazil, the fact that in the democratic transition process direct elections for governor were held in 1982, but not for the presidency until 1989, contributed to the center and demos-constraining nature of the 1988 constitution and the increased decentralization of Brazil's fiscal resources, but it did *not* endanger Brazil's territorial unity.

Spain is a multinational federal polity that contains strong politywide parties with some small but significant provincial parties. Linz and I have argued elsewhere that the fact that the first competitive free elections after the death of Franco were politywide contributed to the creation of strong politywide parties, even in Catalonia and the Basque country (Linz and Stepan 2001). However, Catalonia, the province with sociologically the strongest autonomy movement, is governed by a regional national party coalition. The regional party is also strong in the Basque country. This is a fundamental feature of Spain's "asymmetrical federalism," and it contributes to the iterative bargaining games that occur if no party at the center has a majority.[38]

Russia, like Spain, is a case of asymmetrical federalism, but, as we have seen, it differs from Spain in some very important, and democratically dangerous, respects. Spain is a parliamentary system, and since 1983 after each general parliamentary election a party has achieved a majority or "supported minority" position, and the leader of that party has become the prime minister.

The prime minister is the head of the party and works hard to maintain polity-wide party discipline. But in Russia the system is semipresidential of the "super-presidential" sort. The president's mandate comes from a direct election and is therefore independent of whether he has a majority in parliament or not. In fact, President Yeltsin, as president, never belonged to any political party, never campaigned for political parties in the parliamentary elections, and never, between January 1992 and July 1998, had anything close to a majority in the lower house. Many of the candidates for the Duma and the governorships ran as "independents." Like Spain, Russia's asymmetrical federalism has produced an iterative bargaining game, but a variety that is more impeding of democratic consolidation than that of Spain. The first move in the bargaining game of many Russian subunits is to issue unilaterally their own constitution, which often violates the federal constitution (Stepan 2000b). For the continuum of how parties do, or do not, mitigate the demos-constraining features of a federation, see Table 2.7.

Concluding Reflections

Federal institutions matter for policy at *all* points on the demos-constraining/demos-enabling continuum. Likewise, whether a federation has constitutionally symmetrical or asymmetrical competencies for each state is of great import for matters of policy. At the demos-constraining end, Brazilian senators who represent as little as 8 percent of the electorate have more seats in the Senate than senators who represent more than 90 percent of the electorate.

At the demos-enabling end of the continuum, federalism has a policy impact, especially in "holding together," multinational, asymmetrical federal systems. A unitary system, or a demos-constraining, constitutionally symmetrical, federal system, could not have made as many, and as rapid, linguistic boundary adjustments as were made in India. Likewise, such a system would not have at its disposal the vast repertoire of federal policies that allow the multicultural, multilinguistic, multireligious Indian polity of a billion people to "hold together." The use of creative federalizing devices in India seems simultaneously, in almost all states, to respond to diversity, while reducing secessionist tendencies to small minorities. Democratic federal devolution of power, and the granting of group-specific rights, has not been a slippery

Table 2.7

The Degree to Which Party System Empowers Majority by Creating Politywide Programmatic Discipline

Most						Least
India (1947–67)	Germany	Spain	United States	India (1991–)	Brazil

India (1947–67)	Germany	Spain	United States	India (1991–)	Brazil
Politywide Congress Party always had a strong majority at the center and controlled vast majority of states where it played a major but not coercive role in nominations.	Strong politywide parties control almost all the seats in the lower and upper chambers and exercise rigid discipline on their members. Ideological tradition of trust and mutual aid (*Bundestreue*). When one party, or a "closely connected" coalition of parties, controls both chambers, the majority is strongly empowered.	Disciplined politywide parties control most of lower house, which is key policy-making chamber. But due to Spain's asymmetrical multinational federalism, strong provincial parties exist that are able to negotiate for special status when no party has a majority at the center.	Primary system and self-financing make local and state influence more important than politywide influences for most nominations and elections. Polsby calls the United States a system with "100 state parties flying two banners." Nomination system for president and single-member plurality districts contribute to the two-party system, as does third de facto anti-party	No party at the center has had a majority. Majority of states controlled by a regional party. Thirteen parties, most of them regional but no longer separatist, formed the government at the center in 1996–97, twenty-three in 1999. However, India's	Nominations fundamentally controlled at state and municipal levels. Most campaigns are self-financed. Extremely high score on Pedersen party volatility index (50%). Large number of parties. Laakso-Taagepera index of around 8.

However, if the party or coalition that controls the lower chamber does not control the upper chamber, they are less empowered.

state-level legislation. In federal legislature a two-party system is encouraged by the rules of the congressional committees, which privilege the two major parties. Party discipline grew in the Democratic Party with the end of the Dixiecrats in the 1960s and in the Republican Party due to emergence of the neoconservatives with Reagan.

"regional" parties are becoming in some sense more "centric-regional" than purely regional because they have constituted the governing coalition at the center in 1996–97, and contributed to the BJP-led government coalition in 1998–99, 1999– .

Almost a third of congressmen newly elected to 1992–96 Congress changed parties. "State-nation" so no separatist parties, but many state delegations to the center have strong regional policy agendas.

slope to secession, or to the violation of individual rights, as liberal rights theorists often fear.[39] Once Tamil speakers were given a state, English was retained as a language of the Union, and a regional party won control of the state legislature, the issue of Tamil secession became a nonissue.[40] Democratic elections and devolution in the Punjab in the late 1990s also made violent Sikh secessionist movements almost a nonissue.[41] It appears that India is more decentralized, and more "a state-nation" with a civilizational culture, in the late 1990s than ever before. Multiple and complementary identities that were not the norm for some important Tamil-speaking political leaders in India in the 1950s, or for significant numbers of Sikhs in the Punjab in the 1980s, are now the norm in both areas (Kumar 1997; Singh 1997).[42] Such processes are worth pondering as we develop a new research agenda on democratic federalism in multinational, as well as mononational states.

Spain's "holding together," asymmetrical federalism produces an iterative bargaining game but also helps produce a system of multiple but complementary identities. In 1991, in Catalonia, 73 percent of the population were proud to be Spanish, 82 percent proud to be Catalan, and 83 percent were in favor of increased movement toward confederal formulas in Europe within the European Community (Linz and Stepan 1996b, 102).

Let me conclude with three caveats that have implications for future research. First, some advocates of federalism favor federal, as opposed to unitary, governments because they believe they contribute to liberty, subsidiarity, and democracy. I have seen no systematic evidence to support such presumptions, but they clearly need to be researched. Other scholars and activists argue that, unless a polity is very large, or very multinational, federal institutions are neither necessary nor even useful. Once again, such claims need to be researched, but on grounds of legitimacy, efficacy, and equality, this argument would appear, prima facie, to be a reasonable position.

My second caveat is that, while it may be true that all democracies that are strongly multinational are federal and asymmetrical, some federal practices can be potentially dangerous, especially during moments of transformation in multinational, nondemocratic polities. As we have already discussed, the three formally federal states of Communist Europe fragmented with substantial bloodshed into twenty-three independent countries, many of them ethnocracies. Our research agenda on multinational federalism needs to focus on what political practices and incentives contribute to multiple and complementary identities, civic peace, and democracy, and which practices and incentives contribute to polarizing identities, fratricide, and ethnocracies.

My final caveat is that while I have argued, contra Riker, that federal institutions "do matter," such institutions can, of course, change over time. Of the four variables I have discussed, the most amenable to change is the role of political parties and their impact on federal institutions. As Table 2.7 makes clear, India from 1947 to 1967 was normally ruled at the center, and in the states, by the Congress Party. But since 1996 the three non-Congress ruling coalitions have contained thirteen to twenty-three parties, many of them with a strong base in one, or only a few, states. This factor in itself has altered the political and socioeconomic federal balance in the direction of growing powers for states vis-à-vis the center. In Germany, in the mid-1990s, parties that were in opposition to the governing coalition at the center came to control a majority of the *Länder*, and thus to control a majority in the upper house. De facto, even without a constitutional change, the relative weight of the upper chamber in German federalism increased in this period. Power changes of this sort occur routinely in federal systems. Nonetheless, many decision rules and institutional routines that affect power relations in federal systems are constitutionally embedded—like variables 1, 2, and 3 discussed here—and therefore require supermajorities to change.

Thus, even though preferences may change, there are many consequential, structurally induced regularities in the different types of democratic federal systems, and we must devise better strategies to learn more about such regularities.

NOTES

A previous version of this chapter was published in Stepan (2001).

1. This is, of course, largely a function of the size of federal democracies. The most populous democracy in North America, the United States of America, is federal. The most populous democracy in Western Europe, the Federal Republic of Germany, is federal. The most populous democracy in Asia, indeed, in the world, India, is federal. Other long-standing federal democracies include Australia, Austria, Belgium, Canada, Spain, and Switzerland.

2. These countries are Belgium, Canada, India, and Spain. Switzerland is, of course, a federal democracy, but I will discuss my reservations about calling it "multinational" later in this chapter. Many major polities that are not now democracies, should they ever become so on their existing territories, would be multinational. Countries in this category include Burma, Malaysia, Indonesia, China, and until recently Nigeria. To become democracies most of these countries would probably have to craft workable federal systems. The debates about deepening integration in the Euro-

pean Union and the "democratic deficit" are, of course, debates about multinational federalism.

3. By "demos" I simply mean *all* the citizens of the polity. "Demos constraining" is not meant to imply that "a majority" always exists or is always right. I believe that in some federations, especially multinational or multicultural federations, there can be a role for nonmajoritarian consociational practices which are consensually agreed upon by both the demos at the center and the "demoi" of the subunits of federation. One of the major purposes of this chapter is precisely to assess how different types of democratic federal systems are "demos constraining," whereas some have important "demos-enabling" characteristics.

4. Daniel J. Elazar has written or edited nearly fifteen books that relate to federalism. For political scientists his most influential book is *Exploring Federalism* (1987).

5. Riker published sixteen articles in the *American Political Science Review* in this period, more than any other political scientist. He also led a political science journal citation index in this period. Riker is not just prominent in the judgment of U.S. political scientists. Robert E. Goodin and Hans-Dieter Klingemann, from Australia and Germany, respectively, recently edited the massive *New Handbook of Political Science*. In this handbook Riker is listed as one of the "integrators" of political science in the world and receives twenty-four references in the index, whereas Wheare receives one and Elazar none. See Miller, Tien, and Peebler (1996) and Goodin and Klingemann (1996, 40–41) and the index to their book.

6. This project, of five or six years' duration, will result in our jointly authored book *Federalism, Democracy and Nation*. Also see Linz (1997).

7. Late imperial Germany had a fairly strong rule of law and was a federation, but very important aspects of how power was formed and exercised were still nondemocratic.

8. Indeed, throughout the nondemocratic period of Brazilian twentieth-century history, 1930–45 and 1964–85, federalism remained of some political importance. In Mexico federalism is playing an increasingly important role in the death throes of one of the world's longest reigning nondemocratic party systems.

9. Numerous references on the origins of India's "holding together" federation are to follow. For Belgium's shift from a unitary state to a federal system with consociational characteristics see Hooghe (1993), Senelle (1996), and Swenden (1997). For analysis of the process by which Spain was transformed from a unitary state to a federal state, see Linz (1989) and Agronoff (1994).

10. To be sure, if the partition had not occurred, and if the Muslim territories that are now Pakistan and Bangladesh had sent representatives to the Constituent Assembly, a very different bargaining context would have predominated. In such a context the bargaining power of the princely states, especially the Muslim-ruled princely states in central India such as Hyderabad, would also have been augmented. Once the violent partition began, however, both the Congress Party leaders in the Constituent Assembly and the last British viceroy, Lord Mountbatten, felt that a new geopolitical situation existed. In this new context the Nehru government actually used military force to integrate the largest princely state, Hyderabad, in September 1948. Mountbatten, on numerous informal and formal occasions, let the princely states inside India's new borders know that they no longer had a strong bargaining position. He urged them to join the Indian Union and said that if they did not, the United Kingdom would not let them join the British Commonwealth as indepen-

dent states. Two key books that shed light on the weak bargaining power of the princely states after partition are Menon (1956) and Copland (1997).

11. Modern historical accounts of the 1921–22 period would almost certainly place more emphasis on nationalist resistance in countries such as Georgia and the correlation of military force, especially the Red Army's capacity to conquer Georgia, Armenia, Azerbaijan, and Ukraine, in the absence of international military and diplomatic support for their continued independence. For the Georgia case, see Suny (1993). For the international military balance of power that allowed Soviet military integration efforts to be decisive, see Motyl (1990, esp. 103–18). For the crucial role of the Red Army in inducing "bargains," see Pipes (1954, esp. 193–240).

12. Juan J. Linz and I attempted to do this in our earlier study (Linz and Stepan 1986). See chapters 19 and 20 in the same book. Also see chapter 10 in the present book.

13. In the Linz-Stepan volume, *Federalism, Democracy and Nation,* we will develop this argument with survey data on political identities in numerous countries. In the survey data we will document emerging patterns of conflictual identity polarization in some polities, as well as the emergence of multiple and complementary identities in others.

14. For more detail, see Stepan (2000b).

15. In an earlier version of this chapter I used the phrase "majority constraining" instead of "demos constraining." Scott Mainwaring and Gerry Mackie raised a number of conceptual issues about my use of the term "majority constraining," for which I thank them.

16. For a useful discussion of this normative dimension of U.S. political thought, see Goodin (1996).

17. If supermajorities were to be a requirement for *all* decisions in a federal system, then some "starting points" might be much better than others. For example, if the "starting point" entailed great inequality (such as U.S. slavery based in the South), it would raise more potential problems than in a federal system with a starting point of widely diffused social and economic equalities.

18. Two possible arguments against the thesis that I will advance in this chapter—that Brazil is an extreme outlier on the "demos-constraining continuum"—are that the democratic reforming president Fernando Henrique Cardoso (1995–) is seldom, in fact, blocked from implementing new measures because (1) he uses presidential decree powers and (2) most of the nondecree legislation he formally proposes to Congress actually passes. For an impressive argumentation, and documentation, of this position see Figueiredo and Limongi (1997). I do not challenge any of the data in their meticulous and valuable study. However, I would like to make two observations. First, the fact that President Cardoso, who would like to consolidate the institutions of democracy in Brazil, has to pass so much legislation that is popularly supported and is crucial for the efficacy of government via decrees is an unfortunate way to advance the democratic values of liberty, equality, and efficacy. Under a less able and democratically committed president the demos-constraining element of Brazilian federalism might contribute to what Guillermo O'Donnell calls "delegative democracy." The second observation I would like to make is methodological (and extremely political). Political leaders have only so much political capital and resources. They also know how to count. If a powerful minority win-set opposes many of their preferred policy proposals, they will be parsimonious in the measures they will attempt to get by this formidable blocking win-set. From

this methodological perspective, what is more important? The fact that *most* of the measures that the president proposes to the Congress actually get passed, or the fact that *most* of the measures that the president would like to pass he decides not to formally propose to the Congress because of what he sees as blocking win-sets? Based on my interviews with cabinet ministers at the beginning of the Cardoso administration, and twice later, at two-year intervals, I believe that the latter sequence is the more politically significant.

19. See, for example, Article 79 of the German Basic Law (constitution), which says: "Amendments of this basic law affecting the division of the federation into *Länder* [or] the participation on principle of the *Länder* in legislation . . . shall be inadmissible."

20. The last line of Article 5 of the U.S. Constitution stipulates that "No state, without its Consent, shall be deprived of its equal Suffrage in the Senate." Some constitutional lawyers argue that Article 5 makes the massive malrepresentation of two senators per state, regardless of the size of the populations of the states, beyond revocation by a majority, a supermajority, or even a constitutional amendment.

21. In a private communication David Fleischer (Professor of Political Science at the University of Brasilia) estimates that roughly 40 percent of Brazilian federal senators have been governors (many more than once) and that many of the senators aspire to be governors. Almost no U.S. senators were once governors *and* aspire to return as governors. For powerful documentation that the career paths of federal deputies and senators in Brazil are heavily oriented toward, and influenced by, their states see Samuels and Mainwaring (this volume) and Samuels and Abrucio (2000). Samuels and Mainwaring estimate that in the 1991–94 legislature approximately 35 percent of the sitting deputies either exhibited a preference, or actually gave up their seat, for a state-level executive or electoral post.

22. For an excellent discussion of how and why these compromises were made see Swift (1996, 1–94). Also see Riker (1987, 17–42).

23. The Gini index of inequality simply measures the degree of inequality among variables, where an index value of zero denotes complete equality and an index value approaching the theoretical maximum of 1.0 denotes complete inequality (which would mean here that one state has all the representatives). See Lijphart (1984, 173–75).

24. For a discussion of this serious problem of malapportionment in the lower house see the excellent book by Mainwaring (1999), especially chapter 5. The estimate of 115 deputies for São Paulo in 1997 is by Professor David Fleischer from the University of Brasilia, a specialist on the Brazilian legislature.

25. See Articles 63 and 67 of the German Basic Law.

26. Nearly fifty years after the creation of the Basic Law the Bundesrat today has to consent to approximately 55–65 percent of all federal legislation in a normal legislative session. This increase in the consent ratio of total legislation was partly to compensate for the fact that German federalism became somewhat more "centralized" and "administrative" in character over the years. Another significant factor in increasing the consent ratio was that the *Länder* won the right to vote upon many issues relating to federal integration into the European Union.

27. See the meticulous study by Swenden (2000, chap. 6).

28. On German federalism, and more specifically on the German constitutional concept known as *Bundestreue* (often translated as "federal trust" or "comity"), see de Villiers (1995).

29. The Indian upper chamber at the center, the Council of States, does have some, if not many, blocking powers. For example, Article 249 stipulates that the parliament cannot legislate with respect to an issue that has been allocated as a prerogative of the state legislative assemblies unless two-thirds of the members present and voting in the Council of States approve. Also, Article 368 stipulates that constitutional amendments cannot be passed unless an absolute majority of the members of the Council of States approve, and that two-thirds of those present and voting in the Council of States approve. The article also stipulates that such a parliamentary approved amendment must be ratified by not less than one-half of the state legislatures.

30. For the history and recent evolution of president's rule in India, two useful articles are Marwah (1995) and Mozoomdar (1995). I will develop this point further when I write up the results of my April 1997 trip to India, in which I discussed Article 356 with the former chief justice of the Supreme Court and the former chief minister of Kerala, who had Article 356 used against him. Both the former chief justice and the former chief minister believe that Article 356 can, and should be, used more sparingly.

31. Interview with Alfred Stepan in São Paulo, December 2, 1996, and repeated in a public talk at the University of London, February 1997.

32. In my "Brazil's Decentralized Federalism" (Stepan 2000a) I attempt to explain why this occurred. The short answer is that the constitution of 1988 was constructed after a long period (1964–85) of direct military rule that greatly curtailed the power of the states. In the newly democratizing atmosphere of the Constituent Assembly a discourse predominated that the more all rights were explicitly spelled out and the more power was devolved to states and municipalities, the more democratic Brazil would be. Also, the interests of the federal center were not strongly represented in the Constituent Assembly because Brazil had not had a directly elected president since 1960. However, governors, who had been directly elected since 1982, had great moral and political power in the Constituent Assembly, and the decentralized constitution, which transferred a significant amount of Brazil's total tax revenue from the center to the states and municipalities, served many of their political, financial, and tax interests.

33. I arrive at the calculation in the following way: more than 40 percent of the votes needed to block a constitutional reform are held by senators who represent only 8 percent of the Brazilian population.

34. This point was repeatedly emphasized to me in interviews I held in November and December 1996 with numerous central government officials including the ministers of finance and state administration, the former planning minister, and President Cardoso.

35. For a pioneering analysis of the 1988 constitution and the powers of the governors see Abrucio (1998).

36. For the judicious multifactorial approach that guided what became the world's largest redrawing of linguistic, social, environmental, and political boundaries see Government of India Home Department (1955). For an analysis of the politics of language in India, see Brass (1974). To get an understanding of the secessionist tensions that were building up in the Tamil areas of the

south before the "holding together" linguistic devolution see Barnett (1976). There were also mobilizations and protests in the non-Hindi-speaking south in favor of English being retained as an official language for communications within the Indian Union. See, for example, Forrester (1966). As a result of the politics of democratic federalism English as well as Hindi were retained.

37. Brazil scores near the top on a wide range of indicators concerning party fragmentation or indiscipline.

38. In the March 2000 parliamentary elections, however, the ruling party, the Partido Popular, won an absolute majority and thus will be able to form a government without having to make bargains with regional nationalist parties.

39. For pioneering treatments of the issue of collective rights versus individual rights and liberal theorists' hostility to the former, see the book by the philosopher Will Kymlicka (1995). For a powerful argument by a distinguished legal theorist that group rights are often a precondition of individual rights, see Raz (1986, 193–216). For a political and philosophically acute discussion of these issues in India, see Bhargava (1994).

40. In contrast, if the unitary but multinational state of Sri Lanka, after independence, had crafted a "holding together" federation, with a Tamil-speaking state in the northern part of the country, the now almost unmanageable issue of ethnic violence and democratic breakdown might well have never become an issue. For a compelling analysis of the political construction of polarized identities in Sri Lanka, see Bose (1995).

41. Valuable data on loyalties and identities supportive of democracy in India are contained in a soon to be published survey designed by V. B. Singh and Yogendra Yadev of the Center for the Study of Developing Societies in Delhi. Preliminary results are contained in *India Today* (31 August 1996), pp. 36–53.

42. In this overall context of multiple and complementary identities, and the fact that twenty-three parties are in the ruling coalition in the year 2000, the power of the Hindu fundamentalist party, the Bharatiya Janata Party, is culturally and politically constrained.

BIBLIOGRAPHY

1997. *Whitaker's Almanac.* London: I.Whitaker.

Abrucio, Fernando Luiz. 1998. *Os Barões da Federação: Os Governadores e a Redemocratização Brasileira.* São Paulo: Editora Hucitec.

Agronoff, Robert. 1994. Asymmetrical and Symmetrical Federalism in Spain: An Examination of Intergovernmental Policy. In *Evaluating Federal Systems,* edited by B. de Villiers. Pretoria: Juta.

Anderson, Benedict. 1983. *Imagined Communities: Reflections on the Origin and Spread of Nationalism.* London: New Left Books.

Barber, John. 1997. Opposition in Russia. *Government and Opposition* 32 (4): 598–614.

Barnett, Marguerite Ross. 1976. *The Politics of Cultural Nationalism in South India.* Princeton: Princeton University Press.

Bhargava, Rajeev. 1994. Secularism, Democracy and Rights. In *Communalism in India,* edited by M. Arslan and J. Rayan. Delhi: Manohav.

Bhattacharya, Mohit. 1992. The Mind of the Founding Fathers. In *Federalism in India: Origins and Development,* edited by N. Mukarji and B. Arora. New Delhi: Vikas.

Blaustein, A. P., and G. H. Flanz, eds. 1991–. *Constitutions of the Countries of the World.* Dobbs Ferry, N.Y.: Oceana Publications.

Bose, Sumantra. 1995. State Crises and Nationalities Conflict in Sri Lanka and Yugoslavia. *Comparative Political Studies* 28 (April): 87–116.

Brass, Paul R. 1974. *Language, Religion and Politics in North India.* London: Cambridge University Press.

Copland, Ian. 1997. *The Princes of India in the Endgame of Empire, 1917–1947.* Cambridge: Cambridge University Press.

Dahl, Robert A. 1986. Federalism and the Democratic Process. In *Democracy, Identity, and Equality.* Oslo: Norwegian University Press.

———. 1989. *Democracy and Its Critics.* New Haven: Yale University Press.

de Villiers, Bertus. 1995. *Bundestreue: The Soul of an Intergovernmental Partnership: Comparative Analysis of the Principles Underlying Bundestreue in the Federal Republic of Germany, Switzerland and Belgium.* Occasional Papers RSA. Johannesburg: Konrad-Adenauer Stiftung.

Elazar, Daniel. 1987. *Exploring Federalism.* Tuscaloosa: University of Alabama Press.

———. 1994. *Federal Systems of the World: A Handbook of Federal, Confederal, and Autonomy Arrangements.* 2nd ed. Essex: Longman Group.

Elster, Jon, and Rune Slagstad. 1988. *Constitutions and Democracy.* Cambridge: Cambridge University Press.

Europa World Year Book. 1990. Austria, The Constitution. In *Europa World Year Book 1990.* London: Europa Publications.

———. 1995a. *Europa World Year Book 1995.* London: Europa Publications.

———. 1995b. Germany. In *Europa World Year Book 1995.* London: Europa Publications.

Figueiredo, Angelina Cheibub, and Fernando Limongi. 1997. Medidas Provisórias: Abdicação ou Delegação? *Novos Estudos* 47 (Março): 127–54.

Finer, Herman. 1956. *Governments of Greater European Powers: A Comparative Study of the Governments and Political Culture of Great Britain, France, Germany and the Soviet Union.* London: Methuen.

Finer, S. E., Vernon Bogdanor, and Bernard Rudden. 1995. *Comparing Constitutions.* Oxford: Oxford University Press.

Forrester, Duncan B. 1966. The Madras Anti-Hindi Agitation, 1965. *Pacific Affairs* 39 (Spring): 19–36.

Gellner, Ernest. 1983. *Nations and Nationalism.* Oxford: Blackwell.

Goodin, Robert E. 1996. Institutionalizing the Public Interest: The Defense of Deadlock and Beyond. *American Political Science Review* 90 (June): 331–43.

Goodin, Robert E., and Hans-Dieter Klingemann, eds. 1996. *The New Handbook of Political Science.* Oxford: Oxford University Press.

Government of India. 1951. *Constituent Assembly Debates.* Vol. 2. New Delhi: Government of India.

Government of India Home Department. 1955. *Report of the States Reorganization Commission*. New Delhi: Government of India Press.

Hooghe, Liesbeth. 1993. Belgium: From Regionalism to Federalism. *Regional Politics and Policy* 3 (Autumn): 44–69.

Kumar, Sanjay. 1997. Punjab: A Vote for Change. *Politics in India* (April): 49–40.

Kymlicka, Will. 1995. *Multicultural Citizenship: A Liberal Theory of Minority-Rights*. Oxford: Clarendon Press.

Lijphart, Arend. 1984. *Democracies: Patterns of Majoritarian and Consensus Government in Twenty-one Countries*. New Haven: Yale University Press.

Linz, Juan J. 1978. *The Breakdown of Democratic Regimes: Crisis, Breakdown, and Reequlibration*. Baltimore: Johns Hopkins University Press.

———. 1989. Spanish Democracy and the Estado de las Autonomías. In *Forging Unity Out of Diversity: The Approach of Eight Nations*, edited by R. A. Goldwin, A. Kaufman, and W. A. Schambra. Washington, D.C.: American Institute for Public Policy Research.

———. 1997. Democracy, Multinationalism and Federalism. Paper presented at the International Political Science Association meeting, Seoul, South Korea, August 17–22.

Linz, Juan J., and Alfred Stepan. 1986. Stateness, Nationalism and Democratization. In *Problems of Democratic Transition and Consolidation*. Baltimore: Johns Hopkins University Press.

———. 1996a. The Problem of "Stateness" and Transition: The USSR and Russia. In *Problems of Democratic Transition and Consolidation: Southern Europe, South America and Post-Communist Europe*, edited by J. J. Linz and A. Stepan. Baltimore: Johns Hopkins University Press.

———. 1996b. *Problems of Democratic Transition and Consolidation*. Baltimore: Johns Hopkins University Press.

———. 2001. Political Identities and Electoral Sequences: Spain, the Soviet Union and Yugoslavia. In A. Stepan, *Arguing Comparative Politics*, pp. 200–12. New York: Oxford University Press.

Mainwaring, Scott. 1999. *Rethinking Party Systems in the Third Wave of Democratization: The Case of Brazil*. Stanford: Stanford University Press.

Marwah, Ved. 1995. Use and Abuse of Emergency Powers: The Indian Experience. In *Multiple Identities in a Single State: Indian Federalism in Comparative Perspective*, edited by B. Arora and D. V. Verney. New Delhi: Konark Publishers.

Menon, V. P. 1956. *Integration of the Indian States*. Madras: Orient Longman.

Miller, A. H., C. Tien, and A. A. Peebler. 1996. The American Political Science Review Hall of Fame: Assessments and Implications for an Evolving Discipline. *P.S.: Political Science & Politics* 29 (1): 73–83.

Motyl, Alexander J. 1990. *Sovietology, Rationality and Nationality: Coming to Grips with Nationalism in the USSR*. New York: Columbia University Press.

Mozoomdar, Agit. 1995. The Supreme Court and President's Rule. In *Multiple Identities in a Single State: Indian Federalism in Comparative Perspective*, edited by B. Arora and D. V. Verney. New Delhi: Konark.

O'Donnell, Guillermo. 1994. Delegative Democracy. *Journal of Democracy* 5 (1): 55–69.

O'Donnell, Guillermo, Philippe C. Schmitter, and Laurence Whitehead, eds. 1986. *Transitions from Authoritarian Rule: Prospects for Democracy.* Baltimore: Johns Hopkins University Press.

Pipes, Richard. 1954. *The Formation of the Soviet Union: Communism and Nationalism, 1917–1923.* Cambridge, Mass.: Harvard University Press.

Prezworski, Adam. 1986. Some Problems in the Study of the Transition to Democracy. In *Transitions from Authoritarian Rule: Comparative Perspectives,* edited by G. O'Donnell, P. C. Schmitter, and L. Whitehead. Baltimore: Johns Hopkins University Press.

Raz, Joseph. 1986. *The Morality of Freedom.* Oxford: Clarendon Press.

Riker, William H. 1964. *Federalism: Origin, Operation, Significance.* Boston: Little Brown.

———. 1969. Six Books in Search of a Subject or Does Federalism Exist and Does It Matter? *Comparative Politics* 2 (1): 135–46.

———. 1975. Federalism. In *Handbook of Political Science,* edited by F. Greenstein and N. W. Polsby. Reading, Mass.: Addison-Wesley.

———. 1980. Implications for the Disequilibrium of Majority Rule for the Study of Institutions. *American Political Science Review* 74:432–47.

———. 1982. *Liberalism against Populism: A Confrontation between the Theory of Democracy and the Theory of Social Choice.* Prospect Heights: Waveland Press.

———. 1987. *The Development of American Federalism.* Boston: Kluwer.

———. 1996. European Federalism: The Lessons of Past Experience. In *Federalizing Europe? The Costs, Benefits, and Preconditions of Federal Political Systems,* edited by J. J. Hesse and V. Wright. Oxford: Oxford University Press.

Samuels, David, and Fernando Luis Abrucio. 2000. Federalism and Democratic Transitions: The "New" Politics of the Governors in Brazil. *Publius* 30 (2): 43–61.

Senelle, Robert. 1996. The Reform of the Belgian State. In *Federalizing Europe? The Costs, Benefits and Preconditions of Federal Political Systems,* edited by J. J. Hesse and V. Wright. Oxford: Oxford University Press.

Shepsle, Kenneth, and Barry R. Weingast. 1981. Structure Induced Equilibrium and Legislative Choice. *Public Choice* 37:503–19.

———. 1987. The Institutional Foundations of Committee Power. *American Political Science Review* 81 (1): 85–104.

Singh, Ranbir. 1997. Politics in Punjab: Restoration of Accommodation Model. *Politics in India* (April): 37–38.

Solnick, Steven L. 1996. The Political Economy of Russian Federalism: A Framework for Analysis. *Problems of Post-Communism* 43 (8): 13–25.

Stepan, Alfred. 2000a. Brazil's Decentralized Federalism: Bringing Government Closer to the Citizens? *Dædalus* 129 (2): 145–69.

———. 2000b. Russian Federalism in Comparative Perspective: Problems of Power Creation and Power Deflation. *Post-Soviet Affairs* 16 (2): 133–76.

Stepan, Alfred. 2001. *Arguing Comprehensive Politics.* Oxford: Oxford University Press.

Suny, Ronald Grigor. 1993. *The Revenge of the Past: Nationalism, Revolution and the Collapse of the Soviet Union.* Stanford: Stanford University Press.

Swenden, Wilfried. 1997. Belgium: A Federal State in Search of a Nation. Paper prepared for a Conference on Democracy, Nationalism and Federalism at All Souls College, University of Oxford, June 5–8.

———. 2000. *Federalism and Second Chambers: Regional Representation in Parliamentary Federalism.* Ph.D. dissertation, Oxford University.

Swift, Elaine K. 1996. *The Making of an American Senate: Reconstitutive Change in Congress, 1787–1841.* Ann Arbor: University of Michigan Press.

Truman, David. 1955. Federalism and the Party System. In *Federalism: Mature and Emergent,* edited by A. W. MacMahon. Garden City, N.J.: Doubleday.

Wheare, Kenneth C. 1946. *Federal Government.* Oxford: Oxford University Press.

CHAPTER 3

Strong Federalism, Constraints on the Central Government, and Economic Reform in Brazil

—DAVID J. SAMUELS AND SCOTT MAINWARING

In this chapter, we attempt to contribute to the burgeoning literature on Latin American political institutions by discussing the elements and political consequences of contemporary Brazilian federalism. We hope to make three main contributions. First, at the broadest theoretical level, our analysis addresses the utility and limitations of institutional approaches to explaining political outcomes. Much of our own scholarly production has advanced the institutionalist argument that formal political institutions affect political outcomes, and in this chapter we develop this argument by showing how Brazilian federalism affected the process of economic reforms. We also assert, however, that institutions tell only part of the story. In the Brazilian case, effective political leadership under President Fernando Henrique Cardoso (1995–2002) was able to overcome some of the shackles that federalism imposed on previous presidents.

Second, we intend to contribute to the theoretical discussion of federalism. We portray federalism as a bargaining game between the central government (the president in particular) and states, in which the latter are represented by governors and members of the national congress in their capacity as representatives from the states. We agree with previous analysts (Lijphart 1984, 1999; Stepan, chap. 2; Tsebelis 1995) that federalism usually adds more "veto players" to democratic politics, and hence that major policy reform at the national level is likely to be more difficult in federal systems, other things equal. But rather than focusing solely on how federalism constrains reform initiatives of the central government, we also examine variance in presidential capacity to overcome and even reshape federal institutions. We argue that four institutional features of federalism set broad parameters in the bargaining game between presidents and states. These features enable the state actors to constrain presidential initiatives to varying degrees. Yet in addition, three administration-specific variables account for within-country differences over time. These variables give presidents more or less leverage in their dealings with state actors.

Finally, we illustrate the federalist bargaining game by analyzing the Brazilian case. We focus on the interactions between presidents who wanted to carry out economic reforms that would adversely affect state interests, on the one hand, and governors and members of the national congress who wanted to protect state interests, on the other. All four federalism indicators suggest that Brazilian state actors should have great leverage in their interactions with presidents. We show that between 1985 and 1994, state actors effectively thwarted presidential initiatives in three key policy areas: containing state debts, reining in state banks, and adjusting the allocation of fiscal resources between the national and subnational governments. After 1994 the three administration-specific factors gave President Cardoso a much stronger bargaining position in his dealings with state actors. But because these factors are administration specific, one should not infer that Cardoso's successes in the bargaining game mean a definitive weakening of state actors vis-à-vis the president.

In this chapter we bridge two literatures that often fall into different camps of political science: institutionalism and political economy. We argue that federal institutions sharply constrain what otherwise might be an extremely strong president and that federalism helps explain Brazil's delay in implementing economic reforms.

Federalism, Veto Players, and Policy Reform

Since the 1980s, political scientists have addressed how institutions shape policy outcomes, both at a general theoretical level (Thelen and Steinmo 1992) and specifically with respect to Latin America (Linz and Valenzuela 1994; Shugart and Carey 1992). Nevertheless, until recently relatively little has been written about federalism's policy impact in Latin America. The main reason for this is obvious: only four countries in the region (Argentina, Brazil, Mexico, and Venezuela) are federal republics, and of these four, only in Argentina and Brazil did federalism exercise much impact on political outcomes prior to the 1990s. In Argentina and Brazil, federalism has historically been very important, and it has become more important since the 1980s in Mexico.

Our starting point for analyzing the impact of federalism on policy outcomes is the broader literature on political institutions—especially Tsebelis (1995), Lijphart (1984, 1999), and Stepan (chap. 2). Tsebelis developed the notion of veto players to refer to institutional or political actors whose agreement is required to advance a policy decision. With more veto players, negotiations are more complex and policy stability should be greater, and conversely policy reform should be more difficult to achieve. Tsebelis's argument is relevant to understanding how federalism constrains central governments. Federalism usually adds one or two veto players in the politics of policy reform: the upper chamber and, when they are powerful actors in national politics, state governors. Therefore, all else equal, in federal systems there should be more constraints on central government initiatives.

Lijphart's (1984, 1999) distinction between majoritarian and consensus democracy suggests a similar point. Under majoritarian democracy there are few checks on the majority (in Tsebelis's terms there are fewer veto players). Under consensus democracy, in contrast, supermajorities (i.e., majorities above 50 percent plus one) are required for many policy reforms, and minorities are granted extensive veto powers over policy reforms. Following a logic similar to Tsebelis's, Lijphart notes that federalism pushes democracy in a consensus direction in which multiple and sometimes multiple qualified majorities must concur to bring about policy reforms. These two arguments converge on a fundamental point: both Tsebelis and Lijphart see federalism as imposing constraints on central-government initiatives.[1]

Neither Tsebelis nor Lijphart distinguishes one federal system from another. For other purposes it is important to differentiate *among* federal systems, as Stepan (chap. 2) argues. Just as some countries have stronger presidents and others have weaker presidents, some federal institutions impose powerful constraints while others have little impact. Even if most federal systems create additional veto players, these veto players may have very different consequences from one system to the next. For example, in Mexico until the 1990s and Venezuela until the late 1980s, de jure federalism had marginal policy impact in de facto highly centralized political systems. Conversely, in other cases federalism has very significant policy consequences. Similarly, federalism's policy impact can change significantly in a given country. In Brazil, for example, federalism had much greater policy impact after 1985 than it did under military rule (1964–85), and somewhat less impact under President Cardoso's administration (1995–2002) than between 1985 and 1994.

The Continuum from Weak to Strong Federalism: Four Institutional Variables

We analyze federalism in terms of the interaction between presidents and state-level actors—in particular, governors and members of the national congress.[2] Presidents in all democracies except very small ones engage in negotiations with state-level actors, but the terms of the bargaining games vary greatly across cases. We identify four important factors that help explain, both across countries and across time in a given country, differences in how much state actors constrain initiatives in federal systems.

Federalism Variable 1: The Resource Base of Subnational Governments

Federal systems vary widely in how fiscal resources are allocated among the various levels of government. As the resource base of subnational governments increases, the capacity of state actors to constrain the central government also increases, other things equal. State actors with more resources can pursue their own policies and can more easily undermine (deliberately or not) or constrain the policies of the national government. Conversely, subnational governments that are bereft of fiscal resources have less autonomy to pursue their own objectives and less impact on national politics.

Federalism Variable 2: The Power of Governors

The power of governors in federal systems also varies considerably. If governors have greater power to hire, fire, and tax and spend, they can exert greater constraints on presidents, and subnational governments tend to have greater autonomy. This question is related to but cannot be reduced to the resource base of subnational governments. In some cases, such as the United States, governors have ample resources to implement statewide policies, but they do not significantly influence national legislators. Conversely, if governors wield influence over national policy through the influence of national legislators from their subnational unit, they can more easily veto policy reforms proposed by the president. Governors may wield influence over national legislators from their states by their capacity to affect their reelection and other career prospects.

Federalism Variable 3: The Articulation of Subnational Interests in the National Congress

Members of national legislatures in almost all democracies are simultaneously members of national political parties and representatives of constituents. There are usually inevitable tensions between these two functions. In the former capacity, legislators are responsive to national party interests; in the latter, they usually represent subnational interests. The extent to which national legislators articulate subnational interests as opposed to national party interests varies considerably, depending on the incentives created by institutional design. This variation in the extent to which national legislatures articulate subnational interests is important for understanding negotiations between the president and states.

If subnational interests are strongly articulated in the national legislature, the impact of federalism tends to be greater. The strength of subnational interests in the national legislature depends on the powers of the upper chamber and the forces that shape politicians' careers. All federal systems are bicameral, and most have symmetrical bicameralism (Tsebelis and Money 1997), and many deliberately overrepresent some territorial units in one or both legislative chambers (Samuels and Snyder 2001). These mechanisms give legislators from overrepresented units greater veto power than they would otherwise have.

Regarding the consequences of political career structures, some electoral systems and nomination processes encourage members of the national legislature to focus on subnational interests, while others encourage national legislators to respond to national party leaders, who typically focus more on national policy issues. For example, other things equal, an electoral system in which candidates are nominated by national party leaders ought to encourage more focus on national policy issues. In contrast, a system where candidates are nominated at the local or state level should encourage a focus on subnational interests in the national legislature (Samuels 2003).

Federalism Variable 4: The Distribution of Government Functions across Levels of Government

The distribution of government functions across levels of government varies considerably across cases and time. When subnational governments have more constitutional and para-constitutional powers vis-à-vis the federal government, they can more powerfully constrain the latter. Conversely, when subnational governments have more restricted powers, their ability to constrain or undermine presidential initiatives is weakened.

As an example, assume that the president is committed to improving a country's human rights record but that the federal government has limited power over police, military, and judicial practices in the subnational units. If the leaders of these subnational units are not committed to curbing police violence and other human rights transgressions, the president is likely to enjoy limited success in efforts to effect change. If the president has extensive power to appoint judges and to bring trials against human rights offenders, however, then his or her position in the human rights bargaining game with state-level actors is greatly enhanced.

Presidents and Policy Reform: Three Variables

Thus far, we have followed Stepan's excellent analysis (chap. 2) in arguing that federalism's policy impact depends on institutional features of federal systems. At this point, we add another layer of complexity to our analysis and depart from Stepan's and other analyses that have examined exclusively the institutional determinants of policy stability (or constraints on policy reform) (e.g., Cox and McCubbins 2001; Shugart and Haggard 2001; Tsebelis 1995). Rather than thinking only of the ways in which federalism constrains the central government, we now describe a game between the president (who for reasons of simplicity and parsimony we take to be the embodiment of the central government) and state actors (governors and members of the national congress). Although our starting point is institutional approaches to policy outcomes, we also emphasize the capacity of effective presidents to recraft political institutions.

In this specific game the president's objective is to achieve policy reforms that ad-

versely affect state actors. Some state actors' objective—especially those in opposition to the president—is to block such policy reform. State actors who generally support the president are willing to acquiesce to a reform if the cost of opposing a particular initiative is high but are inclined to block the reform if they calculate that it
can be done at marginal or no cost.

We portray the president as the pro-reform agent for both deductive and empirical reasons. The president is elected by a national constituency and has primary
responsibility for economic policies, and for this reason tends to be more concerned
with macroeconomic results than a Congress that has incentives toward particularism and clientelism (Ames 1987; Mayhew 1974; Shugart and Carey 1992). Governors have weaker incentives than presidents to focus on national-level policy
results and stronger reasons to defend state-level resources even at the expense of
national policy results. Empirically, in Latin America, presidents and not legislatures have been the main agents responsible for pushing for stabilization and state
reform. Not all presidents have been pro-reform agents, but if the president is not
pro-reform, market-oriented economic reform has not occurred at the national
level.

This battle over economic reforms that adversely affect some interests of state actors is an important subset of the games between presidents and state actors. Since
the beginning of concerted efforts at state reform and economic stabilization in
Latin America, it has been the dominant game between presidents and state (or
provincial) governments in Brazil and Argentina. In both countries this particular
bargaining game has had important macroeconomic consequences. For example, in
Argentina the capacity of provincial governors to block provincial-level economic
reform and circumvent the market-oriented reforms that took place at the national
level contributed significantly to economic collapse in 2001–2.

The outcome of this game depends not only on where a particular country fits
in the continuum from weak to strong federalism (i.e., the four variables analyzed
in the previous section), but also on three variables that make particular presidents
more or less powerful in negotiations with Congress and governors. The first variable is the president's (and his or her team's) skill and determination to realize reforms. Leadership variables infrequently get serious scrutiny in comparative politics,
but this variable is crucial to understanding differences across administrations and
countries. Political institutions impose constraints, but effective leaders can negotiate around these constraints far more effectively than ineffective ones or those who
are less committed to undertaking certain reforms. Effective leaders can even change

those institutional constraints, such that there is a feedback mechanism between this leadership variable and the institutional constraints.

The second variable is the extent to which the president has broad and solid backing in the national congress (Mainwaring and Shugart 1997). If the president generally has solid backing in the national congress, it is easier to enact reformist legislation that cuts against the interests of subnational governments. The second variable cannot be deduced exclusively from the size of the president's coalition in Congress or the number of governors who come from the president's coalition or party. This information is useful, but it does not take into account shifts in relationships between Congress and the president that occur because of the impact of presidential performance.

We therefore include a third variable, presidential performance. A strong performance gives the president more leverage in dealing with the national congress and with governors and hence makes it easier for the president to implement reforms that might adversely affect the interests of subnational actors. For present purposes, presidential performance in economic issues is especially relevant because the bargaining games analyzed here have to do with economic reforms.

Whereas the four variables related to federalism tend to remain more or less stable across different presidencies within a democracy, the three variables related to presidentialism can change markedly from one president to the next. The federalism variables set broad parameters for the policy impact of federalism, but the three administration-specific variables mean that there can be important changes in the game between the president and state actors in the former's efforts to obtain economic reforms that state actors oppose.

Adding the relationship between the president and state actors to the analysis of constraints imposed by federalism allows us to capture the dynamic interaction between the two actors and to understand change over time. Analyses such as Lijphart's (1984, 1999), Stepan's (chap. 2), and Tsebelis's (1995) usefully portray the constraints created by federalism, but they do not explain why the bargaining game between presidents and governors sometimes changes markedly from one administration to the next even without a major change in the institutional features of federalism.

Centralization under Military Rule, 1964–1985

Following a military coup in 1964, significant centralization occurred along each of the four variables related to federalism, resulting in a weaker impact of federalism

Table 3.1
Division of the Fiscal Pie in Brazil, 1960–2000

	Share of Total Revenue			Share of Total Expenditures		
Year	Central	State	Municipal	Central	State	Municipal
1960	63.9	31.3	4.7	59.5	34.1	6.4
1965	63.8	30.9	5.9	54.8	35.1	10.1
1970	66.7	30.6	2.7	60.8	29.2	10.0
1975	73.7	23.5	2.8	68.0	23.3	8.7
1980	74.7	21.7	3.7	68.2	23.3	8.6
1985	72.8	24.9	2.4	62.7	26.2	11.1
1990	67.3	29.6	3.1	57.1	28.0	14.9
1995	67.2	28.0	4.8	56.3	27.5	16.2
2000	69.2	26.2	4.6	59.9	25.1	15.0

Source: 1960–1985: Rezende (1995); 1990–2000: Ministério da Fazenda, Secretaria da Receita Federal (2001b).

on national policies. First, soon after taking power the military government centralized the distribution of government revenue and expenditures. The military regime's efforts to centralize resources reduced state and municipal political autonomy, and not until Congress regained some authority in the early 1980s was this trend reversed. Table 3.1 demonstrates the extent of this shift.

The military government also severely restricted the autonomy of state governors. Most importantly, direct gubernatorial elections were eliminated in 1965. From then until 1982, the military government nominated friendly politicians, and the state assemblies rubber-stamped the choice (the progovernment party dominated state assemblies). This move reduced the impact of federalism by eliminating the possibility that opposition to the regime would emerge from control over state government (Medeiros 1986; Sallum Jr. 1996).

Third, the military attenuated the impact of federalism by restricting the powers of Congress through a combination of repression, constitutional changes that strengthened the executive at the expense of the legislature, and an electoral system designed to favor the government party. The government gave itself the power to purge elected officials from office, instilling fear in those members of Congress who were not purged shortly following the coup. In addition, Institutional Act No. 2 reduced the number of congressional votes needed to approve constitutional amendments to a simple majority, transferred all budgetary control to the executive branch, imposed limits on congressional debate on any bill, and gave the government the power to suspend or close Congress, which it did for several months in 1966 and again in 1968–69 and 1977. In a symmetrical bicameral system such as Brazil's, these actions greatly reduced states' capacity to articulate their interests and exert pressure on the executive branch.

Finally, the regime centralized administrative and legal authority. The organs of the central government dramatically expanded their scope and reach during this period (Medeiros 1986), and the government attempted to streamline public administration through the imposition of Decree-Law 200, which gave financial incentives to states and municipalities to follow the central government's lead in administrative organization and procedure (Abrucio 1998). The federal government exercised greater control in most policy areas than it ever had before.

Thus, the four variables related to federalism indicate that subnational governments should have limited capacity to constrain presidential policy initiatives. In addition, the three variables related to the president all point toward great capacity of the executive to initiate reforms that affected state interests until 1982. First, military presidents from 1964 until 1974, and to a slightly lesser extent until 1979, were thoroughly determined to strengthen the central government at the expense of subnational governments. Second, until the early 1980s the military presidents were virtually unchecked by a Congress whose powers were sharply circumscribed. Until the November 1982 elections, they enjoyed an absolute majority of both chambers of Congress. Even after the November 1982 elections, President João Figueiredo (1979–85) retained a two-thirds majority in the Senate and a sizable plurality (235 of 479 seats) in the Chamber of Deputies. Only in 1984 with the defection of droves of members of the governing party to the opposition did the president's rubber-stamp support in Congress erode. Finally, the military presidents' performance on economic issues was generally excellent from 1967 until 1980. A severe recession and escalating inflation from 1981 to 1983 weakened Figueiredo's bargaining position with governors and the Congress—but he still was in a strong negotiating position with state actors given the buttresses of authoritarian power.

Strong Federalism in Post-1985 Brazil: Four Institutional Variables

Federalism Variable 1: The Resource Base of Subnational Governments

The process of democratization in Brazil involved substantial institutional reform of federal arrangements that devolved extensive power to state-based actors. As Table

3.1 shows, beginning in the late 1970s and continuing on into the early 1990s, Brazil underwent a process of extensive fiscal decentralization. This process was first associated with the liberalization of the military regime, which was attempting to curry favor with its civilian allies, and then with the process of democratization itself, as newly elected politicians sought to loosen central-government control over government revenue. From 1975 to 1995, Brazilian state governments' share of total national expenditures increased 17 percent, and municipalities' share increased by 93 percent. Already quite decentralized in comparative perspective, fiscal decentralization transformed Brazil into one of the world's most fiscally decentralized systems. Table 3.2 shows that the resource share of subnational governments in Brazil is larger than that of other countries in Latin America. Brazil has one of the world's most decentralized divisions of revenue across levels of government.

Table 3.2 indicates the portion of revenue each level of government spends but does not tell us how much control each level of government actually has over that revenue. If subnational governments control their own resources, their autonomy increases, whereas if they have significant resources but limited discretion over how to spend them, their capacity to influence central government policy diminishes. Fiscal decentralization in Brazil increased subnational governments' political autonomy because they can use their newfound resources largely as they wish. Most state and municipal gains came through increases in federal revenue transferred through two constitutionally enshrined funds that the central government administers, one for states (the FPE) and one for municipalities (the FPM). Whereas in the United States 90 percent of all central government transfers in 1986 went for specific pro-

Table 3.2

Share of Revenue and Expenditure by Level of Government, Selected Latin American Countries

Country, Year	Share of Total Government Revenue Collected by Level of Government			Share of Total Government Expenditure by Level of Government		
	Central	Intermediate	Local	Central	Intermediate	Local
Argentina, 1992	80.0	15.4	4.6	51.9	39.5	8.6
Brazil, 1995	67.2	28.0	4.8	56.3	27.5	16.2
Chile, 1992	100.0	0.0	0.0	87.3	0.0	12.7
Colombia, 1991	81.6	11.1	7.3	67.0	15.7	17.3
Mexico, 1992	82.7	13.4	3.9	87.8	9.5	2.8
Venezuela, 1989	96.9	0.1	3.1	77.7	15.7	6.5

grams (Bahl 1986, 14), in Brazil 60 percent of all FPE and FPM transfers have no entailments whatsoever, and another 30 percent are only generically linked to education and health (Afonso 1994, 356).[3] This situation gives state governors and mayors of large cities considerable political clout.

Fiscal decentralization in Brazil reflected the malapportionment of state delegations in Congress. As is the case in Argentina (see Gibson et al., this volume), fiscal federalism transfers resources to poorer, less populous, but significantly overrepresented states. During the 1987–88 constitutional convention, heavy pressure from organized state government lobbying encouraged members of the state delegations from the Northeast, North, and Center-West regions of Brazil to unite and disproportionately increased their share of the FPE funds. They could do so because, as we show below, their delegations comprised an absolute majority of seats in the Constitutional Congress. Thus, the percentage of state revenue from FPE transfers declined 24.6 percent in the South and Southeast regions between 1983 and 1992, but it increased 37.4 percent in the three poorer regions (Ministério da Fazenda 1994). Fiscal decentralization thus disproportionately increased the veto power of the poorer states in Brazil's federation.

The policy consequences of fiscal decentralization have been clear. First, extensive fiscal decentralization, combined with Brazil's acute fiscal crisis, reduced the central government's ability to use its own revenue for political purposes. While constitutionally mandated transfers to states and municipalities increased after 1978, unprogrammed, politically manipulable revenue in the central government budget declined (Nogueira 1995, 28). Second, decentralization limited the central government's capacity to balance the national budget and pay off Brazil's huge debt. During the constitutional convention subnational governments grabbed resources yet largely refused to assume new policy responsibilities (Bonfim and Shah 1991). In the 1990s the federal government was forced to search endlessly for nontax sources of revenue that are not necessarily shared with subnational governments (Samuels 2003). Third, fiscal decentralization made the central government's task of establishing and maintaining macroeconomic stability more difficult than it otherwise would have been. In sum, fiscal decentralization gave subnational governments greater autonomy while imposing limitations on the central government's political agility. The consequences of fiscal decentralization bedeviled President Cardoso's reform efforts.

Federalism Variable 2: Federalism and Gubernatorial Power

A second institutional variable strengthening federalism in Brazil emanates from subnational governments themselves: the power of state governors to influence national legislators from their states. When governors exercise such power, they gain influence in national politics. In Brazil state governors command impressive political and economic resources, above and beyond the revenue they have gained over the past twenty years. Because of their influence over deputies and senators from their state, and because presidents need legislative support for many policy proposals, governors can thwart or facilitate presidential designs (Abrucio 1998).

During the transition to democracy, state governors acquired increasing political clout for several reasons. First and most important, in 1982 governors were popularly elected for the first time since 1965. Direct popular election meant that governors needed to be more attentive to state needs even at the expense of being less subservient to the federal government (Abrucio and Samuels 1997).

In the post-1985 period, five additional factors have provided governors with sufficient influence to either proactively influence or reactively veto federal government initiatives: control over hiring and firing at the state level, significant fiscal resources, Brazil's electoral system, control over municipal mayors, and the lack of oversight at the state level. First, governors control access to the resources that politicians need to claim credit and advance their careers. In the absence of strong national party organizations and of a national legislature that controls the purse strings, federal deputies rely on state governors to provide political sustenance. Governors have the power of the pen in the state-level bureaucracy, which can mean control over thousands of political jobs. Governors distribute these jobs, which range from unskilled labor positions to posts as state Secretary of Health or Housing, to deputies or deputies' political cronies. State governors also control nominations to many federal government posts within their state in the lower rungs of the national bureaucracy, a fact not often recognized by students of Brazilian clientelism (Abrucio 1998; Samuels 2003).

Second, although deputies have access to pork-barrel funds in Congress, governors control much larger stocks of pork, and there are few other ways for the average deputy to claim credit from his or her seat in Congress (Samuels 2003, chap. 6). Most deputies need governors to advance their careers. For example, in São Paulo, the richest state in Brazil, the governor announced that in 1997, a pre-election year, he would invest approximately U.S.$1.6 *billion,* aiming to finish visible public works projects to improve his own reelection chances and to help his copartisans and allies. In contrast, in the national congress, each deputy in 1997 could submit U.S.$1.5 *million* in amendments to the budget to use for pork-barrel public works projects. Yet the president has a line-item veto that he uses quite often, and as a result most deputies do not even get credit for a third of the amount they submit (Samuels 2003). In a best-case scenario, the seventy federal deputies from São Paulo could bring home approximately U.S.$100 million, which pales in comparison to the governor's ability to distribute funds according to his political whims.

For deputies from the less-developed regions, the situation is different, but with similar consequences. In the less-developed regions, state governments depend heavily on fiscal transfers from the central government because they have less capacity to raise their own funds. Deputies from these regions, who typically emerge from small groups of elite politicians, serve as ambassadors from their states, as the link between their states and the central government, attempting to obtain funds for their states. Deputies from these regions tend to seek federal funds more than deputies from the more developed regions, but these funds often pass through the hands of the state executive, leaving the deputy reliant on links with the governor to claim the credit for the work he has done.

Control over hiring and firing and the pork barrel gives governors considerable firepower to employ either for or against federal (and state) deputies. Federal deputies must take their governor's preferences into account when taking positions or seeking funds. Because of their potential influence over federal deputies, gubernatorial power in Brazil resonates not only within states but also at the national level.

A third factor that contributes to federal deputies' vulnerability to gubernatorial influence is Brazil's electoral system. An open-list proportional representation system in which states serve as electoral districts forces politicians to compete against members of their own party as well as candidates from other parties for seats. Although some deputies concentrate their electoral bases in a few contiguous municipalities, they can and do seek out votes in any corner of their state. This ability is a double-edged sword, however, because it leaves deputies vulnerable. If a deputy turns against the state governor, or even waffles in his or her support of the governor, the governor can sponsor a competing candidate, feeding plum political jobs or credit for pork-barrel projects in the deputy's bailiwick to the deputy's rival (Abrucio 1998).

Governors also hold power over mayors, whom candidates for federal deputy rely upon to bring out the vote at the local level. Despite their recent gains in fiscal resources, the vast majority of municipal governments in Brazil are tremendously poor. Although mayors can try to obtain funds in Brasília, governors tend to lead the way in coordinating pork, using political criteria for the distribution of resources for public works projects at the municipal level. In addition, the number of municipalities increased 25 percent from 1988 to 1995, from 4,189 to over 5,500. This resulted in increased municipal competition for resources, giving governors the power to divide and conquer if they so desired.

Finally, almost no oversight exists at the state level, giving governors a freer hand. State legislatures across Brazil make little effort to oversee state government spending. Instead, state deputies scramble to enter the governor's party coalition, knowing that if they fail to do so, they will be cut off from the resources they need to advance their careers (Abrucio 1998).[4] Governors control the nominations to organs that oversee state government, ensuring that their actions will never be closely scrutinized. In addition, little public accountability exists at the state level in Brazil: in comparison to municipal or national government, the public cares relatively little about what state governments do (Balbachevsky 1992).

How does the existence of strong governors with significant resources constrain presidential powers? Brazilian presidents need to negotiate policy reforms along two axes: in Congress and with governors. If governors were less central actors in national politics, then presidents would be able to deal with Congress alone. In Tsebelis's (1995) terms, powerful governors add an additional veto player. Governors' influence over federal deputies within their state gives them power that party leaders have in other countries: influence within Congress. National policy proposals, which usually emanate from the executive branch, must pass through negotiations with a Congress fragmented both along party lines and by state delegations that compete to obtain favors from the central government.

Governors are divided by many issues, but they typically unite in defense of state level resources and prerogatives. When they do so, they can thwart presidential reforms even if they do not deliberately coalesce in defense of state interests. For example, the president may attempt to rein in public spending, but because so much public spending in Brazil occurs at the state and local levels, the president faces difficulties accomplishing these objectives without negotiating the reform process with state governors. Moreover, state governors can use their influence to encourage members of Congress from their states to alter or block presidential initiatives that threaten the resource base and autonomy of subnational governments.

Federalism Variable 3: The Articulation of Subnational Interests in the National Legislature

As noted, federal institutions are more likely to articulate subnational interests and thus constrain presidential reforms under two conditions: when bicameralism is symmetrical and when political careers are focused on subnational as opposed to national politics. In Brazil both factors strengthen federalism. First, Brazil is a case of symmetrical bicameralism. Either the Senate or the Chamber of Deputies can initiate a bill, and both must approve it. Both must approve constitutional amendments by the same (60 percent) supermajority twice. The Senate also has broad powers of appointment and approval of appointments (Article 52 of the 1988 constitution). It must approve nominations for ministers of the Federal Accounting Court, presidents and directors of the Central Bank, the attorney general, and a number of other important positions. It must authorize external financial operations, establish the limit to total internal debt, and determine the limits and conditions of internal and external debt of the federal and subnational governments. These powers made the Senate a central player in negotiations regarding state debts to the federal government.

Brazil's combination of symmetrical and incongruent bicameralism (with different methods of selection and marked differences in proportionality between the two chambers), while not uncommon, is far from universal (Lijphart 1984, 90–105; Tsebelis and Money 1997). Relative to unicameral systems or asymmetrical bicameralism, this combination of institutions constrains the central government and enhances the powers of subnational governments, because to pass a policy reform a president must obtain the support of two different majorities from legislative chambers whose electoral bases may diverge markedly. Although the 1988 constitution tilts power toward the executive branch, the Congress can block presidential reforms and can extract many concessions that undermine presidential objectives.

A critical element of the importance of federalism in Brazil is the way in which political career structures strengthen subnational interests in national politics. State-level organizations control access to the ballot for the national legislature. This encourages candidates for the legislature to have a strong orientation toward state and local politics. Given state-level party control over ballot access and alliance decisions,[5] subnational elections tend to drive national elections, not vice versa. In contrast to the presidential coattails effect observed in the United States, in Brazil *gubernatorial* elections exert a strong coattails effect on national legislative elections (Samuels 2003, chap. 5), providing incentives for candidates for national legislative office to coalesce around gubernatorial candidates, not presidential candidates. This dynamic tends to increase governors' influence over their states' congressional delegations. Moreover, state political elites do not generally hold strong ideological-partisan convictions, and except for politicians from the leftist parties they have tended to discount national politics when negotiating electoral alliances. In short, the state-based nature of political competition in Brazil strengthens the policy impact of federalism.

Second, the electoral system for both the Chamber of Deputies and the Senate pushes members of Congress to seek personal votes as opposed to running primarily on the basis of party labels (Ames 1995; Mainwaring 1999). The primary way of obtaining personal votes is by serving local constituents, especially through delivering public goods. Many members of the national congress see their principal function as securing public goods for their home regions and defending subnational interests. Even when serving in the national congress, politicians' desire to maintain and expand their links with state-level machines strengthens the representation of subnational interests in national politics (Samuels 2003, chaps. 3–4).

Third, the turnover in Brazil's Chamber of Deputies reflects the relative lack of interest most politicians have in making a career in national politics. This turnover reflects the dominant trait of political careers in Brazil: a desire to build and maintain a political career at the subnational level or in representing subnational interests in national politics. One can empirically demonstrate the value of subnational positions in the political system by mapping political careers. For example, during democratic periods since 1945, many sitting deputies have abandoned their seats during the legislature to take positions at the state or municipal level. In the 1990s approximately 40 percent of all sitting deputies either took a position outside of Congress or manifested a desire to do so by running for mayor (Samuels 2003, chap. 4). Even if they do not rotate out during the legislature, federal deputies maintain their links with political networks in the states, acting as "ambassadors" of subnational governments, thus increasing the institutional representation of subnational interests.

Because the factors that affect political careers revolve to a great degree around state-level issues, Brazilian politicians must be closely attuned to the interests of state actors. Although a focus on state actors need not preclude the possibility of forging national alliances in the Congress and elsewhere, it creates the possibility of a conflict between national leaders—the president, ministers, national party leaders, and leaders of the national congress—and other members of Congress, who tend to focus more on state-level interests. Moreover, because many of them plan to run for state or municipal office, members of Congress pay greater attention to the fiscal needs of subnational governments than to the needs of the national government. In these ways, politicians' self-interest sometimes serves to impede the president's ability to implement reforms.

In sum, in Brazil political careers tend to revolve around subnational politics, reinforcing the impact of federalism. Members of Congress do not build their careers around being loyal members of national parties, as has been the case in Mexico or Costa Rica, for example. Instead, they tend to focus primarily on state and local needs. Because politicians respond not only to those who helped them win election, but also to those who might help them move up the career ladder, states and municipalities gain a form of institutional representation through members of the national congress. As a result, the strengthening of the national congress fortified the veto power of subnational actors in national politics.

Federalism Variable 4: The Policy Jurisdiction of Subnational Governments

After 1985, many policy areas devolved to local and state governments. The 1988 constitution gave state and local governments ample jurisdiction over many policy areas, including the environment, education, taxes, health, social welfare, and housing (Articles 23–25 and 30). All policy areas that are not explicitly under the domain of the federal government are reserved for the state (Article 25, Section 1). Specifically, state and local governments acquired much greater leeway over education, health, and housing policy, among many other policy domains (Almeida 1995). These policy areas were of direct consequence in the federal government's efforts to rein in inflation and reform the state after 1985.

Policy decentralization in Brazil took on a particular form because of the country's federal institutions. The end of the military regime was associated with a process of fiscal decentralization, a fiscal crisis of the state, and the end of central government "tutelage" of subnational authorities. Together, during the transition to democracy these factors meant that the central government no longer had the political or financial resources to entice subnational governments to follow its dictates. Decentralization also took on a particular form because actors in each level of government sought to preserve benefits while transferring costs onto the other levels. Many states and municipalities sought to obtain resources while leaving responsibility with the central government. In turn, the federal government attempted to transfer responsibilities to subnational governments. Still, in many cases subnational leaders sought policy responsibility as an attempt to implement innovative policies and thus reap subsequent political rewards (Arretche 2000). As the central government's fiscal and political role diminished in the 1980s, federalism provided institutional opportunity spaces for ambitious politicians to experiment with public policies.

Strong Federalism and Constraints upon the Central Government, 1985–1994

In the Brazilian case, the four features of federalism all predict that governors and Congress (as representatives of state interests) would be in a strong bargaining position after 1985, especially after the promulgation of the 1988 constitution. The reinvigoration of federalism in Brazil occurred concomitantly with democratization and with a protracted economic crisis. These three processes significantly affected each other. Political liberalization and democratization reinvigorated federalism as the military devolved power to states and local governments. In turn, political dynamics at the state level increasingly affected liberalization and democratization. The economic crisis was fueled in part by democratization as the military and its civilian allies governing at the state level used public resources to garner political support, thereby creating fiscal imbalance.

Other scholars have addressed the relationship between reinvigorated federalism and democratization (Souza 1996; Abrucio and Samuels 1997; Abrucio 1998); here we focus on the connection between federalism and the economic reforms spurred by the economic crisis. After the return to democracy in 1985, Brazilian presidents attempted to attain economic stabilization and state reform. Yet until the imple-

Table 3.3

Indicators of Economic Performance and Presidential Approval,
Brazil, 1985–2001

	Percentage GDP Growth	Percentage Inflation
1985	7.9%	239%
1986	7.6	59
1987	3.6	295
1988	−0.1	993
1989	3.3	1,862
1990	−4.4	1,585
1991	0.9	476
1992	−0.9	1,149
1993	4.2	2,489
1994	5.8	929
1995	3.9	22
1996	3.1	9
1997	3.5	4
1998	0.1	3
2999	0.7	8
2000	4.5	5

Sources: ECLAC, Preliminary Overview of the Economy of Latin America and
the Caribbean and Economic Survey of Latin America (various years).

mentation of the Real stabilization plan in 1994, successive stabilization plans failed disastrously. Only once between 1985 and 1994 was the annual inflation rate below 250 percent, and it frequently exceeded 1,000 percent (Table 3.3). The succession of failed stabilization plans in conjunction with a long period (1981–92) of no per capita growth led to a growing consensus about the importance of shifting from state-led development to more market-oriented approaches. Yet just as the stabilization policies failed, so did the early efforts at state reform, which lagged behind those in many other Latin American countries (Edwards 1995; Haggard and Kaufman 1995; Packenham 1994).

It is impossible to understand these failures to accomplish economic reform more rapidly without examining the effects of federalism (Sola 1993). As also occurred in Argentina between 1999 and 2002, federalism gave state-based actors—governors and members of the national congress—the capacity to constrain presidential reform initiatives. These constraints partially offset sweeping presidential powers embedded in the 1988 constitution (Shugart and Carey 1992; Figueiredo and Limongi 1994, 1995, 1997; Mainwaring 1997; Power 1998). In what follows, we examine three critical policy areas in which federalism constrained central government reform initiatives in the 1985–94 period: state government debts, state-owned banks, and fiscal decentralization. These policies were crucial for the success of stabilization policies and state reform.

State Debts to the Federal Government

Federalism had a profound impact on stabilization policies and state reform in part by promoting fiscal irresponsibility on the part of the member states. Brazil's state debt crisis originated with the country's foreign debt crisis of the early 1980s. States had contracted large foreign debts which they were no longer able to pay by the early 1980s. The federal government agreed to assume most of these debts, and in return the states agreed to pay back the federal government (Dillinger 1997). On several subsequent occasions, the states again transferred their debts to the federal government. On each occasion, the federal government granted generous repayment terms to the states. States were able to postpone repaying their debts, and in effect they managed to shove their debts onto the federal government. States were able to transfer their debts to the central government because presidents needed state governors to influence their delegations in Congress (Federalism Variable 2 above) and because the executive branch is constitutionally impeded from imposing its will in the fiscal realm (Federalism Variable 4). This practice impeded the central government's ability to reduce Brazil's internal debt and establish macroeconomic stability.

Over a period of twenty years, state governments ran up a debt that totaled U.S.\$139 billion as of late 1997 (*Sinopse,* 3 November 1997). From the early 1980s until Cardoso became president, the central government was unable to limit state indebtedness (Kugelmas, Sallum Jr., and Graeff 1989; Abrucio and Couto 1996). Uncontrolled state spending continuously fueled this debt. Measured as a percentage of the GDP, state and local government payroll expenditures increased 77 percent between 1985 and 1990—an eloquent statement about the lack of fiscal restraint on the part of governors (Werneck 1992, 10).

Several economists identified state debts as a major contributing factor to the lack of federal government control over monetary and fiscal policy in Brazil (Werneck 1992; Bonfim and Shah 1991; World Bank 1990; Werlang and Fraga Neto 1992; Novaes and Werlang 1993). After the Real economic stabilization plan came into effect in 1994, real internal interest rates skyrocketed, making sweeping state debts under the carpet no longer a viable option. Still, states continued to force the central government to assume their debts. Because presidents rely on governors to drum up support in Congress (Federalism Variable 3) and to realize important policy objectives, and because governors have considerable power and autonomy (Federalism Variable 2), presidents from Sarney (1985–90) through Franco (1992–94) never devoted much political capital to forcing state governments to pay their debts to the federal government, although they paid lip service to this objective.

These perverse incentives, in which the central government sought solutions to macroeconomic problems while state governments had stronger incentives to defect (through profligacy) than cooperate, explain a seeming paradox: why state governments remained in difficult financial positions despite the massive infusion of resources after 1988. Because they were able to push debts onto the federal government, most states did not seriously attempt to rein in spending. A few governors were exceptions, believing that fiscal balance would allow them to undertake new initiatives—but the rule was profligacy. States were successful at passing their problems off without agreeing to across-the-board institutional changes. Even when some states signed agreements, no institutional guarantees impeded the next governor from disobeying the terms. The institutions of federalism obstructed a resolution of Brazil's fiscal problems.

Brazil's federal arrangements allowed state governments to gain in three ways: first, they have won favorable loan repayment plans with long-term below-market rates. Second, federal government assumption of their debts gave states budgetary freedom to execute more visible policies that have political payoffs. Finally, while the central government could not avoid paying off these debts without placing the entire country's economic health at risk, states were under no obligation to fulfill their promises and acted as if their irresponsible behavior has no larger ill effects. States signed agreements and then failed to follow through on their part of the bargain.

State-Owned Banks

From 1985 until 1994, banks owned by state governments adversely affected the central government's initiatives regarding economic stabilization. As part of a broad expansion of the public sector, state-government-owned banks proliferated under military rule (Federalism Variable 1). After the military government loosened central control over state finances in the mid-1970s,[6] governors employed state banks for political purposes; state governments borrowed from state banks in order to fund pet political projects, even if they were not economically prudent. The banks became notorious for their autonomy vis-à-vis the central government and for this political manipulation. The governors, using political criteria, chose the directors of the state banks. State-level banks enjoyed broad authority to make their own loans and issue bonds.

As of 1993, twenty-five of Brazil's twenty-seven states (counting the Federal District) owned at least one financial institution (Novaes and Werlang 1993, 16). In comparative perspective, the autonomy of these state banks was exceptional. Because state governments could spend without constraints and cover deficits with state-issued bonds, they had more fiscal and monetary autonomy vis-à-vis the federal government than member countries of the European Union have with respect to the EU. In the EU, member countries must agree to keep their fiscal deficits within a targeted range and will not be allowed to issue new currency as Brazil's state governments effectively did by issuing bonds and pushing the debt onto the federal government. In the United States, no state has its own autonomous publicly owned bank.

Brazil's state banks gained a reputation for profligate spending to bolster the political careers of the politicians who oversee them. With the advent of political liberalization, governors used "their" banks politically. The banks made billions of dollars in unsound loans to state governments. State bank debt totaled U.S.$96 billion as of 1998. Governors used state banks to finance investments and hire personnel for political purposes, often attaching little importance to how economically sound the use of resources was. The benefits of such practices accrued to the governors, the problems to their successors—or more often, to the federal government. As political appointees who would be likely to remain in their positions only as long as the governors did, the directors of state banks functioned with a short-term logic that often violated elementary principles of private banks (Werlang and Fraga Neto 1992). The combination of bad loans (mainly to state governments) and borrowing to build political bases corroded the financial situation of most state banks. With loans from their state banks, governors could embark on spending sprees, and they then refused to pay back the loans, sending the banks into financial ruin. The governors' political use of state banks explains why, as of June 1992, 67 percent of their assets were loaned to state governments (Novaes and Werlang 1993, 16). State banks loaned money to the state government and to public enterprises owned by the state; the state governments and enterprises then spent these funds in politically profitable ways. State governments frequently failed to pay back loans to these banks. For example, by 1995 the government of São Paulo and publicly owned São Paulo companies owed U.S.$13.8 billion to BANESPA, the state bank (Makler 1997). Between 1982 and 1993, the Brazilian Central Bank intervened in sixty of the eighty-seven financial institutions owned by states because they were close to bankruptcy. In 1990 because state banks loaned freely to state governments with little regard for the economic prudence of the loans, 45.3 percent of state bank loans were nonperforming, compared to only 1.7 percent of loans by private-sector banks (Makler 2000, 46).

Until 1995 the federal government regularly bailed out state banks in exchange for political support in Congress; presidents feared gubernatorial wrath and needed congressional support for many measures (Federalism Variables 2 and 3). State governments largely avoided paying for past errors. The state banks effectively pushed the Central Bank to intervene and lend them money, thus transferring debts from the state to the central government. Werlang and Fraga Neto (1992, 3) concluded that the reluctance of the federal government to control state banks led to a situation in which the latter "can emit money, practically without limits and without control from the Central Bank or the National Treasury." Between 1983 and 1987 alone, the Central Bank injected U.S.$33 billion into efforts to rescue state banks (Abrucio and Couto 1996, 25). Despite broad awareness of the high costs of this noncooperative game, the central government failed to rein in state banks until Cardoso's presidency and even failed to prevent the exacerbation of the problem.

Prior to the success of the Real Plan in 1994, the autonomy of the state banks undermined national economic policy and made it difficult for presidents to implement stabilization policies (Bonfim and Shah 1991; World Bank 1990). Despite affirming a commitment to rein in these banks and to prohibit the Central Bank from covering their deficits, the Sarney, Collor, and Franco governments failed to overcome gubernatorial resistance to changes in state-owned banks' organizations or practices.

Efforts to Revise Fiscal Federalism

The substantial decentralization of tax revenue to local and state governments also had a deleterious impact on stabilization from 1985 to 1994. While it mandated specific and substantial transfers of resources to state and local governments, the 1988 constitution was nebulous regarding which levels of government have responsibility for such fundamental issues as health, education, housing, and welfare. The substantial increase in revenue transfers to states and municipalities therefore occurred without a corresponding transfer of responsibilities. This vagueness fueled conflict between federal, state, and local governments, enabling each to claim that certain responsibilities pertain to another. This situation burdened the federal government, leaving it with diminished resources but growing demands (Sola 1993; Tavares de Almeida 1995; Abrucio 1998). Subnational governments lobby the central government to continue to provide all the services and resources it had offered previously, while presidents worked to rein in spending, transfer responsibilities to subnational governments, and curtail concessions to state and local governments.

By the early 1980s, most economists agreed that fiscal imbalance was a major factor behind inflation in Brazil. Successive presidents attempted to rein in spending in order to trim inflation. As part of these efforts, presidents hoped to revise the fiscal decentralization that proved deleterious to the central government in the aftermath of the 1988 constitution. The central government also considered, but did not seriously pursue, measures to push more public sector responsibilities onto state and local governments. Presidents simultaneously faced pressures from state governors, mayors, and federal deputies qua representatives of their states to retain the new status quo that was so favorable to subnational governments (Federalism Variables 1, 2, and 3). Because subnational governments grabbed resources yet only grudgingly assumed new responsibilities, fiscal decentralization made it difficult for the central government to balance the budget (Bonfim and Shah 1991) and reduced the central government's ability to use its resources for political purposes, as was common during the military period.

Presidents Sarney, Collor, and Franco failed to increase the federal government's share of the fiscal pie. Congress and the governors defended the share of state and local governments in federal tax revenues despite a widespread perception that this arrangement contributed to fiscal problems and inflation. For example, President Fernando Collor (1990–92) proposed a fiscal reform that would have shifted resources back to the central government, but his proposal failed in the face of opposition from the states. President Itamar Franco (1992–94) was also thwarted by governors and the national congress in his endeavor to redesign Brazil's fiscal system in favor of the central government. Only under Cardoso did the central government begin to make some headway.

Summary

Abrucio (1997) coined the term "predatory federalism" to characterize the relationship between the federal government and the states between 1985 and 1994. The states preyed on the central government's inability or unwillingness to control sub-national finances. During its apogee (1988–94), the costs of predatory federalism were alarming. State spending and state capacity to push the resulting debts onto the federal government contributed to the inability of successive presidents to tame the fiscal deficit and curb inflation.

Federalism and the Cardoso Administration, 1995–2002

As is suggested by the image of a bargaining game between presidents and state actors, federalism is dynamic. In Brazil the relationship between the federal and state governments changed substantially under President Fernando Henrique Cardoso (1995–2002). The factors that change from one administration to the next all gave President Cardoso greater leeway in dealing with state actors. The differences between the pre- and post-1994 periods are clear: presidential weakness and governability problems characterized the 1985–94 period, while Cardoso's administration marked the emergence of a more coherent executive branch, which enhanced governability. Cardoso controlled inflation and brought economic stability, won broad congressional support, and passed several important economic reforms.

Although the variables that make for strong federalism remained intact during this period, the variables related to presidentialism underwent a significant change. Cardoso's team was more committed to economic stabilization than his predecessors (especially Sarney [1985–90] and Franco [1992–94]), and it devised a clever means of bringing about stabilization—the Real Plan. Until 2002, Cardoso enjoyed broader support in Congress than his predecessors, and he reaped the benefits of better economic performance (Table 3.3).

Table 3.4 shows the percentage of seats in the national congress that Cardoso's coalition controlled. During most of his first term (from April 1996 through December 1998), Cardoso's coalition controlled over 70 percent of the seats in the Chamber of Deputies and 80 percent of the seats in the Senate. In his second term (up through March 2002), his coalition controlled between 63 and 74 percent in the Chamber of Deputies and was of a similar size in the Senate (the size of the coalition varies because politicians frequently change parties). These comfortable majorities fostered Cardoso's ability to win negotiations with state actors, especially since some of his reforms entailed constitutional amendments. In contrast, Sarney's overwhelming majority in 1985–87 eroded severely in 1988–90; during his last eigh-

Table 3.4
Presidential Coalitions in the Brazilian National Congress, 1985–2002

Government	Parties with Cabinet Positions	Percentage of Seats, Chamber of Deputies (Year)	Percentage of Seats, Senate
José Sarney			
3/85 to 2/86	PMDB, PFL, PTB, PDS	94% (1985)	97%
2/86 to 3/90	PMDB, PFL	57 (1986)	50
	PMDB, PFL	78 (1987)	83
	PMDB, PFL	53 (1989)	59
Fernando Collor			
3/90 to 4/92	PMDB, PFL, PRN, PDS	57 (1990)	55
	PMDB, PFL, PRN, PDS	55 (1991)	59
4/92 to 10/92	PFL, PDS, PTB, PL, PSDB	43 (1992)	44
Itamar Franco			
10/92 to 1/93	PFL, PSDB, PFL, PMDB, PSB, PTB	59 (1993)	77
1/93 to 5/93	PFL, PSDB, PFL, PMDB, PSB, PTB, PT	67 (1993)	78
5/93 to 8/93	PFL, PSDB, PFL, PMDB, PSB, PTB	59 (1993)	77
8/93 to 12/94	PMDB, PFL, PP, PSDB	52 (1993)	70
Fernando Henrique Cardoso			
1/95 to 4/96	PSDB, PMDB, PFL, PTB	56 (1995)	69
4/96 to 3/99	PSDB, PMDB, PFL, PPB, PTB, PPS	72 (1996)	80
	PSDB, PMDB, PFL, PPB, PTB, PPS	74 (1999)	80
3/99 to 10/01	PSDB, PMDB, PFL, PPB, PPS	68 (1999)	72
10/01 to 3/02	PSDB, PMDB, PFL, PPB	63 (2001)	71
3/02 to present (6/02)	PSDB, PMDB, PPB	47 (2002)	53

Sources: Amorim Neto (1998, 94), Mainwaring (1997, 77–78), Meneguello (1998), Tables 1, 2, 6; unpublished information obtained from the Departamento de Documentação, Presidência da República, Brasília; unpublished information from Octávio Amorim Neto.

teen months in office, Sarney commanded a slim majority in both chambers. President Sarney presided over a mass migration away from his party, the PMDB (Party of the Brazilian Democratic Movement) and from the PFL (the party of Sarney's closest political allies) toward opposition parties. Collor sometimes had a minority, and Franco's majority in the Chamber of Deputies was a bare 52 percent during sixteen of his twenty-six months in office.

These three administration-specific variables put Cardoso in a stronger position than his predecessors vis-à-vis state governors. Some analysts have even suggested that Cardoso reversed the decentralizing trend that began in the 1980s (Afonso and Mello 2000; Affonso 1998; Montero 2001). Is this argument correct?

After Cardoso came to office, federalism became less predatory in certain ways. Cardoso still needed to deal with governors and subnational interests, but he accomplished many important reforms. The central government curbed states' fiscal autonomy, forced most states to sell off their banks and implemented effective controls over the others, and increased its relative share of fiscal revenue. How did Cardoso bring these changes about? The economic stabilization plan introduced in 1994 when Cardoso was minister of finance, the *Plano Real*, is key for understanding this shift because it provided Cardoso with advantages to leverage concessions from Congress and from governors. As long as inflation persisted, budget deficits at any level of government caused no short-term political problems because governments could reduce real expenditures by delaying disbursements for salaries and government contracts long enough for inflation to erode their value. But mounting debts contributed to inflationary pressures, contributing to a vicious circle. Cardoso's economic plan took aim at the relationship between inflation and fiscal profligacy. The *Plano Real* sought to generate budget surpluses at the national level and eliminate soft budget constraints at the subnational level. The political consequences of the *Plano Real* help account for the central government's increased leverage (Sola, Garman, and Marques 1997; Abrucio and Ferreira Costa 1998). By ending inflation, governments could no longer virtually spend at will. Their expenses were real for the first time in years. Moreover, the plan forced real internal interest rates to skyrocket, which in turn caused subnational debt burdens to increase as well. Sweeping state debts under the carpet was no longer a viable option. For the first time states found themselves in an untenable fiscal position (Abrucio and Ferreira Costa 1998, 80), and they sought immediate relief from debts that began to mount rapidly, with no way to deflate their real value. This gave the central government leverage that it had lacked since the 1970s. Using this leverage, Cardoso tightened restrictions on subnational debt and pushed state governments to sell or restructure their publicly owned banks (Garman, Leite, and Marques 2001).

The *Plano Real* put the central government in an advantageous position it had not enjoyed since redemocratization began. Of the three policy areas discussed in the previous section, the Cardoso administration succeeded in greatly curtailing the pernicious effects of state banks and state-owned debts. In contrast, it made little headway in resolving the problem of fiscal transfers to the states. The reforms Cardoso achieved, however, came at a high cost and were not unilaterally imposed. Subnational interests continued to exert a strong role even when the central government appeared to have the upper hand.

State Debts

The Cardoso government increased the federal government's leverage over states in relation to state debts, and it curtailed states' ability to issue new debt while shoving the bad debt onto the federal government. It began such efforts from its first days in office. In 1995 the financial situation of state governments deteriorated, leaving them more vulnerable to pressures from the federal government (Abrucio and Ferreira Costa 1998; Sola, Garman, and Marques 1997).

Far more so than his predecessors, Cardoso used renegotiations of state debts to the federal government to impose greater restraints on state spending and state banks (Dillinger 1997; Selcher 1998). For example, in 1995 a new law (the "Camata Law") stipulated that as of January 1999, states needed to limit their payroll expenditures to 60 percent of net receipts; otherwise, they would risk losing federal funds. This law gave the federal government leverage in dealing with state governments. Cardoso also pushed state governments to privatize bankrupt state banks. This marked a change in negotiating strategy for the federal government, and it strengthened its hand. When the Cardoso government refinanced state debts in 1997–98, it required states to cease issuing bonds to cover state debts until their total debt was less than one year of tax revenue. Given the magnitude of state debts, this condition had some bite. In June 1998 the National Monetary Council prohibited subnational governments from contracting new foreign debt. The Cardoso government also pushed state governments to privatize their public enterprises, many of which had drained public coffers and borrowed recklessly since 1979.

State debt levels contributed to Brazil's currency crisis at the start of Cardoso's second term and triggered a massive currency devaluation in January 1999 and a renewed determination by the Cardoso administration to curb states' fiscal irresponsibility. Beginning with the state of Minas Gerais's January 1999 moratorium on debt payments to the federal government, the federal government stepped up its efforts to rein in profligate states. It repeatedly blocked federal transfers to the states (e.g., Minas Gerais and Rio Grande do Sul) that failed to meet debt payments. This practice reinforced central government control over state management of debts. For example, in January 1999, in response to the moratorium declared by the governor of Minas Gerais, the government sequestered resources from states' bank accounts to cover arrears on debt payments.

In May 2000 another law, the "Fiscal Responsibility Law" (FRL),[7] aimed to eliminate the perception that states and municipalities enjoyed soft budget constraints. It set strict debt limits for all levels of government and expressly prohibited the central government from refinancing subnational debt. The FRL also required all subnational governments to publish an accounting of revenue and expenditures, and it outlined penalties for public officials who violate the law (Mendes 1999; Afonso and Melo 2000; Cavalcanti and Quadros 2000; Kopits, Jiménez, and Manoel 2000; Miranda 2001).[8]

Although it imposed severe restrictions on subnational policy autonomy, state governors generally favored the bill (the fact that it took only a year to get through Congress indicates the relatively low degree of opposition). Governors did not object to the FRL because the central government had already resolved their debt issues by 1999 and because the law clarifies the conditions under which governors may dismiss employees and / or reduce public employees' salaries. After the *Plano Real* came into effect and inflation was curbed, governors no longer preferred to use the state government as an employment program and are far more reluctant to give pay raises because doing so leaves them without resources to invest in public works projects.

Although Cardoso ultimately succeeded in reining in state profligacy, he did so at a high cost that again underscores the power of state actors in Brazil. In every negotiation over state debts, the central government granted generous terms to the states, authorizing huge rollovers, generous interest rates, and lengthy repayment schedules. In 1997–98, for example, when the central government refinanced $75 billion of state debts (Selcher 1998, 44), it stretched interest payments out over thirty years. It even effectively canceled some state debts. The Brazilian Senate regulates state borrowing, and senators used their power over this policy area to extract huge benefits for the states (Federalism Variables 3 and 4).

State Banks

As was the case with the state debts, Cardoso asserted greater control over state banks than his predecessors (Sola, Garman, and Marques 1997). From the time of the intervention of the state banks of Rio and São Paulo in late 1994, the federal government indicated that it would not continue to bail out failed banks without extracting some leverage in return. The Cardoso government intervened (i.e., put into receivership) and ultimately privatized most of the state banks.

Cardoso had considerable success in controlling state banks, but in order to achieve this success, the federal government paid a high price in negotiations with governors and members of Congress (Abrucio and Couto 1996). The federal government assumed most of the debts that state banks had accrued. When the federal government privatized state banks, it typically refinanced the state's entire debt on terms highly favorable to the governors. Moreover, because of resistance from the governors and members of Congress, the privatization of state banks took several years. Banespa, the state bank of São Paulo, was finally privatized in November 2000, five years after the federal government first began pushing for privatization. Makler (2000, 52) reports that as of January 1999 the Cardoso government had privatized only five of the thirty-four state banks and noted that the heralded privatization effort has gone forward slowly. The main obstacle to faster privatization was the president's need to court the support of governors and state-based interests in the national congress. Overall, refinancing state debts and privatizing and cleaning up state bank finances has increased the central government's own debt level by R$297.7 billion (approximately U.S.$120 billion as of June 2002), almost half of the government's total debt (*O Globo*, 2 June 2002, 35).

Federalism, Fiscal Decentralization, and the Plano Real[9]

To generate the desired budget surpluses at the national level, Cardoso's economic team created what was called the Social Emergency Fund (Fundo Social de Emergência, FSE), a budgetary maneuver that gave the central government increased leeway by disconnecting 20 percent of all central government revenue from any constitutionally mandated spending. Because the FSE altered the distribution of federal tax revenue, it required a constitutional amendment for approval. Constitutional amendments require an absolute majority of 60 percent of both houses of Congress (twice!), and thus Cardoso had to drum up congressional support for this core component of the *Plano Real*.

Because of the need to obtain supermajorities in Congress, Cardoso could not simply impose the *Plano Real* on subnational governments and cause them huge and irrevocable revenue losses. A close look at the FSE reveals that it was not unilaterally imposed, that subnational interests forced the central government to pay a high price for its approval, and that the central government's greater budgetary leeway is *temporary*. The give-and-take of the *Plano Real* illustrates how subnational interests continued to shape national policy even when the central government most demanded political autonomy.

The central government paid a high price to win initial support for and maintain the FSE. In return for governors' support, which helped ensure congressional passage, the central government agreed once again to refinance state banks and purchased state debts on a much larger scale than ever (Abrucio and Ferreira Costa 1998, 47). States did not pay market-level interest rates to the central government; the direct central government subsidy to states for this bailout has been estimated at between R$32 and R$46 billion in 1997 values (Rigolon and Giambiagi 1998, 15). Consequently, although the central government forced subnational governments to commit a portion of their revenue to paying their debts, this subsidy reduced states' debt burden considerably and dwarfs any potential revenue losses that the FSE might have caused. Moreover, the subsidy increased the central government's debt, dramatically restricting its future budgetary leeway.

Even this massive debt subsidy proved insufficient to win the support of state governors for the FSE. The central government also had to agree that states and municipalities would not receive any *less* revenue in transfers from the FPE and FPM than in 1993. Cardoso had initially proposed deep cuts in federal revenue transfers to states and municipalities, but lobbying from mayors and governors forced him to back off. In the end, Cardoso managed only to get Congress to agree that the level of subnational governments' constitutionally mandated transfers would at least stay constant after the FSE was promulgated (Samuels 2003, chap. 9).

Federal transfers to subnational governments actually *increased* in real terms after the implementation of the *Real*. The *Plano Real* did not decrease subnational governments' revenue. The central government's relative share of total government revenue in Brazil did increase in the 1990s and the states' and municipalities' decreased, but all levels of government experienced an absolute increase in revenue. Central government revenue as a portion of GDP increased by 37.4 percent, states' portion by 19.2 percent, and municipalities' by 25.6 percent (Ministério da Fazenda, Secretaria da Receita Federal 2001b). The central government's share of the pie has increased faster than subnational governments' because the government dramatically increased its use of what are called "contributions" in Brazil. Central-government revenue can come from "taxes," "contributions," or assorted other tariffs and fines. In contrast to tax revenue, the central government does not have to share revenue from contributions with subnational governments. Contributions as a portion of central government revenue increased from 27.2 percent in 1990 to 45.5 percent in 2000 (Ministério da Fazenda, Secretaria da Receita Federal 2000, 2001a). Yet revenue from taxes also increased during Cardoso's administration, so much that in real terms FPE transfers actually increased by 106 percent from 1994 to 2000 and FPM transfers increased by 107 percent (Ministério da Fazenda, Secretaria do Tesouro Nacional 2001a, 2001b). (During this period real GDP growth was only 17 percent.) In short, during the 1990s the central government increased its share of the revenue pie mostly because it increased the amount of money that it obtained through the "contributions," not because the FSE decreased transfers to municipal and state governments.

Although the FSE is a constitutional amendment, it is not permanent. Obtaining legislative support for a constitutional amendment in Brazil is difficult enough as it is; presidents must negotiate and provide side-payments or concessions in order to win their passage. Yet the constitutional amendment that enacted the FSE is different because it contains a sunset provision and has already expired and been renewed three times (in 1995, 1997, and 1999). It is set to expire again in 2003. This helps explain why Congress initially accepted the FSE: it was not and is not a permanent reform of intergovernmental fiscal relations. The sunset provision implies not only that the central government has not permanently reversed fiscal decentralization, but also that the president has had to return periodically to the table to renegotiate passage of essentially the same bill. This has given states and municipalities repeated opportunities to force the president to cede his hard line on fiscal matters and offer benefits in exchange for the fund's renewal. The president has had to cede more than if the amendment had been permanent.

In each renegotiation of the *Plano Real,* subnational interests extracted concessions from the executive branch. Although these concessions have not destroyed the foundations of the *Plano Real,* they have made the government's belt-tightening efforts more difficult, and they illustrate that the president has not simply imposed losses on subnational governments. For example, as the fund's first expiration date approached in 1995, Cardoso requested a four-year extension, claiming that he needed more time to complete the work of economic stabilization. Congress approved only an eighteen-month extension, so the fund required renegotiation again just before the 1998 elections. As those elections approached and the fund neared expiration, the government's congressional supporters altered both the length of the proposed fund extension as well as the terms of the president's initial proposal, sending more resources to states and municipalities at the expense of the central government. A similar dynamic recurred in 1999.

The *Plano Real* was the Cardoso administration's most obvious success story. It ended inflation and provided budgetary leeway to the central government. Its consequences put states in a weaker position and allowed the central government to negotiate tighter fiscal controls over subnational governments. However, we must also take into account the costs of these gains and the negotiated nature of the central government's gains. The central government assumed a huge portion of subnational governments' debts, trading off the increased budgetary flexibility of the fund for a heavier debt burden that will limit its own budgetary flexibility far into the future. And although the government has no guarantee that Congress will continue to extend the fund indefinitely, the national debt will live on until paid off.

The central government never achieved its most-preferred outcome, permanently reversing the fiscal decentralization of the 1980s. This would have been a true alteration of the institutions of Brazilian federalism. Deputies and senators refused such a reversal and used the fund's sunset provision to extract concessions to benefit states and municipalities repeatedly. With each renegotiation they successfully reduced states' and municipalities' contribution to the fund, so that presently they contribute nothing. These concessions illustrate that even when the central government was in a relatively advantageous position and even where the central government most demanded political autonomy, subnational interests limited the central government's capacity to alter federal relationships permanently.

Federalism and the Failure of Fiscal Reform

During the Cardoso administration, fiscal reform came to focus on improving the quality of taxation, to reduce the so-called *Custo Brasil* or "Brazil Cost." The objectives of fiscal reform include eliminating "cumulative" taxes (charged at each stage of the production or consumption process without discounting previously charged taxes), spreading the tax base more broadly, reducing the number of taxes, generating incentives to increase tax collection, eliminating state governments' propensity to grant tax exemptions, and changing the way that production and consumption are taxed (Affonso and Silva 1995; Rezende 1996; Afonso, Rezende, and Varsano 1998; Bezerra 1999; Lima 1999).

Across-the-board support for some kind of fiscal reform appeared to exist at the start of Cardoso's administration. In an attempt to follow through on a campaign promise, Cardoso presented a fiscal reform proposal to Congress seven months after taking office.[10] The proposal called for exempting exports, capital investments, and agribusiness from taxes, extinguishing some taxes and fusing others, and unifying the administration of the main state tax (the ICMS), which would simplify taxation of consumption and eliminate states' race-to-the-bottom competition for industry by renouncing tax revenues, known as the "fiscal war." However, in contrast to several other important reforms that Cardoso passed, the proposed fiscal reform went nowhere. Federalism is the main factor that explains this policy inertia.

Despite Cardoso's promise to push for fiscal reform, his administration never expended the political resources to pass a fiscal reform because federal institutions set his government's strategy against it. Every reform proposal suggested reducing or eliminating the so-called "contributions" because of their alleged economic inefficiency. Yet the president had no interest in reforming "contributions" because, in contrast to taxes, Brazil's constitution does not require that the central government share "contributions" with states and municipalities. Cardoso's government, especially given its desire for fiscal responsibility, needed the revenue from contributions to generate budget surpluses.

The constitutional rules that allow the government to reap all revenue from contributions but force it to share tax revenue put the government between a rock and a hard place regarding fiscal reform. Cardoso chose to avoid what he considered the worst outcome of Brazil's revenue distribution system, sharing of tax revenue, and to stick with what he considered a less-worse system that permits Brazil to meet its international obligations and maintain its macroeconomic program even if that system is relatively economically inefficient. A desire to avoid the effects of federal revenue-sharing institutions, imposed by the decentralizing efforts of subnational interests in the 1988 constitution, forced this choice.

The failure of fiscal reform was not simply the executive's fault. Mayors and especially governors opposed fiscal reform, and their influence contributed to the proposals' failure. From states' perspectives, one of the most problematic issues was the proposal to alter the ICMS's general structure and principles. A value-added tax, the

ICMS is the main source of state government revenue apart from transfers from the federal government.[11] States opposed changing two aspects of the ICMS. First, states can set their own ICMS rates (up to a certain point and depending on the product). Second, the ICMS is charged at the point of production, not consumption, which has a particular impact on interstate transactions. State governors can set their ICMS rate at zero if they wish for individual firms or for products.

Governors' ability to manipulate the ICMS rate combined with the fact that the tax is charged at the point of production makes the ICMS an important tool to attract firms that want to invest where tax rates are lowest. In the 1990s governors conducted bidding wars to win new industrial investment, particularly from large multinational corporations. This interstate conflict, known as the *guerra fiscal* or "fiscal war," is a race-to-the-bottom game in which states willingly sacrifice future revenue to win immediate investment (Lemgruber Viol 2001). Exempting firms from the ICMS has become one of states' most important industrial policy tools in an age of privatization and deregulation. By attracting new industrial development through tax exemptions, state governments can claim credit for bringing hundreds or even thousands of well-paying jobs.

Because the ICMS is charged at the point of production, when a state attracts a firm through an ICMS exemption, its taxpayers are not the ones paying the tax. Rather, individuals in other states who consume the product pay the tax, and the revenue is then paid to the state where the item is produced. In most cases, therefore, the fiscal war does not seriously *reduce* a state's tax revenue.

Fiscal reform proposals presented by Cardoso's administration typically suggested eliminating the fiscal war. However, states were reluctant to change the rules of the game because any governor who wins an investment considers the investment a political victory, with minimal economic costs for his or her state. Governors opposed the loss of political autonomy that would accompany the proposed ICMS reforms, and they used their considerable influence to sway members of Congress to favor the status quo. Because of opposition from governors, the government's own support base opposes fiscal reform. States' resistance to *any* change in the ICMS provided the greatest source of opposition from subnational governments to fiscal reform.

Despite the president's repeated statements, the work of well-intentioned members of Congress, and heavy business lobbying, fiscal reform failed to advance. The impact of Brazil's federal institutions was critical to explaining this failure. Revenue-sharing rules that state and municipal interests inscribed in the 1988 constitution limited the executive's interest in broad reform, and state governments feared the loss of political autonomy that would come with reform of the ICMS. Predatory federalism remains active, although in this case states are preying on each other rather than on the central government.

Evaluating the Evolution of Federalism under Cardoso

Beginning in 1995, the Cardoso administration organized coherent and consistent legislative support and promoted several important reforms. There were three keys to Cardoso's success in altering the bargaining games with state actors. First, his administration identified clear priorities with respect to interactions with state actors, identified some of these priorities as absolutely central to the success of its stabilization plan and hence as essential for its own success as a government, and developed relatively coherent and consistent policies for changing the terms of the relationship between the central government and the states. Second, it enjoyed fairly consistent support in Congress—even though it had to compromise on every important controversial issue (Ames 2001). Third, it used its success in taming inflation as further leverage in negotiations with state actors.

However, one should never suppose that the power and legitimacy of today's leader will transfer to tomorrow's. In particular, the relationship between federalism, the party system, and the president's ability to generate legislative support remains potentially problematic in Brazil. The *Plano Real* heralded important political and economic changes. The political consequences of the plan provided the central government with enhanced leverage over subnational governments, forcing a resolution of the subnational debt issue and creating propitious conditions for the privatization and / or restructuring of state banks and the passage of the Fiscal Responsibility Law. For some, these and other policy reforms have permanently eliminated the political incentives that encouraged subnational governments to take advantage of the central government and generally increased the degree of political centralization in Brazil (e.g., Afonso and Mello 2000, 19). This argument implies that the Cardoso administration's policies produced deep and lasting changes in the nature of Brazilian federalism. Although Cardoso's policies attenuated most of the worst aspects of vertical predatory federalism, his emphasis on controlling fiscal profligacy at the subnational level did not fundamentally change most political dynamics of Brazilian federalism. Confronting a legitimate, broadly supported president under relatively stable economic conditions, subnational interests still played a key role in shaping national politics. This suggests that federalism remains an important potential obstacle for future reform-oriented administrations.

If we return to the seven variables that structured our chapter, the four institutional features of federalism have remained fundamentally intact, with only piecemeal changes. What changed markedly during the Cardoso administration were the variables related to a particular president's ability to realize reform objectives. Notwithstanding Cardoso's success in altering the terms of the relationship between the central government and state actors, Cardoso did not irreversibly weaken state actors.

Three points support this conclusion. First, as shown through the exploration of the FSE, even a strong president such as Cardoso could not unilaterally impose his preferences. Policy output instead resulted from negotiations between the central and subnational governments. Subnational interests altered important aspects of the president's agenda and forced Cardoso to abandon key proposals for intergovernmental reform. For example, as Garman, Leite, and Marques (2001) have explained, Congress refused to accept the executive's initial proposal for resolving the state bank crisis and ultimately forced the government to pay a much higher price for a solution. This was also true of the Fundo Social de Emergência, pension reform, administrative reform, fiscal reform, and other policies not discussed here (Abrucio and Ferreira Costa 1998; Souza 1999).

Second, forcing subnational governments to privatize banks or adjust their accounts reveals only one column of the accounting ledger. When evaluating the balance of intergovernmental relations during the Cardoso administration, one cannot simply count subnational losses without also counting the political and economic cost for each central government gain. To encourage states to conform to its vision of the requirements for economic stabilization, the central government assumed the lion's share of the costs of reform. The bottom line included both the billions of dollars in direct subsidies and the assumption of subnational debts, both of which contributed to the rise in Brazil's national debt from 30.4 percent of GDP in 1994 to 49.3 percent in 2000 (*O Estado de São Paulo,* 30 June 2001, B4). This is the policy straightjacket of the *Plano Real*: the government could not maintain confidence in the Real without assuming subnational debt, but the subsequent increase in the national debt weakens the principles of the *Plano Real* and Brazil's long-term macroeconomic health (Giambiagi 2000). The increase in Brazil's national debt imposes a heavy burden on the central government that will restrict its policy mobility far into the future.

Third, Cardoso's ability to shape the agenda was the fruit of contextual factors that may not recur. If not for the palpable threat of a victory in 1994 by leftist presidential candidate Luis Inácio da Silva (Lula), Cardoso might not have been able to construct a broad political coalition and garner the political support for the *Plano Real* in the first place. The stable economy made him an ideal candidate for reelection in 1998, and economic growth boosted tax revenue and helped keep government accounts in the black. Such conditions will be difficult to replicate given Brazil's fragmented party system and the country's continuing exposure to the vicissitudes of the globalized international economy.

On many national policy issues, governors continue to be powerful actors. This is true especially in those cases in which they have common interests—for example, defending state governments' share of tax revenue. It is also true in many other policy areas because governors influence the political careers of members of Congress, upon whose support the president depends for initiating many reforms. Presidents still need to make many concessions to state-based interests. Since redemocratization governors and national legislators in their capacities as representatives from the states have imposed a series of constraints on Brazil's presidents. Federalism constrains the center by forcing presidents to consider the patronage and policy preferences of state governors and the interests they represent in addition to national party interests. Although the modifications that have transpired under Cardoso are meaningful, federalism continues to exert considerable impact in the policy areas examined in this chapter.

Federalism simultaneously constrains the central government and grants autonomy, veto power, and policy initiative to subnational actors. In principle, strong federalism can have many virtues, as Riker (1964), Lijphart (1984, 1999), Stepan (chap. 2), and others have suggested. At its best, strong federalism can encourage innovation at the subnational level. However, greater federal constraints on presidents' policy reforms also bring disadvantages, particularly during periods when maintaining the status quo incurs high costs. In Brazil in the 1980s and first half of the 1990s these disadvantages were generally larger than the advantages. During this time, the Brazilian context was one of poor economic performance, an overloaded and increasingly inefficient state, and the exacerbation of egregious socioeconomic inequalities. Under these circumstances, major constraints upon the president impeded systemic capacity to address the crucial challenges of economic stabilization and state reform. Cardoso was able to overcome several of these constraints. However, as they strive to address other reforms, future presidents will certainly confront subnational interests.

Conclusion

In this chapter we sought to build on the insights of Cox and McCubbins (2001), Lijphart (1984, 1999), Shugart and Haggard (2001), Tsebelis (1995), Stepan (chap. 2), and others on the policy impact of political institutions—especially federalism. Federal institutions contribute to the number of "veto players" in a political system, as Lijphart, Tsebelis, and Stepan have all argued. A first general conclusion of our analysis, following Stepan's earlier chapter in this volume, is that the power of these veto players varies greatly depending on the specific institutional arrangements of federalism. Four institutional factors shape the extent to which federalism constrains the national government: the distribution of resources to subnational governments, the political power of state governors, the articulation of subnational interests in the national congress, and the policy jurisdiction of subnational and national governments. In this respect, although counting the number of veto players may be useful for highly aggregate cross-national comparisons, it can also miss an important part of the picture, namely, that how effective veto players are depends on specific institutional rules.

When we wrote the first draft of this chapter in 1997, we followed institutionalist lines of analysis, focusing on the institutional variables that affect how much state actors can constrain presidential reform initiatives. A second general conclusion of our analysis, reflected in the chapter as it is published in this volume, is that this way of understanding the impact of political institutions on policy outcomes must be complemented by other variables. In particular, presidents' determination and capacity and skill to enact reforms, their ability to cobble together and maintain coalitions, and their performance in office are of fundamental importance in understanding the politics of economic reform. These variables cannot be completely reduced to institutional issues. Our analysis thus used important recent works on the institutional determinants of policy outcomes as a starting point, but it places greater emphasis than strictly institutional analyses on the impact of presidential leadership, coalition building and maintenance, and presidential performance in shaping policy outcomes and in securing reforms of existing institutional arrangements. Cardoso's success indicates that the strength of federalism can vary over time within Brazil—or any country—depending on the relative success of the central government to articulate its own interests.

NOTES

Versions of this chapter were presented at All Souls College, Oxford University, in June 1997, at the Centro de Investigación y Docencia Económicas (CIDE) in Mexico City in June 1999, and at the 2000 meeting of the Latin American Studies Association, Miami. We thank Fernando Abrucio, Barry Ames, Michael Coppedge, Larry Diamond, Edward Gibson, Frances Hagopian, Bolivar Lamounier, Harry Makler, Claus Offe, Alfred Stepan, and the participants at earlier presentations for comments. We also thank Octávio Amorim Neto and Rachel Meneguello for providing data.

1. Some prominent institutionalists (Cox and McCubbins 2001; Shugart and Haggard 2001) do not include federalism in their list of factors that add veto players. We agree with Lijphart (1984, 1999), Stepan (chap. 2), and Tsebelis (1995) that federalism usually has an independent impact in constraining central government initiatives, though as Gibson (introduction to this volume) notes, it does not *always* have such an effect.

2. As we argue later, in some democracies, members of the national congress act above all as representatives of their own subnational unit, whereas in others they act above all as members of national political parties.

3. Additional entailments have recently been introduced, but these remain at a general level (e.g., for "education," but this can mean building schools, paying teachers, buying books, etc.).

4. In fifteen states that Abrucio (1998) studied during the 1991–94 term, no governor initially had a majority in the state assembly, but in fourteen of these states the governor used his influence to construct alliances that gave him one.

5. In this chapter we do not speculate about the consequences of a law issued in 2002 by Brazil's top electoral court that requires interparty alliances for presidential candidates to be replicated in every state.

6. Beginning in 1967 and continuing through the 1975–78 term, the military nominated not only governors but also state secretaries of finance and of public security (positions akin to ministers in state government).

7. *Lei Complementar* No. 101, of 4 May 2000.

8. The FRL supersedes the "Lei Camata," which regulated personnel expenditures at the subnational level, as well as Senate Resolutions 49 and 78, which regulated subnational finances.

9. The next three subsections are based on Samuels 2003, chap. 9.

10. Constitutional Amendment Proposal 175.

11. ICMS revenue varies according to the level of economic activity in each state. São Paulo gen-

erates nearly all its revenue from the ICMS, whereas poorer states rely much more on federal-government transfers.

BIBILIOGRAPHY

Abrucio, Fernando Luiz. 1997. Jogos Federativos: O Modelo Predatório Brasileiro. Unpublished manuscript. São Paulo: CEDEC.

———. 1998. *Os Barões da Federação: O Poder dos Governadores no Brasil Pós-Autoritário.* São Paulo: Editora Hucitec / Universidade de São Paulo.

Abrucio, Fernando Luiz, and Valeriano Mendes Ferreira Costa. 1998. *Reforma do Estado e Contexto Federativo Brasileiro.* São Paulo: Fundação Konrad-Adenauer-Stiftung.

Abrucio, Fernando Luiz, and Cláudio G. Couto. 1996. O Impasse da Federação Brasileira: O Cenário Político-Financeiro e as suas Conseqüências para o Processo de Descentralização. Cadernos CEDEC #58. São Paulo: CEDEC.

Abrucio, Fernando Luiz, and David Samuels. 1997. A "Nova" Política dos Governadores: Política Subnacional e Transição Democrática no Brasil. *Lua Nova* 40 / 41:137–66.

Affonso, Rui. 1998. Coordenação ou Recentralização: O Federalismo Brasileiro na Encruzilhada. Paper presented at the 21st meeting of the Latin American Studies Association, Chicago.

Affonso, Rui, and Pedro L. B. Silva, eds. 1995. *Reforma Tributária e Federação.* São Paulo: FUNDAP / Editora da UNESP.

Afonso, José Roberto Rodrigues. 1994. Decentralização Fiscal: Revendo Idéias. *Ensaios FEE* 15 (2): 353–90.

Afonso, José Roberto Rodrigues, Fernando Rezende, and Ricardo Varsano. 1998. Reforma Tributária no Plano Constitucional: uma Proposta para o Debate. Texto para discussão #606. Rio de Janeiro: IPEA.

Afonso, José Roberto Rodrigues, and Luiz de Mello. 2000. Brazil: An Evolving Federation. Paper presented at the IMF / FAD seminar on decentralization, Washington, D.C.

Almeida, Maria Hermínia Tavares de. 1995. Federalismo e Políticas Sociais. *Revista de Ciências Sociais* 10 (28): 88–108.

Ames, Barry. 1987. *Political Survival: Politicians and Public Policy in Latin America.* Berkeley: University of California Press.

———. 1995. Electoral Rules, Constituency Pressures, and Pork Barrel: Bases of Voting in the Brazilian Congress. *Journal of Politics* 57 (2): 324–43.

———. 2001. *The Deadlock of Democracy in Brazil.* Ann Arbor: University of Michigan Press.

Amorim Neto, Octávio. 1998. Of Presidents, Parties, and Ministers: Cabinet Formation and Legislative Decision-Making under Separation of Powers. Ph.D. dissertation, University of California, San Diego.

Arretche, Marta. 2000. *Estado Federativo e Políticas Sociais: Determinantes da Descentralização.* São Paulo: FAPESP / Editora Revan.

Bahl, Roy. 1986. Design of Intergovernmental Transfers in Industrialized Countries. *Public Budgeting and Finance* 6:3–22.

Balbachevsky, Elizabeth. 1992. Identidade Partidária e Instituições Políticas no Brasil. *Lua Nova* 26:133–65.

Bezerra, Fernando. 1999. Roteiro Seguido Pelo Presidente da CNI, Senador Fernando Bezerra, na Reunião da CESP Que Examina a PEC n:175/95, no dia 04/05/99. Mimeo, office of Senator Fernando Bezerra.

Bonfim, Antulio N., and Anwar Shah. 1991. Macroeconomic Management and the Division of Powers in Brazil: Perspectives for the Nineties. Policy, Research and External Affairs Working Paper. Washington, D.C.: World Bank.

Cavalcanti, Carlos E. G., and Waldemir Luiz de Quadros. 2000. Economia do Setor Público. *Indicadores DIESP* 77 (March/April): 28–31.

Cox, Gary W., and Mathew D. McCubbins. 2001. The Institutional Determinants of Economic Policy Outcomes. In *Presidents, Parliaments, and Policy,* edited by S. Haggard and M. D. McCubbins, 21–63. Cambridge: Cambridge University Press.

Dillinger, William. 1997. Brazil's State Debt Crisis: Lessons Learned. The World Bank Departmental Working Paper 17430, Number 14 (September).

Economic Commission for Latin America and the Caribbean (ECLAC). Various years. *Economic Survey of Latin America.* Santiago, Chile: ECLAC.

———. Various years. *Preliminary Overview of the Economy of Latin America and the Caribbean.* Santiago, Chile: ECLAC.

Edwards, Sebastian. 1995. *Crisis and Reform in Latin America: From Despair to Hope.* New York: Oxford University Press.

Figueiredo, Argelina Cheibub, and Fernando Limongi. 1994. O Processo Legislativo e a Produção Legal no Congresso Pós-Constituinte. *Novos Estudos* 38 (March): 24–37.

———. 1995. Partidos Políticos na Camara dos Deputados: 1989–1994. *Dados* 38 (3): 497–524.

———. 1997. O Congresso e as Medidas Provisórias: Abdicação ou Delegação? *Novos Estudos* 47 (March): 127–54.

Garman, Christopher, Christiane Kerches da Silva Leite, and Moisés da Silva Marques. 2001. Impactos das Relações Banco Central versus Bancos Estaduais no Arranjo Federativo Pós-1994: Análise à Luz do Caso BANESPA. *Revista de Economia Política* 21 (1): 40–61.

Giambiagi, Fábio. 2000. A Política Fiscal depois de 2002: Algumas Simulações. *Revista do BNDES* 7 (14): 3–28.

Haggard, Stephan, and Robert R. Kaufman. 1995. *The Political Economy of Democratic Transitions.* Princeton: Princeton University Press.

Kopits, George, Juan Pablo Jiménez, and Alvaro Manoel. 2000. Responsabilidad Fiscal a Nivel Subnacional: Argentina y Brasil. Paper presented at the XII Seminario Regional de Política Fiscal, CEPAL, Santiago, Chile, January 24–26.

Kugelmas, Eduardo, Brasílio Sallum Jr., and Eduardo Graeff. 1989. Conflito Federativo e Transição Política. *São Paulo em Perspectiva* 3 (3): 95–102.

Lemgruber Viol, Andrea. 2001. *O Fenômeno da Competição Tributária: Aspectos Teóricos e uma Análise do Caso Brasileiro*. Brasília: Secretaria do Tesouro Nacional.

Lijphart, Arend. 1984. *Democracies: Patterns of Majoritarian and Consensus Government in Twenty-one Countries*. New Haven: Yale University Press.

———. 1999. *Patterns of Democracy: Government Forms and Performance in Thirty-six Countries*. New Haven: Yale University Press.

Lima, Edilberto Carlos Pontes. 1999. Reforma Tributária no Brasil: Entre o Ideal e o Possível. Texto para discussão 666. Brasília: IPEA.

Linz, Juan J., and Arturo Valenzuela, eds. 1994. *The Failure of Presidential Democracy*. Baltimore: Johns Hopkins University Press.

Mainwaring, Scott. 1997. Multipartism, Strong Federalism, and Presidentialism in Brazil. In *Presidentialism and Democracy in Latin America*, edited by S. Mainwaring and M. S. Shugart, 55–109. New York: Cambridge University Press.

———. 1999. *Rethinking Party Systems in the Third Wave of Democratization: The Case of Brazil*. Stanford: Stanford University Press.

Mainwaring, Scott, and Matthew S. Shugart. 1997. Presidentialism and the Party System. In *Presidentialism and Democracy in Latin America*, edited by S. Mainwaring and M. S. Shugart, 394–439. New York: Cambridge University Press.

Makler, Harry M. 1997. The Privatization of the Brazilian Banking Sector: Privatization and Some Socio-economic Challenges. Paper presented at the Latin American Sociological Association conference, University of São Paulo, September.

———. 2000. Bank Transformation and Privatization in Brazil: Financial Federalism and Some Lessons about Bank Privatization. *Quarterly Review of Economics and Finance* 40:45–69.

Mayhew, David. 1974. *Congress: The Electoral Connection*. New Haven: Yale University Press.

Medeiros, Antônio Carlos de. 1986. Politics and Intergovernmental Relations in Brazil, 1964–82. Ph.D. dissertation, London School of Economics.

Mendes, Marcos. 1999. Lei de Responsabilidade Fiscal: Análise e Alternativas. Unpublished paper, Instituto Fernand Braudel de Economia Mundial.

Meneguello, Rachel. 1998. *Partidos e Governos no Brasil Contemporâneo (1985–1997)*. São Paulo: Paz e Terra.

Ministério da Fazenda, Secretaria da Receita Federal. 2000. Participação Percentual no PIB (1985–99). Download from www.receita.fazenda.gov.br.

———. 2001a. Carga Tributária do Brasil—2000 (texto). Download from www.receita.fazenda.gov.br.

———. 2001b. Carga Tributária do Brasil—2000 (tabelas). Download from www.receita.fazenda.gov.br.

Ministério da Fazenda, Secretaria do Tesouro Nacional (MF / STN). 1994. *Execução Orçamentária dos Estados e Municípios das Capitais*. Brasília: MF / STN.

———. 2001a. Fundo de Participação des Estados 1991–2000. Download from www.tesouro.fotenda.gov.br.

————. 2001b. Fundo de Participação des Municípios 1991–2000. Download from www.tesouro.fotenda.gov.br.

Miranda, Sérgio. 2001. *Verdades e Mentiras da Lei de Responsabilidade Fiscal*. Brasília: Centro de Documentação e Informação, Coordenação de Publicações.

Montero, Alfred. 2001. Competitive Federalism and Distributive Conflict in Democratic Brazil. Paper presented at the Bildner Center Conference on Brazil, Columbia University.

Nogueira, Júlio Cesar de A. 1995. O Financiamento Público e Descentralização Fiscal no Brasil. Texto para Discussão #34. Rio de Janeiro: CEPP.

Novaes, Walter, and Sérgio Ribeiro da Costa Werlang. 1993. Financial Integration and Public Financial Institutions. Escola de Pós-Graduação em Economia da Fundação Getúlio Vargas, Working Paper #225 (November).

Packenham, Robert A. 1994. The Politics of Economic Liberalization: Argentina and Brazil in Comparative Perspective. Kellogg Institute for International Studies Working Paper #206 (April), University of Notre Dame.

Power, Timothy J. 1998. The Pen Is Mightier Than the Congress: Presidential Decree Power in Brazil. In *Executive Decree Authority: Calling Out the Tanks or Filling Out the Forms?* edited by J. M. Carey and M. S. Shugart. New York: Cambridge University Press.

Rezende, Fernando. 1995. Federalismo Fiscal no Brasil. *Revista de Economia Política* 15 (3): 5–17.

————. 1996. O Processo da Reforma Tributária. Texto para Discussão #420. Rio de Janeiro: IPEA.

Rigolon, Francisco, and Fábio Giambiagi. 1998. "Renegociação das Dívidas Estaduais: Um Novo Regime Fiscal ou a Repetição de uma Antiga História? Unpublished manuscript, BNDES.

Riker, William H. 1964. *Federalism: Origin, Operation, Significance*. Boston: Little Brown.

Sallum Junior, Brasílio. 1996. *Labirintos: Dos Generais à Nova República*. São Paulo: Editora Hucitec.

Samuels, David. 2003. *Ambition, Federalism, and Legislative Politics in Brazil*. New York: Cambridge University Press.

Samuels, David, and Richard Snyder. 2001. The Value of a Vote: Malapportionment in Comparative Perspective. *British Journal of Political Science* 31 (4): 651–71.

Selcher, Wayne A. 1998. The Politics of Decentralized Federalism, National Diversification, and Regionalism in Brazil. *Journal of Interamerican Studies and World Affairs* 40 (4): 25–50.

Shugart, Matthew Soberg, and John M. Carey. 1992. *Presidents and Assemblies: Constitutional Design and Electoral Dynamics*. New York: Cambridge University Press.

Shugart, Matthew Soberg, and Stephan Haggard. 2001. Institutions and Public Policy in Presidential Systems. In *Presidents, Parliaments, and Policy,* edited by S. Haggard and M. D. McCubbins, 64–102. Cambridge: Cambridge University Press.

Sola, Lourdes. 1993. Estado, Transformação Econômica e Democratização no Brasil. In *Estado, Mercado e Democracia,* edited by Lourdes Sola, 235–79. Rio de Janeiro: Paz e Terra.

Sola, Lourdes, Christopher Garman, and Moises Marques. 1997. Central Banking, Democratic Governance and Political Authority: The Case of Brazil in a Regional Perspective. Paper presented at the 17th World Congress of the International Political Science Association, Seoul, South Korea, August 17–21.

Souza, Amaury de. 1999. Cardoso and the Struggle for Reform in Brazil. *Journal of Democracy* 10 (3): 49–63.

Souza, Celina. 1996. Redemocratization and Decentralization in Brazil: The Strength of the Member States. *Development and Change* 27:529–55.

Tavares de Almeida, Maria Hermínia. 1995. Federalismo e Políticas Sociais. *Revista Brasileira de Ciências Sociais* 10 (28): 88–108.

Thelen, Kathleen, and Sven Steinmo. 1992. Historical Institutionalism in Comparative Perspective. In *Structuring Politics: Historical Institutionalism in Comparative Politics,* edited by S. Steinmo, K. Thelen, and F. Longstreth, 1–32. New York: Cambridge University Press.

Tsebelis, George. 1995. Decision Making in Political Systems: Veto Players in Presidentialism, Parliamentarism, Multicameralism, and Multipartyism. *British Journal of Political Science* 25 (3): 289–325.

Tsebelis, George, and Jeanette Money. 1997. *Bicameralism.* New York: Cambridge University Press.

Werlang, Sérgio Ribeiro da Costa, and Armínio Fraga Neto. 1992. Os Bancos Estaduais e o Descontrole Fiscal: Alguns Aspectos. Escola de Pós-Graduação em Economia da Fundação Getúlio Vargas, Working Paper #203 (November).

Werneck, Rogério L. F. 1992. Fiscal Federalism and Stabilization Policy in Brazil. Texto para Discussão 282, Departamento de Economia, Pontifícia Universidade Católica do Rio de Janeiro (June).

World Bank. 1990. The Dilemma of Brazil's State Banking System: An Analysis and Suggestions for Reform. Report Number 8247-BR, Country Operations Division, Brazil Department, Latin America and the Caribbean Region. Washington, D.C.: World Bank.

CHAPTER 4

Legislative Malapportionment in Latin America

Historical and Comparative Perspectives

—RICHARD SNYDER AND DAVID J. SAMUELS

Although scholars vigorously dispute the exact meaning and definition of democracy, wide agreement exists that *free and fair elections* are the cornerstone of any democratic system of government.[1] An essential characteristic of electoral "fairness" in democracies is that the vote of each citizen counts equally. This notion of fairness embodies the well-known principle of "one person, one vote" that theorists such as Robert Dahl consider a necessary ingredient of democracy.[2]

Democratic rule now prevails across Latin America, and many Latin American countries embrace the *principle* of one person, one vote: many constitutions contain provisions that explicitly guarantee the equality of each citizen's vote.[3] Nevertheless, many of these same countries often fall far short of achieving equality of the vote in *practice*. In the lower chambers of their national legislatures, many Latin American countries have high levels of malapportionment—a wide discrepancy between the shares of legislative seats and the shares of population held by electoral districts.

A malapportioned chamber means that the votes of some citizens weigh more than the votes of others. Although a long-standing federalist tradition acknowledges the value of having a bicameral legislature with an *upper* chamber that represents territorial units equally, a situation that usually requires a significant degree of malapportionment, there is a broad consensus that at least one chamber should weigh the votes of citizens equally. Thus there is no normative justification for malapportionment in the lower chamber.

The overall level of malapportionment for upper and lower chambers in Latin America is significantly higher than in the rest of the world. Indeed, Latin America has some of the world's most malapportioned legislative chambers.[4] The entries in Table 4.1 indicate the percentage of seats in the legislature that are not apportioned

Table 4.1
Malapportionment in Latin America, 1999

Country	MAL_{LC}	MAL_{UC}	Federal?
Argentina	0.14	0.49	Yes
Belize	0.08	X	
Bolivia	0.17	0.38	
Brazil	0.09	0.40	Yes
Chile	0.15	0.31	
Colombia	0.13	0.00	
Costa Rica	0.02	X	
Dominican Republic	0.08	0.38	
Ecuador	0.20	X	
El Salvador	0.07	X	
Guatemala	0.06	X	
Honduras	0.04	X	
Mexico	0.06	0.23	Yes
Nicaragua	0.06	X	
Panama	0.06	X	
Paraguay	0.04	0.00	
Peru	0.00	X	
Uruguay	0.03	0.00	
Venezuela	0.07	0.33	Yes
Latin America average	0.08	0.25	
World average without Latin America	0.06	0.18	
United States	0.01	0.36	Yes

Note: LC = Lower Chamber, UC = Upper Chamber.
  Source: Samuels and Snyder (2001).

according to the principle of "one person, one vote." A score of 0.00 represents a perfectly apportioned chamber in which no citizen's vote weighs more than another's. Conversely, a score of 1.00 indicates a fully malapportioned chamber in which all of the legislative seats are allocated to a single electoral district with just one voter. A score of 0.50 means that 50 percent of the seats are allocated to districts that would not receive those seats if there were no malapportionment.

For example, Argentina's Senate (the world's most malapportioned chamber) has a malapportionment score of 0.49, which means that 49 percent of the legislative seats in the Senate are allocated in ways that violate the one person, one vote principle. Similarly, Ecuador's lower chamber (the world's third most malapportioned lower chamber) has a score of 0.20, which means that 20 percent of the legislative seats in the chamber are allocated in ways that violate the one person, one vote principle. Although the table shows that malapportionment is not a problem everywhere in Latin America, a number of prominent countries—Argentina, Bolivia, Brazil, Chile, Colombia, and Ecuador—do have extremely high levels of lower-chamber malapportionment. These countries together account for almost two-thirds of the population of Latin America, underlining how important a focus on malapportionment is for understanding the problems of democracy in the region.

Most democracies have some degree of malapportionment, especially if the legislature has an upper chamber. In fact, the only way to avoid malapportionment is to elect representatives in a single, nationwide district, as in Israel or the Netherlands. Moreover, unless a country employs such a system or already has an automatic reapportionment mechanism in place, it will typically experience rising levels of "natural" malapportionment over time caused by demographic changes across districts (see below).[5]

Despite the tendency for malapportionment to increase over time, many countries have achieved low levels of malapportionment in one or both chambers, an outcome that is especially apparent in the lower chambers of the advanced industrial democracies of Western Europe and North America. The low levels of malapportionment in these cases reflect the implementation of procedures for periodic reapportionment that correct for the tendency of malapportionment to increase over time due to demographic changes. By contrast, the higher levels of malapportionment characterizing both upper *and* lower chambers across Latin America indicate that many countries in the region have not implemented such corrective procedures.

Why do the actual electoral rules and procedures in many Latin American democracies diverge so sharply from the constitutional principle requiring equality of the vote and proportional apportionment of legislative seats according to population? The empirical material analyzed below shows that political elites in many Latin American countries have historically manipulated apportionment as a tool for ensuring "political survival," building electoral and legislative coalitions, and implementing their desired public policies. Manipulation of legislative apportionment has played an especially important role in managing urban-rural cleavages across Latin America. This has resulted in a strong *rural-conservative bias* that persists today in many legislatures, where many countries' urban metropoles remain highly underrepresented. In short, malapportionment has served and continues to serve as a powerful political weapon of conservative elites in Latin America. Consequently, despite the important advances that have been made toward achieving democracy in Latin America, many elections in the region are unfair.

The following section argues that malapportionment should be considered a formal pathology of Latin American political systems, one that raises troubling questions about the performance and quality of democracy in many countries in the region. A subsequent section develops basic conceptual tools for the comparative study of malapportionment. The focus then shifts to an analysis of the evolution of malapportionment in Argentina, Brazil, and Chile. We highlight the different ways that elites have deployed malapportionment as a political weapon for advancing their interests. We also explore some of the important implications of malapportionment for how democracy works in contemporary Latin America. The penultimate section considers alternative strategies for reducing malapportionment, a necessary step for making elections in Latin America more fair.

A Formal Pathology: Malapportionment and the Defects of Democracy in Latin America

Much of the debate about the shortcomings and problems of democracy in Latin America has focused on *informal* rules and practices. For example, in his pioneering work on the limitations of Latin American democracies, Guillermo O'Donnell (1993) has called attention to factors such as "brown areas," where the rule of law is extremely attenuated, as well as the problem of a loose fit between formal rules and actual practice in many new (and old) democracies. Similarly, Jonathan Fox (1994) points to the importance of "semi-clientelist" politics (especially at the local level) as an important hindrance to full-fledged democracy in Latin America.

These kinds of informal defects are clearly important. However, the defects of contemporary Latin American democracy are by no means limited to the informal realm; formal institutions can also diminish the quality of democracy (Shugart and Carey 1992; Linz 1994; Jones 1995; Mainwaring and Shugart 1997). A focus on malapportionment highlights how formalized, detailed, and explicit electoral rules in many countries have resulted in large inequalities in the weighting of citizens' votes. Consequently, the limitations of many contemporary Latin American democracies go beyond the problem that "the games played 'inside' the democratic institutions are different from the ones dictated by their formal rules," as O'Donnell (1996, 41) suggests. Where formal electoral rules result in unfair elections, even games abiding by such rules are undemocratic.[6] In short, democracy in Latin America is impaired not only because of a loose fit between formal rules and actual behavior, but also because the formal rules themselves can have undemocratic consequences.[7]

Our argument challenges the assumption that most Latin American democracies satisfy the procedural criteria for democracy (i.e., inclusive, fair, and competitive elections in addition to freedom of association, assembly, and speech) and that any lingering pathologies have been largely banished to an informal, separate sphere of "brown areas," particularism, and clientelist politics that mainly affect marginalized groups. Because explicit electoral rules in so many Latin American countries flagrantly violate a core criterion of the democratic process—fair elections—the problem of malapportionment should be viewed as a *formal pathology*. Malapportionment is often akin to deliberate institutionally engineered discrimination for or against certain political parties and therefore weakens the quality of democracy in the region.

From a methodological perspective, recognizing this formal pathology offers important advantages. Precisely because it is a formal feature of electoral systems, malapportionment is quite amenable to systematic measurement and to analysis (as an independent or dependent variable) with large-N, statistical techniques. By contrast, informal pathologies, such as "brown areas" and the (un)rule of law, while important, often frustrate scholars because of the difficulty of gathering systematic data beyond fertile anecdotal evidence. Consequently, scholars oriented toward gathering systematic empirical data have tended to dismiss informal, difficult-to-measure elements altogether, a move that creates an unhealthy bias toward crude measures that misclassify as full-fledged democracies countries lacking attributes that many would consider necessary conditions for democracy. By contrast, formal pathologies are far less "fuzzy" than informal ones and can therefore be incorporated more readily into cross-national studies. This possibility provides a basis for such studies to adopt more nuanced conceptualizations of democracy in comparative perspective.

Another important aspect of malapportionment deserves consideration. In part because of its formal, institutionalized nature, malapportionment can serve as a kind of "electoral stealth technology" for engineering bias and maintaining inequalities of influence in a political system. In contrast to traditional "low-tech" methods for rigging elections, such as vote buying and other forms of fraud (e.g., ballot stuffing and tampering with the counting of votes), which are relatively easy for election monitors and opposition parties to observe, malapportionment is less obvious and thus is often not seen as a proximate cause of unfair elections.[8] Moreover, because the mechanisms used to apportion seats are often arcane mathematical functions, they do not provide the kind of vivid material that lends itself to front-page news or to use as a lightening rod for mobilizing mass indignation. By contrast, lurid charges of garden-variety fraud such as ballot stuffing and vote buying are far more attractive bread-and-butter issues for opposition parties, election losers, and international election monitors.

Although differences in the ratio of seats to populations across districts may attract little attention because they are obscured by "juicier" political issues, such discrepancies can nevertheless confer important strategic advantages to political actors, as we demonstrate below. For example, the "gerrymander" is a long-standing and widespread type of malapportionment in which districts are created to bias the vote in favor of one party over another. "Rotten boroughs" (which persisted in England through the mid–nineteenth century) are another type in which some districts have far fewer voters than others.[9]

As is the case elsewhere, such blatant uses of apportionment as a tool for political manipulation seem increasingly unlikely in contemporary Latin America.[10] However, this by no means implies that apportionment decisions have been depoliticized, nor does it mean that apportionment processes are currently fully democratic. In Latin America today, in contrast to the developed Western democracies, high levels of malapportionment in lower chambers of the legislature can readily coexist with the standard set of democratic rules and institutions, such as freedom of association, assembly, and speech, full suffrage, absence of massive fraud, and competitive elections.[11] Consequently, genuinely competitive elections without fraud in a system with full suffrage and where basic civil and political freedoms are effectively guaranteed *may nevertheless be extremely unfair*. In a malapportioned system, all citizens can enjoy a free and equal opportunity to *formulate* and *signify* their preferences yet nevertheless lack the opportunity to have their preferences *weighed* equally.[12] The compatibility between malapportionment and the other core elements of democratic politics makes malapportionment an especially pernicious problem, because it can help sustain a powerful illusion of robust democracy that hides a reality in which some citizens are far more "equal" than others in terms of the value of their votes.

Conceptual Issues in the Comparative Study of Apportionment

Despite the normative and practical importance of malapportionment, to our knowledge only Samuels and Snyder (2001) have analyzed this key dimension of electoral systems in comparative perspective. Consequently, we lack both a basic vocabulary and a set of foundational concepts for cross-national research on malapportionment.[13] This section takes an initial step toward filling the gap.

Natural and Unnatural Malapportionment

Consider the following scenario. The constitutional framers of the bucolic nation of Freedonia are fervently committed to the democratic principle of one person, one vote. Guided by this noble ideal, they meticulously craft an electoral system in which the share of legislative seats allocated to each district corresponds exactly to its share of the national population. Pleased with their perfectly apportioned electoral system, the framers retire from politics and retreat to a tranquil life of contemplation.

Unfortunately, subtle demographic forces soon conspire to undermine the framers' hard work. In the decades after the constitutional convention, Freedonia experiences an unanticipated industrial revolution that causes a gradual yet massive shift of the country's population toward urban areas. Secure that the traditionally sedentary ways of the country's citizens would be a permanent feature of national life, the framers of Freedonia's constitution had myopically failed to create regular procedures for reapportioning legislative seats. Consequently, as people migrated from rural to urban areas, legislative seats did not follow the population, and the perfectly apportioned electoral system crafted by the framers was transformed into a highly malapportioned one that flagrantly violated the cherished one person, one vote ideal.

We call malapportionment that results purely from demographic shifts (i.e., population movement and changes in the size of the overall population) *natural* malapportionment. The point of this vignette is to show that a political decision is not required for a country to have high levels of malapportionment, and not to reapportion may in and of itself be considered a political decision. Indeed, unless measures are taken to periodically reapportion the electoral system, we have a strong basis for expecting most countries to have high levels of malapportionment "by default."[14]

However, not all malapportionment is a natural effect of demographic processes—self-interested politicians often seek to manipulate legislative apportionment. Instead of correcting for malapportionment, reapportionment procedures can actually *increase* malapportionment above its "natural" level. It is therefore imperative to distinguish between natural and politically engineered malapportionment. Understanding how and why malapportionment is politically engineered requires that we explore the tools politicians use to manipulate apportionment procedures.

Engineering Representation: The Nuts and Bolts of Apportionment

We can distinguish (at least) six tools for reapportioning an electoral system: (1) creating *new legislative districts* out of previously unrepresented territory, for example, by adding new states in a federal system; (2) *adding or subtracting* seats to the total number in the legislature; (3) providing a *minimum* number of seats per district, regardless of population; (4) providing a *maximum* number of seats per district, regardless of population; (5) changing the boundary lines of *existing* districts (redistricting); and (6) changing the *distribution of seats* across existing districts without changing their borders or the total number of seats (reseating).[15]

Adding new legislative districts can either reduce or increase malapportionment, depending on whether new districts are created in already overrepresented areas, or whether underrepresented areas are split into new districts and granted additional seats. Adding seats to the legislature reduces malapportionment if the seats are added to underrepresented areas, and subtracting seats reduces malapportionment if the seats are taken away from overrepresented districts.

Providing a minimum number of seats per district guarantees malapportionment in the legislative chamber, because population inevitably varies across districts, and some districts (such as constitutionally recognized federal units) may be indivisible for constitutional reasons. The resulting degree of malapportionment will depend on how small the smaller districts are relative to the average.[16] Likewise, providing a *maximum* number of seats per district necessarily produces malapportionment. For example, in Brazil, where the constitution sets a maximum of seventy deputies per district (Article 45), some voters are effectively prevented from gaining fair representation regardless of other reapportionment rules.[17]

The distinction between the fifth and sixth methods of reapportioning—redistricting and reseating—is especially important, because it helps us separate analytically the "boundary drawing" and "seat allocation" processes. Making this distinction is a key step toward understanding the politics of reapportionment, because different political actors may have authority over the boundary drawing and seat allocation processes. For example, legislative seats in the U.S. House are automatically apportioned to the states according to population after each national census, as per the U.S. constitution. Thus, although the states have no authority over the *number* of districts and seats they have, the constitution stipulates that each state is responsible for drawing the boundaries of its allotted districts (redistricting), a process that involves the state legislative and executive branches. In short, the United States is characterized by a "separation of reapportionment powers" because the authority to reseat (that is, to change the distribution of seats across districts and states) and the authority to redistrict are vested in two distinct institutions.

Whether or not a system is characterized by such a separation of reapportionment powers, the politics of seat allocation is likely to differ in important ways from the politics of boundary drawing. Seats are nondivisible goods, and the fact that a district has gained or lost a seat is difficult to hide. Consequently, reseating is a highly transparent method for redistributing representation in which the winners and losers are clear. By contrast, redistricting can be a far less transparent means for redistributing representation, especially from the perspective of the voters. District boundaries are inherently more "divisible" than seats because they can be nudged in a variety of subtle ways that obscure the political consequences of these changes. It may therefore be quite difficult for voters to discern who wins and who loses from redistricting.

Taken together, these tools can have a variety of effects on malapportionment. Based on this discussion, we distinguish three types of reapportionment:

Progressive Reapportionment

Progressive reapportionment reduces malapportionment and therefore increases the fairness of elections. When progressive reapportionment is achieved by changing the allocation of legislative seats, seats follow the population. For example, progressive reapportionment can involve adding seats to underrepresented areas, subtracting seats from overrepresented areas, or a combination of both methods. When progressive reapportionment is achieved by the method of redistricting, the boundary lines of overrepresented districts may be redrawn so that they have a larger population or, alternatively, the boundary lines of underrepresented districts may be redrawn so that they have smaller populations.[18]

Regressive Reapportionment

Regressive reapportionment increases malapportionment and thus reduces the fairness of elections. When regressive reapportionment is achieved through the method of reallocating legislative seats, seats do not follow the population. Regressive reapportionment can be achieved by adding seats to overrepresented areas, subtracting seats from underrepresented areas, or by a combination of both techniques. In terms of redistricting, regressive reapportionment can be achieved by redrawing the boundary lines of districts so that underrepresented districts experience increases in their populations and overrepresented districts experience decreases in their populations.

Neutral Reapportionment

Neutral reapportionment does not change the overall level of malapportionment in a system. Nevertheless, the distribution of seats and / or the configuration of district boundaries do shift. Neutral reapportionments may be undertaken to ensure representation of ethnic or other minorities, for example.

The Evolution of Malapportionment in Latin America

This section applies the conceptual tools developed above to analyze the historical evolution of malapportionment in Latin America. The discussion focuses on two core issues: (1) Why do many Latin American countries have extraordinarily high levels of malapportionment in their lower chambers? (2) Has malapportionment always been a problem in Latin America? Or, alternatively, is severe malapportionment a feature peculiar to the most recent wave of democratic regimes in the region? We will show that malapportionment has, in fact, characterized many Latin American nations for as long as they have had elections—whether competitive or noncompetitive.[19] Moreover, at many times in Latin America's twentieth-century history, governments have undertaken *regressive* reapportionments for politically strategic purposes. Table 4.2 provides historical data on the evolution of lower-chamber malapportionment in Latin America.[20]

Is there a relationship between country size and malapportionment? Although Samuels and Snyder (2001) found that size was positively associated with malapportionment in a larger cross-national sample, the relationship in Latin America is somewhat ambiguous. In Table 4.3 we classify Latin American countries according to population and whether malapportionment is above or below the world average. Five of the six smaller nations listed in Table 4.3 have achieved below-average levels of malapportionment in their lower chambers, whereas nine of the thirteen medium and larger nations have above-average malapportionment. The absence of a clear relationship between country size and lower-chamber malapportionment (especially among large and medium-sized countries) suggests that the evolution of malapportionment is more a function of political factors. Indeed, the evidence we analyze below indicates that apportionment decisions in Latin America have often been a highly politicized weapon in political elites' arsenal. Because of space limitations, we explore in detail only the cases of Argentina, Brazil, and Chile. However, the evolution of malapportionment has followed a similar course in several other countries in the region.

Argentina

Although Argentina's Congress is among the most malapportioned in the world today, this has not always been the case. In fact, Article 45 of the Argentine constitution of 1860 set the number of congressional deputies per province proportionally according to population and mandated that Congress reapportion seats after each census. Moreover, although Argentina experienced several "natural" increases in malapportionment after 1860, it undertook progressive reapportionments at fairly regular intervals earlier in its history (in 1881, 1898, and 1920). This corrected for internal migration and indicates that Argentine politicians had agreed to abide by the principle of equal representation across provinces up through the 1940s.

However, Argentina began to depart from the path of regular, progressive reapportionment during Juan Perón's first presidency (1946–55). Perón made a con-

Table 4.2

Lower-Chamber Malapportionment in Latin America, Historical Evolution

Year	Argentina	Brazil	Chile	Uruguay	Colombia	Venezuela	Bolivia	Ecuador	Peru	Honduras	Costa Rica
1870											
1872	0.16	0.10	0.12								
1875	0.13	0.10	0.13								
1880	0.13	0.10	0.08								
1885	0.03	0.12	0.07								
1890	0.03	0.12	0.07								
1895	0.18	0.11	0.12								
1900	0.02	0.11	0.12								
1905	0.02	0.10	0.17								
1910	0.02	0.10	0.17								
1915	0.12	0.09	0.06	0.02							
1920	0.13	0.09	0.10	0.02							
1925	0.05	0.09	0.14	0.03							
1930	0.05	0.09	0.10	0.06					0.16		
1935	0.05	0.10	0.04						0.15		

Year											
1940	0.05		0.03						0.14		
1945	0.09	0.11	0.06			0.03			0.09		
1950	0.09	0.10	0.10			0.08		0.20	0.11		0.02
1955	0.05	0.09	0.10						0.11		0.03
1958	0.03	0.10	0.13			0.06			0.09		0.03
1960	0.10	0.10	0.13		0.15	0.06	0.15	0.13	0.09		0.03
1965	0.16	0.08	0.13		0.15	0.03	0.15	0.13	0.09		0.02
1970		0.10	0.17	0.07	0.16	0.08	0.15	0.13	0.09		0.03
1975	0.15	0.12	0.17		0.08	0.05					
1980		0.10		0.07	0.08	0.02	0.15	0.15	0.11	0.07	0.01
1985	0.15	0.10	0.15	0.03	0.08	0.04	0.23	0.17	0.11	0.04	0.01
1990	0.15	0.10	0.15	0.03	0.09	0.04			0.09	0.04	0.02
1995	0.15	0.09			0.13	0.07		0.20	0.00	0.04	0.02
2000	0.14	0.09	0.15	0.03	0.13	0.07	0.17	0.20	0.00	0.04	0.02

Source: Authors' compilation.

Table 4.3
Lower-Chamber Malapportionment and Population in Latin America

	Population over 20 million	Population between 5 and 20 million	Population under 5 million
Malapportionment above world average	Argentina Brazil Colombia Venezuela	Bolivia Chile Dominican Republic Ecuador El Salvador	Belize
Malapportionment at or below world average	Mexico Peru	Guatemala Honduras	Costa Rica Nicaragua Panama Paraguay Uruguay

scious, strategic effort to increase his and his party's electoral and legislative support from the underpopulated hinterlands (Little 1973, 276–80; Sawers 1996, 199–200; see also Gibson and Calvo 2000), and this involved overrepresenting these areas. First, Perón's 1949 constitution ended the proportionality principle enshrined in the 1860 constitution and gave each province a minimum of two deputies, regardless of population (Sawers 1996, 194). Moreover, Perón strategically granted representation to eight sparsely populated, previously unrepresented territories. This initially caused malapportionment to *decline* in the early 1950s, because Perón was granting a legislative voice to a portion of the population that had none before. Yet this situation was soon reversed, because while the populations of the hinterlands stagnated, the province of Buenos Aires experienced rapid population growth (from 26 to 34 percent of the national total from 1947 to 1960). However, Buenos Aires was not granted a similar increase in its share of seats. Consequently, as Table 4.2 shows, malapportionment in Argentina increased dramatically from 1955 to 1960.[21]

Argentina's military rulers from 1966 to 1973 maintained Perón's policy of deliberately underrepresenting the metropolitan provinces (Buenos Aires and the Federal Capital). The military intensified this bias just prior to Perón's return to power in 1973, when the military raised the minimum number of deputies per province from two to three (Law 19862/72) and gave the territory of Tierra del Fuego two deputies (Porto 1990, 183). The military junta in power from 1976 to 1983 continued this practice—just before the return to democracy in 1983, the regime again increased the minimum number of deputies per province, raising it to five (Law 22847 / 83).[22] The logic behind these moves was to further overrepresent conservative provinces and their voters at the expense of urban voters—whether Peronist or not—because the military viewed the more conservative and rural Partido Justicialista (Peronist) and Unión Cívica Radical *caudillos* as less threatening.[23]

Today Argentina's Chamber of Deputies continues to be highly malapportioned, underrepresenting the country's urban core: the provinces that hold just 31 percent of the population control 44 percent of the seats in the Chamber (the situation is even worse in Argentina's Senate). This imbalance provides the less developed and sparsely populated provinces with a legislative veto over reforms that would adversely affect their interests.

In sum, since the 1940s, both democratic and authoritarian rulers in Argentina have manipulated malapportionment for political purposes. Perón converted sparsely populated territories into provinces and increased the minimum number of deputies per province in order to strengthen rural support for his regime. Similarly, the "bureaucratic-authoritarian" military regimes of the 1960s and 1970s used malapportionment to weaken urban electoral and legislative interests, whether Peronist or not.

Brazil

In contrast to the pattern seen in Argentina, where malapportionment in the lower chamber was not an enduring problem until the 1940s, the roots of lower-chamber malapportionment in Brazil reach back to the nineteenth century, when the country was ruled as a constitutional monarchy. Although Brazil's constitution of 1824 did not establish clear procedures for parliamentary representation of the imperial provinces, Table 4.2 shows that Brazil's lower chamber was already highly malapportioned prior to the advent of the highly federalist "Old Republic" in 1890. In the latter half of the nineteenth century, prominent Brazilians argued that the lower chamber ought to be reorganized according to principles of population, as in the United States (Bastos, 172, cited in Porto 1989, 139). Still, while the population of the important states of Minas Gerais, Rio de Janeiro, and São Paulo (especially the latter) began to increase rapidly, malapportionment was never corrected under the empire.[24]

The monarchy was overthrown in 1889, and Brazil's 1891 constitution institutionalized the existing malapportionment by allocating a minimum of four deputies to each state. Nevertheless, during the 1891–1930 period, known as the "Politics of the Governors" for the highly decentralized federal character of Brazilian politics during this phase, the booming states of São Paulo and Minas Gerais, which dominated the country politically and economically, were underrepresented to a *lesser* extent than during any other period (Nicolau 1997, table 2). This pattern jibes well with the standard understanding of the period as the "Coffee and Milk" era, a term that refers to those two states' dominance of the country.

The "Old Republic"—along with the dominance of São Paulo and Minas Gerais—was overthrown in 1930, and in 1933 a constitutional assembly was held using the same seat distribution as in the Old Republic. However, President Getúlio Vargas and his allies at the time aimed to reduce the power of the "Coffee and Milk" state elites, and the members of the constitutional assembly from other states thus decided to decrease São Paulo's and Minas's proportion of seats. This constitution lasted only briefly, as Vargas declared it null and void in 1937 and ruled as dictator for the next eight years.

The prejudice against São Paulo and Minas Gerais continued when competitive elections and mass suffrage were finally established after Vargas's overthrow in 1945. At this point we begin to see striking parallels between the Argentine and Brazilian stories. Elections were held for another constitutional assembly, and the seat distribution used to elect the members of the assembly was the same as for the 1934 constitution, which meant that São Paulo and Minas Gerais were underrepresented prior to the beginning of deliberations for the new constitution.

Fleischer (1994) reports that the apportionment of seats was one of the "hot" issues discussed in the 1946 constitutional convention. Because economic and demographic transformations during the 1930–45 period of Getúlio Vargas's dictatorship had continued to favor Minas Gerais and São Paulo (for example, São Paulo's population increased from 15 to 18 percent of the national total), members of the constitutional assembly from the smaller states "attempted to avoid the return of the "coffee and milk" dynasty (Fleischer 1994, 6) and thus decided to increase the minimum number of federal deputies per state to seven. States would be entitled to an additional deputy for every 150,000 people, up to twenty deputies. In addition, in a jab specifically aimed at São Paulo, if a state were entitled to more than twenty deputies, it received only an additional deputy for every 250,000 people (Nicolau 1997, 444). Thus, the 1946 constitution increased malapportionment relative to the

1934 constitution and particularly prejudiced Brazil's economically most important state.

Malapportionment would have important political consequences during the 1945–64 competitive period. Fleischer (1994, 9) argues that malapportionment, along with nonconcurrent presidential elections, "distanced the executive from the legislative branch . . . resulting in a virtual institutional impasse" at times between the president and the legislature. Citing numerous Brazilian scholars who noticed this pattern, he also notes the impact of malapportionment on the composition of the dominant support base for each branch of government: urban for the executive branch, and rural for the legislative branch. In this way, malapportionment may have contributed to the ongoing executive-legislative tension in Brazil that culminated in a military coup in 1964.

During Brazil's 1964–85 military dictatorship, the government initially attempted to limit the power of both the conservative rural elites and the radical opposition, but following disastrous electoral defeats for its "pet" party (ARENA) to the opposition MDB party in 1970 and especially 1974, the military reversed its policy and implemented a series of changes in the electoral law intended to strengthen their conservative congressional allies and weaken the mainly urban-based opposition (Fleischer 1994, 23).

First, in 1977, they placed a *maximum* on the number of deputies a state could have. In practice, this new ceiling only affected São Paulo, the center of student and labor activism in the 1960s and 1970s, and thus increased the relative weight of the legislative delegations from the poorer and rural regions of the country, where government supporters were stronger. Second, the regime split the state of Mato Grosso into two states, creating the new state of Mato Grosso do Sul, which gave three additional senators and seven deputies to a politically conservative region.

In 1982, just prior to the reinstatement of democratic elections for governors and federal deputies, the military regime made additional adjustments that favored its allies. The military increased the minimum number of seats to eight per state and the maximum number of seats to sixty. This change further advantaged overrepresented states, only marginally improving São Paulo's situation, because under a fairly apportioned system it would have been entitled to 101 seats.[25] In addition, the military created the new state of Rondônia in the poor and generally conservative Northern region, thereby adding another eight deputies and three senators to the ranks of conservatives.

The strategy of regressive reapportionment through increasing the weight of already overrepresented regions in the Brazilian Congress did not end with the demise of the military regime. In 1988 the new democratic constitution increased the maximum number of deputies per state to seventy, although São Paulo would not elect this many deputies until 1994. However, between 1985 and 1990 six new states were created, adding forty-eight deputies (about 10 percent of the total) and eighteen senators (about 20 percent of the total). The creation of these new states added deputies and senators to three less developed, rural regions. By contrast, São Paulo's deputies have been unsuccessful in their efforts to gain further increases in the number of seats allotted to their state, and the state remains sorely underrepresented. Currently, the states that comprise the underdeveloped North, Northeast, and Center-West regions hold 42 percent of the population, yet control 51 percent of the lower-chamber seats (as in Argentina, the situation is much worse in Brazil's Senate).

In sum, lower-chamber malapportionment was already an established part of Brazilian politics in the nineteenth century. While Argentina institutionalized high levels of malapportionment in the 1940s and 1950s, Brazil continued a well-established pattern of severe malapportionment during those decades. In both countries, democratic and authoritarian governments alike used malapportionment to strengthen conservative, rural elites and weaken urban-based, reformist groups.

Chile

The evolution of malapportionment in Chile took a course similar to that in Argentina and Brazil, despite Chile's far smaller population and unitary (rather than federal) institutional design. As in Argentina, progressive reapportionments were carried out periodically in Chile during the nineteenth and early twentieth centuries. As seen in Table 4.2, malapportionment varied over time in Chile prior to the 1930s, by which time Chile had taken steps to reduce malapportionment in the lower chamber.

However, in a pattern of rural bias strikingly similar to that seen in Argentina and Brazil, the primarily urban Santiago province has received an increasingly smaller share of the seats in the lower chamber since the emergence of truly competitive elections in the late 1930s. Despite the fact that Chile's 1925 constitution established clear rules that required a progressive reapportionment of the lower chamber after national censuses (taken in 1940, 1952, and 1960), no such reapportionment was implemented between 1937 and 1973. The absence of progressive reapportionment during this period resulted in "naturally" increasing levels of malapportionment be-cause of Santiago province's faster-than-average population growth (Cruz-Coke 1984, 27). Chile also enacted a slightly regressive reapportionment in 1969, when it added three new seats to already overrepresented districts.

The failure to implement progressive reapportionment in Chile can be explained largely as a consequence of the fears that centrist and rightist political elites had about giving urban interests a greater influence in the national legislature. McDon-ald (1969, 457) writes that Chile's presidents "deviously avoided reapportionment re-sponsibility" and that the censuses were "rejected on technicalities for political rea-sons."[26] He argues that an implicit agreement was reached to avoid redistricting and thereby placate representatives from rural provinces who complained that Santiago was becoming wealthy while the rest of the country stagnated (470).[27]

The consequences of malapportionment in Chile paralleled those seen in other Latin American countries: parties with urban bases were penalized. Caviedes (1979, 53) writes that "From the point of view of distributing a party's political efforts, it required more effort to gather votes from the urban population than to conquer an electoral clientele in the agricultural provinces. . . . [Consequently] the parties that suffered most [from malapportionment] were those that drew their clientele chiefly from urban centers." Loveman (1986, 240) argues that the key to the stability of Chilean democracy through the 1960s was the urban bourgeoisie's fear of outright confrontation with labor and its consequent disposition to compensate rural land-owners. One way this compensation of rural elites may have been accomplished is by ignoring the constitutional requirement for reapportionment, although verifica-tion of this supposition will have to await further research.

The rural bias of the electoral system still exists in Chile. In fact, malapportion-ment in Chile's lower chamber is actually higher now than it was prior to 1973. In part, this increase in malapportionment is a legacy of General Augusto Pinochet's military regime (1973–90). Just before leaving office, Pinochet ordered the design of a new electoral system that favored conservative parties (Garretón 1991). In addition to favoring the second-place finisher (usually a conservative) in each district, the sys-tem also dramatically overrepresented rural areas and discriminated against Santi-ago. Districts with just 35 percent of the population currently control 50 percent of the lower-chamber seats. In addition, although Chile is not federal, its Senate is highly malapportioned.

In short, as in Argentina and Brazil, democratic and authoritarian leaders in Chile have failed to implement progressive reapportionment since the end of the 1930s. Instead, when political elites have acted to reapportion the electoral system, they have done so in a regressive way that deliberately overrepresents rural areas and underrepresents urban areas.

Strategic Uses of Apportionment

The empirical material above shows that malapportionment has served as an important weapon in the strategic arsenals of Latin American politicians for more than a century: elites have used their control over legislative apportionment to weaken opposition and strengthen supporters, and to build "strange bedfellows" coalitions.

Malapportionment can serve as a powerful tool for weakening opposition groups. The bureaucratic-authoritarian regimes in Argentina, Brazil, and Chile in the 1960s and 1970s provide perhaps the most vivid examples of how malapportionment can serve as a tool for weakening progressive opposition forces. In each country we see striking examples of how malapportionment undercut the electoral influence of urban groups.

The flip side of malapportionment's weakening of politically progressive opposition groups is its strengthening of conservative forces. In all three cases malapportionment served to increase the representation of less developed, more rural areas that tended to send conservative representatives to the national legislatures. Frequently, these regressive reapportionments occurred just prior to the military regimes' exit from power and were obviously intended to institutionalize a strong conservative bias in the political arena. If Latin American lower chambers had been fairly apportioned in the past, history might have been different.

Yet malapportionment has also been used (or, conversely, a decision to reapportion has been avoided) under democratic auspices in Latin America, and there is no clear correlation between the "type" of democratic leader or party and the "progression" or "regression" of malapportionment. For example, although Argentina, Brazil, and Chile have had populist, socialist, moderate, and conservative presidents since 1945, none have taken significant steps to correct malapportionment, and many have acted to make it worse. Apportionment has thus been utilized by both democratic and authoritarian elites in Latin America to penalize urban, progressive interests or, as in Perón's case, to bolster a populist national coalition.

The use of malapportionment by politicians of different political orientations points to another important way that malapportionment has been utilized by political elites in Latin America: malapportionment has served as a key political weapon for building "strange bedfellows" legislative coalitions. Scholars have highlighted Perón's explicit attempt to include Argentina's rural, poor, and sparsely populated regions in his "populist" project, and a similar alliance has characterized the PRI in Mexico (Gibson 1997). Likewise, in Brazil, the attack on São Paulo during the 1946 constitutional convention was part of a strategy that Vargas and his allies adopted that aimed to deactivate and fragment São Paulo labor while simultaneously activating labor elsewhere. Vargas organized the urban labor–based Partido Trabalhista Brasileiro (PTB) and attempted to control this party and thereby channel labor demands (Campello de Souza 1976). However, Vargas never focused the PTB's organizing efforts on São Paulo. Although São Paulo had the largest labor movement, it was historically more independent of state direction. Moreover, São Paulo was the center of communist party activity. Consequently, the PTB was never strong in São Paulo. Like Perón, Vargas also attempted to tie the fate of his populist political party (that is, the PTB) to a conservative rural-based organization (the Partido Social Democrático, PSD) (Delgado 1989), albeit with much less success.

We would thus extend Gibson's "strange bedfellows" notion to Brazil, Chile, and potentially elsewhere. Malapportionment appears to have been one tool that governing elites in Latin America used to "contain" urban-popular pressures during the 1950s and 1960s. Today, after decades of rural-urban migration, malapportionment continues to enhance the power of rural politicians in national legislatures. In cases such as Argentina, Chile, Brazil, Ecuador, Bolivia, and Mexico, politicians with metropolitan support bases still cannot hope to govern without forming an alliance with politicians from peripheral regions. The next section elaborates this theme.[28]

Malapportionment and the Quality of Democracy

In addition to the important normative issues raised by the problem of unfair elections, malapportionment also has major practical consequences for how democracy works in contemporary Latin America. Specifically, the high levels of malapportionment in many Latin American countries have fostered (1) a rural-conservative bias in legislatures, (2) estrangement of the executive and legislative branches, (3) the proliferation of subnational authoritarian enclaves, and (4) a strong capacity for subnational elites to "hold the center hostage" with regard to major policy issues.

Rural-Conservative Bias

Our evidence shows that malapportionment characterizes many Latin American national legislatures. This has resulted in a heavy legislative overrepresentation of rural interests, and not just in the upper chambers, where it might naturally be expected.[29] This rural-conservative bias is not only a result of centuries-old domination by conservative landed elites who engineered an institutional bias against emerging urban classes, but also of the military bureaucratic-authoritarian regimes of the 1960s and 1970s in Argentina, Brazil, and Chile. These regimes left a strong institutional legacy of rural bias in legislatures that has persisted in the contemporary democratic period.[30] Thus, a variety of factors conspire to maintain a *rural-conservative* bias in many lower chambers of Latin American legislatures.

Moreover, in malapportioned systems, an increase in the share of the total population residing in urban districts can paradoxically *strengthen* the hand of rural interests, because the amount of pork-barrel funds required to "purchase" legislative support should decrease as rural areas acquire relatively smaller populations. For example, as an overrepresented rural district loses people, the "cost" in terms of pork of buying the district's support should decrease, thereby making it an attractive source of "cheap" support for coalition builders at the national level.[31] The pro-rural legacies of existing malapportionment combined with out-migration from rural to urban areas has greatly strengthened the influence of rural-conservative interests in many Latin American legislatures.

Estrangement of the Legislative and Executive Branches

Some scholars have praised presidential systems for their ability to combine distinct kinds of representation—for example, the legislature can be "representative of the diversity of the society and polity" (Shugart and Carey 1992, 286), while the executive can represent the nation as a whole. However, the evidence from Latin America suggests that where legislatures are malapportioned, such combinations can foster paralyzing impasses among branches of government. Malapportionment in Latin America fosters a "ruralization" of lower chambers, yet presidential elections in the region are organized in ways that conform far more closely to the one person, one vote principle, typically relying on a single, national district.[32] Because the president's district is essentially the entire nation, presidential candidates have strong incentives to build their electoral coalitions in regions with the largest absolute number of voters, which over the course of the last century have increasingly been urban areas. Consequently, presidents seek and gain most of their support from urban constituencies, whereas legislatures are dominated by rural interests. This difference in bases of support can contribute to an estrangement of the legislative from the executive branch.[33]

The urbanization of the executive branch and the contrasting ruralization of the legislative branch may help explain the stalemate and gridlock that so often characterize legislative-executive relations in Latin America, both in the past and in the contemporary period. In systems with severe malapportionment that advantages rural areas in legislative elections, presidents often face powerful tensions between the dual imperatives of building an urban-based *electoral coalition* and forging a rural-based *governing coalition*.[34] For example, in Brazil, no presidential candidate can hope to win without doing very well in São Paulo, Rio de Janeiro, and Minas Gerais, which together comprise 43 percent of the electorate. If a candidate concentrates his campaign in those three states and wins, he may have earned significant legislative support from those states, but those states only control 33 percent of the seats in the Chamber of Deputies. Constructing a viable governing coalition may thus require newly elected presidents in countries with high levels of malapportionment to overcome the challenge of incorporating new rural allies without alienating the urban constituencies that brought them to power.

A failure to manage this challenge can have profound consequences for democracy. For example, the distinct geographic support bases for the Brazilian legislative and executive branches led to a distancing between the two branches that contributed to the breakdown of democracy in 1964 (Fleischer 1994). A similar problem existed in Chile—Loveman (1986, 239) argues that Chilean presidents were forced to moderate their electoral promises once in office because of their "dependence on the Right for essential legislation." This dynamic also occurred in Argentina, Ecuador, Bolivia, and Mexico. Ruralization of legislatures as a result of severe malapportionment may also help explain why many recent Latin American executives so often bypass legislatures and rule by decree.[35]

The task of building a governing coalition that caters to rural interests—a requirement that stems from the ruralizing effects of malapportionment in the national legislature—creates strong incentives for presidents to channel patronage payoffs to rural areas in order to purchase legislative support (Ames 1987; Gibson 1997;

Gibson, Calvo, and Falleti, this volume). To avoid a paralyzing estrangement of the legislative and executive branches, presidents in countries that heavily overrepresent rural areas may thus find themselves compelled to retreat from their campaign promises and resort to clientelist politics of appeasement toward rural interests.

Proliferation of Subnational Authoritarian Enclaves

Malapportionment also has an important impact on subnational politics in Latin America. In new democracies overrepresentation of rural districts can contribute to the maintenance—and even proliferation—of nondemocratic enclaves at the subnational level. Malapportionment can compel pro-democratic elites at the national level to tolerate subnational authoritarian enclaves because these elites rely on overrepresented regions to secure the national legislative majorities they need to achieve their policy goals. Ironically, the ability of leaders at the national level to implement and consolidate democratic reforms in a highly malapportioned system may therefore depend on winning the overvalued support of subnational authoritarian elites.[36] At the same time, overrepresentation of subnational authoritarian enclaves in national legislatures may strengthen the ability of these subnational elites to fend off efforts by external groups seeking to reform local politics.[37] Such a dynamic has been especially apparent in the case of Brazil, where, as Alfred Stepan (2000, 165) notes, "many of the states that are overrepresented in the federal legislature are precisely those states with particularly unequal income distribution and strong traditions of local oligarchic control."

Holding the Center Hostage

Federalism may allow less populated regions to "hold the center hostage" to its desires, because the senate in federal systems typically overrepresents less populated regions and can thus exercise a policy veto. We would add that lower-chamber malapportionment serves the same purpose, in both federal (e.g., Argentina and Brazil) *and* nonfederal systems (e.g., Chile, Colombia, Ecuador, Bolivia). The overrepresentation of rural constituencies strengthens the capacity of politicians from the periphery to extract fiscal favors from the center (that is, from national-level elites). This extractive capacity can contribute to the construction and maintenance of "peripheral populist" regimes even in the face of an overall national policy environment characterized by fiscal austerity and neoliberal budget shrinking.[38] As illustrated by the Mexican and Argentine cases, the possibility for subnational populist regimes seems especially strong in federal systems with severe malapportionment.[39]

Can Latin America Achieve Fair Elections? Strategies for Reducing Malapportionment

The pernicious normative and practical consequences of malapportionment in Latin America highlight the importance of considering possible "treatments" for this formal pathology. What strategies exist for reducing malapportionment? In addressing this question, we limit our discussion to methods for reducing malapportionment that have actually been used, and we focus specifically on two strategies: (1) establishing judicial oversight of reapportionment, and (2) electoral law reform.

Judicial Oversight of Reapportionment

Judiciaries have become involved in reapportionment decisions in several countries, most notably the United States. Prior to 1962, significant *intrastate* malapportionment existed in the U.S. House of Representatives. Near-zero malapportionment in the House has only been achieved since the U.S. Supreme Court affirmed in a series of decisions beginning with *Baker v. Carr* in 1962 that the votes of all citizens must count equally, which meant that all districts must (to the degree possible) have equal populations (Cain 1984; Balinski and Young 1982).[40]

After the Supreme Court's decisions of the early 1960s, either a federal or a state court could declare a state's districting plan null and void. This right of judicial review over districting plans dramatically altered the strategic situation facing politicians involved in the reapportionment process (i.e., incumbent state legislators and governors). If the courts declared a districting plan null and void, they gave the legislature and the governor a deadline, and if the legislature and governor failed to reach an agreement by the deadline, the court would impose a plan. Sometimes the plan to be imposed was clear ex ante, sometimes not—a situation that created tremendous uncertainty for all incumbent legislators, from both parties. All politicians sought to limit their individual uncertainty. In states that lost seats they knew *somebody* would lose, but they wanted to have some control over their own futures rather than have a random outcome imposed by the courts. In short, judicial review of apportionment decisions forced a situation in which all the political actors involved in the reapportionment process had a powerful incentive to agree to a plan for progressive reapportionment in order to avoid having the decision fall to the courts.[41]

High courts have also influenced apportionment in Japan and Germany (Hata 1990). Prior to 1993, Japan had a serious problem with malapportionment, and the Japanese Supreme Court acknowledged that this problem violated the country's constitution. However, elections continued to be held under "unconstitutional" rules, and the court refused several voters' requests to halt elections or vacate their results. Moreover, the court never attempted to force the Diet to carry out a progressive reapportionment. Japan enacted a progressive reapportionment only when it altered its entire electoral system in 1993.

The judicial option for controlling malapportionment proved feasible in Germany, however, where the court found in favor of a suit challenging the 1961 election results because of egregious malapportionment. The court did not invalidate the previous election but declared that it would invalidate the 1965 election unless the Bundestag reapportioned its seats, which it did in 1964 (Hata 1990).

What are the implications of the U.S., Japanese, and German cases for how malapportionment could be reduced in Latin American countries? First, it should be noted that the notion of judicially mandated progressive reapportionment presupposes that courts (whether local, state, or national) are insulated from partisan influence. Otherwise, the prospect of judicial review would not necessarily induce politicians to act to avoid the legally defined default outcome (as happened in Japan until 1993). If the courts are exposed to political pressures and operate as reliable agents of partisan interests, then judicial oversight of the reapportionment process is unlikely to serve as an effective mechanism for reducing malapportionment. In such a scenario, court-imposed plans—like politically engineered plans—are likely to manipulate malapportionment in order to generate strong partisan biases.

The cases of the United States, Japan, and Germany also demonstrate that unless the courts can credibly threaten either to redraw the districts themselves or invalidate an election, the judicial option for regulating malapportionment will have little effect (except in the unlikely instance that incumbent politicians are more concerned with fairness than with their own political careers). Thus we remain skeptical of the judicial oversight option in Latin America, where the relative weakness of most judiciaries poses serious obstacles to the successful implementation of progressive reapportionment through a challenge to the electoral law.

A Latin American perspective also reminds us that judicial autonomy should not be taken for granted. In many Latin American countries, courts are notorious both for their politicization and for their weakness.[42] Consequently, most Latin American judiciaries may simply lack the autonomy needed to define a credible legal default point that could induce politicians to implement progressive reapportionment. The strategy of reducing malapportionment through judicial oversight, therefore, does not seem especially promising in contemporary Latin America.

However, it should be emphasized that the Latin American cases do show that an autonomous judiciary is by no means a necessary condition for implementing progressive reapportionment: countries such as Honduras, Paraguay, Uruguay, and Peru have achieved remarkably low levels of malapportionment despite having judiciaries that are certainly no more autonomous than those in Latin American countries with high levels of malapportionment.

Since the judicial oversight strategy for reducing malapportionment does not seem especially feasible in contemporary Latin America, a more promising alternative would be to create a neutral, nonpartisan electoral commission that is legally obligated to reduce lower-chamber malapportionment. This strategy for reducing malapportionment has been employed effectively in Mexico, where the Federal Electoral Institute (IFE) has exercised full authority over redistricting decisions since 1996 and has helped compensate for the weakness of the Mexican judiciary. In July 1996 IFE's top governing body, the General Council, unanimously approved a lower-chamber redistricting plan—designed by a committee of nonpartisan technical experts with impressive academic and professional credentials—that significantly reduced malapportionment in anticipation of the 1997 elections. Mexico's political parties also played a key role in designing the plan. Their representatives were invited to comment on drafts of the plan, and some of their suggestions were incorporated into the final version, contributing to the plan's undisputed acceptance (Lujambio and Vives, 2000).

This approach to reducing malapportionment could work in other Latin American countries, where the judiciary lacks the capacity to enforce the "one person, one vote" principle. In assessing the prospects for replicating the "IFE model" in other countries, it is important to highlight that IFE had its roots in the allegedly stolen presidential victory of Institutional Revolutionary Party (PRI) candidate Carlos Salinas in 1988. In exchange for recognizing Salinas's legitimacy, the opposition National Action Party (PAN) successfully demanded a package of electoral reforms, including the formation of an independent electoral commission (Domínguez and McCann 1995, 118–19), which suggests that effective independent, nonpartisan electoral commissions emerge out of partisan competition and may require an inter-party pact.

Electoral Law Reform

Here we focus on three potential options for electoral law reform: reapportionment, the adoption of a single-district chamber system that elects all representatives in an at-large election, and the adoption of a mixed-member electoral system like Germany's.

Reapportionment

The most obvious method for correcting malapportionment is simply to reallocate seats across districts. However, in the absence of judicially mandated reapportionment, these decisions are politically difficult to engineer. Indeed, because reapportionment is such a volatile issue, reapportionments may be feasible only as part of a larger electoral reform package. Such agreements typically require complex negotiations and cross-partisan agreement to avoid a "winner-take-all" situation where losers would face permanent disenfranchisement and would therefore have compelling incentives to undermine any proposed agreement. For example, Britain's extensive reapportionment in 1885 was but one piece of the Third Reform Act, which included a broad expansion of suffrage and was the product of a negotiated inter-party pact (McLean and Mortimore 1992).

To our knowledge, reapportionment initiatives have not been linked to broader proposals for electoral and institutional reform in Latin America, but this could be a viable strategy for reducing malapportionment. Such reform proposals might even include provisions for creating the kind of nonpartisan electoral commission discussed above to manage the apportionment process in a neutral fashion. Because the problem of malapportionment in countries like Brazil seems so closely connected with other institutional flaws, such as a fragmented party system and overly decentralized federalism, correcting malapportionment could become part of a wider package of reforms that would significantly enhance the quality of democracy, economic efficiency, and socioeconomic justice.[43]

Single-District Chambers

Another potential option is to abandon an electoral system with multiple districts by adopting a single nationwide district, as Israel and the Netherlands have done. In Latin America only Peru has adopted this system for its lower chamber. In 1993 President Fujimori abolished Peru's Senate and created a unicameral national legislature by executive fiat, thereby eliminating malapportionment altogether. Three other Latin American countries have eliminated malapportionment in their Senates by moving from a multidistrict to a single-district format (Colombia, Paraguay, and Uruguay). Is this a viable option for reducing malapportionment?

Before answering that question, we should first ask whether there are advantages to having chambers with multiple, territorially defined electoral districts rather than a single national district. Should the goal of perfect apportionment be balanced against other objectives that require multidistrict chambers? Although they eliminate malapportionment, single-district chambers may also weaken "citizen control" over representatives by making it more difficult for voters to assign clear responsibility to specific legislators and punish specific legislators for their actions.[44] Such a weakening of citizen control raises troubling issues with regard to the accountability of elected officials: because each legislator is accountable to everyone (i.e., the entire electorate) she or he may, in fact, be accountable to no one. Because citizens lose the sense that a particular legislator "belongs" to them, they should have relatively fewer incentives to monitor and punish the performance of individual legislators selectively. Thus the ability of the "electoral connection" to serve as a mechanism of accountability may be severely attenuated in systems with single-district chambers. This would be especially unfortunate in countries where accountability is already a crucial problem (O'Donnell 1994). The achievement of perfect apportionment and fair elections via the strategy of moving to a single-district chamber may therefore be purchased at the significant price of weakening the accountability of incumbents to constituents.[45] This tension deserves further study.

Another, more practical problem exists: the fact that seven of the eight countries in our sample that opted for single national districts in one or both chambers are fairly small in size and population suggests that the ideal of "perfect apportionment" may not work for larger countries, because of historic or constitutional attachments to representation of territorial units.[46] However, this does not mean that lower chambers ought to *overrepresent* certain territorial units, particularly in bicameral systems.

Another practical problem involves the politics of converting a multidistrict system into a single-district chamber. In a single national district, every candidate competes in an at-large election. Given the strong aversion that incumbent legislators who compete in a subnational district would have against competing in an at-large election (see above), it is puzzling that legislators would gleefully accede to the elimination of "their" districts.[47] Of course, eliminating *all* members' districts may be a less thorny task than selectively eliminating only *some* members' districts. One can therefore imagine a bargain in which each incumbent agreed to give up his or her district as long as all other incumbents were compelled to do the same. Still, the relative benefits that individual incumbents would have reaped from making such a move are unclear. In this regard, an in-depth study of Uruguay's move to a single national district in the Senate in 1938, as well as Colombia's and Paraguay's more recent adoption of a single national district for their senates, would be interesting.

The Peruvian case illustrates an alternative path from multi- to single-district chambers. As noted above, Fujimori imposed this institutional reform by executive fiat. This authoritarian mode of eliminating malapportionment underscores the point that just as high levels of malapportionment can coexist with key components of the democratic process (as discussed above), perfect apportionment can also coexist with decidedly undemocratic processes. Whether Fujimori's authoritarian reapportionment has ironically left a strong foundation for fair elections in the wake of his removal remains to be seen.

Although a single national district fully eliminates malapportionment, such a system may be impractical for many countries and also counterproductive for the goal of ensuring fair democratic representation. Thus, we do not generally advocate this option.

Adding Tiers: The German Model

Several Latin American countries have recently adopted a "two-tiered" electoral system that combines elements of both single-member district (SMD) systems and proportional representation (PR) systems. For example, Mexico elects three hundred deputies in a tier of SMDs and two hundred additional deputies in a second tier of five forty-member PR districts. Venezuela and Bolivia have recently adopted similar systems, and mixed-member proportional systems are often proposed as an alternative to Brazil's open-list PR framework.

Countries do not typically adopt such systems with the goal of reducing malapportionment. Rather, the objective is to guarantee the representation of minority parties that would fail to win a plurality in any single district because their base of support is geographically dispersed. Nevertheless, a mixed system could serve to reduce malapportionment, depending on the number of seats added to the second tier and whether or not the second-tier seats are allocated to a nationwide district (see Samuels and Snyder 2001).

Mixed systems significantly reduce malapportionment only if the number of seats in the second tier is substantial. For example, adding a tier with twenty seats elected in a nationwide district to a malapportioned legislature with three hundred seats would have only a slight effect on the overall level of malapportionment. Moreover, a mixed system will reduce malapportionment only if the upper tier allocates seats exclusively to a nationwide district (as in El Salvador and Nicaragua). By contrast, tiers that distribute seats to *subnational* (provincial, state, or regional) districts may actually *increase* overall malapportionment (as in Bolivia and Venezuela).[48] For example, if Brazil adopted a system at the state level, and maintained the distribution of seats across states, malapportionment would remain about the same. On the other hand, if a country elected national deputies in a single at-large district in addition to deputies in SMD or PR districts, malapportionment would be attenuated.

The strategy of allocating a large number of seats to a nationwide district has several advantages. First, it can be implemented in the context of a chamber with multiple, territorially defined electoral districts. Consequently, a far greater degree of citizen control over legislators is possible than in the case of a single-district chamber. Second, a tier of new seats can easily be added to the legislature without taking away any existing seats. This possibility reduces the likelihood of opposition from incumbent legislators concerned about protecting their districts. In short, because courts generally lack the capacity to supervise the reapportionment process in a nonpartisan fashion, the strategy of adding a tier may offer the best solution to the problem of malapportionment in Latin America.

Conclusion

Malapportionment pervades lower chambers in many Latin American legislatures. This violates one of the principal tenets of democratic theory, that all citizens' votes should be weighed equally. Consequently, many elections in contemporary Latin America are unfair. We have therefore argued that malapportionment is an important, formal flaw of Latin American democracies.

This chapter provided conceptual tools for the comparative study of malapportionment and analyzed the historical evolution of malapportionment across several Latin American countries. The comparative analysis highlighted the varied ways in which elites have deployed malapportionment as a political weapon for advancing their interests. We also explored the troubling implications of malapportionment for how democracy works in contemporary Latin America. Finally, we considered alternative strategies for reducing malapportionment, a necessary step for making elections in Latin America more democratic.

Our critique of malapportionment is anchored in the view that elections should, first and foremost, represent the will of individual citizens. Of course, alternative conceptions of representation exist—for example, that legislators should represent corporate or territorial units. Although few instances of corporate representation remain in Latin America,[49] the constitutions of many Latin American countries do explicitly provide for representation of territorial units in the upper chamber. Such "territorial" chambers are intended to protect the interests of less populated regions. A high degree of malapportionment may be necessary to achieve this objective, which is certainly a legitimate democratic goal.

Yet while malapportionment may be warranted in the upper chamber, there is no normative justification for unfairness in the lower chamber. The lower chamber should be based upon "one person, one vote," with citizens represented as political equals. Because many Latin American countries have high levels of malapportionment in both their upper and lower chambers, they essentially have *two* territorial chambers, and *none* in which citizens' votes count equally. As we have argued, this situation has had a negative effect on the quality of democracy in the region. Latin America's democracies should transform the *principle* of one person, one vote into *practice* by solving the problem of malapportionment in their lower chambers.

APPENDIX: CONSTITUTIONAL APPORTIONMENT RULES IN LATIN AMERICA

- Argentina: Article 45 of the 1860 constitution stipulates that each province shall have one deputy for every 33,000 inhabitants or fraction that exceeds 16,500 inhabitants. The constitution declares that after each census Congress can set a different number, with the stipulation that it can increase but not decrease the ratio between population and the number of deputies.
- Belize: no such constitutional rule.
- Bolivia: Article 60 of the 1967 constitution states that single-member districts shall be based on population and that the National Electoral Court will delimit the single-member districts. Furthermore, the constitution states that the distribution of seats to each department shall be determined by law, with the population of each department serving as the basis for the calculation, in accordance with the last national census. The constitution adds that a law shall assign a minimum number of seats to those departments with a lower population and a lower degree of economic development.
- Brazil: Article 45 of the 1988 constitution stipulates that each state shall have a minimum of eight and a maximum of seventy deputies. A supplementary law may reapportion the number of deputies to each state in accordance with population.
- Chile: no such constitutional rule.
- Colombia: Article 176 of the constitution states that there shall be a minimum of two representatives for each territorial circumscription, plus an additional deputy for each 250,000 inhabitants and fraction larger than 125,000 that exceeds the first 250,000.
- Costa Rica: Article 106 of the constitution states that seats shall be apportioned to provinces according to their population, that each province shall have a minimum of one representative, and that after each new census, the High Electoral Court shall conduct a reapportionment.
- Dominican Republic: Article 24 of the constitution states that each province shall have one deputy for every fifty thousand inhabitants, or fraction larger than twenty-five thousand inhabitants, but in no case shall a province have fewer than two deputies.
- Ecuador: Article 126 of the constitution states that each province shall elect a

minimum of two deputies and one more deputy for each 200,000 inhabitants or fraction larger than 150,000 that exceeds the first 200,000. The number of inhabitants that serves as the basis for the election shall be established by the most recent national census, which shall be conducted every ten years.

- El Salvador: no such constitutional rule.
- Guatemala: Article 157 states that each electoral district shall have a minimum of one deputy, and that a law shall establish the number of deputies for each district according to each district's population.
- Honduras: Article 202 of the constitution states that seats shall be apportioned to provinces according to their population, that each province shall have a minimum of one representative, and that Congress shall have the power to change this law.
- Mexico: Article 53 of the constitution states that the demarcation of the three hundred single-member districts shall be based on the most recent general census, with the stipulation that no state can have fewer than two deputies.
- Nicaragua: no such constitutional rule.
- Panama: Article 141, sections 1–5 states that each department shall have a minimum number of deputies, and that each department shall gain an additional deputy per thirty thousand persons or fraction greater than ten thousand persons after the first thirty thousand.
- Paraguay: Article 221 of the constitution states that each department shall be represented by at least one deputy. The Superior Tribunal of Electoral Justice, prior to each election and in accordance with the number of registered voters in each department, shall establish the number of seats in each department.
- Peru: the unicameral legislature is elected in a single, nationwide district.
- Uruguay: Article 88 of the constitution states that each department shall have at least two representatives. A law can modify the number of representatives, but this requires a two-thirds vote of all members of each house of Congress.
- Venezuela: Article 151 of the constitution stipulates that each state shall elect at least two deputies, and each territory shall elect one deputy.

NOTES

The authors share equal responsibility for this work. We thank Sebastian Mazzuca, Gerardo Munck, and Matthew Shugart for comments.

1. On democracy as an "essentially contested concept," see Collier and Levitsky (1997). According to Huntington (1991, 9), "Elections, open, free, and fair are the essence of democracy, the inescapable sine qua non."

2. Dahl (1971, 2) writes that the "unimpaired opportunit[y]" of all full citizens to "have their preferences weighed equally" is a necessary condition for a democracy. Dahl also emphasizes as a "key characteristic" of democracy that citizens be considered "political equals." Dahl (1989, 109–11) includes "voting equality" as one of his "five criteria for a democratic process." He writes that "At the decisive stage of collective decisions [i.e., voting], each citizen must be ensured an equal opportunity to express a choice that will be counted as equal in weight to the choice expressed by any other citizen" (109). He notes that voting equality is crucial because without it, "citizens would face the prospect of an infinite regress of potential inequalities in their influence over decisions, with no final court of appeal in which, as political equals, they could decide whether their interests, as they interpreted them were given equal consideration" (109–10). See also Rokkan (1970).

3. The following countries explicitly guarantee each citizen an equal vote in their national constitutions: Argentina (Article 37), Bolivia (Article 219), Brazil (Article 14), Chile (Article 15), Ecuador (Article 27), El Salvador (Article 78), Honduras (Article 44), Nicaragua (Article 2), Panama (Article 129), Paraguay (Article 118), Peru (Article 31).

4. See Samuels and Snyder (2001) for a study of the degree of malapportionment in seventy-eight countries.

5. Only five of seventy-eight countries in our sample have single, national districts—Israel, Peru, Namibia, the Netherlands, and Sierra Leone.

6. Because the rule of "equal representation" is part of the constitution in many Latin American countries (see the Appendix), the fit between one level of rules—the constitutional rules—and the actual electoral rules is loose. This is a formal-formal slippage, rather than a formal-informal slippage, as analyzed by O'Donnell et al. A focus on malapportionment highlights the gap between formal electoral rules that *are* applied and formal constitutional rules that are *not* applied.

7. Indeed, a looser fit between formal electoral rules of this type could actually strengthen democracy in some circumstances.

8. It should be noted that the idea that the effects of formal rules may be *less* visible than those of informal processes is somewhat counterintuitive.

9. At their worst, rotten or "pocket" boroughs had only one voter. See Cox (1987, 10).

10. The crafting of electoral rules in Latin American countries (and other developing countries) has been increasingly transformed into a "science," as teams of professional political scientists and mathematicians play larger roles in the design of electoral systems. This professionalization and technological upgrading of the process of designing electoral systems suggests that the strategic use of malapportionment to confer political advantages occurs in a far less blatant manner than in the past. This point can be seen in the differences between Mexico's electoral reform of 1989 and 1994, as analyzed by Balinski and Ramírez Gónzalez (1996). They note that although the 1994 reform is a much more sophisticated and technically competent document, it nevertheless "reinforce[s] the advantages conferred on the one big political party [i.e., the PRI], though in not so evidently blatant a manner" (204). The principal-agent issues of accountability and control between

politician principals and their technician agents who are actually charged with writing the electoral rules are interesting to consider.

11. By contrast, *informal* pathologies, such as clientelism and particularism, may be less compatible with the procedural criteria of democracy. As Gunther, Diamandouros, and Puhle (1996, 159) point out, such factors may be "incompatible with the unhindered exercise of suffrage." The fact that malapportionment is less directly corrosive of these other elements may make it more difficult to detect.

12. Here, we follow Dahl's (1971, 1–3) threefold distinction between the formulating, signifying, and weighing of citizens' preferences.

13. Of course, a large number of single-country studies of malapportionment exist. See the references in Samuels and Snyder (2001).

14. The phenomenon of "reverse migration" out of the city and to the countryside or to provincial cities would be fascinating to consider. Moreover, even if a country *does* have regular procedures for reapportionment and uses these procedures to keep average malapportionment at low levels (e.g., the United States, Great Britain), it may nevertheless experience creeping malapportionment because citizens move around *between* reapportionments. For example, although the United States has very low average levels of malapportionment, the ten-year lag between federal censuses (which form the bases for reapportionment) causes significant variation in levels of malapportionment across congressional elections. The first postcensus election, which usually occurs in the second year of each decade, typically takes place under conditions of significantly lower malapportionment than the last precensus election (that is, the last election of each decade). Consequently, even in a system with robust, politically insulated procedures for correcting malapportionment, some elections are fairer than others in terms of the equality of the vote. In systems that lack such procedures, the problem of unfair elections can be much more acute.

15. Obviously, these tools are by no means mutually exclusive and are frequently used together.

16. In the United States, where the average population per seat is approximately 570,000, the smallest state (Wyoming) has a population of 480,000, about 80 percent of the average. In contrast, in Brazil the smallest state (Roraima) has a population that is only 4 percent of the average.

17. The largest district, the state of São Paulo, has seventy seats and a population 145 times larger than the smallest district, the state of Roraima, which has eight seats. This makes a vote in Roraima worth seventeen times as much as a vote in São Paulo.

18. As noted, the politics of increasing the total number of seats is obviously different from the politics of taking away seats, and *ceteris paribus* we would expect the former to be less contentious and, thus, politically preferable. The politics of taking away seats may be accompanied by "blame avoidance" strategies, such as obfuscation of responsibility for the fact that a seat has been lost, as well as by compensatory efforts on the part of those doing the taking away.

19. During certain periods, some countries (e.g., Argentina and Chile) established effective mechanisms for keeping malapportionment at relatively low levels.

20. We calculated malapportionment as per Samuels and Snyder (2001), using published electoral and census data, and used the most recently taken census prior to the year of the election, or,

if no census was available, the best population estimates available in published sources. Gaps in the data indicate either no election was held or data were unavailable.

The constitutions of all countries in this analysis except for Paraguay and Uruguay explicitly require that apportionment for lower chambers be based on district population. Paraguay's constitution apportions deputies according to the number of registered voters in each department (Article 221). Uruguay's constitution does not mention the issue, and we used the number of registered voters.

21. Perón's constitution was annulled when he was overthrown in 1955. Nevertheless, the principle of providing each province with a minimum number of deputies was maintained in Law 15264/59 of 1959 (Porto 1990, 182). Like many countries, Argentina gave territories some representation in the lower chamber even though they were not recognized as provinces. Further research is needed on the Frondizi presidency to discover why Buenos Aires province was not granted additional seats and why Perón's policies were continued and even exacerbated.

22. The military also stipulated that no province could have fewer deputies than it had as of 23 March 1976, when Perón was deposed (Porto 1990, 183).

23. Personal communication with Professor Mark Jones, 11 January 1999.

24. Scholars of Brazilian political history have attributed the origins of malapportionment to interstate political rivalries: in the last three decades of the nineteenth century the emperor strategically attempted to undercut the increasing influence of antimonarchical elements, which emerged primarily in the heavily populated states of São Paulo and Minas Gerais (Fleischer 1994, 3). On a more mundane note, Porto (1989, 139) argues that the primary reason for malapportionment was the infrequency of censuses and their poor quality when taken.

25. However, by this time, Minas Gerais was no longer dramatically underrepresented because its population had not grown as rapidly as São Paulo's. Only São Paulo was seriously disadvantaged.

26. For example, President Videla (1946–52) postponed the scheduled 1950 census until 1952 to avoid conflict, and President Alessandri (1958–64) delayed "official completion" of the 1960 census until 1964, "too late to implement a reapportionment for the 1965 congressional elections" (McDonald 1969, 458).

27. McDonald is not explicit about who was involved in this implicit agreement or who rejected the censuses—the president or congressional leaders.

28. In their intriguing essays on the role of federalism in nation-building processes, Alfred Stepan (2001) and Juan Linz (1997) point to another strategic use for malapportionment. Stepan and Linz suggest that federal institutions can serve the purposes of "bringing together" and "holding together" political units that might not otherwise cohere as a single nation. Could malapportionment have played a similar role in helping stitch together Latin American nations in the nineteenth century? The deliberate creation of inequalities of representation through malapportionment may have given underpopulated regions a larger stake in joining a new nation where, in the absence of some kind of guaranteed overrepresentation, they stood to be permanent losers to more populated regions in the national political arena. The Brazilian case suggests the kind of role that malapportionment played in nation-building processes. As noted, Brazil's lower chamber was highly

malapportioned virtually since it was created in the early nineteenth century. In the context of the country's constitutional monarchy, the emperor strategically manipulated the distribution of seats in the legislature in order to undercut the strength of antimonarchical, centrifugal forces clustered in the heavily populated states of São Paulo and Minas Gerais, thus potentially helping to hold together the nation.

29. This rural bias almost always means a conservative bias; hence, we refer to rural-conservative bias.

30. Interestingly, the kind of rural bias created by malapportionment also characterized many European nations at an earlier stage of their history. Thus, Rokkan (1970, 165) notes that in Europe conservative urban elites in the cities found important allies in the countryside and preferred to stay underrepresented as long as their rural allies could help them in their fight against urban radicals.

31. See Gibson and Calvo (2000), who make a similar point with their notion of "low-maintenance" constituencies. Although the amount of resources from the national budget needed to buy the support of overrepresented, "low-maintenance" rural constituencies may indeed be small, buying these provinces can turn out to be extremely expensive over time, because of fiscal profligacy in these provinces, which raises interest rates and public debts. For example, the provinces in Brazil that defaulted on their debts in the late 1990s and raised the risk premium on Brazilian bonds were overrepresented rural ones. Similarly, in Argentina fiscal profligacy by overrepresented provinces contributed to the macroeconomic crisis that has nearly paralyzed the country in recent years. Thus initially cheap support from low-maintenance constituencies in malapportioned systems may become quite costly over time when, as occurred recently in Brazil and Argentina, this political support generates "negative economic externalities" that destabilize the national economy. The macroeconomic implications of electoral malapportionment merit further investigation. We thank Sebastian Mazzuca for calling this point to our attention.

32. Until 1994 Argentina employed an electoral college that overrepresented rural areas, thus mitigating the problem of estrangement between an urban executive branch and a rural legislative branch. See Cabrera (1997).

33. Of course, such urban / rural cleavages are not the *only* cause of legislative-executive estrangement. Nor does legislative-executive estrangement only occur in countries with high levels of malapportionment.

34. This is similar, but not entirely equivalent to, Gibson's (1997) distinction between "electoral" and "policy" coalitions.

35. O'Donnell (1994) describes this situation of legislative bypass as "delegative democracy." See also Shugart and Carey (1992) on executive decree authority.

36. Conversely, low levels of malapportionment might work against such dependence, thereby weakening the potential for the emergence of subnational authoritarian regimes.

37. On the issue of how national-level political and economic liberalization can contribute to the maintenance of subnational authoritarian regimes, see Snyder (1999, 2001a) and Fox (1994).

38. As noted, the extractive capacity of overrepresented peripheral elites may also contribute to macroeconomic crisis, as has occurred recently in Argentina and Brazil.

39. On the possibilities for peripheral populism in the context of a neoliberal center, see Snyder (1999, 2001b) on the Mexican case, as well as Gibson, Calvo, and Falleti on "reallocative federalism" in this volume.

40. One of the key mechanisms for enforcing this procedure is the "reversion point," the legally defined default, if the state's legislature and governor fail to agree on a new districting plan. According to the Supreme Court rulings, if the state legislature and governor cannot agree on a new plan, then the federal district court has full jurisdiction over the reapportionment decision. Rather than actually redrawing the district lines themselves, the federal courts usually choose to hold at-large elections for the federal legislature, a worst-case outcome from the perspective of most incumbent legislators and governors. Prior to the Supreme Court rulings of the early 1960s, if a state legislature and governor failed to agree on a new districting plan, either the old districting plan was retained, or, if new congressional seats had been added to the state, the new members would be elected at-large, thereby preserving all the old districts. In the case of states that had lost seats, however, a different reversionary scenario existed: if the state government failed to achieve a new districting plan, then *all* members would be elected at-large. According to Cox and Katz (1999), this difference helps explain why the bulk of pre 1960s redistricting occurred in states that lost seats in Congress: incumbents in such states were subject to the extremely unpalatable outcome of at-large elections for all members if they failed to agree on a redistricting plan (under an at-large election, incumbents would lose the benefits of "barriers to entry" that district lines create). By contrast, incumbents who failed to agree on a redistricting plan in states that did not lose seats faced the far less threatening prospect of preserving the old districts.

41. At the same time, we should not overlook the fact that there is still a considerable degree of slack in the U.S. system. We observe some malapportionment in the U.S. House, and malapportionment does tend to creep up between censuses. The degree to which the malapportionment we observe in the United States is merely the result of demographic flux between reapportionments (i.e., natural malapportionment) or reflects some other kind of slippage in the institutional arrangements for enforcing progressive reapportionment is an interesting question.

42. See Méndez, O'Donnell, and Pinheiro (1999) on the "unrule" of law in Latin America.

43. For years several politicians in Brazil have advocated a mixed-member PR system, yet they have not included reapportionment in their reform proposals.

44. The term "citizen control" is from Powell (1989). See also Shugart and Carey (1992, 273).

45. By contrast, a virtue of this method for reducing malapportionment is that it can obviously be implemented in the absence of an autonomous judiciary.

46. Other questions that should be addressed include: What are the strengths and limitations of the hybrid approach of combining a single-district chamber with a (malapportioned) multidistrict chamber (e.g., Colombia)? Is the option of *two* perfectly apportioned chambers (e.g., Holland) desirable for Latin American countries? What lessons can Latin American countries learn from non–Latin American countries that have implemented single national districts (e.g., Israel, Holland, Namibia, Sierra Leone)?

47. Although such a move might be less curious in systems with strong, centralized parties and / or weak incentives for politicians to cultivate a personal vote.

48. It should be noted, however, that in Venezuela, as in Germany, "extra" seats can be allocated to different states to make the party results proportional.

49. One such instance is the automatic granting of a Senate seat to ex-presidents in some Latin American countries (Chile and Venezuela, for example).

BIBLIOGRAPHY

Ames, Barry. 1987. *Political Survival: Politicians and Public Policy in Latin America.* Berkeley: University of California Press.

Balinski, Michael, and H. Peyton Young. 1982. *Fair Representation: Meeting the Ideal of One Man, One Vote.* New Haven: Yale University Press.

Balinski, Michel, and Victoriano Ramírez González. 1996. A Case Study of Electoral Manipulation: The Mexican Laws of 1989 and 1994. *Electoral Studies* 15 (2): 203–17.

Cabrera, Ernesto. 1997. Multiparty Politics in Argentina? Electoral Rules and Changing Patterns. *Electoral Studies* 15 (4): 477–95.

Cain, Bruce. 1984. *The Reapportionment Puzzle.* Berkeley: University of California Press.

Campello de Souza, Maria do Carmo. 1976. *Estado e Partidos Políticos no Brasil (1930–64).* São Paulo: Editora Alfa-Omega.

Caviedes, César. 1979. *The Politics of Chile: A Sociogeographical Assessment.* Boulder: Westview Press.

Collier, David, and Steven Levitsky. 1997. Democracy with Adjectives: Conceptual Innovation in Comparative Research. *World Politics* 49 (3): 43–51.

Cox, Gary. 1987. *The Efficient Secret: The Cabinet and the Development of Political Parties in Victorian England.* Cambridge: Cambridge University Press.

Cox, Gary, and Jonathan Katz. 1999. The Reapportionment Revolution and Bias in U.S. Congressional Elections. *American Journal of Political Science* 43 (3): 812–41.

Cruz-Coke, Ricardo. 1984. *Historia Electoral de Chile 1925–73.* Santiago: Editorial Jurídica de Chile.

Dahl, Robert. 1971. *Polyarchy: Participation and Opposition.* New Haven: Yale University Press.

———. 1989. *Democracy and Its Critics.* New Haven: Yale University Press.

Delgado, Lucília de Almeida Neves. 1989. *PTB: Do Getulismo ao Reformismo.* São Paulo: Editora Marca Zero.

Domínguez, Jorge, and James McCann. 1995. *Democratizing Mexico.* Baltimore: Johns Hopkins University Press.

Fleischer, David V. 1994. Manipulações Casuísticas do Sistema Eleitoral Durante o Período Militar, ou Como Usualmente o Fetiço Voltava contra o Feitiçeiro. Cadernos de Ciência Política 10. Brasília: Universidade de Brasília, Depto. de Ciência Políticas e Relações Internacionais.

Fox, Jonathan. 1994. The Difficult Transition from Clientelism to Citizenship: Lessons from Mexico. *World Politics* 46 (2): 151–84.

Garretón, Manuel. 1991. The Political Opposition and the Party System. In *The Struggle for Democracy in Chile, 1982–1990,* edited by P. Drake and I. Jaksic. Lincoln: University of Nebraska Press.

Gibson, Edward L. 1997. The Populist Road to Market Reform: Policy and Electoral Coalitions in Mexico and Argentina. *World Politics* 49 (3): 339–70.

Gibson, Edward L., and Ernesto Calvo. 2000. Federalism and Low-Maintenance Constituencies: Territorial Dimensions of Economic Reform in Argentina. *Studies in Comparative International Development* 35 (3): 32–55.

Gunther, Richard, P. Nikiforos Diamandouros, and Hans-Jürgen Puhle. 1996. O'Donnell's Illusions: A Rejoinder. *Journal of Democracy* 7 (4): 151–59.

Hata, Hiroyuki. 1990. Malapportionment of Representation in the National Diet. *Law and Contemporary Problems* 53 (2): 153–70.

Huntington, Samuel P. 1991. *The Third Wave: Democratization in the Late Twentieth Century*. Norman: University of Oklahoma Press.

Jones, Mark. 1995. *Electoral Laws and the Survival of Presidential Democracy*. Notre Dame, Ind.: University of Notre Dame Press.

Linz, Juan J. 1994. Presidential or Parliamentary Democracy: Does It Make a Difference? In *The Failure of Presidential Democracy: The Case of Latin America*, edited by J. J. Linz and A. Valenzuela, 3–87. Baltimore: Johns Hopkins University Press.

———. 1997. Democracy, Multinationalism, and Federalism. Paper prepared for the Conference on Federalism and Democracy, Oxford University.

Little, Walter. 1973. Electoral Aspects of Peronism, 1946–54. *Journal of Interamerican Studies and World Affairs* 15 (3): 267–83.

Loveman, Brian. 1986. The Transformation of the Chilean Countryside. In *Military Rule in Chile: Dictatorship and Oppositions*, edited by J. S. Valenzuela and A. Valenzuela. Baltimore: Johns Hopkins University Press.

Lujambio, Alonso, and Horacio Vives. 2000. Nota Sobre la Redistritación. Unpublished ms.

Mainwaring, Scott, and Matthew S. Shugart, eds. 1997. *Presidentialism and Democracy in Latin America*. Cambridge: Cambridge University Press.

McDonald, Ronald. 1969. Apportionment and Party Politics in Santiago, Chile. *Midwest Journal of Political Science* 13 (3): 455–70.

McLean, Iain, and Roger Mortimore. 1992. Apportionment and the Boundary Commission for England. *Electoral Studies* 11 (4): 293–309.

Méndez, Juan E., Guillermo O'Donnell, and Paulo Sérgio Pinheiro, eds. 1999. *The (Un)Rule of Law and the Underprivileged in Latin America*. Notre Dame, Ind.: University of Notre Dame Press.

Nicolau, Jairo M. 1997. As Distorções na Representação dos Estados na Câmara dos Deputados Brasileiros. *DADOS: Revista de Ciências Sociais* 40 (3): 441–64.

O'Donnell, Guillermo. 1993. On the State, Democratization, and Some Conceptual Problems: A Latin American View with Glances at Some Post-communist Countries. *World Development* 21 (August): 1355–70.

———. 1994. Delegative Democracy. *Journal of Democracy* 5 (1): 55–69.

———. 1996. Illusions about Consolidation. *Journal of Democracy* 7 (12): 34–52.

Porto, Alberto. 1990. *Federalismo Fiscal: El Caso Argentino*. Buenos Aires: Editorial Tesis.

Porto, Walter Costa. 1989. *O Voto no Brasil: Da Colônia à Quinta República.* Brasília: Gráfica do Senado Federal.

Powell, G. Bingham, Jr. 1989. Constitutional Design and Citizen Electoral Control. *Journal of Theoretical Politics* 1 (2): 107–30.

Rokkan, Stein. 1970. *Citizens, Elections, Parties: Approaches to the Comparative Study of the Processes of Development.* New York: David McKay.

Samuels, David, and Richard Snyder. 2001. The Value of a Vote: Malapportionment in Comparative Perspective. *British Journal of Political Science* 31 (4): 651–71.

Sawers, Larry. 1996. *The Other Argentina: The Interior and National Development.* Boulder: Westview Press.

Shugart, Matthew, and John Carey. 1992. *Presidents and Assemblies.* Cambridge: Cambridge University Press.

Snyder, Richard. 1999. After the State Withdraws: Neoliberalism and Subnational Authoritarian Regimes in Mexico. In *Subnational Politics and Democratization in Mexico,* edited by W. A. Cornelius, T. Eisenstadt, and J. Hindley. La Jolla, Calif.: Center for U.S.-Mexican Studies, University of California, San Diego.

———. 2001a. Scaling Down: The Subnational Comparative Method. *Studies in Comparative International Development* 36 (1): 93–110.

———. 2001b. *Politics after Neoliberalism: Reregulation in Mexico.* Cambridge: Cambridge University Press.

Stepan, Alfred. 2000. Brazil's Decentralized Federalism: Bringing Government Closer to the Citizens? *Daedelus* 129 (spring): 145–69.

———. 2001. Toward a New Comparative Politics of Federalism, (Multi) Nationalism, and Democracy: Beyond Rikerian Federalism. In *Arguing Comparative Politics,* 315–61. Oxford: Oxford University Press.

CHAPTER 5

Reallocative Federalism

Legislative Overrepresentation and Public Spending
in the Western Hemisphere

—EDWARD L. GIBSON, ERNESTO F. CALVO, AND TULIA G. FALLETI

Do institutional features of federal systems have an independent impact on politics and public policy? For a long time the debate was somewhat closed. William Riker's suggestion that federalism and its institutions had no significant impact on public policy was largely unquestioned in the three decades since he first pronounced himself on the subject.[1] However, recently this claim has come under scrutiny. In this volume Alfred Stepan challenges Riker's position explicitly, and other contributions (Samuels and Mainwaring, Penfold-Becerra, and Ochoa-Reza) provide implicit criticism of Riker's skepticism about the independent effects of federal institutions on political outcomes. These authors' works tackle the issue from a variety of perspectives, but a common thread that links them concerns the relationship between the institutional features of federal systems and the underlying asymmetries of federal countries. All federal countries are characterized internally, and in varying ways, by asymmetry. Asymmetries in population, size, and economic power exist between

173

the constituent territories of a federal union. Federal institutions interact with these underlying asymmetries by granting particular political rights, obligations, and representation in national governing bodies to the constituent units of the federation. In some cases these institutions compound underlying asymmetries, and in others they compensate for them. Federal institutions contain power asymmetries of their own as well: they exist between the governmental bodies of the federation, between upper and lower chambers of the national legislatures, or between constitutional prerogatives assigned to central and subnational governments (or often *between* subnational governments). The design of federal institutions thus has implications for how power is distributed between key actors in a federal system. They shape (and reshape) the spatial distribution of power between territorially based actors and the institutional distribution of power between actors located in different "levels" of the federal polity. As a result, it should be expected that key outcomes, from the structuring of patterns of political representation to the distribution of public goods and resources, are at least in part shaped by the varying institutional features observable across federal systems.

This chapter contributes to this research agenda by exploring the impact of an institutional feature that, while intrinsic to most federal systems, has received relatively little attention in the literature on the politics and political economy of federalism: the overrepresentation of subnational territorial units (provinces or states) in national legislatures. All federal systems reflect internally the tensions between norms of territorial representation and norms of population (or citizen) representation. Each reflects, in the structure of its constitution, a historically determined balance between these norms. Federal systems across the world display significant variations in the primacy of one norm over the other.[2]

The basic question to be explored here is, does the overrepresentation of territories (states or provinces) in national legislatures of federal systems affect the territorial distribution of public spending by federal governments? The hypothesis to be tested is that it does, and that territorial overrepresentation produces a distortion of federal spending that benefits populations living in overrepresented territories.[3] We also introduce a conceptual distinction to capture this connection between territorial overrepresentation and the nonproportional distribution of public funds. Countries where this connection exists are identified as cases of *reallocative* federalism, whereas countries with territorial patterns of public spending that are proportional to population are identified as cases of *proportional* federalism.[4] This chapter is therefore an inquiry into the political economy of federalism. It explores the extent to which institutional features of federal countries shape the distribution of economic resources between their constituent territorial units. Our evidence is drawn from subnational-level data (at the provincial / state level) from the Western Hemisphere's four largest federal countries: the United States of America, Brazil, Mexico, and Argentina.

The analysis will be divided into three sections. First, we provide descriptive data comparing overrepresentation in the legislatures of our four countries, contrasting overrepresentation in national senates and lower houses. We also provide data comparing regional distortions in public spending in each of the countries. Although in theory lower houses are meant to represent populations rather than territories, these four cases exhibit striking variations in adherence to that norm. The United States and Mexico tend to allot seats to states in proportion to their populations. Brazil and Argentina significantly overrepresent several provinces in the lower chamber. In this latter group, therefore, a dual structure of territorial overrepresentation exists, with the lower chamber's regional allocation of seats compounding the overrepresentation inherent in the senate's role as an arena for territorial representation. The second section will analyze the above-mentioned relationships through pooled data from our group of countries. We will argue that lower-house overrepresentation has a greater impact on federal spending distortions than all other variables (including senate overrepresentation) and explains the difference between the "reallocative" federalisms of Brazil and Argentina and the "proportional" federalisms of the United States and Mexico. In the final section we will provide a more in-depth perspective through a case study of public spending and electoral coalition building in Argentina, one of our cases of "reallocative" federalism.

Overrepresentation and Revenue Sharing: Patterns in the United States, Mexico, Brazil, and Argentina

As federal countries, each of the cases we analyze overrepresents states in their national legislatures to varying degrees. All countries possess national senates where territorial overrepresentation is deliberately built into the allocation of the bodies' seats. This is a common characteristic shared by all four federal systems. However, they do not overrepresent to the same degree. As can be seen in Table 5.1,[5] the Brazilian, U.S., and Argentine senates overrepresent states considerably more than the Mexican Senate.[6]

Table 5.1
Overrepresentation and Public Spending Descriptive Variables

	Country	N	Range	Minimum	Maximum	Mean	Std. Deviation
Senate	Argentina	24	19.73	0.11	19.84	3.44	4.07
Overrep.	Brazil	27	25.8	0.18	25.98	3.93	6.1
	Mexico	32	7.8	0.26	8.03	1.96	1.8
	United States	50	21.89	0.33	22.22	5.24	5.3
House	Argentina	24			9.59	1.85	1.8
Overrep.	Brazil	27	9.89	0.63	10.52	1.92	2.31
	Mexico	32	0.79	0.91	1.7	1.04	0.137
	United States	50	0.56	0.72	1.28	1	0.086
Fund	Argentina	24	6.44	0.58	7.02	2.22	1.6
Ratio	Brazil	27	17.25	0.05	17.3	3.25	4.68
	Mexico	32	1.65	0.69	2.35	1.08	0.37
	United States	50	1.53	0.65	2.19	1.06	0.3

Note: Senate Overrep. and House Overrep. = ratio of state's percentage share of total seats to state's percentage share of national population. A score of 1 means seat allotments are proportional to population. Fund Ratio = ratio of state's percentage share of federal transfers to state's percentage share of the population. A score of 1 means funds received are proportional to population.

The data also show that considerable distortion exists in Brazil, Argentina, and the United States. All three have large ranges between the most underrepresented state and the most overrepresented states, and their mean ratios are at least three times that which would reflect proportional representation. Furthermore, all three have yawning gaps between the amount of votes required to elect a senator in the most underrepresented and most overrepresented states. In Argentina one vote in Tierra del Fuego is equal to 180 votes in Buenos Aires. In Brazil one vote in Roraima is worth 144 votes in São Paulo, and in the United States one vote in Wyoming is worth sixty-seven votes in California. In contrast, Mexico, whose Senate does allocate seats disproportionately between states, comes in a distant fourth, where one vote in Baja California Sur is worth thirty-one votes in the state of Mexico.[7]

Table 5.1 also shows the degree of overrepresentation present in the lower chambers of these countries' legislatures. Here the results show a division of the cases into two clusters. Brazil and Argentina demonstrate a striking deviation from the norm of proportionality in the regional allocation of lower-chamber seats to individual states. They both exhibit a substantial range between the most underrepresented and overrepresented states (substantial for a supposedly proportional body), and the average ratio of seat share to population share for each is nearly two to one. In contrast, the Mexican and U.S. lower houses are highly proportional in the allocation of seats between the states. For both, the average ratio of seat share to population share is, for all intents and purposes, one to one.[8]

Finally, the data in Table 5.1 provide measures of deviation (from proportionality) in the distribution of revenue-sharing funds allocated by the central government to the states. Once again, the four cases separate into two opposing clusters. Argentina and Brazil show considerably more regional distortion than Mexico and the United States.[9] Brazil shows the most distortion, with a range between most benefited state to least benefited state that towers over the rest, and is almost three times its closest contender, Argentina. Nevertheless, Argentina's range is four times those of Mexico and the United States, whose average ratios of share of federal funds to share of population are close to complete proportionality.

In sum, from a political economy standpoint Brazil and Argentina present cases of reallocative federalism, whereas Mexico and the United States approximate models of proportional federalism. What accounts for the regional distortions of federal spending patterns, and what factors best explain differences between proportional and reallocative federalism? We will attempt to answer these questions in the following section, while at the same time providing a picture of key associations between overrepresentation and socioeconomic conditions of subnational territorial units.

Overrepresentation and Public Spending: Pooled Comparisons

Table 5.2 provides individual correlations between measures of overrepresentation and selected public spending and socioeconomic variables. As mentioned earlier, these are generated by the pooled data set of the 133 states of the five countries under study. Among these variables, "senover" and "houseover" are the measures of overrepresentation presented earlier. Similarly, "fundratio" is the ratio presented in the preceding section of the states' share of nondiscretionary federal transfers to their percentage share of the national population. "Discratio" is another measure of regional spending distortion and represents discretionary transfers from the federal government received by individual states.

The data in Table 5.2 show very strong positive correlations between senate and house overrepresentation and the two measures of spending distortion, and the cor-

Table 5.2
Overrepresentation, Public Spending, and Selected Socioeconomic Variables

Variable	Houseover	Senover	Fundratio	Discratio
Houseover	1.000	0.638[a]	0.824[a]	0.820[a]
Senover	0.638[a]	1.000	0.529[a]	0.352[a]
Fundratio	0.824[a]	0.529[a]	1.000	0.907[a]
Discratio	0.820[a]	0.352[a]	0.907[a]	1.000
Perlocal	−0.315[a]	−0.023[a]	−0.334[a]	−0.256[a]
Pubemp	0.530[a]	0.262[a]	0.386[a]	0.615[a]
Poverty	0.069	−0.088	0.211[b]	−0.136
Income	−0.195[b]	0.163	−0.258[a]	−0.025

Note: The Pubemp variable represents state (provincial) public-sector employees for Brazil, Argentina, and the United States and both state and municipal public employees in Mexico. The Poverty variable represents the percentage of the population living below the official poverty line in the United States and uses a proxy for poverty, percentage of population that is illiterate, for Brazil, Argentina, and Mexico (which correlates very highly with the poverty indexes we have available). Income represents median monthly household incomes measured in US$. All data were gathered from official government publications and Internet sites. U.S. data are taken from U.S. Census Bureau Statistical Abstracts for 1994 and 1997. Argentine data are from INDEC (1997) and Ministerio de Economía y Obras y Servicios Públicos (1994). Mexican data are from INEGI (1995). Brazilian data are from IBGE (http://www.ibge.gob.br) and Ministerio de Fazenda (http://www.fazenda.gov.br) as well as the Ministério da Administracao Federal e Reforma do Estado (1997). $N = 133$, for all correlation coefficients except those with Discrat ($N = 105$, Brazil not included).
[a]Correlation is significant at the 0.01 level (2-tailed).
[b]Correlation is significant at the 0.05 level (2-tailed).

relation coefficients registered for lower-chamber overrepresentation are considerably higher than those for senate overrepresentation. The lower-house overrepresentation variable is far more robust when compared to the performance of other variables that might represent alternative explanations for regional spending distortions, primarily public policy objectives aimed at addressing the poverty or socioeconomic deprivation of fiscally favored states. The correlations in the table suggest at best a moderate public policy drive behind regional allocations of federal transfers. Both "poverty" and "income" show a moderate and significant relationship with nondiscretionary spending distortions, in the direction that would be expected if redistributive and the other poverty alleviation objectives were behind such flows. The "income" variable, which represents monthly median incomes of individual states (measured in U.S. dollars), has a negative relationship with the measure of spending distortion, while the "poverty" variable has a positive relationship. However, discretionary spending has no significant relationship with either poverty or income, suggesting that other political factors are behind the regional distribution of such transfers.

Finally, the data in Table 5.2 provide an interesting glimpse into the relationship between reallocative federalism and the fiscal aspects of local political economies. The data suggest that local fiscal realities are molded by federal spending distortions. The "perlocal" variable, which represents the share of total state revenues generated through local taxation, shows a significant negative correlation with both the "fundratio" and "discratio" variables. This suggests that states that receive disproportionate shares of federal funds are also states whose budgets are least funded by local tax revenues. Similarly, as suggested by the significant positive relationships registered between the public-sector employment ("pubempl") variable and the measures of spending distortion, they are also the states that have the highest shares of state public-sector employees as a percentage of local populations. It can be assumed that federal transfers in overbenefited states are relatively important sources of funding for public-sector-dependent economies. This provides a more nuanced view of the stake that politicians have in maintaining the status quo of reallocative federalism, a fact that has implications for coalition building between central and local governments in periods of economic reform. This issue will be explored in more detail in the Argentina case study presented later.

In sum, the findings presented in Table 5.2 provide support for the hypothesis that legislative overrepresentation produces federal spending distortions in favor of overrepresented territories. Furthermore, they also lend support to the proposition that lower-house overrepresentation is more important than senate overrepresentation in accounting for differences in spending distortion levels. However, they can at best be considered suggestive. As individual correlations they do not control for other variables or give a measure of the relative impact of specific variables on federal spending patterns.

Tables 5.3 and 5.4 present the results of multiple regression analyses that incorporate key variables that on their own could explain deviations from the norm of proportionality in federal spending patterns. In essence, they seek to explore the extent to which regional federal spending distortions are the results of overrepresentation or are the results of public policy objectives aimed at redressing socioeconomic inequalities between states. Regarding overrepresentation, the analyses seek to establish whether overrepresentation in the senate or the lower chamber best accounts for variations in federal spending distortions across the federal systems in our sample.

The results of the analyses are suggestive. Both overrepresentation and public

Table 5.3
Overrepresentation, Poverty, and Federal Spending Distortion
Nondiscretionary Transfers (multiple regression analysis)

Independent Variables	Model 1	Model 2
(Constant)	-0.216^a	-0.813^b
	(0.093)	(0.233)
Houseover (ln)	1.019^b	0.873^b
	(0.110)	(0.113)
Senover (ln)	0.187^b	0.236^b
	(0.043)	(0.043)
Poverty	0.009^b	0.015^b
	(0.003)	(0.003)
Income	0.00000047	0.00026
	(0.000)	(0.000)
Argentina		0.659^b
		(0.183)
Brazil		0.334
		(0.241)
Mexico		0.368^a
		(0.148)
Adjusted R^2	0.645	0.683
	(0.425)	(0.402)
F	60.11	41.02
N	130	130

Note: Reported values are the B (nonstandarized) coefficients. Standard errors of the estimates are shown in parentheses. Dependent variable: "fundratio" = ratio of state's percentage share of federal funds to its percentage share of national population.
   [a]Significant at the 0.05 level (2-tailed).
   [b]Significant at the 0.01 level (2-tailed).
   $N = 131$.

policy appear to influence the distribution of federal transfers between states. Although the results presented in Table 5.4 for the "poverty" and "income" variables suggest that discretionary spending distortions are not driven by redistributive public policy considerations, the performance of the "poverty" variable in Table 5.3 suggests that deviations from proportionality in the distribution of funds are driven partly by local poverty levels for nondiscretionary federal transfers. However, both tables confirm that overrepresentation plays the most significant role in reallocative spending patterns, whether for nondiscretionary or discretionary transfers. In addition, of the two measures of legislative overrepresentation, the "houseover" variable trumps all others in the model by a considerable margin.

Table 5.4

Overrepresentation, Poverty, and Federal Spending Distortion

Discretionary Transfers (multiple regression analysis)

Independent Variables	Model 1	Model 2
(Constant)	-0.435^a	-1.497^a
	(0.127)	(0.265)
Houseover (ln)	1.541^a	1.091^a
	(0.172)	(0.179)
Senover (ln)	0.136^b	0.211^a
	(0.054)	(0.051)
Poverty	0.0014	0.003
	(0.005)	(0.004)
Income	0.00026^b	0.00082^a
	(0.000)	(0.000)
Argentina		1.084^a
		(0.216)
Mexico		0.545^a
		(0.167)
Adjusted R^2	0.556	0.641
F	33.19	31.71
N	103	103

Note: Reported values are the B (nonstandarized) coefficients. Standard errors of the estimates are shown in parentheses. Dependent variable: "discratio" = ratio of state's percentage share of federal discretionary transfers to its percentage share of the national population.

[a]Significant at the 0.01 level (2-tailed).

[b]Significant at the 0.05 level (2-tailed).

Thus, two conclusions can be drawn from this analysis. First, territorial overrepresentation in national legislatures plays a substantially higher role than public policy considerations in producing the federal spending distortions characteristic of reallocative federalism. Whether federal spending is governed by pre-set distributional formulas or whether it is discretionary, territorial overrepresentation is a powerful determinant of the regional distribution of federal largesse toward the states. Second, overrepresentation in the lower chamber of the legislature is a stronger predictor of federal spending distortions than is senate overrepresentation. By extension, it accounts for a significant part of the variation between the reallocative and proportional federalisms in the four countries in our sample.

The analysis so far has provided a statistical and superficial glimpse of the relationship between legislative overrepresentation and fiscal federalism in four American countries. In the following sections we provide a more detailed look at how territorial overrepresentation interacts with the political economy of policy making and the geography of coalition building in one of our cases of reallocative federalism, Argentina, between 1990 and 1995.

Overrepresented Territories, Discretionary Spending, and Electoral Politics in Argentina[10]

The bulk of Argentina's population and productive structure are located on and around an expansive and fertile plain known as the *Pampas* region. Argentina's largest city, the city of Buenos Aires, is a federal district encrusted in the agriculturally rich Buenos Aires province. The city of Buenos Aires is surrounded by a massive industrial and urban belt that makes the greater Buenos Aires urban area the population and economic hub of the nation.[11] In addition, the greater Buenos Aries urban area is one end of a string of three industrial cities that stretch to the city of Rosario, in adjoining Santa Fe province, and on to the city of Córdoba, the capital of Córdoba province. Together these three provinces account for 73 percent of total industrial production and 65 percent of the national population. If Mendoza, the country's fourth most prosperous and urbanized province is added, the total share of the "metropolitan" provinces' industrial production and population rises to 78 and 70 percent, respectively.[12]

As mentioned in the previous sections, Argentina's federal system overrepresents poor and underpopulated territories more than most federal systems in the world. In 1995 the nineteen provinces designated as comprising the "peripheral region" of the country contained 30 percent of the national population but held forty of forty-eight seats in the Senate—83 percent of the total. This overrepresentation also extends to the lower chamber of the Congress, the Chamber of Deputies, where peripheral region provinces hold 52 percent of the seats.

The Argentine constitution of 1856 established that seats in the Chamber of Deputies would be allocated proportionally to district population. However, this principle was abandoned in the twentieth century when both Peronist and military governments, each for their own political reasons, introduced amendments that bolstered representation of the traditionally conservative peripheral regions in the lower chamber. The first departure from direct proportional representation was in 1949, when a constitution drafted by the government of Juan Perón established a minimum of two deputies per province, regardless of population. In 1972 the minimum number was increased to three (Sawers 1996). In 1983 the departing military government of General Reynaldo Bignone increased that number to five deputies per province. As a result, a congressional candidate in the city of Buenos Aires is required to obtain almost seven times the number of votes as those required by his or her counterpart in Tierra del Fuego (Cabrera and Murillo 1994).

This institutional overrepresentation meant that no national winning electoral or legislative coalition could be put together without the support of the regional structures of power in the periphery. Given the highly contested electoral contexts in the more developed and urbanized regions, the national party that won electorally would be that party that possessed institutional ties with the networks of regional power brokers capable of delivering the vote in the "interior" regions of the country. The party that proved most successful at this task after the 1940s was the Peronist Party. Peronism's seeming invincibility at the polls—what came to be known by supporters and detractors alike as the "iron law" of Argentine elections—was due not to organized labor in the metropolis but to its ties to clientelistic and traditional networks of power and electoral mobilization in the periphery.[13]

The protagonism of overrepresented peripheral provinces in the national Peronist coalition has continued to the present day, and during President Menem's first term they provided a major base of support in the national legislature. Furthermore, the peripheral region's political weight in Menem's governing coalition was bolstered by the Peronist Party's coalition building with provincial conservative parties. Such parties play an important role in local politics in several provinces, and during Menem's first term they became full partners in government, occupying high government positions, providing progovernment voting blocks in the Congress, and endorsing the president's reelection bid in 1995.

As can be glimpsed in Table 5.5, the Peronist Party controlled the lion's share of

Table 5.5
Composition of the Argentine Senate, 1992–1995

	Metro Region	Non-Metro	Total	Percentage of Seats
Peronist Party	5	25	30	63%
Radical Party	5	6	11	23
Provincial Parties	0	7	7	15
Total	10	38	48	101[a]

[a]Does not add to 100% due to rounding.

Source: Dirección de Información Parlamentaria, Argentine National Congress (http://proyectos .senado.gov.ar/images/historico/historico.html).

Table 5.6
Composition of the Argentine Chamber of Deputies, 1993–1995

	Metro Region	Non-Metro	Total	Percentage
Peronist party	69	59	128	50%
Radical Party	49	34	83	32
Conservative/				
Provincial	8	21	29	11
Other	16	1	17	7
Total	142	115	257	100

Source: Fraga (1995).

seats from nonmetropolitan provinces in the national senate. This majority was turned into outright control of that body by the party's alliance with conservative provincial parties. The combination of Peronist senators and provincial party senators effectively gave President Menem a 78 percent majority of seats in the Senate.

In the Chamber of Deputies the overrepresentation of smaller provinces also gave the peripheral region an advantage over the metropolitan provinces. With 30 percent of the population the peripheral provinces held 45 percent of the seats. As can be seen in Table 5.6, this overrepresentation, coupled with the Peronist Party's electoral strength in those regions, worked to the advantage of the Peronist Party during Menem's presidency.

The Peronist Party dominated other parties in both metropolitan and nonmetropolitan delegations to the lower house of Congress. Yet its near-majority in the Chamber of Deputies owed much to its edge in seats from the peripheral provinces. The ruling party controlled 51 percent of the seats from those provinces, compared to 48 percent of the seats from the metropolitan provinces. Furthermore, it was in the peripheral regions where the Peronist alliance with conservative provincial parties gave the ruling party its lock on the legislative body. Together Peronists and provincial parties controlled 70 percent of the nonmetropolitan delegation to the Chamber of Deputies, compared to 54 percent for the Peronist-conservative blocks from the metropolitan provinces. In sum, even in the Chamber of Deputies the peripheral coalition delivered greater political leverage to the ruling party than its population size would have indicated. With 30 percent of the electorate, peripheral provinces gave the Peronist–provincial party alliance a total of seventy seats in the Chamber of Deputies. The metropolitan region, with 70 percent of the electorate, yielded a total of seventy-seven seats.

How did this regional structure of the Peronist Party coalition shape the management of economic reform between 1990 and 1995? In essence, it led the Menem government to shield its politically overrepresented peripheral constituencies from the more ravaging effects of the reforms while bringing the day of reckoning to the metropolitan regions of the country. This goal was achieved by postponing public-sector employment cuts in the provincial public sectors and by increasing subsidy flows from the central government to provincial public coffers (which made the strategy of maintaining provincial public employment levels possible). In this chapter we will focus on the regional patterns of federal government spending.[14]

Resource transfers to provincial governments from the national government take place primarily through two channels. The first is a mechanism for sharing national tax revenues, known as "coparticipation," which systematically favors peripheral region provinces according to an automatic revenue-sharing formula. The second is a cluster of discretionary flows, including national treasury contributions to provincial governments, a fund to aid provinces in "fiscal disequilibrium," and federal grants and credits for housing, public works, health, and education.[15]

As the figures in Table 5.7 show, total federal transfers to the provinces more than doubled between 1990 and 1995.[16] However, automatic revenue-sharing flows were not the only disbursements that increased during this period. Discretionary flows also kept pace, nearly doubling between 1990 and 1995.[17] Although federal funding is important to all provinces, the greater dependence of peripheral region economies on the national state can be seen in Table 5.7, which contrasts subsidy patterns in metropolitan and peripheral provinces. Total public spending in individual metropolitan provinces greatly exceeds that for peripheral region provinces, but peripheral provinces have a much larger share of their budgets subsidized by the federal government. The federal government subsidized an average of approximately 43 percent of metropolitan provincial budgets, mostly through the institutional mechanism of coparticipation. In contrast, 78 percent of expenditures of peripheral provinces were financed by the national government, with discretionary funds taking up 18 percent of total federal subsidies (compared to 7 percent for the metropolitan region).[18]

These data also give an indication of the political dimensions of discretionary spending on the provinces during the Menem government and of the potentially greater political payoff to the ruling party from every dollar spent on low-maintenance constituencies in the interior. In absolute terms federal transfers to

Table 5.7
Federal Expenditures and Public Employment by Province

Province	Percentage of Provincial Budget Financed by Federal Govt. 1994	Total Federal Transfers 1990 (millions, U.S.$)	Total Federal Transfers 1995 (millions, U.S.$)	Federal Transfers 1995 (U.S.$ per capita)	Discretionary Transfers 1990 (millions, U.S.$)	Discretionary Transfers 1995 (millions, U.S.$)
Federal District[a]	6.16					
Buenos Aires	46.04	1,292	3,544	282	164	290
Córdoba	55.16	514	1,007	363	63	68
Mendoza	58.57	306	611	432	25	37
Santa Fe	52.28	989	2,031	725	104	97
Metro (mean)	43.64	775	1,798	451	89	123
Catamarca	90.88	198	339	1,282	53	30
Chaco	87.97	311	596	1,105	69	70
Chubut	79.98	182	395	629	40	99
Corrientes	85.71	260	501	709	65	70
Entre Rio	70.74	306	638	625	58	62
Formosa	92.44	235	497	1,247	53	99
Jujuy	74.46	303	392	765	153	54
La Pampa	62.59	124	302	1,161	21	67
La Rioja	84.04	172	530	2,401	51	259
Misiones	82.35	220	468	593	52	72
Neuquén	68.55	359	608	1,563	66	123
Rio Negro	66.16	289	401	791	111	74
Salta	71.14	271	535	617	34	64
San Juan	82.97	214	449	849	41	64
San Luis	76.19	159	321	1,120	41	56
Santa Cruz	76.30	224	426	2,665	43	97
Santiago del Estero	85.63	243	548	815	43	89
Tierra del Fuego	71.58	90	236	3,402	33	92
Tucumán	76.42	323	613	536	62	58
Periphery (mean)	78.22	235	463	1,204	57	84

[a]Federal District is not a province, and thus did not participate in federal revenue-sharing programs.
Sources: 1990 figures, INDEC (1991); 1994 figures, Ministerio de Economía (1995).

metropolitan provinces far exceeded those to peripheral provinces (Table 5.7). However, the per capita spending figures in Table 5.7 show just how favored populations living in the periphery are in federal transfer schemes. The federal government spent, on average, three times as much per person in the periphery than in the metropolis.

If we look at the more politically driven discretionary funding patterns, we see a marked peripheral bias to the Peronist government's spending during this period. Discretionary transfers increased in both regions; however, the rate of growth in the periphery was well over double that in metropolitan provinces. Furthermore, the figures in Table 5.8 show the substantially greater local impact discretionary spend-

Table 5.8
Federal Transfers, Unemployment, and Votes

	Discretionary Federal Transfers 1995 (U.S.$ per capita)	Ratio: Voters Needed to Elect a member of Congress over the National Average (1 = natl. avg.)	Percentage Growth in Discretionary Transfers, 1990–1995	Unemployment Growth, 1989–1995	Peronist Presidential Vote Percentage, 1995	Percentage Change in Peronist Presidential Vote, 1989–1995
Federal District				9.10	41.5%	5.20%
Buenos Aires	23.03	1.75	76%	12.60	51.8	1.90
Córdoba	24.58	1.74	7	6.40	48.2	3.60
Mendoza	26.02	1.53	48	2.40	5.2	9.90
Santa Fe	34.66	1.75	−7	6.50	46.8	−4.80
Metro (mean)	27.07	1.69	31	7.40	48.38	3.16
Catamarca	113.54	0.52	−43	2.00	52.3	−3.60
Chaco	83.37	0.66	147	4.10	56.8	5.10
Chubut	277.16	1.14	8	2.90	57	14.40
Corrientes	87.98	1.16	0	7.20	46	3.90
Entre Rio	60.77	1.19	7	2.80	46.2	−5.40
Formosa	248.49	0.9	87	−3.80	49.5	−8.50
Jujuy	105.40	0.75	−64	5.60	44.2	1.10
La Pampa	257.70	0.56	220	2.30	50.3	−1.20
La Rioja	1,173.38	0.44	407	5.20	76.1	9.50
Misiones	91.26	1	38	3.50	49.5	−3.20
Neuquén	316.33	1.18	86	8.10	53.5	14.30
Rio Negro	146.02	0.85	−33	3.70	44	−3.20
Salta	73.89	1.14	88	10.60	54.1	12.90
San Juan	121.05	0.88	56	5.20	59.8	11.40
San Luis	195.49	0.6	37	3.20	51.7	5.40
Santa Cruz	606.86	0.35	126	2.40	58.4	3.70
Santiago del Estero	132.44	0.95	107	0.00	64.6	−.30
Tierra del Fuego	1,326.24	0.15	179	−0.20	61.1	18.40
Tucumán	50.78	1.42	−6	7.30	45.5	4.20
Periphery (mean)	288.78	0.83	76	3.79	53.37	7.63

Sources: Unemployment figures, INDEC (1995); electoral figures calculated from data supplied by the Ministry of the Interior.

ing had in peripheral provinces. In 1995 the average per capita amounts transferred to peripheral provinces was *ten times* that sent to metropolitan provinces. Furthermore, as the figures in Table 5.8 suggest, the potential political payoff from this spending for the ruling party's legislative coalition was magnified by the relatively lower cost in votes required to elect a member of Congress in the periphery.

Table 5.8 also provides another glimpse of the potential political benefits of the Menem government's subsidy of provincial government budgets. The more relatively heavily subsidized, but less costly, provinces in the periphery experienced smaller increases in unemployment than their less subsidized metropolitan counterparts.

How significant, however, was this political investment of public spending in the overrepresented periphery for the Menem government's ability to maintain a winning legislative coalition during the period of economic reform? The regression analyses displayed in Tables 5.9 and 5.10 attempt to answer this question. First, we seek to identify the potential causes of the changes in regional discretionary spending patterns displayed in Tables 5.7 and 5.8. We assume, in line with the working hypothesis of this paper, that overrepresentation affected the strategic delivery of discretionary funds by the central government. However, we also assume that discretionary spending sought to reward or bolster the central government's provincial partisans, and that the results of prior elections (namely the Peronist Party's performance) also affected the flow of discretionary funding to individual provinces. The model in Table 5.9 thus includes territorial overrepresentation in the lower chamber ("houseover") as well as the Peronist Party's vote totals in the 1989 presidential election and the 1991 elections for the national Chamber of Deputies ("PJ89pres" and "PJ91house," respectively).

The results suggest that, although the flow of discretionary funding was indeed affected by the results of earlier elections, overrepresentation was a stronger pre-

Table 5.9
Overrepresentation, Elections, and Discretionary Spending Shifts (multiple regression analysis)

Model	B	Std. Error	Beta	t	Sig.
(Constant)	−361.882	122.441		−2.956	0.008
Houseover	24.604	9.157	0.440	2.687	0.015
PJ89pres.	4.276	2.327	0.310	1.837	0.082
PJ91house	4.253	1.845	0.390	2.305	0.033

Note: N = 22, Adj. R^2 = .412, Std. error = 78.702.
  Dependent variable: Change in discretionary spending, by province, 1990–95.

Table 5.10
Discretionary Federal Spending, Unemployment, and the 1995 Chamber of Deputies Election
(multiple regression analysis)

Model	B	Std. Error	Beta	t	Sig.
(Constant)	27.134	8.76		3.1	0.006
Chdisc	0.051	0.020	0.429	2.6	0.019
PJ91house	0.482	0.215	0.372	2.2	0.037
Unemploymt. Ch.	0.923	0.510	−0.270	1.8	0.086

Note: $N = 22$, Adj. $R^2 = 0.519$, Std. error $= 8.5$.
    Dependent variable: Peronist vote percentages, 1995 Chamber of Deputies election.

dictor of the allocation of discretionary funds than prior Peronist Party electoral performance. That is, while local Peronist Party officials were likely to reap the rewards of central government largesse if they did well electorally, they were likely to see more of this largesse if they lived in overrepresented provinces.

In the second regression analysis (see Table 5.10) we seek to gain a sense of the impact of discretionary spending shifts on the Peronist Party's electoral performance in the 1995 Chamber of Deputies elections. On the assumption that prior electoral performance affects subsequent electoral results, the model incorporates a variable measuring the party's performance in prior legislative elections.[19] In addition, the model incorporates a contextual economic variable, changes in provincial unemployment levels, to control for its impact on Peronist electoral performance.[20]

The results suggest that the strongest relative impact on Peronist electoral performance in the 1995 legislative elections came from increases in discretionary spending to the provinces. Taking both regression analyses into account, we can infer that strategically placed federal disbursements to overrepresented provinces played a major part in the maintenance of President Menem's legislative coalition during the period of market reform. Turbulence in the metropolis was made politically affordable by federal spending in the overrepresented periphery.

Conclusion

This chapter establishes that territorial overrepresentation affects the regional distribution of central government fiscal transfers in federal systems. The evidence presented supports our hypothesis that territorial overrepresentation promotes a reallocation of federal revenue-sharing funds and discretionary spending that benefits overrepresented states. However, we also note variation in this relationship across federal systems: some federal governments distribute funds to states proportionally to population, and some do not. We thus introduce a conceptual distinction between "reallocative federalism" and "proportional federalism" to capture this divergence.

Within our group of countries, Brazil and Argentina are classified as cases of "reallocative federalism," whereas the United States and Mexico are labeled cases of "proportional federalism." We also seek to explore possible reasons for this divergence in these four countries. The examination of pooled state-level data on federal spending patterns, legislative seat allocations, and socioeconomic factors leads to the conclusion that the territorial overrepresentation in the lower house of the national congress best explains the variation between our cases of reallocative federalism and proportional federalism. The lower chamber, not the senate, is the driving force behind the reallocation of federal transfers in favor of overrepresented states and provinces.

This finding runs counter to widely held assumptions about the centrality of the senate in shaping the nonproportional features and outcomes of federal systems. It suggests that more attention needs to be paid to the effects of lower-house overrepresentation on politics and public policy in federal systems.[21] The senate, as the constitutionally sanctioned body for territorial representation, has taken the lion's share of attention in scholarly treatment of the subject.[22] The results of this study suggest that senate overrepresentation per se is a weak explanatory variable for spending variations *between* the federal systems we have analyzed, most of which contain a significant element of territorial overrepresentation in their senates.[23]

The results of this study also beg a question that was only partly addressed here: what are the causal mechanisms behind the relationship between overrepresentation and federal spending distortions? Although the comparative analysis of our four cases establishes associations without exploration of causal mechanisms, our case study on Argentina provides some insights into this question. Regarding strategic and pork barrel transfers, our case study on Argentina provides a glimpse into the causal logic of reallocative federalism. Put simply, overrepresented territories tend to yield a high political payoff from investments of political spending. This introduces a "low-maintenance constituency" dynamic that has implications for the uses of public funds for coalition building (Gibson and Calvo 2000). Since the economic investment required for one unit of political support from an overrepresented territory is far lower than the investment required for an underrepresented and high-population territory, the dynamics of selecting between "low-maintenance" and "high-maintenance" constituencies come into play. In Argentina, the relatively small size of state-dependent peripheral economies makes political spending on those regions affordable. Furthermore, political overrepresentation of the periphery provides the ruling party a substantial political payoff from relatively small investments of political spending.

This logic operates in a context where the national executive plays the decisive role in determining the regional allocation of short-term federal spending. However, in contexts where the legislature plays a decisive role the causal mechanisms will obviously be different. This suggests that the "policy scope" in budgetary matters of different governmental bodies, specifically the relative importance of the national executive and legislature in structuring the regional distribution of federal spending, is a topic that merits further research. If the Congress plays a major role in determining such flows, overrepresentation may induce *legislatively* driven reallocations of federal spending, where overrepresented states themselves effect such reallocations thanks to their leverage in budgetary committees. For example, David Samuels (2002) details how Brazilian legislators from overrepresented states manage to reproduce their overrepresentation in legislative chambers onto key congressional budgetary committees, thus inducing reallocations of public funds to their states. This legislative-driven model contrasts with the executive-driven model we detail for Argentina, where the central government directs federal spending toward overrepresented states to shore up its majority in the Congress.

The causal mechanisms for constitutionally mandated federal transfers, or federal revenue sharing according to preset formulas, is also worthy of further research, as they will in all likelihood be different than those for discretionary transfers. Historical research on the negotiations that established revenue-sharing formulas could yield interesting insights into how the balance of power between the central government and the states, and between the states themselves, structured the fiscal framework of federal arrangements. In contexts of strong central authority, or in contexts of alliance between the federal government and prosperous states, more proportional revenue-sharing arrangements would probably result from these negotiations. Different configurations of power and alliance between the central government and the states, as well as between the states, would thus plausibly have yielded different configurations of federal revenue-sharing arrangements.

The same can be said for the origins of lower-house overrepresentation. Overrepresentation is often used as a measure of the "robustness" or "peripheralizing" nature of federal systems,[24] but this begs the question of whether overrepresentation is a result or a cause of the peripheralized nature of federal systems. It also leaves open the question of whether such overrepresentation was the work of the states themselves or of a central government eager to shore up supporters in specific regions of the country (as was the case with Perón and subsequent military leaders in Argentina).[25]

In sum, the institutional features of federal systems do make a difference for politics and policy making. The political economy of federalism is not independent of the political structures of federal systems. This chapter has sought to shed light on one such area of interdependence. As research agendas on federalism continue to develop, we hope that further light will be shed on the causal mechanisms behind these relationships as well as on their significance for politics and political development.

NOTES

1. See Riker (1964). His arguments are developed further in such later publications as Riker (1975, 1987).

2. See Stepan (2001) and Samuels and Snyder (2001) for quantitative evidence of these variations.

3. A semantic note: throughout the paper we will use the term "overrepresentation" rather than "malapportionment," which is customarily used in the literature. We do so to avoid the negative connotations of malapportionment. It is not our contention that territorial overrepresentation is a "bad" feature of federal systems. In fact, overrepresentation may well be beneficial to the stability and territorial integrity of federal systems, particularly those with significant economic and demographic asymmetries between their subnational units. Territorial overrepresentation can function as a compensatory mechanism between otherwise unequal units, providing political leverage to weak states or provinces that would otherwise be unavailable to them in the face of the economic or demographic clout of dominant states or provinces.

4. Federal revenue-sharing programs, by definition, have a redistributive function, since by allocating funds proportionally to population they effect a redistribution of national tax revenues from wealthier to poorer states. We thus adopt the term "reallocative federalism" to address the extent to which territorial overrepresentation promotes a regional allocation of public funds that deviates from the norm of proportionality.

5. Both senate and lower chamber overrepresentation are measured by an index that is the ratio of a state's percentage share of seats to its percentage share of the national population. A ratio

of 1 means that the percentage share of seats is equal to the state's percentage share of the national population.

6. And they probably do so more than these data indicate, since as of 1996 the Mexican Senate has three senators allotted per state and thirty-two senators elected on the basis of proportional representation, thus tempering the territorial nature of that body's representation. The senators elected by proportional representation are not included in the data presented here. In a later version of this chapter we will explore whether these can be incorporated into the measures used here. For a recent suggestive discussion of Mexican federalism, see Marván (1997).

7. In his contribution to this volume Alfred Stepan uses a single measure to rank federal systems, the "Gini coefficient of representational inequality." He ranks each of these countries' senates from most overrepresentative to least as follows: Argentina, Brazil, the United States, and Mexico.

8. Again, the Mexican lower house combines deputies elected by single-member districts allotted to states with deputies elected by proportional representation in five multistate districts. Three hundred deputies represent the former and two hundred the latter. For the time being, data presented here include only the three hundred deputies from state-level single-member districts. For details on the Mexican electoral system see Instituto Federal Electoral (1997).

9. The measure of distortion for federal spending is similar to that of senate and lower-house overrepresentation. It is a ratio of the share of federal funds received by the state to its share of the national population. A coefficient of 1 indicates a completely proportional allocation of funds.

10. Some of the material presented in this section appeared previously in Gibson and Calvo (2000).

11. With a population of nearly 11 million, the greater Buenos Aires area comprises one-third of the national population.

12. Throughout this section we divide Argentina into a "metropolitan" region—comprising the five most economically developed and populated provinces, Buenos Aires, the Federal District, Santa Fe, Córdoba, and Mendoza—and a "peripheral" region, comprising the remaining nineteen provinces. Population figures taken from Instituto Nacional de Estadísticas y Censo (INDEC 1991) and economic figures taken from Instituto Nacional de Estadísticas y Censo (INDEC 1994).

13. For a more detailed discussion, see Gibson (1997).

14. Between 1990 and 1995 the Menem government cut public-sector jobs substantially, but these jobs were in the national public sector, 80 percent of whose employees were located in metropolitan regions. Provincial public-sector rolls were not touched and, in fact, increased slightly between 1990 and 1995. For more detailed treatment and evidence, see Gibson and Calvo (2000).

15. For details on central government revenue-sharing arrangements with the provinces, see Inter-American Development Bank (1994) and World Bank (1993). The revenue-sharing formula was last modified in 1988. This last modification placed the bulk of resource transfers under the "coparticipated" funds category, and reduced the discretionary flow component of total federal transfers.

16. This increase was in large part a boon to the provincial public sector from the national reforms carried out by the Menem government, notably a substantial increase in federal tax collec-

tions during the government's first years. This meant that, according to automatic tax revenue-sharing arrangements established in 1988 under the previous government of President Alfonsín, "coparticipated" transfers to provincial governments would increase substantially in the early 1990s.

17. As a result of increased federal funding, the provinces' beleaguered public finances improved somewhat. However, the enhanced flows were a major disincentive for local public-sector reforms, and these were well avoided by local governments throughout Menem's first term in office (see World Bank 1993, 1996). In 1992 the Menem government transferred education and health functions from the national government to the provinces, which did increase the fiscal burden on those provinces and offset some of the increased revenue flows. However, the increase in revenue sharing represented more than double the expense of services transferred to the provinces (Sawers 1996).

18. According to one source, nearly 70 percent of public spending goes to salaries of public-sector personnel in peripheral provinces, compared to 55 percent in metropolitan provinces (Sawers 1996).

19. The prior election used in the model is the 1991 election. It would have been better to use the 1993 election, but for the moment we do not have the data for that election.

20. Unemployment rose to historically unprecedented levels during President Menem's first term in office. It was arguably the most important issue discussed publicly during the 1995 elections.

21. The importance of this suggestion seems all the greater given Snyder and Samuels's findings on the prevalence of malapportionment in lower houses throughout federal and unitary systems in Latin America.

22. For example, Alfred Stepan's chapter in this volume focuses almost exclusively on the senate in his measurements and theoretical treatment of overrepresentation in federal systems.

23. One possibility that has not been explored in this study is that senate overrepresentation may be a more powerful predictor in pools of cases that include more proportionally designed senates, such as the German, Indian, or Austrian systems. These bodies do overrepresent subnational units, but they do not allocate the same number of senate seats to all states. A comparative study of fiscal politics that included federal systems with more proportionally structured senates would be most interesting.

24. See, for example, the Samuels and Mainwaring and Stepan chapters in this volume.

25. For some answers to these questions, see the chapter by Snyder and Samuels in this volume.

BIBLIOGRAPHY

Cabrera, Ernesto, and María Victoria Murillo. 1994. The 1993 Argentine Elections. *Electoral Studies* 13 (2): 150–56.

Dirección de Información Parlamentaria, Argentine National Congress. Http://proyectos.senado .gov.ar/images/historico/historico.html.

Fraga, Rosendo. 1995. *Argentina en las Urnas, 1916–1994*. Buenos Aires: Editorial Centro de Estudios Unión para la Nueva Mayoría.

Gibson, Edward L. 1997. The Populist Road to Market Reform: Policy and Electoral Coalitions in Mexico and Argentina. *World Politics* 49 (3): 339–70.

Gibson, Edward L., and Ernesto Calvo. 2000. Federalism and Low-Maintenance Constituencies: Territorial Dimensions of Economic Reform in Argentina. *Studies in Comparative International Development* 35 (3): 32–55.

IBGE. Http://www.ibge.gov.br.

INDEC. 1991. Instituto Nacional de Estadísticas y Censo, Ministerio de Economía y Obras y Servicios Públicos. *Censo Nacional de Población y Vivienda, 1991*. Buenos Aires, Argentina.

———. 1994. Instituto Nacional de Estadísticas y Censo, Ministerio de Economía y Obras y Servicios Públicos. *Censo Nacional Económico, 1994*. Buenos Aires, Argentina.

———. 1995. Instituto Nacional de Estadísticas y Censo, Ministerio de Economía y Obras y Servicios Públicos. *Censo Nacional Económico, 1995*. Buenos Aires, Argentina.

———. 1997. Instituto Nacional de Estadísticas y Censo, Ministerio de Economía y Obras y Servicios Públicos. *Anuario Estadístico, 1997*. Buenos Aires, Argentina.

INEGI. 1995. *Anuario Estadistico de los Estados Unidos Mexicanos*. Mexico City: INEGI.

Instituto Federal Electoral. 1997. *The Mexican Electoral System and the Federal Election*. Mexico: Instituto Federal Electoral.

Inter-American Development Bank. 1994. La Descentralización Fiscal en América Latina, Problemas y Perspectivas: El Caso de Argentina. Washington, D.C.: Inter-American Development Bank.

Marván, Ignacio. 1997. Reflexiones sobre Federalismo y Sistema Político en México. *Política y Gobierno* 4 (1): 149–66.

Ministério da Administração Federal e Reforma do Estado. 1997. *Boletim Estatístico de Pessoal*. July.

Ministerio de Economía y Obras y Servicios Públicos. 1994. *Situación de las Provincias Argentinas: Ccierre de 1994 y Perspectivas para 1995*. Buenos Aires: Ministero de Economía y Obras y Servicios Públicos.

———. 1995. *Argentina en Crecimiento, 1995–1999*. Buenos Aires: Secretaría de Programación Económica. Internet version.

Ministério da Fazenda. Http://www.fazenda.gov.br.

Riker, William H. 1964. *Federalism: Origin, Operation, Significance*. Boston: Little, Brown.

———. 1975. Federalism. In *Handbook of Political Science*, edited by F. Greenstein and N. W. Polsby. Reading, Mass.: Addison-Wesley.

———. 1987. *The Development of American Federalism*. Boston: Kluwer.

Samuels, David. 2002. Progressive Ambition, Federalism, and Pork-Barreling in Brazil. In *Legislative Politics in Latin America*, edited by S. Morgenstern and B. Nacif. Cambridge: Cambridge University Press.

Samuels, David, and Richard Snyder. 2001. The Value of a Vote: Malapportionment in Comparative Perspective. *British Journal of Political Science* 31 (4): 651–71.

Sawers, Larry. 1996. *The Other Argentina: The Interior and National Development*. Boulder: Westview Press.

Stepan, Alfred. 2001. Toward a New Comparative Politics of Federalism, (Multi) Nationalism, and Democracy: Beyond Rikerian Federalism. In *Arguing Comparative Politics*. Oxford: Oxford University Press.

World Bank. 1993. *Argentina: From Insolvency to Growth*. A World Bank Country Study. Washington, D.C.: World Bank.

———. 1996. *Argentina: Cordoba-Public Sector Assessment and Proposals for Reform*. Latin America and Caribbean Regional Office. Washington, D.C.: World Bank.

CHAPTER 6

Federalism and Institutional Change in Venezuela

—MICHAEL PENFOLD-BECERRA

In spite of its label as a federal system, until recently Venezuela's political system retained many unitary features. When the Venezuelan legislature approved the direct
election of regional governors and local mayors in 1989, however, it activated a federal system that had been dormant for over a century. As a result of this political reform, new actors in regional and local politics emerged, and they modified the
boundaries of the central government's field of action. Moreover, political decentralization transformed the existing party system and led to the eventual collapse of
the two dominant parties, the Acción Democrática (AD) and the Comité de Organización Política Electoral Independiente (COPEI). In other words, the activation of
federalist institutions contributed to a fundamental restructuring of the political institutions that characterized Venezuela's forty-one-year-old democratic regime.

The reforms enacted in 1989 help to explain the nature of institutional change in
Venezuela during the last decade.[1] The purpose of this chapter is to demonstrate the

causal links between the activation of a federal system and the transformation of Venezuelan politics and to elucidate how the Venezuelan case sheds light on federalism's effect on the evolution of party systems. Several authors writing on federalism have stated that a federal system can have a decentralizing effect on political parties by modifying incentives, levels of fragmentation, and party discipline (Geddes and Benton 1997; Riker 1964; Stepan 2001). Given Venezuela's lengthy history as a democracy characterized by highly centralized and disciplined political parties, it is an especially good case for tracing the effect of federalism on party systems.[2]

I argue that the activation of federal institutions played an integral role in the demise of Venezuela's long-standing party system. When elections were held in more than twenty states and three hundred municipalities, the highly centralized structure that characterized AD and COPEI became inadequate, and party leaders lost control of the political careers of their cadre. The initiation of the direct election of governors and mayors in 1989 increased the competitiveness of elections and modified the strategies of political actors as they built their careers. In addition, the possibility of reelection led governors and mayors to establish their support base at the municipal level and to build on this base of support to vie for positions at the state and the national levels. Since governors and mayors could now be reelected without the support of the national party organization and competed based on their performance, the hold of national party leaders on party members weakened. The process of political decentralization created incentives to personalize the vote and reduced the importance of the party label at the regional and local levels, while rewarding performance and increasing accountability. Consequently, the central leadership of AD and COPEI faced numerous internal conflicts, and prominent members broke away to form alternative parties. In addition, a host of regionally based parties emerged to compete in these new electoral arenas. The activation of federal institutions is therefore a primary cause of the demise of the AD-COPEI duopoly in Venezuelan politics and paved the way for the rise of Hugo Chávez Frías.

While the activation of federal institutions made the rise of Chávez possible, once in power he attempted to recentralize power and to weaken aspects of the federal system. However, he did not succeed in reversing the activation of federal institutions, since the enduring power of federal actors allows them to resist recentralization. Federal institutions continue to shape the incentives faced by political actors at different levels of the political system and will therefore affect the future development of Venezuela's evolving party system.

Federalism and Party Systems

Many political scientists have explored the relationship between federalism and party systems, and one variable examined is the impact of party centralization on the sustainability of federal institutions. According to Riker, for example, the maintenance of the federal bargain depends on the existence of a decentralized party system that allows politicians representing regional and local constituencies to veto any attempt by the central government to change the rules underpinning this political arrangement (Riker 1964). In contrast, federal arrangements embedded within a centralized party system, in which representatives are more accountable to party leaders, can be more easily subverted by politicians at the national level since they do not have vested interests in maintaining the bargain at the regional and local level. Interestingly, Riker also thought that federalism created incentives for centralized political parties to decentralize but failed to explain why this would be the case.

Josep Colomer (1999) has also explored the relationship between the federal bargain and institutional variables such as the existence of nonconcurrent elections, bicameralism, and the number of states. In addition, Colomer mentions the possibility that these same variables affect the party system and the behavior of politicians. Colomer claims, for example, that large federations with nonconcurrent elections tend to foster more decentralized and less cohesive party systems. In a similar vein, Alfred Stepan (2001) has argued that federalism generates a decentralizing pressure on political parties and increases the level of fragmentation. However, Stepan has observed correctly that other institutional factors—ideology, parliamentary systems, proportional electoral systems with closed lists, the absence of primary elections, district magnitude, and campaign funding sources—can offset the decentralizing impulse.[3] Finally, Geddes and Benton (1997) have commented that when federalism reaches a stable equilibrium, with actors accepting the institutional context imposed by it, federalism will start to shape the nature of the party system. Once federalism has been consolidated, provincial parties will begin to protect the states from national political actors attempting to usurp their domain.

The decentralizing impact of a federal constitution on the party system is mediated by a number of institutional variables. First, the electoral rules used to elect national legislators can hinder the ability of national party leaders to control party nominations, which encourages legislators to personalize the vote and become more accountable to regional and local interests. In these cases, the party system will be able to internalize federalist considerations into the decision-making process at the national level. Second, the separation of national elections from regional and local elections and the possibility of reelection fosters a higher level of political autonomy for governors and mayors, as these public officials are not elected on the basis of coattail effects from the presidential race. Instead, election and reelection are based on government performance and on their ability to control political resources. These dynamics create pressures for party decentralization. Third, the size of the federal system influences the level of electoral competition and the number of spaces in which political parties can participate. The larger the size of a federal country, the more costly it will be to have a centralized party organization, and the more difficult it will be for these types of organizations to adapt to changing political realities in different states. Large federations create incentives to form decentralized political parties in order to compete more effectively at the regional and local levels. Fourth, higher levels of fiscal autonomy provide governors and mayors with economic resources to act independently from national political actors. In contrast, federal arrangements in which states and municipalities are more dependent on intergovernmental fiscal transfers controlled by the central government face harder constraints. Therefore, federal systems that promote fiscal decentralization provide politicians with more fiscal autonomy to build an independent party base, creating more favorable conditions for the consolidation of a less centralized party system.

As will be described below, in Venezuela the election of governors and mayors had a decentralizing impact on the party system, but other institutional factors heightened this effect. The Venezuelan case shows how the introduction of nonconcurrent elections and the reelection rules for subnational actors, particularly governors, set in motion a series of changes in the power relationships of the party system. The activation of this particular federalist institutional feature amplified the decentralizing pressures within the traditional centralist political parties. The empowerment of regional and local political actors unleashed conflicts within the parties and helped to accelerate the decline of AD and COPEI, which faced strong public demands to reform internally and to deepen democratization. The increase in the number of electoral arenas in which these two parties competed also augmented these decentralizing pressures. The emergence of elected officials who became increasingly accountable to their regional and local constituencies for reelection in turn created more favorable conditions for increasing the fiscal autonomy of the states, despite the fact that most legislators were still more accountable to national party leaders. In short, in Venezuela the strengthening of certain federalist features, in particular the incentives created by the electoral system for governors and mayors, is an important factor in explaining the transformation and eventual collapse of the party system.

The relationship between party systems and federalist institutions is one of the key theoretical issues in the study of federalism, and the recent changes in Venezuela demonstrate how federalism shapes party systems. The Venezuelan case confirms Colomer's and Stepan's arguments that institutional features can mitigate or exacerbate the decentralizing impulse of federalism on the party system. I argue that the increased electoral competition and opportunities at the subnational level, the reelection of governors and mayors, changes in rules for electing national legislators, and deepening fiscal federalism played an important role in the process of institutional change and the unintended collapse of the party system in Venezuela.

The Emergence of a Federal System

During the twentieth century federalism in Venezuela was a legal formality. Under both authoritarian and democratic governments, the president appointed governors.[4] In fact, throughout the twentieth century intellectuals perceived that limiting the power of the *caudillos* at the state level was a positive step toward the consolidation of the state.[5] In order to avoid the caudillo era that had characterized Venezuela's politics during the nineteenth century, the Venezuelan political elite believed that federalism needed to be repressed until the necessary conditions for its proper functioning developed. Some also argued that a strong central government contributed to the political stability needed for economic development (Vallenilla-Lanz 1990). In addition, the emergence of strongly disciplined and centralized political parties since the 1930s contributed to the postponement of the actualization of federalism.

In 1958 the three principal parties (AD, COPEI, and URD) signed a political pact known as the *Pacto de Punto Fijo* to guarantee the consolidation of Venezuela's democracy.[6] In the negotiations for the pact, the political elite did not consider strengthening federal institutions. The political parties involved in the pact did not believe that the necessary conditions for the political reestablishment of federalism existed, and they stipulated that democracy at the national level should be consolidated first (Mascareño 2000). Accordingly, although the 1961 constitution created a federal system, it also gave the president the prerogative to appoint state governors personally. Nevertheless, the same document established the transitory nature of this decision by stating that "[t]he law can establish the direct election and removal of governors stipulated in Article 3 of this Constitution. Both chambers must accept the bill by a two-thirds majority. The law is not subject to the President's veto. Meanwhile, governors will be freely named and removed by the President."[7] During the years 1945–48 and 1958–89, the leaders of Venezuela's democracy did not question the validity of limiting federal institutions. Until the legislative approval of the 1989 law that established the direct election of governors and mayors every three years, the president appointed state governors without congressional approval. The 1989 law also created the mayoral position, which was not mentioned in either constitution.

The changes to the electoral system in 1989 activated the federal framework within the 1961 constitution. However, the 1961 constitution limited the incorporation of federalist priorities in the democratic decision-making process. The Senate guaranteed equal territorial representation to the states, but parties received additional seats proportionate to the party's share of the vote at the national level.[8] In addition, the 1961 constitution did not grant the Senate, the territorial chamber, exclusivity over legislative matters that affected the states. On the contrary, the most important Senate functions concerned national affairs such as the nomination or approval of public officials.[9] The Senate acquired the exclusive right to approve individual contractual agreements between the national government and the states for the administrative transfer of concurrent social services such as education and health care only in 1989, and this was accomplished without a constitutional reform.[10]

The constitution did not assign important fiscal and administrative responsibilities to the states. The states' fiscal responsibilities, for both income and expenditures, were residual. Only those fiscal matters not assigned to the central government or to the municipal governments were left to the states. As a result, the states had little capacity to produce revenue, and their administrative responsibilities were equally limited. Nonetheless, the 1961 constitution assigned the states fiscal resources by an automatic budget allocation equivalent to at least 15 percent of the nation's ordinary income. The constitution established the following distributive formula: 30 percent was assigned equally to all states, and 70 percent was allocated proportionally according to population. Fifty percent of these resources had to be transferred from the states to the municipalities, and the same formula applied.[11] The states' inability to produce additional income through taxation made them further dependent on intergovernmental fiscal transfers, which reinforced the centralist features of the party system.

If we also take into account the incentives created by the party system, as suggested by Stepan, we can explain some of the constraints facing political agents attempting to activate and deepen federalist arrangements. Traditionally, political parties like AD and COPEI had a centralized structure. Since the political system was based on a proportional representation (PR) system with closed lists, party leaders controlled the nomination process for the designation of candidates at every level of government. The parties were characterized by strict internal discipline that did not necessarily reflect local and regional interests. The party machinery responded primarily to the priorities of the national party leaders, and the centralized nomination system allowed them to maintain close control over party members. The party system therefore did not create incentives for party leaders to include federalist considerations in the democratic decision-making process.

In the 1980s public opinion and social movements became increasingly critical of the party system, in particular its rigidity and hegemony over public affairs. Some minority parties, NGOs, and factions with the dominant political parties began to discuss the possibility of electoral reform as a mechanism to improve accountability, and the direct election of governors and mayors emerged as a possible solution.[12] These groups harshly criticized the restriction of citizens' democratic choice to just the election of the president and congress. AD and COPEI party elite had complete control over the nomination process for candidates to both houses of Congress, state assemblies, and municipal councils; they also had the power to nominate and appoint judges. Under this regime the multitiered political organizations at the national, state, and municipal levels responded to the disciplinary directives of the national party leaders.

As the critical pressure for reform mounted, the AD candidate for the presidency in the 1983 elections, Jaime Lusinchi, endorsed a campaign platform that called for an open dialogue between political parties and civil society in order to create a new agenda for political and social reform (Navarro 1993). Once in office, Lusinchi created by decree the Presidential Commission for State Reform (COPRE). Seventeen members represented the political parties (AD: 9, COPEI: 5, Movimiento Al Socialismo (MAS): 1, URD: 1, and MEP: 1), and eighteen members were nonpartisan intellectuals. COPRE consulted with social, political, and economic groups, and these discussions became the basis for the formulation of specific political reforms. COPRE recommended reforms in several political and administrative areas, most notably the direct election of governors and mayors, reform of the closed-list proportional system, and administrative decentralization (COPRE 1986). These reforms, particularly the changes in the electoral system, would diminish the ability of the party barons to control the nomination process. COPRE claimed that abandoning the system of closed lists for electing legislators and the introduction of direct elections for regional and local public officials would help to increase accountability and promote the democratization of the political parties.

The proposals met with a negative response from AD's central committee, the Comité Ejecutivo Nacional (CEN). The party leaders considered COPRE's recommendation to be too radical and against party interests. The AD secretary general, Manuel Peñalver, commented, "COPRE's reforms are too modern for Venezuela, as we are not Swiss" (El Nacional, 27 January 1987). Gonzalo Barrios, AD's president, publicly rejected the reform proposals, in particular the direct election of governors and mayors, with the words, "This country is not historically prepared for these reforms" (El Universal, 26 June 1986). AD controlled both houses of Congress, and the legislators decided to postpone the discussion until the country could reach a consensus about the viability of the reforms. President Lusinchi aligned himself with the party and opted to downplay the importance of COPRE's recommendations.

The issue of reform, however, would not go away. During the 1988 presidential campaign, the AD and COPEI candidates, Carlos Andrés Pérez and Eduardo Fernández, promised to support political reform. Fernández proposed that a reform package to improve the electoral system and strengthen local governments should be approved in Congress regardless of the electoral results. Pérez suggested that the reform be passed immediately through a political pact.[13] As COPRE had recommended, reform needed to address the democratization of the political parties, the reform of the electoral system, and the direct election of governors and mayors.

Pérez based his support for these reforms on his need to weaken the power base of the AD party elite, CEN. With the support of grassroots leaders such as Claudio Fermín, Antonio Ledezma, and Hector Alonso López, he was elected through an electoral convention rather than the national party leaders.[14] Federalism would increase the power of these new local leaders by providing them with spaces to compete as well as access to public offices. Federalism, then, would also undermine the power of the CEN (Penfold 1999a). Factional politics plagued COPEI during the presidential race as well. For example, Eduardo Fernández fought for control over the party machinery against established party leaders like Rafael Caldera, Hilarión Cardozo, and Luis Herrera Campins. The electoral reform that aimed to activate

Venezuela's federalism therefore became an object of political struggle. Political leaders within the parties sought to activate federalist institutions to their own political advantage in order to create an electoral base that could weaken the power of the party barons that obstructed their political careers.

COPRE immediately took advantage of this political opportunity and acted as the intermediary for the political parties (AD, COPEI, MAS, URD, and MEP) in order to reach an agreement on the content of the political pact proposed by Pérez. Once AD agreed to join the pact, the CEN also supported these reforms in Congress, as public opinion favored the AD candidate's commitment to reform (Penfold 1999a). In June 1988 Congress approved three important bills: the creation of the mayoral position, which was to be elected directly at the municipal level; the reform of the electoral system from proportional with closed lists to a mixed system; and the strengthening of the fiscal responsibilities of municipal governments. Although Pérez's political move forced the CEN to abandon its traditional opposition to political reform, the AD used its majority in Congress to minimize the political effects of the reforms. The AD blocked the direct election of governors and secured the postponement of the implementation of the new electoral system until the 1994 congressional elections.

Social pressure, however, derailed AD's plans. In February 1989 one month after Pérez's inauguration as president, massive urban riots led AD to change course to support the direct election of governors and the transfer of administrative and fiscal responsibilities to the states (Penfold 1999a). The social upheaval lifted the mask of "democratic stability" and provided the impetus for wholesale reforms of the existing political order. Although in public politicians blamed Pérez's neoliberal program as the cause of the riots, in private they recognized that the majority of citizens had lost touch with existing political institutions. Party barons within AD and COPEI abandoned their reluctance to act and approved the direct gubernatorial elections in 1989. This reform brought about dramatic changes in the incentives that politicians faced at the national level and contributed to the transformation of Venezuela's party system and its eventual unintended collapse.

The Transformation of the Party System 1989–1998

In its statements COPRE perceived federalism as an efficacious means to increase political accountability and to yield a more efficient distribution of public expenditure. The congressional approval of COPRE's reforms promised to bring citizens closer to their regional and municipal leaders and to allocate public goods and services in line with the preferences of citizens. These reforms, however, were also driven by more explicitly political agendas, as they empowered political agents at the regional and local levels, allowing them to confront political actors at the national level. According to a member of COPRE, "The movement toward the decentralization of the state brings with it a necessary decrease in the discretionary power of the party leaders. As centralization lessened the discretionary power of the national party directorates would also diminish" (Edgar Paredes Pisani, COPRE's executive secretary, as quoted in Arenas and Mascareño 1996, 16–17). Most of COPRE's members believed that internal party reform aimed at deepening democratization within the parties was impossible and would therefore have to be achieved indirectly by way of political and fiscal decentralization, which in turn would strengthen federalism. The activation of federal institutions in Venezuela affected the party system in two important ways. First, it increased competition and electoral opportunities at the subnational level, and second, the reelection and nonconcurrent scheduling of national and subnational elections changed the political career paths for politicians.

Increasing Competition and Electoral Opportunities at the Subnational Level

Increased subnational competition threatened the traditional political parties and required them to make important organizational changes in order to adapt to the federal political system. Previously, the competitive electoral opportunities were few: the presidential and congressional elections were concurrent, and the contest for seats in the municipal councils was held immediately afterwards. Moreover, the electoral system with closed lists allowed party leaders to tightly control these electoral processes.

After 1989, the political parties had to compete in three different contests, each with its own logic—the municipal, state, and national elections. Political parties such as AD and COPEI, whose internal organizational structures were hierarchical and inflexible, had to adapt to a more competitive electoral process in the municipalities and states. In order to compete more effectively in these contests, the parties needed to loosen central control, in particular with regard to nominating procedures. Theoretically, an increase in the number of regional and local elections would generate pressure on the parties to adapt to these changes by creating a more decentralized organization and provoke their eventual internal transformation.

Federalism also led to a lowering of the entry barriers to the democratic system. Political parties that lost in the national elections now had the option of competing for public posts in the states and municipalities. Those organizations that found national level elections to be very costly could modify their strategies and concentrate at the subnational levels. The activation of federalism, therefore, opened a window of opportunity for new actors to enter the political scene.

The effects of these changes became evident, particularly after 1992. In 1989 the traditional parties, especially AD, dominated the electoral market in the states and municipalities, but during the nineties their supremacy waned. At the state level, AD went from 55 percent (11) of the governorships in 1989 to only 35 percent (8) in 1998 (see Table 6.1). COPEI's decline was even more dramatic, from 35 percent (7) of the governorships in 1989 to only 22 percent (5) in 1998. AD and COPEI both experienced an important decrease in the number of electoral spaces that they were able to control at the state level, which opened opportunities to other political parties such as MAS, La Causa R, Proyecto Venezuela, and later the Movimiento Bolivariano Revolucionario (MBR-200). This decrease was not only an effect of federalism but also the consequence of a multifaceted process during which both parties were losing power at the national level.[15] Nevertheless, the activation of the federalist features of Venezuela's democracy created a new institutional context in which control of the regional governments became much more difficult for parties like AD and COPEI.

The increase in gubernatorial electoral opportunities permitted such emerging parties as Causa R, Proyecto Venezuela, and MBR-200 to take advantage of these contests and become important players on the Venezuelan political scene, while established small parties like MAS increased their presence at the regional and local

Table 6.1
Share of Governorships by Political Party in Venezuela

	1989	1992	1995	1998
AD	55% (11)	36.4% (8)	54.5% (12)	34.7% (8)
COPEI	35 (7)	31.8 (7)	13.6 (3)	21.7 (5)
MAS	5 (1)	27.3 (6)	18.4 (4)	13 (3)
LCR	5 (1)	4.5 (1)	4.5 (1)	—
Proyecto Venezuela	—	—	4.5 (1)	4.3 (1)
Convergencia	—	—	4.5 (1)	4.3 (1)
MBR-200	—	—	—	17.7 (4)
MERI	—	—	—	4.3 (1)

levels. MAS expanded its share of governorships by forming alliances with many other political parties, from 5 percent (1) in 1989 to 13 percent (3) in 1998 (see Table 6.1). During this period, many political parties built their power bases in the regions. For example, Causa R became a Bolívar-based party with a strong foundation in the union movement. Following the electoral triumphs in the statewide contests, the party sought to conquer other offices throughout the country. Andrés Velásquez, Bolívar state's governor from Causa R from 1989 to 1993, competed in the presidential elections of 1993 and received a significant number of votes based on his successful administration in Bolívar.[16] In Carabobo state, Governor Henrique Salas Romer broke with COPEI during the 1992 regional elections and created a state-based party, the Proyecto Carabobo, which won the 1992 and 1998 gubernatorial elections. In 1998 Salas Romer changed the party name to the Proyecto Venezuela and ran for president, placing second and receiving 43 percent of the presidential vote, 16 percent of the seats in the Chamber of Deputies, and 6 percent of the Senate. Hugo Chávez Frías's party, MBR-200, later renamed the Movimiento V República (MVR), also demonstrated its strength at the regional level before competing in presidential elections. In 1998, supported by the popularity of their presidential candidate, the MBR-200 won 17.7 percent (4) of the governorships.

The invigoration of federalism also altered the alliance strategies pursued by political parties. The traditional parties, AD and COPEI, and even MAS turned increasingly to the creation of alliance-bloc systems as a tactic to protect their regional leaderships. In 1989 AD established alliances with an average of 2.18 parties per state for the gubernatorial elections, but in 1998 they allied on average with 7.5 parties per state (see Table 6.2). COPEI and MAS benefited more from alliances than AD. COPEI had established alliances with an average of 5.57 parties in 1989 and nine in 1998. The electoral premium—the percentage of votes contributed by other parties supporting the gubernatorial candidate that COPEI obtained from these alliances— averaged 7.07 in 1989 but rose to 20.6 points in 1998. COPEI therefore became more reliant than AD on the formation of these alliances to ensure an electoral victory at the state level. MAS was the most dependent on the formation of bloc systems, going from six political parties in 1989 to nine in 1998. MAS's electoral premium rose from 1.72 points in 1989 to 32.69 in 1998. MBR-200, Chávez's political movement, also used alliances in the 1998 regional elections, which allowed the organization to win in four states, an impressive accomplishment considering that this was its first time competing in regional elections.[17] On average, alliances provided the MBR-200 with 18.27 points.

Table 6.2

Average Number of Parties in Alliance for Gubernatorial Elections

	1989		1992		1995		1998	
	No. of Parties in Alliance	Electoral Premium Alliance	No. of Parties in Alliance	Electoral Premium Alliance	No. of Parties in Alliance	Electoral Premium Alliance	No. of Parties in Alliance	Electoral Premium Alliance
AD	2.18	0.67	7.125	2.5	5.41	4.43	7.5	6.76
COPEI	5.57	7.07	14.42	7.83	10.33	6.93	9	20.6
MAS	6	1.72	7.83	11.08	9	21.83	9	32.69
LCR	1	—	1	—	2	2.84	—	—
Proyecto Venezuela	—	—	—	—	5	—	3	15.64
Convergencia	—	—	—	—	7	7.79	9	4.65
MVR	—	—	—	—	—	—	8	18.27
MERI	—	—	—	—	—	—	9	36.61

Finally, many incumbent governors formed coalitions to ensure their reelection without the support of the national party. These governors expanded and changed the alliance bloc in order to maximize the probability of victory.[18] Their behavior during this period is another indication of the increasing independence of regional leaders from the national party.

The Reelection of Governors and Mayors

The reelection of mayors and governors in contests held nonconcurrently with national elections also affected the party system. Both governors and mayors could now run for reelection for an additional three-year term in office, creating incentives to disassociate themselves from the national party leaders and capture the subnational party organization and its followers. These dynamics increased the bargaining power of governors and mayors vis-à-vis the national party's leaders. Since reelection depended on the performance of the municipality or state government and the control of existing local party machinery, the continuation of political careers no longer depended exclusively upon the support of national politicians. During the 1992 regional elections, eighteen incumbent governors vied for reelection, and eight were reelected (45 percent). In 1995 three governors were up for reelection, and two of them gained reelection. In 1998 twenty-one governors ran for reelection, and seventeen were successful (see Table 6.3). These events demonstrate a consoli-

Table 6.3

Reelection of Governors, 1989–1998

Political Affiliation (party that provided largest share of votes)	1989 Total	1992				1995			1998		
		Incumbents	Reelected	Total before Repetition	Total after Repetition	Incum-bents	Reelected	Total	Incum-bents	Reelected	Total
AD	11	9	6	7	8	1[b]	1	12	11	7	8
COPEI	7	6	6[a]	11	8	2[c]	1	3	4[d]	4	5
MAS	1	1	1	3	5			4	3	3	3
LCR	1	1	1	1	1			1			
Convergencia								1	1	1	1
Proyecto Carabobo / Vzla								1	1	1	1
MBR-200											4
MERI									1[e]	1	1
Total	20	17	14	22	22	3	2	22	21	17	23

[a]Ovidio González, who was reelected as governor of Anzoátegui in 1992 (COPEI), did not finish his second term in office. In 1994 new elections were conducted and won by Dennis Balza Ron (AD).

[b]In 1995 Dennis Balza Ron, who had been elected as governor of Anzoátegui in 1994, was reelected with the support of AD.

[c]In 1995 Lolita Aniyar, who won the election in Zulia in 1993 (after Oswaldo Alvárez Paz resigned to become COPEI's presidential candidate), was not reelected.

[d]This count includes Francisco Arias Cárdenas, who had received COPEI support for reelection in the state of Zulia. For this election COPEI provided a larger share of the vote than La Causa R.

[e]Emery Mata Millán has been elected three times as the governor of Delta Amacuro. COPEI provided the largest share of the vote for his first victory, but he could nor finish his term. In 1992 AD supported his candidacy and provided more votes than COPEI. Finally, in 1995 Mata Millán created his own political party, called MERI, which provided the largest share of the vote.

Source: Author's calculations based on information from Venezuela's National Electoral Council (CNE).

dation of federalism throughout Venezuela, as communities rewarded governors for their performance.

The possibility of reelection at the local and regional levels also changed political career paths in Venezuela. Prior to these reforms, politicians usually built their political careers within the structure of the party machinery where they were rewarded (or punished) with access to places on the closed lists of congressional or municipal candidates nominated by the party bosses. As the process of political decentralization advanced, a growing number of politicians sought to build their careers starting from the positions won in municipal and state elections and progressing to the national level. Now the path was reversed, and political careers could start from the subnational level, rising to the national level. In fact, successful politicians needed to demonstrate administrative and political success as mayor or governor in order to grow within the party and gain public attention. Governorships and the mayoralty of such important metropolitan centers as Caracas were now considered to be a springboard to the presidency. The separation of regional and local contests from the national elections exacerbated this tendency and increased internal tensions within political parties with centralized structures, as it strengthened local actors' independence from national political actors.[19] For the first time in Venezuelan history, these dynamics produced strong incentives to personalize the vote at the subnational level.

The changing political incentives associated with the strengthening of Venezuela's federal system thus increased the conflicts within the traditional political parties. Conflict and competition arose between old guard national party leaders and the regional and local leaders positioned to take control of the subnational tiers of the party organization. In the case of COPEI, national leaders were willing to support new regional leaders as presidential candidates—Oswaldo Alvarez Paz in 1994 and Irene Saez in 1998[20]—but they expected to maintain full control of nominations of candidates to Congress as well as the party machinery in exchange. As a result, the organization's electoral structure collapsed, and over time COPEI became an empty shell. Increasingly, party members created alternative regionally based organizations. For example, Henrique Salas Romer, the governor of Carabobo (Venezuela's richest state), favored his own political party, as did Enrique Mendoza, the governor of Miranda. Caldera, a founding member of COPEI, even decided to found a new political movement, Convergencia, and later won the presidency with a platform of opposition against the traditional parties and Pérez's neoliberal economic program. The lack of control of Caldera, a former party baron, over an increasingly decentralized political party, drove him to abandon COPEI, since he could no longer construct a political base to win the presidential candidacy within the party.

The national AD party leaders reacted similarly. Although they supported the former mayor of Caracas, Claudio Fermín, as the party's presidential candidate in 1994, the party leaders denied him control over nominations for candidates to Congress and attempted to maintain their hegemony over the party machinery. In 1998 national party officials, on the defensive, refused to support any of the subnational leaders, most notably Claudio Fermín or Antonio Ledezma. AD nominated the party's eighty-year-old power broker, Secretary General Alfaro Ucero, as their presidential candidate. Before the decision was even taken, Claudio Fermín left AD and founded a political organization named Renovación to support his campaign for the presidency. In response to the Alfaro Ucero candidacy, several AD governors also withdrew their support of his candidacy as the threat of Chávez's victory became apparent. The AD governors threw their support to the eventual runner-up in the presidential race, Henrique Salas Romer of Proyecto Venezuela.

The increasing federalization of Venezuela's democracy took place within a party system that still responded to past incentives created by centralized and hierarchical political parties. Consequently, factional politics now stemming from the disputes between regional and national politicians became more acute. Regional politicians started to perceive that federalism, in the context of a decaying party system, created strong incentives to split off from parties like AD and COPEI, or at least created strong incentives to seek support through an alliance system beyond their own political party. Politicians also began to perceive that it was possible not only to gain independence and even split off if necessary but also to build regional-based political parties, such as La Causa R, Proyecto Venezuela, and Renovación. In other words, federalism in Venezuela promoted unintended dual dynamics: the formation of new regional parties and split-off parties from AD and COPEI.

Federalism in Venezuela modified legislators' behavior within Congress as well. In the past, party leaders dictated legislative decisions, but now representatives began to specialize and participate in commissions that represented their regional interests. The modification of the electoral system from a PR system with closed lists to a mixed system for the House of Representatives during the 1994 election also increased the personalization of the vote. The representatives from Nueva Esparta, Anzoátegui, and Sucre began to participate actively in the tourism committee, the most important economic activity in these states.[21] Likewise the representatives of the oil states, Zulia and Monagas, were active on the energy committee. Finally, representatives from Apure, Barinas, and Portuguesa took a strong interest in the agriculture committee (Maggi 1998). The weakening of the national party leaders, along with the beginning of a federal logic, created incentives for legislators to specialize in issues associated with their regional interests.

Parties with a strong regional base such as Proyecto Venezuela, Causa R, and MAS participated increasingly in Congress, which accelerated the fragmentation of the party system during the 1990s. Venezuela became an unstable multiparty system instead of an almost perfect biparty system.[22] This fragmentation was the result of both changes in voters' preferences and the new political incentives created by the emergence of a federal system (Molina and Baralt 1996).

Strengthening Fiscal Federalism

Federalism's transformation of the party system also led to the expansion of fiscal federalism. Newly empowered regional actors increasingly took advantage of the changing environment at the national level to push for fiscal decentralization. The 1961 constitution limited the ability of governors to raise their own revenues, making states dependent on the Situado Constitucional, a constitutional proviso that automatically transferred at least 15 percent of ordinary income from the central government to the states and municipalities. In 1989 national politicians agreed to raise this intergovernmental transfer to 20 percent, although the transfer of administrative responsibilities over public services like education and health care was initiated a few years later. Politicians at the national level accepted this reform in order to strengthen the fiscal autonomy of the newly elected governors and mayors. Although municipal governments, unlike those at the state level, could levy taxes, their administrations were equally dependent on the Situado. Since they could not collect taxes, fiscal arrangements embedded in the 1961 constitution inhibited the ability of the governors to act autonomously.[23]

Governors and mayors organized collectively after 1989 to pressure Congress to transform the structure of revenues at the regional and local levels. Once governors and mayors could be reelected, they acquired more autonomy when facing national political actors. After 1989, the National Association of Governors became an important forum for regional politicians to organize and defend the process of decentralization, independently of their political affiliation. In 1993, for example, the association succeeded in obtaining a significant share of the value-added tax. They met every six months and actively presented bills to Congress to reform the electoral system at the national level, increase intergovernmental transfers, and lobby for the decentralization of administrative responsibilities.[24]

In 1993 the central government confronted serious political and economic problems. A failed coup d'etat and the impeachment of President Pérez created political instability, and in early 1993 Ramón J. Velásquez, an independent politician and well-known historian, was appointed interim president by Congress for a nine-month period. Velásquez confronted a dire fiscal situation. Oil prices had declined, and the only responsible way to finance the budget for the following years was to pass a law to introduce a value-added tax. Venezuelans had previously resisted paying taxes, as public expenditure in Venezuela had traditionally been financed by oil revenues and public debt. The population also perceived that VAT revenues would be stolen by the same rent-seeking politicians that Lieutenant Chávez had tried to depose. Governors took advantage of this situation and threatened, through the National Association of Governors, to oppose the value-added tax unless they received at least half of the revenue that it generated (Penfold 2000).

Congress, in order to avoid the political costs of this reform, delegated extraordinary powers to President Velásquez to pass this law via a presidential decree. Velásquez, in turn, needed the political support of the governors to enact the decree, since the voters believed that the governors would spend these resources more responsibly than national politicians.[25] In exchange for their support of the presidential decree, governors were given up to 30 percent of VAT revenues. The presidential decree set the revenue-sharing system for governors and mayors at 10 percent for 1994, gradually increasing to a maximum of 30 percent by 2000 (Fides 1996). As a compromise, these funds were to be administered by an intergovernmental agency called FIDES. States and municipalities could obtain the resources only after the submission and approval of investment projects, which ensured that governors and mayors would spend VAT revenues on public investments such as hospitals, schools, infrastructure, and housing.

After the presidential election of Rafael Caldera (1994–99), governors and mayors continued to pressure Congress to deepen fiscal decentralization. The fragmentation of the party system and the decline of the power of national party leaders increased the ability of governors and mayors to push for these types of legislative reforms. In 1996 the governor of Zulia and Chávez's former 1992 coup mate, Francisco Arias Cárdenas, introduced a bill in Congress to transfer oil royalties to the state, the most important oil-producing region in Venezuela. In Congress a parliamentary fraction composed of Zulia-based politicians from AD and COPEI supported Arias Cárdenas's bill, although the national party leaders of both parties resisted. The Zulia-based fraction proposed to include other oil-producing states such as Monagas and Anzoátegui in the scheme in order to gain more political support, further undermining party discipline on this particular policy dimension. However, the rest of the legislators opposed the bill since it favored only oil-producing states. As a result, those legislators supporting the bill agreed to provide non-oil-producing states with a percentage of oil royalties, which immediately gained the necessary support to approve this new intergovernmental transfer. The law obliged the central government to transfer at least 20 percent of oil royalties to the states starting in 1997, increasing to 30 percent in 2000.[26] Oil-producing regions received 70 percent of the transfer, while the others received 30 percent. Although FIDES administers these funds, the states had more discretion over them than the VAT funds. This reform further increased regional and local politicians' access to fiscal resources, which also enhanced their political and economic independence.

The creation of these two new intergovernmental transfers changed dramatically the structure of revenues for the states. In 1990, 99 percent of state revenues came from the Situado Constitucional (see Table 6.4), but in 1999, states received only about 63 percent from this source. According to Table 6.4, intergovernmental transfers such as FIDES—which represented more than 8 percent of the states' revenues in 1999—caused this decline. Similarly, the Asignaciones Económicas Especiales comprised more than 10 percent of the states' revenues in 1999. However, despite this transformation in the public finances of the regional governments the revenues collected by the states themselves never surpassed 2 percent from 1996 onward (see Table 6.4). The reason, as argued earlier, is that states confronted constitutional restrictions on collecting their own taxes.

Finally, this change in the composition of the states' revenues also reflects the increasing responsibility that governors have in the administration of social services such as education and health care. Between 1989 and 1999 the central government, with the approval of the Senate, initiated the transfer of administrative responsibilities to the states. As of 1998, most of the regional governments had already acquired the responsibility for the administration of the public health care system. In educa-

Table 6.4

Revenue Structure for States (percentage of total state revenue)

Revenue	1990	1991	1992	1993	1994	1995	1996	1997	1998	1999
Situado	98.5	95.2	94.8	92.7	81.6	83.9	71.8	58.5	60.4	63.3
FIDES							4.6	5.8	8.6	8.9
Asignaciones especiales										
Special contributions for the administration of social services	1.1	0.7	1.7	2.6	9.3	12.9	22.2	2.3	10.4	10.7
								31.8	18.8	15.7
Total transfers	99.6	95.9	96.5	95.3	90.9	96.8	98.7	98.5	98.1	98.5
Own revenues	0.4	4.1	3.5	4.7	9.1	3.2	1.3	1.5	1.9	1.5

Sources: OCEPRE, IESA.

tion only certain states such as Aragua, Lara, and Nueva Esparta had decided to take over this service. The central government has transferred the necessary budgetary resources to these governments. According to Table 6.4, since 1995 these budget transfers have represented on average more than 20 percent of the states' revenues.

During the nineties the new dynamic created by federalism in Venezuela not only dramatically changed party politics but also resulted in important fiscal reforms aimed at increasing the availability of resources for mayors and governors. These fiscal reforms were politically motivated and promoted by both governors and mayors responding to their constituencies. These reforms also relied on the support of national legislators who were willing to contradict party barons and back their regional and local counterparts on certain issues. As a result, the deepening of fiscal federalism in Venezuela made it possible for these politicians to gain economic independence from party leaders, create and finance their political networks, and start protecting their own political interests.

Federalism and Constitution Making in Venezuela

Hugo Chávez Frías's election as president was an unintended effect of federalism's weakening of the Venezuelan party system. During the 1990s political organizations such as Proyecto Venezuela, MAS, Convergencia, Causa R, and MBR-200 gained power at the expense of traditional parties, while AD and COPEI leaders faced difficulty in disciplining party members. These emerging political organizations began to rely on the strength, performance, and leadership of their governors all over the country.

By the 1998 presidential election, AD and COPEI were no longer real contenders. Indeed, by then the choice was between two candidates from nontraditional parties: Salas Romer, the governor of Carabobo from Proyecto Venezuela, and Hugo Chávez Frías, backed by MBR-200, MAS, Patria Para Todos (PPT), and Partido Comunista (PCV). In the face of Chávez's overwhelming strength, Salas Romer accepted the support of AD and COPEI.[27] These two parties feared Chávez's threats to replace the political actors of the *puntofijismo* and to create a new institutional arrangement. Chávez promised to abolish all existing political institutions and to elect a National Constituent Assembly to draft a new constitution. According to him, it was imperative to weaken and abolish the entrenched parties that had harmed the existing political institutions. In April 1999 Chávez called for a referendum to ap-

Table 6.5
Composition of the Constituent Assembly

Party	Members	Party Coalition
MVR	53	Polo Patriótico
Chavistas (running on an individual basis)	36	Polo Patriótico
MAS	12	Polo Patriótico
PPT	12	Polo Patriótico
PCV	2	Polo Patriótico
27-N (Military)	2	Polo Patriótico
Opposition	6	
Indigenous Groups	3	
Others	5	
Total	131	

prove the election of a National Constituent Assembly, and three months later a National Constituent Assembly was elected.[28] In the elections, the Polo Patriótico (PP), a coalition of political parties (MVR, MAS, and PPT) supporting the president, obtained 122 seats (93 percent) out of 131 with only 56 percent of the total number of votes (see Table 6.5). The candidates of the opposition, most of them running on an individual basis and without the support of established political parties, obtained only six seats. The remaining three seats were allocated to indigenous groups. It is important to highlight that this electoral outcome was also the unintended result of the plurinominal electoral system used to elect the Constituent Assembly.[29]

Such unbalanced representation resulted in the drafting of a constitution that was insufficiently debated, unnecessarily lengthy, inconsistent, and overly presidentialist. The new constitution gives the president important powers and very few checks. The most prominent features of Venezuela's presidentialism are (1) the ability of the president to call for national referendums to dissolve existing powers and call for another Constituent Assembly, (2) the president's direct control over promotions in the armed forces, (3) the president's broader decree and veto powers over legislative matters, and (4) the extension of the presidential term to six years with reelection. These characteristics may further erode Venezuela's prospects for democratic consolidation. The dissolution of the party system, explained to a certain extent by the activation of federalism and the weak and disorganized presence of opposition forces during the Constituent Assembly, opened the way for Chávez to impose these constitutional powers.

Interestingly, this presidentialist tendency was weakest on policy issues related to federalism. Most representatives from the alliance Polo Patriótico had a federalist bias, since MAS and PPT (formerly the Causa R) had strong roots in states such as Aragua, Bolivar, Lara, Sucre, and Zulia. According to the electoral system, 82 percent of these representatives were elected in state districts and had to prove residency.[30] The debates regarding the institutional design that would regulate the federal arrangement were undoubtedly the most interesting in the National Constituent Assembly. The representatives of the Polo Patriótico were convinced about the need to deepen federalism through the delegation of fiscal authority to the states. Similarly, they agreed to increase the governors' and mayors' tenure from three to four years with a possibility of reelection. Therefore, representatives in the Constituent Assembly, despite Chávez's ambition, managed to approve constitutional reforms aimed at protecting the powers of governors and mayors.

The new constitution also guarantees the states the right to have their own taxes and even allows for the possibility of decentralizing central taxes to the regions. Representatives of the Constituent Assembly included in the constitution an obligation for the National Assembly to approve a law during 2001 in which taxes would be transferred to the states and fiscal federalism would be pursued further. Obviously, this law will confront the president's resistance given his centralist bias, and he will threaten to veto such legislation. The constitution maintains the Situado Constitucional figure provided in the constitution of 1961, yet it establishes that this figure cannot surpass 20 percent of the ordinary revenues.

In addition, the constitution eliminated the bicameral nature of the Venezuelan federal system despite the fact that the president retained this important characteristic in his constitutional project. Surprisingly, the heated debates regarding this subject did not focus on the key role of the senate as an institutional mechanism to protect federalism. Instead, the representatives that voted in favor of the elimination of the senate advanced the idea that the upper house had become a refuge for the traditional political parties, which prevented the adoption of important institutional reforms, in particular further transfers of administrative responsibilities to the states.[31] To guarantee an equal representation within the federal system, each state was given the right to have a minimum of three representatives within the assembly.

The constitution also envisages the creation of a Federal Council of Government, headed by the vice president and composed of all the governors and one mayor for each state. In theory, this new institutional mechanism will coordinate the discussion and activities related to the transfer of administrative functions and the distribution of resources from an Intergovernmental Compensation Fund created by the constitution.[32] If this Federal Council is not properly regulated by law, it could be used by the central government as a means to divide the governors through the political use of resources accumulated in this fund.

Once the constitution was approved in another national referendum, one of Chávez's first moves was to request special powers through an enabling law in order to legislate economic and institutional matters. These special powers were aimed at regulating federal questions such as the Law on Fiscal Federalism, the Intergovernmental Compensation Fund Law, and the Federal Council Law. Although the National Assembly supported the enabling law, it opposed giving the executive power over the resources and revenues to be decentralized to the states. The assembly exclusively delegated to the executive the Federal Council Law, but with a clear guiding principle that prevents the executive from legislating issues related to the Compensation Fund. As of 2001, neither of these laws had been approved. The National Assembly also retained all the features related to the Law on Fiscal Federalism and the creation of the Intergovernmental Compensation Fund. A few months later, the MVR proposed a bill to decentralize taxes such as the gasoline sales tax and to create mechanisms that would promote mutual participation for the income tax. This bill is still being discussed in the national legislature.

It is too early to predict the future of Venezuelan federalism, but the incentives established in 1989 remain and still condition the new legislators' behavior. Features such as the increasing fiscal independence of the states, the extension of governors' and mayors' electoral period from three to four years with reelection, and the division of the presidential and the National Assembly elections might sooner or later help counterbalance the presidential power and induce unpredicted changes in the Venezuelan weak party structure. Federalism was one of the main causes of the collapse of the *puntofijista* system and will remain an important source of future changes in Venezuela's democratic system.

Conclusions

The effect of federalism on the party system in Venezuela largely confirms the intuitions of the literature. As expected, in Venezuela federalism contributed to the fragmentation of the party system and to the personalization of the vote during the

1990s. These changes were achieved mainly through enhanced political competition, the division between regional / local and national elections, the reelection of governors and mayors, and an increase in their financial autonomy vis-à-vis national party leaders.

The Venezuelan case also shows how federalism can unleash key political dynamics between national, regional, and local political actors. Governors and mayors took advantage of the windows of opportunity that the enactment of Venezuela's federalist arrangements provided, in the context of a decaying centralized party system, to enhance their own political power and debilitate traditional party barons. However, federalism also had unintended consequences for the party system. National politicians who first supported the direct election of governors and mayors in 1989 never anticipated that institutional reforms that enhanced competition within and among political parties, increased accountability, and fostered the personalization of the vote would also contribute to the weakness of their political parties. The activation of federalist institutions brought out a number of internal contradictions within these organizations. In addition, political actors outside the traditional political parties took advantage of these changes in the party system to gain access not only to regional and local offices but also to the presidency and the national legislature. In other words, federalism is a fundamental part of the story of explaining and understanding the collapse of the party system in Venezuela over the past decade.

Therefore, it is important to note that the victory of Hugo Chávez Frías in 1998 took place in the context of a party system in which federalism had already changed many of its most important features. Once elected as president, Chávez managed to change the constitution and increase his presidential powers. However, Chávez was not able to reverse federalism. Although the new constitution eliminated the Senate and concentrated power in the hands of the president, it still maintains the direct election of governors in twenty-three states and of mayors in more than three hundred municipalities, separates regional and local elections from the presidential race, and provides the states with the capacity to levy taxes in the future. Therefore, Venezuela's federal system might help counterbalance presidential power, continue to modify legislators' behavior, and even undermine the coalition that keeps Chávez in power. It is still too early to tell the impact of federalism on the eventual shape of Venezuelan democracy, but evidence indicates that federalism will remain a critical source of political change in the country.

NOTES

I would like to thank Javier Corrales, Edward Gibson, Virginia López Glass, Rosa Amelia González, Robert Kaufman, Janet Kelly, Francisco Monaldi Marturet, and Moisés Naím for their helpful comments on earlier versions of this chapter.

1. Very few studies have explored the impact of the activation of Venezuela's federalism on the party system. For studies that stress economic performance and other political variables see Naím (1993), McCoy and Smith (1995), and Penfold (2001).

2. For the traditional description of Venezuela's party system as centralized and extremely hierarchical see Coppedge (1994).

3. According to Alfred Stepan (2001, 46), "There are many countervailing factors, including ideology, that can contribute to such polity-wide unity despite the inherent fragmenting pressures found in all federations. For example, if there are no primary elections, and there is either closed list proportional representation (in which parties rank the candidates), or a single member district in which the polity-wide party selects the party-nominees, if the polity-wide party provides the vast majority of campaign funding for its nominees, and if the system is parliamentary, there will be a strong set of structural and rational choice incentives—despite federalism—to produce disciplined polity-wide parties."

4. For historical background on Venezuela's federal arrangements during the nineteenth century see Gabaldon (1988).

5. Laureano Vallenilla-Lanz (1990) was the first Venezuelan intellectual to articulate this idea in the early twentieth century. Vallenilla-Lanz helped to justify the authoritarian regime of Juan Vicent Gómez (1908–36), which marked the end of the *caudillo* era in Venezuela.

6. For a description and explanation of Venezuela's *Pacto de Punto Fijo* see Levine (1973), Rey (1980), and Karl (1986).

7. 1961 Venezuelan Constitution, Art. 22.

8. 1961 Venezuelan Constitution, Art. 148.

9. 1961 Venezuelan Constitution, Art. 150.

10. I am referring to the Ley de Delimitación y Transferencia de Competencias Administrativas, approved during that same year.

11. 1961 Venezuelan Constitution, Art. 229.

12. For a complete description of these social and political demands see Calcaño and Maya (1990).

13. For a complete account of these events see Penfold (1999a).

14. All of these politicians worked for Carlos Andrés Pérez during his presidential campaign in 1988 and later ran as AD candidates for regional and local positions.

15. For an analysis of the process of electoral dealignment that was taking place at the national level see Molina and Baralt (1996) and Alvarez (1996).

16. Velásquez received 21.95 percent of the presidential vote.

17. It is interesting that after winning the 1998 presidential elections on the promise of eliminating the traditional political parties, Hugo Chávez Frías began to view federalism warily. One of the reasons is that AD seemed to be relatively stronger than MBR-200 at the regional and local level.

Chávez's political party proved him wrong by winning more than 50 percent of the states after the approval of the 1999 constitution.

18. Aldo Cermeño (former COPEI's governor in Falcón), William Dávila (former AD governor in Mérida) and Enrique Mendoza (COPEI's governor in Miranda) are the best examples of regional political leaders that formed alliances with other political parties without necessarily having the approval of national party leaders.

19. The elections for mayors and governors were not heavily influenced by the coattail effect created by presidential candidates. The elections held after the approval of the 1999 constitution and the presidential and gubernatorial elections in 1998, which were not concurrent but were held during the same year, are exceptions.

20. Oswaldo Alvarez Paz was the governor of Zulia between 1989 and 1992 and Irene Saez was the mayor of Chacao (1992–98), the richest municipality of Venezuela, located in Caracas.

21. For an excellent account of the transformation of legislators' behavior within Congress during this period see Maggi (1998).

22. Following the Lasko-Taagepera index, the number of effective parties grew from 2.38 in 1988 to 5.12 in 1993 to 7.34 in 1998. See Penfold (2001, 45).

23. For an excellent analysis of the Situado Constitucional and its fiscal impact see De la Cruz (1994).

24. For a detailed description of the importance of the National Association of Governors as a coordinating device see Penfold (2000).

25. According to a poll conducted by Datanalisis and published in El Nacional (15 June 1993, D-1), 73 percent of the respondents believed that governors were more efficient and responsible than their national counterparts.

26. For an analysis of this law see Barrios (1999).

27. In an attempt to enfeeble the Chávez candidacy, six months prior to the elections legislators from AD and COPEI decided to separate the presidential from the gubernatorial and congressional elections. Legislators believed that if governors and congressmen were elected two months prior to the presidential race, then Chávez's popularity would be affected negatively given the stronger footing of parties like AD at the regional level. In addition, it would allow political parties to avoid the coattail effects of the presidential race, enabling candidates from AD and COPEI to Congress to be elected with the support of their governors.

28. The legal grounds used by Chávez to convene the Constituent Assembly were highly contested. The Supreme Court ruled that the president had the right to call for a national referendum and submit to the people the question of whether they wished the convocation of a national Constituent Assembly with the power to redraft the constitution and revoke the powers of existing public branches.

29. For an analysis of these electoral results and their negative impact on Venezuela's prospects for democratic consolidation see Penfold (1999b). See also the reports written by Penfold as an observer for the Carter Center during the National Constituent Assembly and published in Newman and McCoy (2001).

30. See Penfold (1999b) for an early analysis of the incentives created by the electoral system used for the Constituent Assembly.

31. Part of the reason for this belief is that the electoral system, despite several reforms during the nineties, never reformed the way senators were elected. Most reforms touched the electoral system for electing politicians in the House.

32. The fiscal sources and distribution criteria of this fund will be determined by a law that is still under discussion by the legislature.

BIBLIOGRAPHY

Alvarez, Angel. 1996. La Crisis de Hegemonía de los Partidos Políticos Venezolanos. In *El Sistema Político Venezolano: Crisis y Transformaciones,* edited by A. Alvarez. Caracas: UCV.

Arenas, Nelly, and Carlos Mascareño. 1996. *Descentralización y Partidos Políticos en Venezuela.* Caracas: ILDIS.

Barrios, Armando. 1999. Riesgos Latentes en el Arreglo Institucional para la Descentralización en Venezuela. IESA, Centro de Políticas Públicas.

Calcaño, Luis Gómez, and Margarita Lopez Maya. 1990. *El Tejido de Penelope: La Reforma del Estado en Venezuela.* Caracas: CENDES.

Colomer, Josep. 1999. Las Instituciones del Federalismo. Cuadernos de la Facultad Latinoamericana de Ciencias Sociales, México D.F.

Coppedge, Michael. 1994. *Strong Parties and Lame Ducks: Presidential Partyarchy and Factionalism in Venezuela.* Stanford: Stanford University Press.

COPRE. 1986. *Documentos para la Reforma del Estado.* Caracas: COPRE.

De la Cruz, Rafael. 1994. Finanzas Públicas y Descentralización: La Teoría Inacabada del Federalismo Fiscal. In *Federalismo Fiscal,* edited by A. Barrios and R. De la Cruz. Caracas: Nueva Sociedad.

Fides. 1996. *Fides: Una Experiencia Positiva.* Caracas: Fides.

Gabaldon, Eleonora. 1988. *La Convención de Valencia (La Idea Federal) 1858.* Caracas: Instituto Autónomo Biblioteca Nacional.

Geddes, Barbara, and Allyson Benton. 1997. Federalism and Party System. Paper prepared for the conference "The Transformation of Argentina: Democratic Consolidation, Economic Reforms and Institutional Design," Universidad de San Andrés.

Karl, Terry Lynn. 1986. Petroleum and Political Pacts: The Transition to Democracy in Venezuela. In *Transitions from Authoritarian Rule: Latin America,* edited by G. O'Donnell, P. C. Schmitter, and L. Whitehead. Baltimore: Johns Hopkins University Press.

Levine, Daniel. 1973. *Conflict and Political Change in Venezuela.* Princeton: Princeton University Press.

Maggi, Daniel Paravisini. 1998. Efectos de las Reformas sobre el Parlamento Venezolano: Especialización y Representación de los Intereses Regionales. Paper presented at the Latin American Studies Association meeting, Chicago.

Mascareño, Carlos. 2000. *Balance de la Descentralización en Venezuela: Logros, Limitaciones y Perspectivas.* Caracas: ILDIS.

McCoy, Jennifer, and William C. Smith. 1995. Democratic Disequilibrium in Venezuela. *Journal of Interamerican Studies and World Affairs* 37 (2): 113–80.

Molina, José, and Carmen Pérez Baralt. 1996. Los Procesos Electorales y la Evolución del Sistema de Partidos en Venezuela. In *El Sistema Político Venezolano: Crisis y Transformaciones,* edited by A. Alvarez. Caracas: UCV.

Naím, Moisés. 1993. *Paper Tigers and Minotaurs: The Politics of Venezuela's Economic Reforms.* Washington, D.C.: Carnegie Endowment.

Navarro, Juan Carlos. 1993. En Busca del Pacto Perdido: La Fallida Búsqueda del Consenso en la Venezuela de los 80 y los 90. In *Venezuela la Democracia Bajo Presión,* edited by A. Serbin et al. Caracas: Editorial Nueva Sociedad.

Newman, Laura, and Jennifer McCoy. 2001. *Observando el Cambio Político en Venezuela: La Constitución Bolivariana y las Elecciones 2000.* Atlanta: Series de Reportajes Especiales, Carter Center.

Penfold, Michael. 1999a. Institutional Electoral Incentives and Decentralization Outcomes: Comparing Colombia and Venezuela. Ph.D. dissertation, Columbia University.

———. 1999b. Presidencialismo, Sistema de Partidos y Cambio Electoral: Notas Sobre la Naturaleza de la Transición Política Venezolana. *Debates IESA* 5:25–42.

———. 2000. Federalism and Decentralization: Analyzing State Reform in Venezuela. Paper presented at a conference on decentralization in Latin America, University of Minnesota.

———. 2001. El Colapso del Sistema de Partidos en Venezuela: Explicación de una Muerte Anunciada. In *Venezuela en Transición: Elecciones y Democracia 1998–2000,* edited by J. V. Carrasquero, T. Maingnon, and F. Welsch. Caracas: REDPOL-CDB Publicaciones.

Rey, Juan Carlos. 1980. El Sistema de Partidos Venezolanos. In *Problemas Socio-Políticos de América Latina.* Caracas: Editorial Ateneo.

Riker, William H. 1964. *Federalism: Origin, Operation, Significance.* Boston: Little Brown.

Stepan, Alfred. 2001. Toward a New Comparative Politics of Federalism, (Multi) Nationalism, and Democracy: Beyond Rikerian Federalism. In *Arguing Comparative Politics.* Oxford: Oxford University Press.

Vallenilla-Lanz, Laureano. 1990. *Cesarismo Democrático.* Caracas: Monte Avila Editores.

CHAPTER 7

Unity by the Stick

Regional Conflict and the Origins of Argentine Federalism

—EDWARD L. GIBSON AND TULIA G. FALLETI

The acts of making federal constitutions should display the main feature of bargains generally, which is that all parties are willing to make them.

William Riker (1987)

Haremos la unidad a palos
(We will forge unity by the stick)

Aide to Argentine President Bernardino Rivadavia, 1827

How do rivalries between territorial units of a federation shape the institutional evolution of federalism? More specifically, how do federal countries resolve the problem of a regional hegemon within the federation? Our chapter explores these questions in a case study of the creation and evolution of federalism in Argentina. In addition to providing a new perspective on the origins of federalism in Argentina, we seek to make a number of theoretical contributions to the comparative historical study of federalism.

First, the comparative literature on federalism has tended to focus on conflict between levels of government (i.e., between the national and subnational governments) to explain change in federal systems. In this chapter we provide a theoretical framework that adds an *interprovincial* conflict dimension to the intergovernmental conflict dimension traditionally found in explanations of centralization or decentralization in federal systems.[1] This provides a fuller understanding of the internal power dynamics of federal systems than approaches focusing unidimensionally on intergovernmental conflict. Conflict between regions and conflict between levels of government operate simultaneously in federal systems, and they jointly affect important outcomes in the institutional development of federalism and its degree of centralization. In this chapter we therefore develop a regional conflict perspective to analyze the origins of Argentine federalism and to explain the institutional power relationships that emerged from the nineteenth-century cauldrons of interprovincial strife.

We also develop theoretical insights about the origins and formation of federal regimes. We distinguish between three outcomes of federal system formation that tend to be conflated in the contemporary literature: national unification, the decision to adopt a federal (versus unitary) regime, and the degree of centralization of that federal regime. Each of these represent separate stages in the emergence and evolution of federal systems, and the sequences between these stages (the U.S. "ideal type" notwithstanding) have varied empirically across historical cases. In addition to being sequential, these three outcomes also involve a distinct causal mechanism.

Regarding the Argentine case, our theoretical framework explains how nineteenth-century interregional conflicts simultaneously determined the balance of power between the national and provincial governments as well as the balance of power between the provinces themselves. The struggle over political centralization, we contend, was less a struggle over how a national government would dominate local governments than over how the provinces would dominate one another. Having first experienced subordination to Buenos Aires province, the regional Goliath, in a decentralized federal order we categorize as *hegemonic federalism,* coalitions of weaker provinces fought for a strong and autonomous central government to check the union's most powerful province. While giving peripheral provinces strong representation in national political institutions, they created a federal system that centralized considerable power in the national government. A *centralized plural federalism* emerged in the early 1880s in which a national government, empowered and monitored collectively by the provinces, nevertheless retained considerable discretionary power in its actions toward individual provinces.

Theoretical Considerations and the Argentine Case

William Riker and the Origins of Federalism

A logical theoretical point of departure for a search for the origins of Argentine federalism is William Riker's (1964) classic work on the origins and evolution of federal systems. Drawing his theories from the experience of the late-eighteenth-century North American colonies, Riker saw the international security context as a driving force for the formation of federal systems. In what Alfred Stepan has characterized as a "coming together" theory of federalism, Riker suggests that political entities with actual or presumptive claims to sovereignty agree to come together in a federation to meet a joint security threat or foreign military opportunity that they are unable to meet on their own. The constituent units of the federation willingly trade sovereignty for security and military power in a "federal bargain" (Riker 1964, 11–14).

In describing his "law of federal origins," Riker lists two conditions predisposing leaders to enter a "federal bargain": (1) the "expansion condition" (the opportunity for aggression by the federation) and (2) the "military condition" (the desire for protection from an external military threat). He goes on to write that "these two predispositions are *always* present in the federal bargain and that each one is a necessary condition for the creation of federalism" (Riker 1987, 13–14).

Riker's "universal" theory of federalism draws heavily on the case of the United States, which results in several shortcomings when applied to the study of Argentine federalism. The first shortcoming is that the international threat / opportunity condition does not apply to the nineteenth-century geopolitical context that gave rise to the Argentine federation. As we will discuss below, international wars took place, and security threats existed, but none of these applied consistently to all or even most of the eventual constituent units of the federation at any particular time. Furthermore, none of those events or threats was salient at the two major moments of federation building, the 1831 pact that gave rise to the Confederación Argentina (Argentine Confederation) and the constituent assembly of 1853 that inaugurated the Argentine Federal Republic.

A more significant shortcoming in Riker's theory, however, is the blurring of distinctions between three analytically separate phenomena: the causes of national unification, the adoption of a federal regime, and the subsequent degree of centralization of that federal regime. In Riker's own account of the origins of federalism in the United States these three factors tend to converge. National unity and the adoption of a federal regime are treated as simultaneous and analytically equivalent events (caused also by the same international security variable). The confusion is further compounded when Riker shifts the outcome under study to the *centralization* of the federal system rather than the *origin* of the federal system itself.[2]

Concepts and outcomes are thus conflated in Riker's treatment of federalism, constraining its usefulness as a road map for the study of Argentine federalism. In the following pages we look at the historical origins of that federal system by systematically addressing the three analytical stages mentioned above (causes of national unification, decision to adopt a federal regime, and its degree of centralization). We suggest that each dimension has its own causes. First, the union of separate sovereign or semisovereign provinces was driven by mutual economic needs, but these by themselves did not determine a federal outcome. Second, the choice of a federal regime was determined by the inability of one powerful region to impose its dominion over the others through a unitary project. Federalism emerged only after decades of failed constitutional projects, intermittent secessionist challenges, and continuous military conflict.[3] Finally, the emergence of a "centralized federalism"[4] was similarly the outcome of regional conflicts in which victorious elites from poor provinces sought a strong and autonomous central government that would prevent one province's dominion over the others in the union. A "federal bargain," driven by economic need and global economic opportunities, would indeed be struck between separate governmental units, but its provisions would be enforced by a third party to that bargain: a relatively autonomous federal state working on behalf of the union against encroachments by any single member.

Governmental Centralization and Interprovincial Conflict:
An Analytical Framework

In the regional conflict explanation presented in the following pages the rise of centralized federalism is seen as an outcome of conflict between two sets of provincial actors, "centralizers" and "peripheralizers." While it is difficult to assert ex ante whether a province will prefer centralization or peripheralization, we will venture to say that strong provinces' first preference will be a unitary arrangement. If strong provinces cannot impose a unitary government on the other provinces of the union, they prefer "hegemonic federalism," an arrangement in which a regional hegemon dominates the government of the union (and by extension, the other provinces in that union). Weak provinces, in turn, prefer the institutional arrangements that mitigate that domination.[5] These preferences may change, however, based on the strategic choices faced in the struggle between powerful provinces seeking to dominate the union and weaker provinces seeking to avoid their domination.

At this point a bit of chronology is required in order to make sense of the theoretical discussion that follows. We separate the historical discussion in this paper into five phases. During the first period, 1810–31, the postindependence union was beset by conflicts over the form of regime (unitary or federal) to be adopted. In the second period, 1831–52, a decentralized confederation was established following the victory of federalist "peripheralizers," which very soon succumbed to the hegemonic control of Buenos Aires province. In the third period, 1853–62, a federal constitution was promulgated granting important powers to a central government, but Buenos Aires refused to join. After a series of military conflicts, Buenos Aires eventually prevailed and joined the federation in a position of paramountcy. During the fourth period, 1862–68, a modern state was built under the presidency of Bartolomé Mitre of Buenos Aires, and a centralized federalism emerged under Buenos Aires's domination. In the final period, 1868–80, the interior provinces engaged in successful institutional coalition building that gradually increased their influence in the federation. Buenos Aires rebelled, and the process culminated in the 1880 military defeat of the province and the removal of the last important vestiges of its control over the national government.

In the Argentine case, contending provinces shifted their preferences about centralization across historical periods. During the early struggles over regime type (1810–31), as Buenos Aires pushed forward with its schemes for unitary domination, the weaker "federalist" provinces of the interior were the union's "peripheralizers," raising the banners of subregional autonomy in successful resistance to unitarist centralization. The victory proved to be Pyrrhic, however, as the decentralized confederation that ensued did not protect the weaker provinces from economic and political subordination to the union's regional hegemon, Buenos Aires (1831–52). Having tasted the fruits of this Pyrrhic victory, the interior provinces became the federal union's centralizers. They sought a strong central government with sufficient autonomy to protect them collectively against the union's provincial giant. Buenos Aires, on the other hand, embraced centralization when it could control the central government and advocated peripheralization when faced with the prospect of a central government with autonomous powers.

The regional conflict explanation provided in the following pages therefore argues that the creation of a centralized or peripheralized federal system is an institutional outcome of conflict between the territorial units of the federation (rather than between central and subnational governments). The literature on the origins and evolution of federalism, from Riker to the present, tend to characterize the driving conflict as one between a central government, on the one hand, and the constituent governmental units on the other. The main axis of conflict within a federation is thus conceived as between a national government and the provinces as a whole.[6] Issues

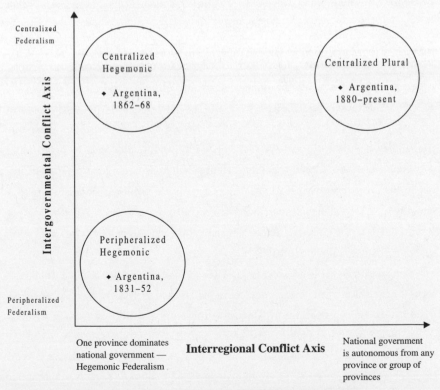

Fig. 7.1. Intergovernmental Conflict, Interprovincial Conflict, and Federalism

Table 7.1
Types of Federalism

	Peripheralized	Centralized
Hegemonic	Argentina 1831–52	Argentina 1862–68
Plural		Argentina 1880–Present

of *interprovincial* conflict and domination have no place in this conceptualization, nor do they have a potentially explanatory role in the origins of particular federal systems. To correct this we add another dimension of conflict to this scheme: conflict between constituent territorial units of the federation. Federal systems are thus measured not only according to the relationship between the national government and the provinces, but also according to their relationship to interprovincial domination.

Thus, to Riker's "centralized federalism–peripheralized federalism" continuum we add another continuum: *hegemonic federalism–plural federalism.* At the "hegemonic" extreme of this continuum one province dominates the national government—that is, the central government exercises little or no independence from a provincial hegemon. At the plural end, the central government is autonomous from any particular province or group of provinces. It acts on behalf of the union as a whole, rather than of any constituent member or group of members. Figure 7.1 attempts to capture the interactions between an axis measuring conflict between levels of government and an axis measuring conflict between provinces. Different moments in the institutional evolution of Argentine federalism are placed in corresponding locations on the two-dimensional space. These distinctions could also be conceptualized dichotomously, as in Table 7.1 where hegemonic or plural federalisms are classified as subtypes of the peripheralized or centralized federalisms. A country could be classified as a centralized federalism and then placed in a subtype indicating whether it is hegemonic or plural.

At this point we see the usefulness of these conceptualizations as heuristic devices for the study of the origins and evolution of federal systems and for providing systematic ways of integrating the intergovernmental and interregional dimensions of conflict. The conceptualizations offer better understandings of "federalism" in both of its key historical dimensions: as a system for managing conflicts between levels of government and as a system for managing conflict between regions.

La Unidad a Palos: National Union and the Creation of a Federal Regime

From the very beginning Buenos Aires was at the heart of controversy between the "provinces" that had once formed the Spanish Vice-Royalty of the River Plate.[7] The juridical political entity that linked them prior to independence was a construct of Spanish colonial administration, which linked vast territories, stretching from Tierra del Fuego to the present-day northern borders of Bolivia and Paraguay, under a viceroy located in Buenos Aires. Between 1810 (the start of the wars of independence) and 1853, this assembly of territorial political units lacked a formal constitution and a permanent national government—but it was not for a lack of trying. Between 1810 and 1831 political leaders organized at least seven national governments and four constitutional assemblies, and they sought to promulgate two constitutions (Chiaramonte 1993). Both were unitary constitutions, and they were immediately rejected by regional *caudillos* distrustful of the hegemonic intentions of their Buenos Aires–based rivals (Rock 1985).[8]

Buenos Aires's dominance over the provinces of the ex–vice-royalty was political, administrative, and economic. As the seat of the Spanish vice-royalty, the city of Buenos Aires developed a political and administrative infrastructure unrivaled by any other province, which made it the "natural" center of government to early aspiring nation builders. Located at the mouth of a giant network of navigable rivers linking the provinces to one another and to global markets, Buenos Aires was able to control the flow of domestic and international trade. Its hold over customs and ports gave it command over trade and customs revenues, as well as the ability to impose tariffs on other provinces. The city's paramount position during the early decades after independence would be compounded by the explosive nineteenth-century agricultural development of the province of Buenos Aires. The development of the *Pampas* plains made the province the domestic pivot of an internationally driven model of development that made Argentina one of the richest countries in the world well into the twentieth century, and further heightened the economic disparities between Buenos Aires and its provincial counterparts.

Freedom from domination by the provincial colossus thus became the rallying cry of "federalist" provinces throughout the former vice-royalty of the River Plate. In the early years of the republic, as the peripheral northern corners of the old vice-royalty seceded and international conflict led to the separation of present-day

Uruguay from the Argentine territory, the remaining constituent units of the vice-royalty of the River Plate battled for domination.

Given the bloody and bitter nature of these conflicts, the provinces' continuing desire to form a union does seem surprising. The vast geographic distances and cultural divides separating them made them unlikely partners in the building of an Argentine "nation."[9] However, the unhappy union, a product of Spanish administrative design, would be held together in the face of repeated secessionist experiments and autonomist insurrections up to the 1880s for economic reasons.

The provinces of the periphery that experimented with autonomy did so at their economic peril. The price paid for secession was not military conquest or absorption by another power but poverty and economic isolation. Almost all outlets to foreign trade passed through Buenos Aires, and the revenues controlled by that province were often vital to local economic well-being. Furthermore, the provinces of the interior, whether the poor provinces of the north or the more prosperous ones adjoining Buenos Aires, had a clear interest in ensuring that the fluvial choke-points of the River Plate remained open to them rather than controlled by a hostile or isolated foreign power. Thus, recalcitrant provinces eventually returned to some kind of national union, and the subject of national unity remained active on the agenda of interprovincial discussions and debates. The provinces desperately needed the economic dynamism Buenos Aires could provide, but they feared with equal desperation the political price of union with the regional hegemon.

From the perspective of Buenos Aires, national union offered the expansion of markets and trade revenues under its control. The economic incentives of union increased dramatically for Buenos Aires during the nineteenth century as the wool and cattle boom on the *Pampas* and international demand for Argentine agricultural products pushed development northward and westward into adjoining provinces in an expanding search for new lands and settlement. Buenos Aires's ability to seize the opportunity offered by the boom in global demand was thus increasingly tied to its political interactions with the provinces of the interior (Burgin 1946; Rock 1985).

These factors provide a more compelling and consistent explanation for the persistence of a national unity project than international military risks or opportunities. International security risks did appear during the four decades between independence and the 1853 federal regime, but they were either too localized or too ephemeral to have sustained the union by themselves. The wars of independence from Spain did provide an important impetus for union, but these resulted in neither a permanent union nor a federal regime. Furthermore, the threat of a Spanish reconquest, along the lines of that provided by Great Britain against the fledgling United States of America, simply did not exist after 1820. By Riker's (1964, 41–42) theory, then, the Argentine federal union should have broken apart once the military need for it had subsided.[10] Nevertheless, in spite of bitter interregional conflicts, the push for union continued, and federalism in its peripheralized variant was established in 1831.

Other military conflicts after independence also fail to explain this trend. In the late 1820s the provinces of the River Plate went to war against Brazil in a conflict that eventually resulted in the creation of Uruguay as an independent buffer state. However, this war did not involve much of the federation. The main combatants were the province of Buenos Aires and to a lesser extent the provinces adjoining Brazil to the north of Buenos Aires. In 1866 Argentina went to war (this time allied with Brazil) against Paraguay in a bloody war that did much to consolidate the Argentine state and its fledgling federal army. However, by this time a federal government had been formally constituted for fifteen years, rendering this particular "foreign military opportunity" unsuitable as an explanation for the origins of Argentine federalism.

This leads us, therefore, to restate our basic rejoinder to Riker's theory. National union and federal regime creation were two distinct processes that had different causes: international economic need and opportunities for the former, and subnational territorial conflict for the latter. Furthermore, in neither case were the international security variables mentioned by Riker the driving forces for either national union or the creation of federalism.

Leviathan or Hegemon? The Creation of Peripheralized Federalism, 1831–1852

A situation of mutual distrust combined with growing mutual need shaped the early decades of the Argentine union. Against a backdrop of permanent interprovincial war and conflict between "unitarists" and "federalists" the hapless political leaders of the "United" Provinces of South America sought to craft political arrangements that would impart institutional order to their union. The eventual proposals that emerged usually reflected momentary balances of power wrought on the battlefield. Buenos Aires, the economic and military colossus, dominated most national governments fashioned during the 1810–31 period and served as the hotbed of unitarist designs for national union. The weaker provinces of the "interior," hotbeds of "federalist" agendas, were unable to impose their constitutional projects of limited government and provincial autonomy from Buenos Aires.[11] Yet their resistance was enough to undermine successive unitarist schemes launched by Buenos Aires. During this period the concept of a strong central government, embodied in the unitarist schemes of the day, was inseparable from the notion of a nation dominated by its richest province. The "federalism" of the times, therefore, represented resistance to both the idea of a central government and the idea of a Buenos Aires–dominated national union.

It was only with the eventual military triumph of "federalist" forces throughout the territory that the fledgling union's first federal arrangement became accepted by all of its constituent units. The key to this development was a successful federalist insurrection in Buenos Aires province itself. Juan Manuel de Rosas, a prominent cattleman and general in the Buenos Aires militia, unfurled the federalist banner against the urban-led unitarist leadership in his province.[12] Forming an alliance with federalist *caudillos* in the interior, he defeated the Buenos Aires government in 1829 and ruled the province with an iron hand until his ouster in 1852. His rise to office shifted the national balance of power in favor of the federalists. Reinforced with the material and political support of the nation's provincial giant, federalist forces in the interior soon subdued the last bastions of unitarist armed resistance. In 1831 a *Pacto Federal* (Federal Pact) was accepted by all Argentine provinces and became the legal basis for the newly named Confederación Argentina (Argentine Confederation).[13] Unitarism was now defeated militarily. Argentina formally became what Riker would consider a "peripheralized" federal system.

The *Pacto Federal* was not a constitution. It was a pact meant to have temporary binding force, pending the drafting of a constitution by a constitutional convention. The confederation bore some resemblance initially to another hemispheric experiment in peripheralized federalism, the short-lived Confederation of the United States of America. However, in design and actual practice this longer-lived experiment would prove even more peripheralized than its northern counterpart. As in the U.S. confederation, the signers of the *Pacto Federal* did not create a national executive or judiciary. Instead, they delegated powers to a national "Representative Commission" of the provinces exclusively to raise armies for the national defense. A constitutional convention scheduled later would decide on more permanent arrangements regarding the division of powers between the central and subnational governments, as well as thornier questions of national tax collection and the sharing of revenues from trade between Buenos Aires and the provinces (Sampay 1975). However, the constitutional convention never convened. Buenos Aires had little interest in weakening its control over trade revenues and formalizing revenue-sharing schemes that would diminish its discretionary control over its confederated allies. Nor did it have much interest in granting legal powers to a national government vis-à-vis the provinces that might mitigate its sway over the federation.

The *Pacto Federal* would thus remain in a state of "provisional permanence" for over two decades as the Argentine federation's legal framework (Chiaramonte 1993, 82). However, it would become a rather empty shell for a loose alliance of provinces that soon succumbed to the de facto control of its provincial hegemon. Within a year of the pact's signing Buenos Aires engineered the dissolution of the confederation's only national organ, the "Representative Commission" of the provinces. Rosas emerged as the dominant political figure of the Argentine confederation, eclipsing the provincial federalist *caudillos* that cofounded the union and crushing sectionalist rebellions within the federation's borders. The government of Buenos Aires assumed control over national military affairs and external relations, and it dominated the union through military force, control of international and interprovincial trade, and the discretionary use of subsidies to resource-starved provincial allies (Rock 1985, 104–13).[14]

The Confederación Argentina put into bold relief that regardless of the regime type adopted, the issue of Buenos Aires's political domination upon the other provinces would not go away. Many had seen the "federal-unitary" distinction as the dividing line between pluralism and hegemony, yet it had proven inadequate for capturing the dilemmas of nineteenth-century regional conflict. The root of the problem was that neither federalist nor unitarist leaders of the early postindependence period had been able to imagine a national government that was not controlled by Buenos Aires. Federalists, therefore, sought the absence of central government. When Rosas turned Buenos Aires into a bastion of federalism, all provinces converged for once on the common institutional device of a peripheralized federalism under the Argentine confederation. However, it would be a common device for different purposes. The *caudillos* of the interior saw it as a way to gain the benefits of union without the domination of Buenos Aires. The supreme *caudillo* of Buenos Aires saw it as a way to maximize his province's own structural advantages vis-à-vis the union unencumbered by institutional counterweights and constraints.

Rosas proved the most prescient of the group. A federal union without a central government was little different than a unitary government controlled by Buenos Aires. The key was not the type of regime but the relationship of central authority to the union's richest province. The bitterly ironic lesson learned by the provinces during the Argentine Confederation was that, after decades of fighting a unitarist Leviathan, they were now at the mercy of a federalist hegemon.

The Development of Centralized Plural Federalism 1853–1880

The Constitution of 1853 and the Struggle against Hegemonic Federalism

A key moment in the evolution of any federal union is when the national government becomes separated from the government of the union's most powerful province. This may occur relatively early in the union's history, or it may take decades of struggle, but it is a vital step in federalism's institutional evolution. It produces a "relatively autonomous" central government that acts on behalf of the collectivity of provinces rather than of any single constituent member or members.[15] "Hegemonic federalism," where the government of the union is dominated by a provincial primus inter pares, gives way to plural federalism, where in its ideal form a national government exercises equal sovereignty over all the constituent governmental units of the federation. This move from one form of federalism to another is an outcome of interprovincial conflict. Where successful, however, it also marks a shift from the axis of intraregional conflict toward the intergovernmental conflict axis. In other words, the conflict between provinces is increasingly displaced by sovereignty conflicts between levels of government.

In Argentina the struggle took nearly seventy years. It culminated spectacularly (once again) in 1880, in the military conquest of Buenos Aires by a federal army. The victorious forces subjugated the government of the province and wrested away its crown jewel, the city of Buenos Aires. The city, with its ports, customs revenues, administrative infrastructure, cultural heritage, and economic wealth, was made a federal district, controlled by the national government and officially declared the patrimony of the Argentine nation. The powerful governor of the province and his staff were forced to set up a new provincial capital in the sleepy River Plate town of La Plata, sixty miles from the new federal district.[16]

The 1880 military denouement, however, marked the endpoint of a struggle that in the previous two decades had become increasingly institutional. Military and economic power had been gradually displaced by the coalition building of the weaker provinces in the newly created federal institutions. The process evolved slowly, starting in 1852 when a military coalition of provinces led by the Entre Ríos *caudillo* Justo José de Urquiza defeated "the Caligula of the River Plate," Governor Juan Manuel de Rosas. The victorious forces held a constitutional convention in the province of Santa Fe and in 1853 promulgated a federal constitution that created both a high degree of provincial representation in national political institutions and a powerful central government.

In spite of deep partisan and regional hostilities, the economic impetus for union was stronger than ever. A boom in international demand for Argentine wool and cattle products was underway and had transformed much of the country's agricultural landscape. The provinces were desperate for a piece of the boom, and they needed Buenos Aires for access to it. Buenos Aires, on the other hand, also needed land and markets in the interior. As Rock (1985, 123) writes, "both the provinces and Buenos Aires—one wanting trade outlets and investment funds, the other seeking new land—had reasons to support peace and cooperation." Nevertheless, the terms of that union continued to be problematic. Intellectuals and political leaders on both sides of the provincial divide were converging on the need for national union and, more importantly, for a central government that could bring order and facilitate the nation's international economic integration.[17] However, these modern state builders could not agree on the government's role in the regulation of interprovincial domination.

The federal constitution of 1853 represented a solution to many in the Argentine political elite. The constitution embodied fundamental changes in Argentine federalist thought wrought by the experience of hegemonic federalism under Governor Rosas's rule. Botana (1993) has characterized the 1853 constitution as a fusion of unitarist and federalist ideals, embodying the unitarist ideal of a powerful presidentialist central government and the federalist principles of provincial autonomy and representation in national political institutions. What this "fusion" also represented was a clear revalorization by federalists of the functional and strategic uses of a central government. Functionally, as mentioned above, the architects of the constitution saw the values of a central state for maintaining order and providing the organizational bases of Argentina's integration into the international economy. Strategically, however, the creation of an autonomous central government would introduce an institutional counterweight to Buenos Aires. The federalist "peripheralizers" of the past were now the "centralizers" of the Argentine federation. The federalist provinces that had once seen a strong central authority as the agent of their domination by the union's giant now embraced it as their deliverer from that domination.

The new constitution established a federal regime, a bicameral legislature, and an independent judiciary. On one hand, the new constitution provided for a high level of provincial representation in national political institutions. A national senate, invested with considerable policy-making influence, would be composed of two senators per province, each elected by provincial legislatures. This arrangement also ensured an important national role to provincial governors, whose control of local legislatures would give them a central role in determining the composition of their province's two-member delegation to the Senate. In addition, the constitution created a president with a six-year term of office without immediate reelection. An electoral college of provincial delegates would elect that president.

The new federal constitution, on the other hand, also introduced a high level of centralization. One of the most important institutional provisions that the interior's new centralizers created was the power of "federal intervention."[18] Copying the United States's constitutional clause by which the federal government can intervene in its member states to guarantee the republican form of government, the Argentine "founding fathers" also granted the federal government such a power in Article 6 of the constitution.[19] However, from the very beginning, the issue of federal interventions raised many questions about when and how they should be used and about the capacities of the federal government vis-à-vis the provinces before and during the interventions. In the constitutional convention of 1853, the preferences of centralizers and peripheralizers were reflected in two competing proposals regarding federal interventions. The provinces of the interior wanted a strong central government and sided with Juan Bautista Alberdi's proposal that, in case of sedition, the federal government could intervene in the provinces without their request in order to reestablish order.[20] The province of Buenos Aires instead preferred a federal government with limited powers and sided with Domingo Faustino Sarmiento's proposal to prohibit the federal government from intervening without the explicit request of the local authorities.

The final text of the 1853 constitution permitted interventions with and without local requests and failed to specify if the national executive needed the approval of congress to declare an intervention. Thus, the constitution of 1853 left the door open for the national executive to use federal interventions according to its discretion and convenience. Indeed, soon after the constitution was promulgated, federal interventions in Argentina became widely used and one of the most important institutional mechanisms to control subnational governments and political actors. Between 1853 and 1860, the center intervened in all provinces but Entre Ríos and San Luis—some of them on two occasions—and all interventions were decided by presidential decree.[21]

The 1853 constitution that would govern the República Argentina was signed by all the governments of the interior provinces that had defeated Juan Manuel de Rosas, but Buenos Aires, suspicious of the interior's designs on its capital city and control over international trade revenues, refused to subscribe to the new constitution. The provinces of the new union thus set up their capital in the city of Paraná, metropolitan center of the province of Entre Ríos, the second power of the Argentine union.[22] For the next six years the relationship between Buenos Aires and the union remained in a legal state of limbo. Much of that time the city of Buenos Aires was under siege by the armed forces of the Republic;[23] the province and the federal government refused to recognize each other's claims to political authority and harassed one another with economic blockades and discriminatory tariffs. The first break in the logjam came with the military defeat of Buenos Aires in the 1859 battle of Cepeda. A reluctant Buenos Aires agreed to the terms of the 1853 constitution (after an 1860 constitutional convention incorporated certain reforms favorable to the province) and pledged large monthly subsidies to the other provinces in the union (Oszlak 1985, 236).[24]

In yet another of the dizzying reversals of fortune that characterized nineteenth-century Argentine regional conflicts, an ever-defiant Buenos Aires turned the tables again on the union less than a year later. The Buenos Aires militia, led by Bartolomé Mitre, defeated the allied provincial militias in the Battle of Pavón in 1861. In 1862 Mitre was unanimously proclaimed president of the newly named República Argentina by an electoral college of delegates from the provinces (Botana 1993, 234). Mitre, who had become governor of Buenos Aires only in 1860, was a zealous defender of Buenos Aires interests. Nevertheless, he was also a prominent local advocate for unity with the Argentine provinces. Along with his counterparts in the intellectual elite that drafted the 1853 constitution, he saw the region's future great-ness as best ensured by a union led by a modern national state. He thus sought unity, but on different terms from those advocated by his contemporaries in the Argentine federation. As Rock (1985) writes, "whereas Urquiza sought to reduce the power of Buenos Aires and impose an equitable sharing of revenues, Mitre's conception of unity endorsed the paramountcy of Buenos Aires."

Mitre's triumphs thus paved the way for a new project of hegemonic federalism led by Buenos Aires, this time under a federal government with considerable pow-ers over the provinces. Exhausted by stalemate, and desperate for an end to the eco-nomic hardships imposed by interregional strife, the other provinces of the federa-tion acquiesced. A military victory had once again set the terms of national union. In the next six years of Mitre's presidency, Buenos Aires's economic powers and a booming global demand for Argentine agricultural products would make those terms palatable to the provinces and consolidate support for the union throughout the territory.[25] However, during this time a less visible but nevertheless important story that would ultimately undermine Mitre's project of hegemonic federalism was being played out in the nation's fledgling institutions.

The 1862–68 presidency of Bartolomé Mitre was an institutional watershed for the country. For the first time in its history, a central government became consoli-dated, governing effectively over all the provinces of the territory. This is not to say that the central government ruled unopposed. During Mitre's six-year presidency there were a total of 107 uprisings in the interior against the central government (Botana 1980), and 117 "unscheduled" local changes of government.[26] Mitre's gov-ernment dealt with these challenges through a variety of means. The economic boom provided ample resources for dispensing subsidies to the provinces and build-ing alliances with *caudillos* whose militias maintained order and crushed antigov-ernment military challenges. Eventually the central government formed a network of provincial allies that helped enforce its authority throughout the territory.

The government also availed itself liberally of the powers of federal intervention granted by the constitution, demonstrating the power of this constitutional device for consolidating centralized presidential authority. As Oszlak (1985, 127–28) has ob-served, with continued use and with practically no constitutional limitations on how or when they could be used, federal interventions became the indispensable tool for Mitre and his immediate successors for imposing central authority over the union.

Since the rebellions and uprisings were usually local, and only occasionally spread to other provinces, the principle of *divide et impera* permitted the government to prevent coalitions from forming and to confront the provinces one on one with a clear asymmetry of power. In this process of continuous learning, the national government was able to develop and fine-tune an invaluable instrument that would wipe out all federalist vestiges that opposed its quest to concentrate and centralize political power.

Between 1860 and 1880, as the system of centralized federalism was crystallizing, four presidents intervened a total of twenty-nine times in the provinces. Only five of those interventions were passed by congressional law. The rest were the result of presidential decrees (Comisión de Estudios Constitucionales 1957, 26–28).

The centralization of power facilitated another institutional accomplishment during Mitre's presidency: the creation of a national state. When Mitre assumed office the three branches of the national government were located together in the national capital for the first time. In addition, Mitre's government created a national legal system, a taxation system, and a national bureaucracy.[27] In its early years the administration created a national treasury and a customs office, followed shortly thereafter by a national judiciary. Midway through his presidency, Mitre also embarked upon the building of a modern national army. By the end of his term the federal army was fifteen thousand men strong, and it would gradually eclipse all provincial militias that challenged the central government's supremacy throughout the territory (Botana 1993, 236).

The imposition of central authority and the construction of a national state were thus major advances in the consolidation of Argentina's federal regime. However, Mitre's was a hegemonic centralized federalism, and it was a one-sided affair. The central government's powers increased vastly over those of the provincial governments of the interior, but not over the union's strongest province. All interventions during Mitre's presidency were directed at the interior provinces. The province of Buenos Aires, in contrast, continued to enjoy considerable autonomy vis-à-vis the central government, as did the province of Entre Ríos, the junior hegemon of the union. As Botana (1980, 109) has written, "Argentina was governed by a political regime whose most significant characteristics can be summarized as follows: two regional powers—Buenos Aires and Entre Ríos—jealously guarding their autonomy and privileges before the national government, and a periphery of provinces that had experienced the effects of federal intervention. The national government thus had two faces, because if on the one hand it suffered from major weaknesses before the strong provinces, on the other hand it had managed to impose its sovereignty on the rest of the provincial constellation."

In the end, hegemonic federalism would be undermined not by provincial military insurrections or civil war but by the fledgling institutions of the federal regime itself. While Mitre consolidated central authority, built the national state, and coordinated the nation's domestic and international economic integration, the institutions of federalism were silently shifting the coalitional landscape against his home province. The constitution of 1853 had invested tremendous powers in the presidency. However, it had also created important national arenas for the representation of provincial interests whose clout was not initially evident in the heady days of Mitre's hegemonic federalism. The Senate, the Electoral College that elected the president, and the informal networks of gubernatorial alliances were forums that privileged numbers and coalitions over sheer power. They were also organs that had the institutional authority to decide presidential succession. During Mitre's tenure they became the crystallizing points of interprovincial coalitions that would defeat the continuity of his hegemonic project and expand the interior provinces' influence over the federal system.

Institutional Conflicts and the Transition to Centralized Plural Federalism

The trick for outflanking Buenos Aires institutionally lay in an electoral college coalition, crafted by senators and governors, between a majority of interior provinces and an anti-Mitre dissident faction in Buenos Aires.[28] The quid pro quo between these regional actors was the vice presidency for the Buenos Aires faction in exchange for support in the electoral college for a president from the interior. The first test of this arrangement came in the succession struggles of 1868. San Juan province's Domingo Faustino Sarmiento (one of the centralizing federalists who had crafted the constitution of 1853) defeated Mitre's handpicked successor in the electoral college. The coalitional formula proved its staying power. Starting with Sarmiento, the interior provinces would win the presidency in four consecutive elections.

By manipulating federal institutions during Mitre's presidency provincial elites won the greatest institutional prize: the presidency of the republic. This institutional conquest provided them with the means to consolidate their project of centralized plural federalism. Between 1868 and the final military explosion of 1880, Argentine presidents moved the federal project ahead on two fronts. The first front was interprovincial relations, where the central government redirected economic resources toward the development of the interior and expanded the interior provinces' influence in national political institutions. Economically, the government invested heavily in infrastructure projects for the interior, established protectionist schemes for key industries, and scaled back the Buenos Aires provincial government's control over customs revenues and international trade (Balán 1978; Oszlak 1985). Politically, the interior's influence was advanced through the consolidation of the coalitions built in the 1860s in national political institutions. New institutional layers were grafted onto the federal system that increased the interior's hold over the political process. The electoral alliance that brought Sarmiento to power evolved into a national political party (of sorts) known as the Partido Autonomista Nacional (PAN). The PAN functioned as a network of alliances between the president, the senate, and an informal yet powerful *liga de gobernadores* (league of governors). The PAN served both as a transmission belt for political decision making between the president and provincial governmental elites, and as a mechanism deciding presidential successions.[29] Regarding the latter, the PAN ensured continued control by the dominant coalition of interior provinces over the presidential selection process. Over the strenuous protests of Buenos Aires (and Entre Ríos in 1874), the electoral coalition engineered the electoral college victories of Nicolás Avellaneda in 1874 and Julio A. Roca in 1880, both from Tucumán Province.

The second front concerned relations between the central government and provincial governments. The now dominant coalition of provincial elites expanded the centralization of the federal system and gradually asserted the supremacy of the central government over provincial governments. Just as Mitre had before them, the presidents from the interior availed themselves liberally of the powers of federal intervention to crush challenges to the national government's sovereignty. They also expanded the federal army's reach throughout the national territory. Not surprisingly, these federal weapons were routinely applied against *díscolos* (malcontents) among the poorer provinces of the largely subordinated interior. However, the ultimate triumphs of centralized federalism came with the subordination of the country's powerful and still defiant provinces. One by one the central government asserted its authority over these provinces. The first triumph came against the province of Entre Ríos, which rebelled against the central government shortly after the electoral college selection of Nicolás Avellaneda in 1874.[30] A federal army defeated and disbanded the Entre Ríos provincial militia, dissolved the provincial government, and put an end to the interior's last bastion of defiance against the central government. Now, as Botana (1980, 109) observed, the last remaining obstacle to the consolidation of federal authority lay in the "undefined relationship between two centers of power: the national government and the province of Buenos Aires."

The opportunity came over yet another dispute over presidential succession. In 1880 the PAN proclaimed Julio A. Roca its presidential candidate, and Roca won the election handily in the electoral college. Buenos Aires rebelled and was defeated by the federal army in a series of bloody confrontations. The decisive military defeat of Buenos Aires's provincial militia put an end to all significant provincial challenges to centralized federalism. The federal government promptly dissolved the Buenos Aires provincial militia and shortly thereafter, in a resounding affirmation of central government supremacy, banned all provincial militias. In an act as important symbolically as it was substantively, the federal government officially "intervened" in the government of the province and dissolved all its branches. It also abolished several economic privileges enjoyed by the province, such as its access to customs revenues and its power to issue currency. Most importantly, however, by federalizing the city of Buenos Aires, it rendered unambiguous the separation between the national government and the province of Buenos Aires. With the final bloodbath of 1880 an institutional framework for interprovincial domination was triumphant throughout the union. Argentina entered the era of centralized plural federalism.

Conclusion

The construction of federalism in Argentina was a blood-soaked and protracted process that bears little resemblance to the theoretical scenario of federalism as a "bargain" between consenting territorial actors in pursuit of common foreign policy goals. We would suggest that the Argentine case is not unique but is representative of broader patterns that can be understood with greater clarity through some of the theoretical contributions made by this chapter.

First, we provide an analytical framework for studying the origins and evolution of federal systems, based on the interactions between two axes of conflict: conflicts between regions or provinces and conflicts between central and subnational governments. "Levels of government" conflicts have predominated in studies of federalism. This has obscured important phenomena relevant to the categorization of federal systems and to our understanding of causal sequences behind the evolution of federal systems. In this chapter we provide the means to measure and understand federalism in both its operational dimensions: as a system for managing conflicts between levels of government and as a system for managing conflicts between regions. Thus, to William Riker's original distinction between "centralized federalism" and "peripheralized federalism," which measures the balance of power between the central and subnational governments of a union, we have added a distinction between "hegemonic federalism" and "plural federalism," which measures the balance of power between the union's constituent territorial units. Federal countries can thus be compared along two dimensions of power, intergovernmental and interregional, providing a richer picture of their internal power dynamics.

By incorporating interprovincial conflict as one of the theoretical axes of conflict in federal systems we are also in a better position to explain not only key sectional outcomes but the degree of institutional centralization in federal systems as well. A perspective that explains centralization (or decentralization) in federal systems exclusively as an outcome of conflicts between actors defined as a "central government" and "the subnational governments" obscures the enormous impact that these outcomes have for the balance of power between the subnational units of a federation. Where sectional conflicts exist, the battles over how much power to grant the central government are essentially battles over interprovincial domination. The outcomes will tell us as much about the balance of power between the territorial units of the federation as they will about the state of relations between levels of government.[31]

This chapter also demonstrated the usefulness of distinguishing between three outcomes that tend to be conflated in theories of federal formation: national unity, the choice of a federal system, and the degree of centralization of the federal regime. The Argentine case, where these developments occurred separately and interactively, may be more representative of other cases than the U.S. case analyzed by Riker, in which federalism and the birth of the American state were nearly simultaneous events.[32] In much of Latin America, the formation of nation-states took place well before the choice of federalism versus unitarism was made. In fact, the region's two other large federal republics, Brazil and Mexico, began their existence as sovereign states as unitary systems, and conflicts between "federalists and unitarists" were endemic to both countries well after their adoption of federal regimes in later years.

The distinctions between these three developmental outcomes thus provide a useful heuristic for organizing the comparative analysis of federal system formation and for permitting a more precise separation of the causes of federalism from those of other key stages in the formation of nation-states. Our study suggests that, contrary to Riker's "law" of federal origins, the adoption of federalism is driven more by internal political dynamics than external military threats or opportunities. The choice of federalism is fundamentally a regime choice, and as such, it is strongly subject to conflict, deliberation, strategic interaction, and, quite often, open warfare between domestic political actors.[33] The international stimuli stressed in Rikerian theories may be an effective explanation for national unification or integration of countries that subsequently became federal, but the causes of each outcome are not the same.[34]

The creation of the Argentine nation-state by reluctant territorial leaders was driven by economics. International economic opportunities, and the advantages of national unity for meeting those opportunities provided the impetus for unification between the fractious members of the former Vice-Royalty of the River Plate. The subsequent emergence of centralized federalism and the eventual victory of its plural subtype in Argentina were an outcome of interprovincial conflict. The struggle was framed in terms of conflict between the central and provincial governments, but until the relationship between Buenos Aires and the national government could be resolved it was fundamentally an issue of interprovincial domination. In a prolonged confrontation that culminated in 1880, provincial "centralizers" prevailed over their "peripheralizing" counterparts in the struggle to determine the relationship between the union's regional hegemon and central authority. The outcome was a relatively autonomous central government, monitored collectively and institutionally by a majority of provinces, and invested with considerable powers to act against any single member on behalf of the union.

In the seventy-year struggle that culminated in the conquest of Buenos Aires there was a rather surprising role reversal between the poorer and richer provinces regarding preferences over centralization. The federalist peripheralizers of the 1810–52 period become the federalist centralizers of 1853–80. And Buenos Aires, once the breeding ground of unitarist and centralist designs for the union, became its last bastion of provincial independence from central authority. The reason for this lay in the parties' shifting perceptions about the relationship of political institutions to interprovincial domination. The bitter lesson learned by the peripheralizing provinces of the immediate postindependence period was that a union without a central government was still a union dominated politically and economically by Buenos Aires. Once they got their second chance to design a regime for the union, they perceived the central government not as a problem but as a solution. The system they devised was thus an institutional double-edged sword. The central government could act against any of them at any time, and for the weaker provinces of the interior this did indeed become a permanent threat. However, the eventual victory of centralized plural federalism universalized that threat, and by doing so it rescued the provinces of the interior from the permanent political hegemony of Buenos Aires. There was nothing the interior could do to eliminate the overwhelming structural advantages enjoyed by Buenos Aires. However, the political system they designed and later crafted through bloodshed, institution building, and sheer political manipulation brought about, to an important degree, a separation of national political power from regional economic power.

The rise of centralized plural federalism in Argentina also provides an eloquent demonstration of the power of institutions as strategic tools in conflicts between political actors. As the debates between the constitution's designers made clear, they certainly had theoretical notions about how its institutional features might affect power relations between the provinces. Nevertheless, it was economic and military power between the provinces that first set the terms of the union during the hegemonic federalism of Bartolomé Mitre's presidency. However, once created, these institutions, through the many arenas and mechanisms for provincial representation and coalition building, provided the weaker provinces with means for countering the hegemon's political hold on the union. Ironically, Mitre's own state building made the prize of their institutional maneuvering all the greater. The presidency that the coalition of interior provinces captured and held after 1868 possessed significant constitutional powers, an increasingly effective national bureaucracy, and a federal army that in 1880 proved equal to the task of subduing its most indomitable provincial foe. This was an irony well captured by historian Rock (1985): "Eighteen years earlier the province of Buenos Aires had supported a national government in the belief that the nation would be its captive; but in 1880 the province instead became the last and greatest prize of its own creation."

NOTES

The authors want to thank Nancy Bermeo, Natalio Botana, Teri Caraway, Kent Eaton, Dietrich Rueschemeyer, David Samuels, Richard Snyder, Alfred Stepan, and Kathleen Thelen for their helpful comments on previous versions of this chapter.

Epigraphs: See Riker (1987, 13); Rock (1985, 102).

1. For the sake of simplicity we will refer to the intermediate level of government (between the central and local levels) as "provinces," whether referring to Argentina (where this term is used) or

to other countries where such terms as "state," "canton," or "republic" denote this type of subnational entity.

2. This would presumably be the regime governed by the Articles of Confederation. This system is described by Riker as a "peripheralized" federal regime, on the continuum from centralized to peripheralized federal systems, rather than an entirely different form of regime. It should be noted that the cause of both the Articles of Confederation and the constitution of 1787 appears to be the same in Riker's book, namely, the disposition of political elites to enter into a federation to meet an international military threat or opportunity.

3. In fact, this proposition is consistent with one aspect of Riker's (1964) theory. He states that the politicians offering the federal "bargain" to their regional counterparts do so because they are unable to expand by conquest, "because of either military incapacity or ideological distaste" (12). We would suggest that this statement constitutes the nub of a regional conflict explanation for the formation of federal systems. In other words, regardless of the external stimulus (international security or international economics) the adoption of a federal form of government is the outcome of a military or political stalemate between subnational units of the federation, which prevents a dominant region from imposing a unitary regime.

4. Defined in terms of Riker's centralized federalism–peripheralized federalism continuum. A centralized federal system is one in which the central government possesses independent decision-making power vis-à-vis the subnational governments in a high number of issue areas.

5. Assuming, of course, that the option to secede is either undesired or unattainable.

6. This can be seen in the works of Riker (1964), Stepan (chap. 2), and Weingast (1995). To Riker, the movement between "centralized" and "peripheralized" federalism results from the continuous struggle between "the rulers of the federation and the constituent governments," where movement toward either end of the continuum implies one party "overawing" the other (6–7). Stepan, on the other hand, categorizes federal systems according to the degree to which the constituent governmental units "constrain" the central government's range of action, resulting in either "demos-constraining" or "demos-enabling" federations. Weingast's sovereign-constituency transgression game, which accounts for a federal system's survival, is played between the center or sovereign and groups of citizens (equivalent to the subnational level) that respond on an equal footing to actions undertaken by the center.

7. We place the term "provinces" in quotes because of the ambiguous juridical status of the current-day provinces between the start of the wars of independence and the 1853 federal republic. The Vice-Royalty of the River Plate was divided into governorships and municipalities that fragmented into new political units during and after the wars of independence. Until the constitution of 1853 their legal status remained ambiguous; although at all times some form of union was in place or under discussion, at some moments these political units appeared to be sovereign entities linked to one another via military and political alliances. At other times they were linked together via confederate arrangements, with their subservience to a presumed central authority more theoretical than real. For a discussion of the theoretical and historical dimensions of these arrangements, see Chiaramonte (1993).

8. As José Carlos Chiaramonte (1993) suggests, the very name of the union at that time, the

"United Provinces of the River Plate," denoted the region adjoining the River Plate, which is largely Buenos Aires, and was clearly visualized in the writings and statements of its early leaders as a broad union under the dominion of the River Plate region. Similarly, the very name "Argentina," a derivation of the Latin word for silver (*plata* in Spanish) connotes the supremacy of the River Plate region.

9. Argentina is over four times the size of France, and the economic differences separating Buenos Aires from the "interior" provinces are compounded by major cultural and sociological differences. For discussions of these contrasts see Gibson (1996) and Scobie (1971).

10. Riker acknowledges that Argentina stayed together as a federal system, in contrast to other early South American federalisms, which either broke up into separate unitary countries or fell under the rule of "centralizing dictatorships" once the external military condition that had brought them together vanished. But he fails to explain why. His general explanatory remarks for "Spanish-American federalisms" are utterly inadequate for the Argentine case. In his own words, "all these remarks demonstrate that the second condition, namely, that the receivers of the federal offer be motivated by a military goal, applies to all the Spanish American federalisms. . . . When the concern over Spanish reconquest died down, federalism waned because few national leaders were willing to offer the necessary bargain to the *caudillos*. In those cases in which a strong national leader ultimately appeared (e.g., Chile, Colombia), federalism was changed to unitary government. But when no strong national leader appeared, the federation simply dissolved into constituent units." In contrast to Riker's argument, the first triumph of Argentine federalism actually occurred *after* the threat of Spanish reconquest receded, not before. Moreover, although strong national leaders appeared in Argentina after the creation of the federal republic, the federal system was preserved.

11. Federalist provincial leaders held two constitutional conventions but failed to produce a constitution. See Chiaramonte (1993).

12. Beyond sectional cleavages, intraprovincial federalist-unitarist alignments were often shaped by the urban-rural cleavage in Buenos Aires and much of the country as well. Unitarist sentiment, strongly urban, was naturally strongest in its most urban province, Buenos Aires. However, the explosive expansion of cattle ranching in that province in the nineteenth century gradually eroded the urban monopoly of political power. As Rock (1985, 105) writes, "the rise of Rosas expressed first and foremost the accession to power of the new ranching interests, developing since 1810, and the displacement of the mercantile clique that had sustained Rivadavia [unitarist president in 1827]."

13. The *Pacto Federal* was originally the basis for a military alliance known as the "Liga del Litoral" between the federalist-controlled provinces of Buenos Aires, Santa Fe, and Entre Ríos. After the final defeat of unitarist forces, however, the remaining provinces agreed to the pact. See Chiaramonte (1993).

14. A sense of the bitterness of the federalist-unitarist conflicts can be garnered from official statements and documents of the time, which were usually prefaced by the slogan *mueran los salvajes unitarios* (death to the savage unitarists). In a turn toward the absurd, one federalist governor, a close ally of Rosas, went so far as to issue a decree proclaiming all unitarists in his province insane. See Correas (1999).

15. In a Poulantzian sense, but applied to interprovincial conflict rather than class conflict.

16. Botana (1980) provides a moving and fascinating account of the battle for Buenos Aires and the politics of the period.

17. This convergence can be seen not only in the writings of such illustrious provincial members of the "Generation of 1837" intellectual elite, but also in the thought of Bartolomé Mitre (1859), Buenos Aires's most prominent political leader at that time. In his opus *Historia de Belgrano y de la Emancipación Argentina,* published in 1859, he laid out a vision for a strong federal government bringing stability and international glory to the Argentine nation.

18. Although federal interventions have received very little theoretical and empirical attention, these constitutional devices have an important impact on intergovernmental relations as well as on the political party system. When the federal government intervenes, its agents have the capacity to remove all elected subnational offices and judges, call for elections, and hand over the government to the new authorities. Federal interventions suppress the dual sovereignty that is theoretically intrinsic to the federal arrangement. Sovereignty of the intervened territory resides solely in the federal government. Thus, federal interventions nullify the constitutional autonomy of the subnational units in the sense that they suspend federalism for certain periods in certain parts of the nation. Furthermore, in terms of *inter* and *intra* partisan competition, the capacities of the national government and / or the national executive to decide upon when and how to intervene, to select and appoint the intervener, and to prepare and schedule the new elections, all of these attributes, can lead to favorable political outcomes for the political party that controls the presidency if used strategically.

19. See Constitution of the United States of America, Article IV, Section V.

20. Alberdi's *Bases y Puntos de Partida para la Organización Política de la República Argentina* proposes the following: "[The confederation] intervenes without requisition in its territory for the purpose of reestablishing the order perturbed by sedition" (as quoted in Comisión de Estudios Constitucionales 1957, 19).

21. The number of interventions between 1853 and 1860: Catamarca 1 intervention, Cordoba 1, Corrientes 2, Jujuy 2, La Rioja 2, Mendoza 1, Salta 1, San Juan 2, Santa Fe 2, Santiago del Estero 1, Tucumán 1, Rosario 2. See Comisión de Estudios Constitucionales (1957, 25–26).

22. We say "metropolitan" with some reluctance. At that time Paraná had a population of ten thousand, compared to that of 100,000 for the city of Buenos Aires (Córdoba, the second largest city of the union, had twenty-five thousand inhabitants at that time). This provides yet another indication of the demographic and economic asymmetries between Buenos Aires and the rest of the country. Nevertheless, at that time the wool, cattle, and agriculture boom had transformed Entre Ríos, which in many ways had become a miniature replica of the province of Buenos Aires, and gave it sway over its federalist provincial allies in the country's interior.

23. In actual fact, these forces were the militia of Justo José de Urquiza, president of the Republic between 1854 and 1860 and *caudillo* of Entre Ríos province.

24. Among the reforms discussed in 1860 was the issue of federal interventions. As in 1853, the province of Buenos Aires saw federal interventions as a device for an arbitrary central government

to encroach upon its autonomy and to threaten political and economic resources under its control. Although the text of Article 6 on federal interventions was amended to accommodate the province's concerns, the interpretation of the new article confronted similar ambiguities as the 1853 version. The new wording of Article 6 left ample room for presidential interpretation and maneuvering. It was not clear who constituted the "federal government": was it the president, congress, or both who had the right to declare an intervention in the provinces? Furthermore, according to the text, the "federal government" could intervene without local request to "guarantee the republican form of government." Provincial request was necessary if the causes of the intervention were sedition or invasion from other province, but nothing was said about which provincial power—executive, legislative, or both—should request federal intervention. See Sommariva (1929).

25. Again, quoting Rock (1985, 126), "During its first delicate years the main pillars of national unity were thus high export earning and a matching land boom, foreign investment, and handouts from Buenos Aires to the provincial landed classes."

26. Several of these rebellions were minor disputes over central government subsidies and tariffs. However, others involved important secessionist challenges and interprovincial warfare and were crushed only with massive military force. Among the most noteworthy challenges were those led by *caudillos* from the Northwest provinces, mainly La Rioja's Vicente Peñaloza, and later Felipe Varela, from the same province. They were eventually defeated by armies led by a family clique of *caudillos* from Santiago del Estero province, the Taboadas, who were allied with, and handsomely subsidized by, Bartolomé Mitre's government. For accounts of these *caudillos'* colorful careers, see Lafforgue (1999).

27. For a detailed account of state building under Mitre, see Oszlak (1985).

28. This minority faction was led by Adolfo Alsina, a former autonomist (not to say secessionist) governor of Buenos Aires, and implacable Mitre rival.

29. And, of course, for the administration of patronage, control of elections and electoral fraud, and settlement of interprovincial conflicts. See Gibson (1996).

30. The details of this rebellion are somewhat more complicated. Justo José de Urquiza, the province's long standing *caudillo,* had been assassinated shortly before, casting the province's internal politics into a spiral of instability. His successor attempted to break with Urquiza's policy of cooperation with the federation and mounted an autonomist challenge to the central government, which culminated in the 1874 uprising.

31. Studies by Bensel (1984, 1990) on the United States capture this idea dramatically.

32. Especially if we consider that the "centralized federalism" analyzed by Riker was adopted four years after the cessation of hostilities with the British former colonial power.

33. The more recent evolution of unitary states toward federal or quasi-federal arrangements, in what Alfred Stepan calls "holding together" patterns of federal formation (Spain and India, for example), provide additional confirmations of this proposition.

34. Furthermore, we would add the additional caveat that the driving international stimuli for Argentine unification were economic rather than military, a finding that suggests the need for an additional modification of Riker's theory of federal origins.

BIBLIOGRAPHY

Balán, Jorge. 1978. Una Cuestión Regional en la Argentina: Burguesías Provinciales y el Mercado Nacional en el Desarrollo Agroexportador. *Desarrollo Económico* 18 (April / June): 49–87.

Bensel, Richard. 1984. *Sectionalism and American Political Development, 1880–1990*. Madison: University of Wisconsin Press.

———. 1990. *Yankee Leviathan: The Origins of Central State Authority in America, 1859–1877*. New York: Cambridge.

Botana, Natalio. 1980. La Federalización de Buenos Aires. In *La Argentina del Ochenta al Centenario*, edited by G. Ferrari and E. Gallo. Buenos Aires: Editorial Sudamericana.

———. 1993. El Federalismo Liberal en la Argentina: 1852–1930. In *Federalismos Latinoamericanos: México / Brasil / Argentina*, edited by M. Carmagnani. Mexico City: El Colegio de México.

Burgin, Miron. 1946. *The Economic Aspects of Argentine Federalism, 1820–1852*. Cambridge, Mass.: Harvard University Press.

Chiaramonte, José Carlos. 1993. El Federalismo Argentino en la Primera Mitad del Siglo XIX. In *Federalismos Latinoamericanos: México / Brasil / Argentina*, edited by M. Carmagnani. Mexico City: El Colegio de Mexico / Fondo de Cultura Económica.

Comisión de Estudios Constitucionales. 1957. *Materiales para la Reforma Constitucional*, vol. 6: *Intervención Federal*. Buenos Aires: Argentine Republic.

Correas, Jaime. 1999. Pasión y Luchas del Fraile Aldao. In *Historias de Caudillos Argentinos*, edited by J. Lafforgue. Buenos Aires: Alfaguara Editores.

Gibson, Edward L. 1996. *Class and Conservative Parties: Argentina in Comparative Perspective*. Baltimore: Johns Hopkins University Press.

Lafforgue, Jorge, ed. 1999. *Historias de Caudillos Argentinos*. Buenos Aires: Extra Alfaguara.

Mitre, Bartolome. 1859. *Historia de Belgrano*. Buenos Aires: Libreria de la Victoria.

Oszlak, Oscar. 1985. *La Formación del Estado Argentino*. Buenos Aires: Editorial Belgrano.

Riker, William H. 1964. *Federalism: Origin, Operation, Significance*. Boston: Little Brown.

———. 1987. *The Development of American Federalism*. Boston: Kluwer.

Rock, David. 1985. *Argentina 1516–1982: From Spanish Colonization to the Falklands War*. Berkeley: University of California Press.

Sampay, Arturo Enrique. 1975. *Las Constituciones de la Argentina, 1810–1972*. Buenos Aires: EUDEBA.

Scobie, James. 1971. *Argentina: A City and a Nation*. New York: Oxford University Press.

Sommariva, Luis H. 1929. *Historia de las Intervenciones Federales en las Provincias*. Buenos Aires: El Ateneo.

Weingast, Barry R. 1995. The Economic Role of Political Institutions: Market-Preserving Federalism and Economic Development. *Journal of Law, Economics, and Organization* 11 (1): 1–31.

CHAPTER 8

Multiple Arenas of Struggle

Federalism and Mexico's Transition to Democracy

—ENRIQUE OCHOA-REZA

Conventional wisdom is easy to follow but occasionally wrong. Political science journals and the international media commonly assert that the recent election of a new president in Mexico ended more than seventy years of national authoritarian rule by the Institutional Revolutionary Party (PRI). Although the statement accurately describes Mexico's authoritarian political situation prior to 1977, it does not accurately explain the decades leading up to the presidential elections of 2000. Long before the momentous victory of Vicente Fox, Mexico's political regime had undergone vast transformations and democratized substantially.

In the late seventies Mexico had a party-state system in which all sixty-four senators and 196 out of 237 federal deputies were PRI members. The same party governed all thirty-one states and Mexico City. In addition, the PRI held supermajorities in all state congresses and ruled 99 percent of the localities. Twenty-three years later, on the eve of the 2000 presidential elections, Mexico's political map differed dramatically. No single party had the majority in the Chamber of Deputies, the PRI held only 60 percent of the seats in the Senate, and non-PRI governors ruled in ten of Mexico's thirty-one states and Mexico City, which together accounted for almost half of the country's GDP. Opposition parties also held over 51 percent of the seats in state congresses, and more than 50 percent of the population lived under non-PRI mayors.

The election of Vicente Fox as president of Mexico therefore did not suddenly give birth to democracy but made visible fundamental changes that had taken place under a cumulative dynamic in which local struggles interacted with national-level politics to produce the Mexican democratic transition. The social, political, and economic dynamics of this process have been well documented,[1] and scholars have also increasingly noted the "subnational" characteristics of the mobilizations and power struggles of the period (Cornelius 2000; Snyder 2001; Weldon 1997). However, one little-noticed fact is that Mexico's long political transition took place in the context of a federal political system. It is a central contention of this chapter that neither the process nor the outcome of the Mexican democratic transition can be properly understood without attention to the transition's embeddedness in a federal institutional system. Federalism profoundly shaped Mexico's democratization process.

This chapter thus seeks to analyze how federal features played a major role in the Mexican transition, and how, in turn, the political transition reshaped the institutional structure of Mexico's federal system. In so doing I also hope to shed new light on theoretical connections between federalism and democratization. I argue that a series of electoral reforms, beginning in 1977, created the conditions for freer and fairer elections. Federalism pluralized competition into multiple subnational arenas. As members of a party different from the president's were elected to significant state and local positions, the relationship between the center and the periphery changed, transforming a purely legal federal framework into a functioning federal system. This, in turn, redistributed power between actors located at different institutional points in the country's territorially decentralized polity, providing opportunities for mobilization, countermobilization, and negotiations between regionally organized actors. The push and pull between these actors transformed politics at all levels of the political system and in many cases evolved into a virtuous cycle. New political spaces in Mexico allowed locally based politicians to compete for power and to mobilize civil society when electoral violations occurred. The capture of local power by opposition parties gave them leverage to push for additional reforms at the national level, which once in place increased the degree of free and fair elections in the states and localities. By the 1990s, local politicians became national actors. Indeed, mayors, state congresses, governors, and the Senate were institutional driving forces for democratic transition. This virtuous cycle evolved throughout the twenty-three years of the Mexican transition (1977–2000), although its pace varied among the nation's thirty-one states, since each state's constitution and electoral law establishes the system of election for local and state authorities, which affected the speed and uniformity of democratization across states.[2]

Although the variation in democratization between states is an important issue, for our analysis the national orientation of the country's party system, which strongly influenced the politywide effects of the federally driven transition, is even more critical. The combination of cumulative electoral reforms and the incentives of the party system prompted local elites to create or consolidate regional branches of *national* parties rather than to initiate regional opposition parties, which resulted in the evolution of a politywide, relatively disciplined, and programmatic party system. The constitutional reforms from the center opened spaces for political contestation that were occupied mostly by local opposition members of national parties, which appeared across the country united under a common political banner. At the same time, reforms to the federal system bolstered the relative positions of national opposition parties. Most notably, the reforms in the allocation of seats in both houses of the national legislature (the expansion of proportional representation seats in the lower house and the addition of national constituency senators in the upper house) tempered the territorial bases of representation in the federalizing political system.

In effect, the "federalization" of electoral competition led to the strengthening of national opposition parties, not to the regional fragmentation of the party system. It also led to institutional reforms that, while empowering new political actors at the subnational level (particularly governors) and activating once-dormant federal institutions, also mitigated potentially "demos-constraining" outcomes in the development of Mexico's federal system.[3]

Cycle I: The Electoral Reforms of 1977 and 1983

Before 1977, Mexico's party system was exclusive and noncompetitive. Although parties other than PRI existed, they held only forty-one out of 237 seats in the Chamber of Deputies and no seats in the Senate. The lone opposition party was the National Action Party (PAN), and no new parties had appeared in the political arena in the five federal elections prior to the 1977 reforms.[4] As with most transitions to democracy, the opening shot of the democratic process initiated a sequence of events unanticipated and uncontrolled by those who started them. The leaders of the Mexican political regime in the late 1970s sought to open spaces for political participation to adjust the political system to a rapidly changing and increasingly restless society. President Jose López Portillo (1976–82) was aware that social agitation was not yet a threat to the stability of the state, but he also knew that social diversity was not matched by political representation. In President López Portillo's words, "It was indispensable to deepen the country's democratization process by establishing political reforms that would enrich, in line with our society's diversity, the spaces of political representation, so as to legitimize the responsible struggle of minorities and dissidents in our political institutions" (quoted in Becerra, Salazar, and Woldenberg 2000, 87). However, PRI also sought to maximize its control over the political process and, if possible, to increase its electoral prospects under the evolving institutional order. The aim of reform was therefore to increase opposition participation in the system while safeguarding the PRI's hegemonic position. After eight months of civil and legislative work, Congress approved a constitutional electoral reform on 6 December 1977, initiating (in retrospect) the Mexican transition to democracy. Two weeks later, in order to deepen and materialize the new constitutional principles, the Federal Law of Political Organizations and Electoral Processes (LOPPE) was also approved.

The Reforms

Although López Portillo succeeded in passing an electoral reform, the few soft-liners within the regime faced constant opposition from hard-liners, who saw little reason to concede political space to other parties. Soft-liners therefore pursued a two-pronged strategy. On the one hand, through the introduction of proportional representation (PR) seats they opened new spaces of public contestation in the three levels of the federal structure. On the other hand, they increased the number of seats elected by plurality in all the assemblies, bolstering the PRI's position, since they traditionally held these seats. In this way, although PRI members had more political spaces in which to pursue their careers, the overall presence and influence of opposition parties at the local, state, and federal levels increased.[5]

The 1977 reform included three constitutional provisions that opened new spaces for political contestation (see Table 8.1). These reforms activated federal institutions by allowing opposition parties to gain a foothold at multiple levels of government. The first provision introduced PR seats for local councils in towns with populations greater than 300,000. At the time, only ten cities met this criterion, but the introduction of PR seats was an experimental measure that became a general rule for all city councils in the 1983 reform. Some states took full advantage of their legislative autonomy and interpreted the population threshold as a recommendation and included PR seats in city councils with fewer inhabitants (Lujambio 2000, 94),[6] opening more spaces for political contestation at the local level than were constitutionally required.

The second provision introduced PR seats in state congresses, allowing each state's legislature to establish the number of PR seats in their congresses and the minimum percentage of votes required for a party to gain a seat. Consequently, each state developed a particular mixed system in its legislative branch, introducing different degrees of political contestation across states. However, in all cases additional arenas of contestation emerged, although the level of increase was greater in some states than in others.

The third provision modified two aspects of the electoral system for the federal Chamber of Deputies. The first introduced one hundred PR seats, which were assigned by a formula among the political parties who did not win at least sixty plurality seats.[7] The second modification increased the number of plurality seats in the Chamber of Deputies from 196 to 300. Although the introduction of the PR seats guaranteed at least 25 percent of the seats in the Chamber of Deputies for opposition parties, the increase in the number of plurality seats ensured the continued dominance of the PRI.

In addition to reforms aimed at increasing contestation, the 1977 reform included three constitutionally embedded conditions that created conditions for free and fair elections. First, national parties could now compete in elections at the state and local levels. Prior to this, local elites often prevented electoral competition at the subnational level by establishing electoral requirements that national parties other than PRI had difficulty meeting. Before this reform, parties could often participate at the federal level but not at the local and state levels. Second, new political parties could compete in federal elections under a "conditional registration," which could be turned into a permanent registration if the party received at least 1.5 percent of the

Table 8.1
Main Aspects of the Constitutional and Legal Electoral Reforms 1977–1990

Type of Reform	1977	1986	1989–1990
Reforms that opened new spaces for political contestation	Introduction of proportional representation (PR) seats for local councils in towns with population above 300,000 inhabitants. Introduction of PR seats for state congress. Plurality seats (usually won by PRI) in the Federal Chamber increased from 196 to 300. 100 PR seats also added to increase minority party representation.	Introduction of PR seats for all local councils. Creation of an Assembly of Representatives for Mexico City formed by 40 plurality seats and 26 PR seats. Increase in the number of PR seats in the federal Chamber of Deputies from 100 to 200.	Any single party limited to 350 seats (70%) in the federal Chamber of Deputies. Nevertheless, the party winning a majority of plurality seats is guaranteed enough PR seats to secure a majority in the Chamber.
Reforms that created conditions for free and fair elections	Reduction in legal obstacles for national parties to compete in state and local elections. Incorporation of new political parties to the system with conditioned registration. New parties incorporated into the national electoral authority (without a vote).	Different parties allowed to present common candidates. Conditioned registration eliminated. PR introduced into the national electoral authority. Court of Electoral Claims (TRICOEL) created. However, all 11 members named by the PRI majority of the Chamber of Deputies.	Creation of Federal Electoral Institute (IFE) responsible for organizing federal executive and legislative elections. Creation of the Federal Electoral Register (RFE) Creation of the Federal Electoral Court (TRIFE)

1993–1996

Type of Reform	1993	1994	1996
Reforms that opened new spaces for political contestation	Any single party limited to 315 seats (63%) in the federal Chamber. Senate reformed. Number of senators increased from 64 to 128 (4 per state). In each state the party winning a plurality of the vote received three seats, with one seat held for second-place party.		Mayor of Mexico City chosen by popular vote. Any single party limited to 300 seats (60%). Senate reformed. PR (from a national list) introduced for 32 seats out of 128. For the remaining 96 seats (3 per state), the party winning a plurality of the vote in each state receives two seats, with one seat held for the second-place party.
Reforms that created conditions for free and fair elections	IFE authorized to review spending of political parties and their candidates. IFE authorized to monitor media coverage of elections and political parties. TRIFE established as constitutional legal authority with powers to make binding and definitive decisions.	State and local electoral institutes (analogous to IFE) established throughout the country. "Citizen Counselors" appointed by the Chamber of Deputies gain majority control of IFE. Political parties stripped of vote. Transparency of elections improved: a picture ID issued for all voters, electoral ballots numbered, all parties given access to voter registration lists. Campaign advertising prohibited 20 days before election.	Autonomy and scope of sub-national electoral institutes expanded. Independence of IFE strengthened. Creation of the Electoral Court (TEPJF) as the top electoral legal authority.

national vote in the following election. This reform allowed for the creation of new political parties, including the Communist Party, which included significant elements of the left. Third, the reform increased the responsibilities of the institution in charge of organizing the elections, the Federal Electoral Commission (CFE), and included in its deliberative sessions a representative of both parties with registration and those with "conditional registration." However, parties with conditional registration could participate but not vote, so the final decisions remained under PRI majoritarian control.

The 1977 reform not only initiated Mexico's democratic transition by opening arenas for political contestation and creating conditions for free and fair elections but also simultaneously initiated the activation of the federal system through two reinforcing dynamics. On the one hand, multiparty contestation at the local, state, and federal levels became constitutionally embedded, slowly reforming the one-party state that in political practice simulated a unitary system. On the other hand, by using PR seats to open the door to the opposition, the reform promoted the formation of national parties and established incentives for party discipline, which resulted in cohesive behavior across federal features to oppose slowly the powerful centralist presidential role.

Effects of the Reforms on Mexico's Federal System

After 1977, state and local elections became the source of three essential elements for democratization. First, the state and local levels turned into continuous arenas for political competition between opposition parties and the PRI. Second, as a result of the capacity to compete in local and state elections and the addition of PR seats in the federal legislature, opposition parties had greater access to political positions, public resources, and the local and national media. Third, the persistence of electoral abuses provoked political mobilization in states where the economic elite participated in an opposition party. Although mobilizations rarely changed the outcome of elections, they consolidated the opposition leaderships at the state and local levels, as well as the regional branches of national parties. Furthermore, the persistence of nondemocratic elections created legitimacy problems for the elected government, which were both costly and time-consuming. By the end of this cycle, eight states around the country had already experienced significant civil mobilizations, setting the stage for further reforms.

The outcomes of the first comprehensive electoral reform of the transition can be analyzed at the various levels of Mexico's federal system. The country meticulously followed an intensive electoral calendar at the three levels of government, so the opposition had many opportunities to test the electoral reforms in the thirty-one states. Slowly but surely, elections at all levels of the federal system became more competitive and opposition parties expanded their presence in elected office.

The increased level of competition in the Mexican polity is evident in the number of effective political parties, which can be calculated on the basis of vote shares or seat shares.[8] Markku Laakso and Rein Taagepera devised a formula to measure the "number of hypothetical equal-size parties that would have the same total effect on fractionalization of the system as have the actual parties of unequal size" (Laasko and Taagepera 1979, 4). As the number of effective parties (N) increases in any given system, we can assume that the degree of political contestation increases too. When N equals 1, the system is a one-party state, and when N is equal to or greater than 1.5, the political system is competitive. As N reaches 2, a two-party system is in place, and when N is greater than 2.5, a multiparty system exists.

At the local level, the development of political contestation among city mayors increased consistently but slowly. In the first years after the reform politicians from the left won initial positions, but after the severe economic crisis of 1982 well-known local business leaders joined the PAN to oppose the regime. These new politicians ran as PAN mayoral candidates in the northern states of Sinaloa, Chihuahua, Baja California, and Durango in 1983, but PRI candidates still won more than 97 percent of the local elections. However, future national PAN figures were elected as mayors in two capitals (Durango and Chihuahua) as well as in an important border city with the United States (Ciudad Juárez, Chihuahua) in 1983. Candidates from PAN also won the capital of Sonora, the capital city of San Luis Potosí, and Michoacán's second most important city, Uruapan, in 1983. The United Socialist Party of Mexico (PSUM) won the mayoral election of Juchitán, an important city in the southern state of Oaxaca, and the Democratic Mexican Party (PDM) captured the capital city of Guanajuato in 1982. By 1983, eight out of thirty-one states had an effective number of parties greater than 1.5 at the local level, which was unheard of before 1977 (see Table 8.2). In 1986 the opposition performed better at the local level. Thirteen states held elections for mayors, city councils, and state congresses, and opposition parties won in twenty-five cities.

Competitiveness at the state level also increased quickly. A year before the 1977

Table 8.2

Effective Number of Parties for Mayors and City Councils per State (Laakso/Taagepera Index), 1980–1998

State	1980	1981	1982	1983	1984	1985	1986	1987	1988	1989	1990	1991	1992	1993	1994	1995	1996	1997	1998
Ags.	1.15			1.68			1.45			1.68			1.67			2.26			2.38
Bc.	2.17			2.25			2.38			2.30			2.29			2.28			2.25
Bcs.	1.25			1.57				1.37			1.87			1.97			2.36		
Camp.			1.07			1.11			1.28			1.49			2.00			2.39	
Coah.		1.40			1.63			1.41			1.67			1.97			2.11		
Col.			1.31			1.33			1.73			2.07			2.23			2.70	
Chis.			1.22			1.21			1.34			1.35							2.38
Chih.	1.27			1.60			1.69			1.55			1.90			2.24			2.17
Dgo.	1.28			1.69			1.81			1.66			1.98			2.46			2.75
Gto.			1.59			1.66			1.98			2.26			2.29			2.82	
Gro.	1.26			1.31			1.37			1.97				2.02		2.18		
Hgo.		1.04			1.10			1.07			1.51			1.63			2.09		
Jal.			1.64			1.61			1.73				1.86			2.20		2.60	
E.Mex		1.16			1.41			1.54			1.97			2.18			2.65		
Mich.	1.17			1.46			1.34			2.13			2.16			2.53			2.54
Mor.			1.34			1.21			1.38			1.82			1.99			2.76	
Nay.		1.44			1.41			1.27			1.49			2.08			2.18		
NL.			1.13			1.20			1.26			1.35			1.94			2.11	
Oax.	1.08			1.10			1.10			1.22			1.17			2.02			2.07
Pue.	1.15			1.25			1.19			1.51			1.61			1.92			2.02

Qro.			1.12			1.20			1.41			1.45						2.47	
Qroo.		1.13			1.10			1.19			1.42						2.02		
SLP.			1.30			1.32			1.52			1.68			2.08			2.57	
Sin.	1.39			1.51			1.57						1.93			2.31			2.40
Son.			1.24			1.38			1.19			1.41			1.79			2.09	
Tab.			1.10			1.11			1.42			1.77			2.05			2.30	
Tam.	1.22			1.28			1.26			1.56			1.81			2.01			1.95
Tlax.			1.35			1.40			1.67			1.66			2.07		2.13	2.52	
Ver.			1.28			1.36			1.67			1.68			2.12			2.59	
Yuc.		1.19			1.20			1.17			1.45			1.71			1.87		1.85
Zac.			1.19			1.18			1.54			1.85			2.33			2.60	
Avg.	1.31	1.23	1.28	1.52	1.31	1.31	1.51	1.29	1.51	1.72	1.63	1.67	1.84	1.87	2.02	2.2	2.22	2.49	2.3
No. Cases	11	6	14	11	6	14	10	7	14	10	7	12	11	8	11	13	8	11	13
N = 1.5	1	0	2	6	1	2	4	1	7	9	4	7	10	7	11	13	8	11	13
N = 2.0	0	0	0	1	0	0	1	0	0	2	0	2	2	3	7	11	8	11	11
N = 2.5	0	0	0	0	0	0	0	0	0	0	0	0	0	0	0	1	1	6	4

Note: Laakso / Taagepera index, as discussed in Laakso and Taagepera (1979).
Source: Author's calculations and data from de Remes (2000a).

Table 8.3

Effective Number of Parties for State Congress per State (Laakso/Taagepera Index), 1976–1999

State	1976	1977	1978	1979	1980	1981	1982	1983	1984	1985	1986	1987	1988	1989	1990	1991	1992	1993	1994	1995	1996	1997	1998	1999
Ags.		1.37			1.70			1.66			1.70			1.66			1.53			2.48			2.04	
Bc.		1.00			1.34			1.48			1.43			2.98			2.79			2.14			2.49	
Bcs.			1.28			1.51			161			1.51			1.38			1.99			2.46			3.04
Camp.		1.00			1.00			1.19			1.29			1.50			1.52		1.78				2.37	
Coah.	1.00			1.68			1.68			1.51			1.8			1.86			2.27			2.78		
Col.	1.00			1.58			1.58			1.64			1.91			1.94			2.29			2.53		
Chis.	1.00			1.50			1.72			1.72			1.71			1.34				2.15			2.15	
Chih.	1.00				1.28			1.74			1.28			1.56			2.25			2.08			2.23	
Dgo.		1.00			1.73			1.51			1.53			2.22			2.57			2.70			2.59	
Gto.	1.00			1.70			1.70			1.85			2.09			2.04			1.66			3.03		
Gro.			1.18			1.37			1.29			1.64			1.88			1.92			2.01			
Hgo.			1.00			1.57			1.72			1.72			1.72			1.89			2.04			2.16
Jal.		1.00			1.64			1.63			1.61			1.83			1.83			1.89			2.30	
E.Mex			1.44			1.70			1.64			1.57			2.39			2.37			3.40			
Mich.		1.12			1.00			1.70			1.71			2.96			1.94			2.54			2.30	
Mor.	1.00			1.53			1.53			1.53			1.53			2.07			1.68			2.84		
Nay.			1.68			1.68			1.61			1.89			1.91			1.94			2.01			
NL.	1.00			1.90			1.60			1.92			1.83			1.89			2.26			2.26		
Oax.		1.00			1.71			1.70			1.72			1.73			2.04			2.40			2.17	
Pue.			1.52			1.65			1.59			1.67			1.69			1.67			2.22			2.04
Qro.	1.00			1.00			1.47			1.51			1.99			1.86			2.24			2.77		

Qroo.													1.51	1.67	1.80	1.80	1.82	1.84		2.32	2.24
SLP.	1.00	1.00					1.73	1.72	1.60	1.72	1.69		2.01						2.42	2.21
Sin.		1.00		1.55	1.90	1.65	1.53			1.85		2.06	2.03				2.38			2.16
Son.			2.10						1.73		1.87		1.94						2.88	
Tab.	1.00				1.74	1.23	1.24	1.72		1.43		1.64				1.85		2.22	1.99	2.16
Tam.	1.00						1.72				1.77			1.64						
Tlax.		1.22	1.77	1.77	1.80	1.77	1.77		1.77		1.74	1.74				2.53			2.84	
Ver.		1.39	1.77	1.77		1.77		1.96	1.92		1.88				1.88				2.35	
Yuc.	1.15		1.47		1.30		1.57		1.73		1.84				1.67		1.99		2.13	
Zac.		1.00		1.00		1.43	1.43	1.63	1.86		1.84		1.84		2.02				3.16	
Avg.	1.02	1.08	1.29	1.44	1.61	1.62	1.58	1.63	1.66	1.55	1.68	1.83	1.95	1.79	1.88	2.00	1.92	2.22	2.34	2.69	2.36	2.3
No. Cases	9	13	9	13	9	13	9	13	9	9	13	9	9	9	9	13	9	8	8	8	15	5
N = 1.5	0	0	3	7	7	8	9	9	9	9	9	9	12	9	8	13	9	8	8	8	15	5
N = 2.0	0	0	0	1	0	0	0	0	0	0	0	1	3	1	3	5	2	8	1	8	14	5
N = 2.5	0	0	0	0	0	0	0	0	0	0	0	0	2	0	0	3	0	1	1	6	3	1

Note: Laakso/Taagepera index, as discussed in Laakso and Taagepera (1979).
Source: Author's calculations and data from Lujambio (2000).

Table 8.4

Party Distribution in the Chamber of Deputies, 1976–2003

Party	1976–1979		1979–1982		1982–1985		1985–1988		1988–1991		1991–1994		1994–1997		1997–2000		2000–2003	
	No. Seats	Percentage Total	No. Seats	Percentage Total	No. Seats	Percentage Total	No. Seats	Percentage Total	No. Seats	Percentage Total	No. Seats	Percentage Total	No. Seats	Percentage Total	No. Seats	Percentage Total	No. Seats	Percentage Total
PAN	20	8.4%	43	10.8%	51	12.8%	38	9.5%	101	20.2%	89	17.8%	119	23.8%	121	24.2%	208	41.6%
PRI	195	82.3	296	74.0	299	74.8	292	73.0	260	52.0	320	64.0	300	60.0	239	47.8	209	41.8
PRD											41	8.2	71	14.2	125	25.0	51	10.2
PARM	10	4.2	12	3.0			11	2.8	30	6.0	15	3.0						
PPS	12	5.1	11	2.8	10	2.5	11	2.8	32	6.4	12	2.4						
PCM			18	4.5														
PSUM					17	4.3	12	3.0										
PMS									19	3.8								
PDM			10	2.5	12	3.0	12	3.0										
PST/PFCRN			10	2.5	11	2.8	12	3.0	34	6.8	23	4.6						
PRT					6	1.5	6	1.5										
PMT					6	1.5	6	1.5										
PT													10	2.0	7	1.4	9	1.8
PVEM															8	1.6	15	3.0
PSN																	3	0.6
CD																	3	0.6
PAS																	2	0.4
Coalitions									24	4.8								
Total	237	100.0	400	100.0	400	100.0	400	100.0	500	100.0	500	100.0	500	100.0	500	100.0	500	100.0

Note: Proportional representation was introduced in the Chamber of Deputies in 1979, through the 1977 electoral reform.

Source: Data for the period 1976–97 from Becerra et al. (2000, 649). Data for the period 2000–2003 from Instituto Federal Electoral (IFE) at www.ife.org.mx.

electoral reform the average effective number of parties in the state congresses elected in 1976 was equal to 1.02, a clear indication of a one-party state. Six years later, by 1983, over two-thirds of the states had a competitive political system, as the effective number of parties in twenty-four state congresses was equal to or greater than 1.5 (see Table 8.3). The state average increased from 1.02 in the 1974–77 period to 1.61 in 1980–83. Furthermore, the nine highest ranking states extended over the whole territory: Chiapas and Oaxaca in the south, Veracruz and Tamaulipas in the Gulf of Mexico, Sonora and Chihuahua in the north, and Michoacán, Estado de Mexico, and Guanajuato in the center. As with the local level, the political left (mainly the PCM) increasingly gained state legislative seats. The main opposition party on the right, PAN, increased its number of seats as well but at a slower rate.

At the federal level, opposition parties reached the highest level of participation in history in the Chamber of Deputies, although PRI still held almost 75 percent of the seats, which was more than the two-thirds majority needed to amend the constitution (see Table 8.4). Nevertheless, representation in the chamber opened the possibility for members of the opposition to protest against the unfairness experienced at the state and local electoral processes in a national forum, and they energetically embraced this opportunity.[9]

Mobilization

While opposition politicians eagerly embraced opportunities to run for office in these new political spaces, opposition parties often had to resort to political mobilization in order to keep the momentum of reform going. In the early 1980s a number of conditions facilitated the capacity of politicians to mobilize support. The populist management of the economy under President López Portillo's administration resulted in a severe economic crisis in 1982, which included the nationalization of the banking system. After six years of confrontation between the private sector and President Luis Echeverría (1970–76), López Portillo's management of the economy drove important members of the local economic elite to join the regional branches of PAN.[10]

In 1983 regional cases of civil mobilization in response to electoral irregularities made the national news. The new PAN leaders and candidates had the money and ability to organize movements of civic resistance in several states. In Sinaloa, Baja California, and Puebla these movements included massive demonstrations in public plazas, protest walks, and the shutdown of public offices. One year later, the election in the northern border state Coahuila caught the attention of the international press, and PAN's local leaders and candidates organized several acts of protest against the results in three cities. After protesters repeatedly obstructed highways and even set the headquarters of a city council on fire, the national army intervened to normalize the situation. In 1985 an important local businessman ran as the PAN candidate for governor in Mexico's third most important state, Nuevo León. Although the PRI candidate won, PAN-affiliated local organizations mobilized, unsuccessfully, against the outcome.

In 1986 the most important civic resistance movement during the administration of President Miguel de la Madrid (1982–88) developed in the northern state of Chihuahua, where elections were held for mayors, state congressmen, and the governor. Civil resistance started a year before the election when the local electoral law was modified by a majority PRI Congress. However, opposition parties held 30 percent of the seats in Chihuahua's congress (the effective number of political parties was 1.74), and they made a public case against the legislative reforms. Local PAN officials promptly joined in, leading a twenty-two-day hunger strike and a "Walk for Democracy" from Chihuahua to the central state of Querétaro, over a thousand miles away. The PAN candidate for governor lost after a bitter campaign, and when PRI candidates claimed 98 percent of the offices contested in the election, civil mobilization started again. At the local level PAN officials held a forty-day hunger strike and sponsored rallies in public plazas and the obstruction of custom bridges, while at the federal level PAN presented a claim to the Supreme Court seeking the nullification of the electoral authority report. The Chamber of Deputies frequently discussed the Chihuahua case, and several meetings were held in the Ministry of Government in an attempt to resolve the electoral dispute. Although in the end PAN did not succeed, the mobilization in Chihuahua was a model for further civil protest around the country. Furthermore, its development throughout the second half of 1986 evolved simultaneously with the negotiation process in Mexico City of the second cumulative electoral reform of the transition.

Before I start the analysis of the 1986 electoral reform, it is important to highlight the influence of federal features in the first decade of the Mexican transition. The 1977 and 1983 reforms activated federal institutions by opening new arenas of contestation at multiple levels of the federal system. The opposition embraced these opportunities and began to compete with the PRI for political power at the subnational level. When electoral practices impeded their success, subnational leaders of the opposition mobilized the population, and opposition members at the federal level raised their concerns in national fora, further propelling additional reforms.

Cycle II: The 1986 Reforms

The Reforms

The 1986 reforms represented both a step forward and a step backward (see Table 8.1). Two reforms opened new spaces for political contestation. First, a constitutional amendment increased the number of PR seats in the Chamber of Deputies from one hundred to two hundred. Although PR seats now accounted for 40 percent of the seats, the reform also allowed the party with the plurality of seats an allocation of PR seats that gave it a majority in the chamber. This change rolled back part of the 1977 reform, which excluded parties that obtained more than sixty plurality seats from the distribution of PR seats and violated the original purpose of PR seats, which was to reduce overrepresentation in the political system. Once again, PRI softliners opened new spaces for political contestation but secured positions for PRI members in order to achieve the support of the regime's hard-liners. Second, an Assembly of Representatives for Mexico City was established, with sixty-six members, forty elected by plurality and twenty-six by PR. Both of these reforms created new opportunities for the opposition to increase its power at multiple levels of government.

Regarding the reforms to create conditions for free and fair elections, the 1986 reform authorized parties to present common candidates. However, the 1986 reform also eliminated the "conditional registration" of new political parties, which slowed down the ongoing expansion of the party system, and introduced PR in the Federal Electoral Commission (CFE). In the CFE, parties were awarded representatives in proportion to their share of the national vote, which favored PRI, and this system of organization was replicated at the state and local levels. In addition, the Ministry of Government had the authority to appoint the main local and state electoral administrative officials, giving the CFE little credibility. Finally, the government created the first autonomous organization to solve electoral claims. Although the nine members

Table 8.5

Non-PRI Governors in the Mexican Transition 1977–2000 and Governor Elections since the 2000 Presidential Election

State	Election Date	Period of Gov.	Name	Party/Alliance[a]	Percentage Natl. Pop.	Percentage Natl. GDP
Baja California	July 2, 1989	1989–95	Ernesto Ruffo	PAN	2.3%	2.8%
Guanajuato	August 18, 1991	1991–95	Carlos Medina	PAN	4.8	3.4
Chihuahua	July 12, 1992	1992–98	Francisco Barrio	PAN	3.1	4.0
Jalisco	February 12, 1995	1995–2001	Alberto Cárdenas	PAN	6.6	6.5
Guanajuato	May 28, 1995	1995–2001	Vicente Fox	PAN	4.8	3.4
Baja California	August 6, 1995	1995–2001	Héctor Terán Terán	PAN	2.3	3.1
Mexico City	July 6, 1997	1997–2000	Cuauhtémoc Cárdenas	PRD	9.3	22.6
Querétaro	July 6, 1997	1997–2003	Ignacio Loyola Vera	PAN	1.4	1.8
Nuevo León	July 6, 1997	1997–2003	Fernando Canales	PAN	3.9	6.9
Zacatecas	July 5, 1998	1998–2004	Ricardo Monreal[b]	PRD	1.5	0.8
Aguascalientes	August 2, 1998	1998–2004	Felipe González	PAN	0.9	1.2
Tlaxcala	November 8, 1998	1999–2005	Alfonso Sánchez Anaya[b]	PRD/PT/PVEM	1.0	0.5
BCS	February 7, 1999	1999–2005	Leonel Cota Montaño[b]	PRD/PT	0.4	0.5
Nayarit	July 4, 1999	1999–2005	Antonio Echevarría Domínguez[b]	PAN/PRD/PT/PVEM	1.0	0.6
Presidential Election, July 2, 2000						
Mexico City	July 2, 2000	2000–2006	Andrés M. López Obrador	PRD	8.8	22.7
Morelos	July 2, 2000	2000–2006	Sergio Estrada	PAN	1.6	1.4
Guanajuato	July 2, 2000	2000–2006	Juan Carlos Romero Hicks	PAN	4.8	3.3
Chiapas	August 20, 2000	2000–2006	Pablo Salazar Mendiguchía[b]	PRD/PAN/PT/PVEM	4.0	1.7
Jalisco	November 12, 2000	2001–7	Francisco Ramírez Acuña	PAN	6.5	6.4
Yucatán	May 27, 2001	2001–7	Patricio Patrón Laviada	PAN/PRD/PT/PVEM	1.7	1.3
Baja California	July 8, 2001	2001–7	Eugenio Elorduy Walter	PAN	2.6	3.3
Tabasco	August 5, 2001	2001–7	Manuel Andrade	PRI	1.9	1.2
Michoacán	November 5, 2001	2001–7	Lázaro Cárdenas Batel	PRD	4.9	2.4

[a]In the cases of multiparty alliances, the party listed first is the party to which the governor is member or with which the governor is mostly identified.

[b]All these governors were significant PRI members until just before their election, when they formed multiparty opposition coalition.

Sources: Author's calculations and data, as well as data from Lujambio (2000) and the web sites of the PRI, PAN, and PRD. Population data for 1995 from INEGI (1996) and for 2000 INEGI (2000). For the state's percentage of the national GDP see INEGI's web site. All population and economic data can be found in Mexico's National Institute of Statistics, Geography and Information (INEGI) web page: www.inegi.gob.mx.

of the Court of Electoral Claims (TRICOEL) were appointed by majority vote in the Chamber of Deputies, under PRI control, the institution became the target of future reform and became a central institution in the transition.

Effects of the Reforms on Mexico's Federal System: Increased Contestation at the Subnational Level

By 1989 every state and city in the nation had held at least one election under the 1986 framework. Although the 1986 reform failed to guarantee fully free and fair elections at the national level, it had a positive impact on political contestation at all levels of the federal system.

In the three years following the reforms, major strides were made in improving the level of competitiveness at the local level: seventeen out of thirty-one states reached the competitive level for mayors and city councils (see Table 8.2). In 1989 the ten states that held local elections reached the highest average level of competitiveness ever, with an effective number of parties of 1.72. However, only one state surpassed the two-party threshold, Baja California, and none achieved the multiparty cutoff, 2.5.

The gains at the state level were also impressive. In the 1987–89 period, thirty out of thirty-one states reached the competitive level in the number of effective parties in state congresses. The average for the period was an historic high of 1.82. Moreover, four states reached the bipartisan level, and two passed the multiparty level. And in a development of major substantive and symbolic significance, Baja California became the first state to elect a non-PRI governor in 1989 (see Table 8.5).

As a result of the bold opposition gains in state legislatures, opposition parties could now act as veto players for local constitutional amendments and legislation in some states, which forced the majority party in the state congress and the governor to negotiate.[11] In the congresses of Baja California, Durango, Guanajuato, and Michoacán no political party could amend the local constitution by itself. More negotiation also occurs when opposition parties in state congresses become veto players for all legislative work, and in the 1987–89 period, this happened in the states of Baja California and Michoacán. These two states had the highest number of effective political parties in their state congresses, with 2.98 and 2.96, respectively.

In addition, opposition gains in the state legislatures and gubernatorial races led to more divided and juxtaposed governments. A divided government implies a situation where a party or an alliance of parties different from the party that holds executive power holds the majority of seats in the legislature—for example, if the governor is from PRI but the opposition controls the legislature. Juxtaposed governments occur when the party that governs the smaller territorial unit (state, city mayor, or city council) is different from that which governs the larger territorial unit (the federation, state, or state congress)—for example, a PAN governor and a PRI mayor (de Remes 2000a). Both divided and juxtaposed governments help strengthen checks and balances and cooperation between regime and antiregime political leaderships. Divided and juxtaposed governments do not mean that states or localities control national decisions, but they do mean that the federal government cannot control all state and local decisions. As juxtaposed and divided governments arose in Mexico, multiparty competition across and within the federal structure transformed the formal federal framework into a functioning federal system.

At the national level, three viable candidates competed in the 1988 presidential elections—a first in Mexico's modern history. One of the candidates, Cuauhtémoc Cárdenas, had led a democratizing movement within PRI called the Corriente Democrática (Democratic Current). After PRI expelled most members of the Corriente Democrática in 1987, Cárdenas decided to run for the presidency. He drew support from most leftist civic organizations and was nominated by four of the eight political parties that competed in the election. PARM, PPS, and PFCRN created the Frente Democrático Nacional (National Democratic Front), naming Cárdenas as their candidate. From the right, PAN put forward Manuel Clouthier, a former local and national business leader who ran unsuccessfully for governor in the northern state of Sinaloa in 1986, where he organized a significant civil mobilization against fraudulent electoral practices. Clouthier represented the new generation of PAN leaders and candidates, drawn from regional businessmen that were increasingly disappointed with the government's economic performance. PRI's candidate was a successful career bureaucrat from the budget ministry, Carlos Salinas.

Mobilization

Although the election was peaceful, late that night the CFE declared that it could not announce the electoral results because the telephone and computer systems for receiving electoral results had crashed. The suspicious nature of this incident, when combined with reports of voter intimidation, multiple voting by PRI supporters, segregation of opposition poll watchers, and stuffed ballot boxes, immediately discredited the electoral process. The CFE finally announced five days later that Carlos Salinas had received 50.36 percent of the vote, Cuauhtémoc Cárdenas 30.8 percent, and Manuel Clouthier 17.07 percent. Although the postelectoral problems were "resolved" within the timetable established by the law, many of the opposition parties considered the electoral results to be illegitimate. The regional branches of the main parties organized civil mobilizations across the nation, especially in Mexico City and the states where the opposition had a strong base: Coahuila, Chihuahua, Durango, and Sinaloa in the north; Jalisco, Michoacán, Estado de México, and Morelos in the center; and Puebla, Oaxaca, Tabasco, and Veracruz in the south. The regional branches of the national parties, after gaining strength as a result of the 1977 and 1986 electoral reforms, played a significant role in winning votes for the opposition presidential candidates and the mobilization of civil society after election day. Most of these states had an effective number of parties at the state and local levels above the competitive landmark of 1.5 before the 1988 election.

In the period between the federal election in July 1988 and President Salinas's swearing-in ceremony on 1 December 1988, four state elections sparked civil mobilizations. In the northern state of Sinaloa and the central state of Puebla, local offices of PAN organized several protests, while the members of the leftist Frente Democrático Nacional organized six months of mobilizations in the central state of Michoacán and the southern state of Guerrero.[12]

These local and state mobilizations created pressures to which the new national government had to respond. Initially the opposition presented a cohesive position against the PRI and the government, but as negotiations evolved the strategies of PAN and the Frente diverged. Cárdenas insisted that President-Elect Salinas should resign, that Congress should name a provisional government, and that a fair election should be held next year. PAN faced a more difficult choice. Although it described the presidential election as questionable, it accepted the legality of the electoral results for Congress, which gave them their historically high number of seats. However, PAN continued to push for additional reforms, arguing that the illegitimate president could achieve legitimacy by using presidential power to promote democratization, social justice, and national sovereignty. If President Salinas was willing to achieve legitimization through this secondary mechanism, the PAN would not stand in the way, and PAN's willingness to work with Salinas inaugurated a type of coalition government between the PAN and the Salinas administration.

In sum, as a consequence of the 1977 and 1986 electoral reforms and the multiple spaces for political contestation available through the federal structure, Mexico was far more democratic in 1990 than it had been in 1977.[13] The increased success at the subnational level created divided and juxtaposed governments, and debates between the PRI and opposition parties over federal, state, and local responsibilities developed. Increasingly, negotiations over the allocation of state and local budgets required the consensus not only of the political elite within one party but also of other parties. Plural negotiations over public policy became, slowly but consistently, day-to-day business at the state and local levels. Moreover, the introduction of PR seats at the local, state, and federal levels created incentives for the opposition elites in the regions to build constituencies. Furthermore, the PR system of election and the inability to run for reelection created strong incentives for elites to pursue their careers through national parties. Soon enough, as these local politicians claimed national offices, bipartisan and multiparty agreements would also be needed between the national and subnational levels.

Cycle III: The 1989–1990 Reforms

By the late 1980s, regional politicians that emerged in the first half of the transition began to compete for national political office. The multiparty political contestation present in several states in the late seventies and eighties became common in the federal legislative chamber in the next decade.

Since the PRI no longer had the capacity to amend the constitution on its own, the Salinas administration needed to build a multiparty consensus to achieve policy change. In September 1988, President-Elect Salinas proposed a four-point national agenda stressing the need for reforms regarding electoral laws and institutions, external debt, public security, and poverty. After seven months of multiparty negotiations the national congress approved a comprehensive reform in August of 1989 with the support of PRI and PAN. One month later, a multiparty consensus in the Chamber of Deputies and PRI's supermajority in the Senate also approved the new Federal Code of Electoral Institutions and Procedures (COFIPE). Let us now turn to an examination of the content of these reforms.

The Reforms

The 1989–90 reform created new spaces for political contestation by establishing that no party in the Chamber of Deputies could have more than 350 seats (70 percent of the Chamber). Although this reform guaranteed opposition parties at least

150 seats of the Chamber, it still allowed for the possibility that a party could achieve enough seats (two-thirds) to amend the constitution. Moreover, the PRI insisted on retaining the article introduced in the 1986 reform that entitled the party that won the majority of plurality seats to receive enough PR seats to achieve the overall majority in the Chamber. When combined with the electoral circumstances of the time, PRI was almost guaranteed the control of the majority of the Chamber of Deputies in the late 1980s and early 1990s and could thus avoid a divided government at the federal level.

Two important reforms significantly improved the conditions for free and fair elections in Mexico: the creation of a reliable electoral authority and a new system of voting registration. The Electoral Federal Institute (IFE) was created as a public and autonomous organism responsible for the organization of executive and legislative elections at the federal level. For the first time in the transition, the government and the PRI yielded control of the federal electoral authority. In the new twenty-three-member council, only seven members were PRI members or federal bureaucrats, while six others were citizens nominated by the president but approved by a two-thirds majority in the Chamber of Deputies, which required multiparty support, given the electoral results of 1988. The remaining ten seats were representatives of the opposition parties. The Federal Electoral Register (RFE) created a new electoral roll and a new personal voting identification. The IFE had the responsibility of creating the RFE in order to guarantee every citizen the right to vote and to guarantee every party that any given citizen would vote only once. This reform decreased the government, and the PRI's capacity to commit electoral fraud.

Effects of the Reforms on Mexico's Federal System

Contestation

Elections at the local level continued to become more competitive. In the 1990–93 period, twenty-four out of thirty-one states reached the competitive level and seven states passed the bipartisan threshold (see Table 8.2). Of the thirty most populated cities in the country, opposition parties governed in nine, and an opposition party had governed at least once in ten of thirty-one capitals. Electoral gains also continued at the state level. In the 1990–93 period all thirty-one states reported an effective number of political parties in their legislatures above the competitive level of 1.5, and one-third of them registered a number above the bipartisan threshold of 2 (see Table 8.3). The opposition also captured additional governorships (see Table 8.5). In Chihuahua former mayor Francisco Barrio, who had led the 1986 civil mobilizations as the losing candidate, became the third governor from PAN in 1992, and his party won the majority of the state congress as well. By 1993, PAN governed three states and about 10 percent of the national population. In that same year, opposition parties had gained enough seats in eight states to prevent the PRI from unilaterally changing the constitution. Divided governments existed in three states— Guanajuato, Baja California, and Baja California Sur.

At the federal level the electoral results in 1991 reflected the popularity of Carlos Salinas. The PRI recovered its comfortable majority in the Chamber of Deputies (320 out of 500) and retained a strong, although decreasing, overrepresentation in the Senate. However, concurrent subnational elections generated civic mobilizations that captured national attention and created incentives for further electoral reforms at the center.

Mobilization

In 1991 state elections for governor were held in eight states concurrently with the federal congressional elections. In spite of an impressive recovery by PRI in the federal congressional elections, the elections were uneventful and most results were accepted as legitimate. PRI gubernatorial victories in Guanajuato and San Luis Potosí, however, generated local mobilizations.[14] These mobilizations, led mainly by PAN, soon reached the national arena. Vicente Fox, a federal congressman and former businessman, ran as the PAN candidate for governor in Guanajuato. Officially he lost by almost 20 percent against the PRI candidate and former mayor of Mexico City, Ramón Aguirre. The results were questioned because of numerous electoral violations. Civil mobilization arose immediately, declaring that Fox was the legitimate winner. Soon after, Ramón Aguirre resigned as the governor-elect. The congress of Guanajuato appointed Carlos Medina, the PAN acting mayor of the industrial city of León, as the state governor. In exchange, Medina, the second non-PRI governor of modern Mexico, appointed a PRI former supreme justice as Secretary of State. This unexpected solution sent the message that party-led civil mobilizations not only could promote future legal and institutional reforms but could also change the outcome of the elections. Furthermore, it created the third divided government in the history of modern Mexico.

A similar protest occurred in San Luis Potosí, resulting in the resignation of a PRI governor, and serious civil disobedience occurred in Tabasco as well, following an overwhelming PRI victory late in 1991. Andrés Manuel López Obrador, a local PRD leader and former PRI official, led the mobilizations in Tabasco. Although the protests did not change the electoral outcome, López Obrador gained national exposure. He later became the National President of PRD and in the landmark 2000 election he was elected mayor of Mexico City. In the 1992 election in Michoacán, the PRI candidate officially won the election but the PRD candidate claimed that the result was the product of electoral fraud. Civil mobilizations ensued for months and did not cease until the PRI victor stepped down from his post. The state congress appointed a local PRI politician as governor, and PRD agreed to negotiate the conditions for a new election.

In conclusion, the 1989–93 period had significant results for the democratization process. First, the participation of political actors from the opposition at the subnational level evolved from occupying minority roles through PR to gaining the majority of seats in state assemblies or getting elected to significant executive positions at the state and local levels. This phenomenon resulted in an increasing number of divided and juxtaposed governments, which developed political dynamics between the center and the periphery that were absent under the party-state system. Second, after the first half of the Salinas administration and three cumulative electoral reforms that improved the conditions for free and fair elections, the PRI notably increased its voting share at the federal level and won several state elections with the recognition of the opposition. However, postelectoral problems arose in several states, and repeatedly the president and the national leadership of the PAN reached a negotiated solution outside the procedures established by the law. This practice, popularly known as "concertacesion," made evident that the legal framework needed modifications to prevent and solve future electoral problems. Once again subnational political conflicts provided national debates and eventually led to the electoral reforms of 1993 and 1994.

Cycle IV: The Reforms of 1993 and 1994

As the presidential election of 1994 approached, Salinas sought to avoid the disruptive electoral conflicts that had occurred in previous years and therefore acknowledged that some aspects of the electoral framework required further adjustments.

Consequently the parties in Congress discussed a new electoral reform in 1993. Although the PRD, PPS, PARM, and PFCRN abstained, the reforms approved by the PRI and the PAN produced important achievements. Once the fourth electoral reform of the transition was enacted, and as the presidential race drew closer, many political actors, including the PRI's presidential candidate, Luis Donaldo Colosio, argued for another round of reforms that would satisfy those parties that disagreed with the 1993 reform. A further reason to pursue further reforms was the Zapatista rebellion that broke out in Chiapas in January 1994. As the fifth electoral reform of the transition was being approved by a multiparty vote in Congress, Mr. Colosio was assassinated. The dramatic events in the first three months of 1994 fostered the fifth electoral reform of the transition, which should be analyzed in conjunction with the 1993 reform, since they had a cumulative impact on the following national, state, and local elections.

The Reforms

The 1993 reform included two changes that opened new spaces for political contestation. First, the constitution was amended so that no party in the Chamber of Deputies could have more than 315 seats (63 percent of the Chamber), preventing any single party from amending the constitution. The opposition was therefore guaranteed at least 185 seats. Second, the size of the Senate was doubled from sixty-four seats to 128 seats (four seats per state), and its system of election was also transformed. Three senators were to be assigned to the political party that achieved the plurality of votes and the fourth to the party that placed second in the election. This reform had a triple effect. First, it guaranteed that opposition parties would hold at least one-fourth of the seats in the Senate. Second, it reduced the level of overrepresentation between the winner and the runner-up of a Senate election, and third, it added thirty-two more seats to be awarded by the majority rule, which pleased the PRI. The 1994 reform did not open new spaces for political contestation.

Regarding the creation of conditions for free and fair elections, both reforms were deep. The 1993 reform empowered the electoral authority, the IFE, to determine the spending limits for political parties and their candidates. Previously, there was no electoral financial regulation. Although the law did not equalize expenditures between parties, it allowed some equalizing legislation through further reforms. The IFE was also empowered to provide general guidelines to the National Chamber of

Radio and Television to reduce the inequalities in electoral coverage between parties. Finally, the Tribunal Federal Electoral (TRIFE) was established as a juridical authority with constitutional rank, and its decisions were not subject to review by the Supreme Court.

The 1994 reform promoted significant changes in the composition of the General Council of the IFE and in the system for the election of its members. The parties agreed to withdraw their right to vote in the General Council's sessions and instead legislated that six citizens, appointed by two-thirds of the Chamber of Deputies, hold the majority on the eleven-member Council. This structure was replicated at the state and local councils of IFE. Every party retained a seat in every national, state, or local IFE council but without the right to vote their positions lost their deliberative power. Regarding actions to promote conditions of equality for the electoral process, a picture identification card was issued for every voter. All political parties had open access to the electoral roll, the ballots were numbered to avoid double counting and double voting, and twenty days before the election all social governmental propaganda was suspended.

Effects of the Reforms on Mexico's Federal System

Contestation

As the intensive subnational electoral calendar unfolded, political contestation at the state and local levels increased. The combination of the cumulative effect of electoral reform and economic crisis resulted in important defeats across the nation for the PRI. At the local level, in the 1994–96 period seventeen of the thirty most populated cities in the country were governed by non-PRI mayors, and the effective number of parties for mayors and city councils was above 2.0 for twenty-five out of thirty-one states (see Table 8.2). At the state level, the average effective number of parties for state congresses was 2.18; all states surpassed the competitive level (1.5), and four of the thirty-one states reached the multiparty level (2.5) (see Table 8.3). In the previous three years of the transition only ten states had registered an effective number of parties above 2, but in the 1994–96 period this number rose to twenty-three out of thirty-one states. In 1995 five states held elections for governor, and in three—Guanajuato, Jalisco, and Baja California—PAN candidates won (see Table 8.5). In the other two, Michoacán and Yucatán, the PRI candidates won in elections widely regarded as legitimate. By the end of 1995, more than 17 percent of the national population lived in the four states governed by PAN—Baja California, Guanajuato, Chihuahua, and Jalisco (Mexico's third most important state).

This increase in the number of effective political parties produced more divided and juxtaposed governments, as well as unified opposition governments. By 1996 five states had divided governments—Baja California Sur, Chihuahua, Guanajuato, Aguascalientes, and Estado de México. Two states, Jalisco and Baja California, had unified governments under PAN. In nineteen states no party had enough seats to reform the constitution by itself, and the number of juxtaposed governments more than doubled from 239 in 1991–1993 to 579 in 1994–96 (de Remes 2000a).

In a year of political violence and economic turmoil the 1994 presidential and congressional elections on 21 August were remarkably peaceful. Since no significant civil mobilizations followed, the process was generally acknowledged as the most open and transparent ever. President Ernesto Zedillo (1994–2000) of PRI received 51 percent of the vote, and although PRI retained the majority in both houses of Congress, it remained unable to reform the constitution by itself. In addition, three-fourths of the 128-seat Senate was replaced. Although the PRI held ninety-five seats overall, its highest number ever, the 1993 reforms decreased its overrepresentation rate from 33 to 24 percent, and decreased the PAN's underrepresentation rate from 19 to almost 6 percent.[15]

Mobilization

From this point forward, the character of the cycles changes slightly. As the opposition secured political power at all levels of government, they increasingly pursued further reform through formal political institutions rather than through pressure in the streets. Moreover, the increased freedom and fairness of elections meant that PRI victories were now widely recognized as legitimate.

Cycle V: The 1996 Reform

Since his first days as president-elect, Ernesto Zedillo had promoted a new round of debates to reach what he called a definitive electoral reform. On 30 January 1996 Zedillo outlined his expectations for the ongoing round of reforms by arguing that the electoral process by which he had come to power was *legal pero no equitativo* (legal but not equal).[16] President Zedillo expressed his desire to establish new electoral rules that would ensure equity in financial resources, electoral campaigns, and access to the media. Although various parties withdrew from negotiations at one time or another, all parties participated in the final negotiations for the reform in both the Chamber of Deputies and the Senate. On 30 July 1996 both houses of Congress unanimously approved the sixth and final constitutional reform of the transition.

The Reforms

The 1996 electoral reform is more comprehensive than the two previous ones. The goal was to establish an institutional and legal framework to promote free and fair elections and to prevent postelectoral protests. The 1996 reforms opened new spaces for political contestation in three ways. First, for the first time in over fifty years the inhabitants of Mexico City could elect their mayor. Previously, the president appointed the mayor. Second, in the Chamber of Deputies no single party could hold more than three hundred seats—60 percent of the Chamber. In addition, no party could be overrepresented by more than 8 percent unless it was the result of winning plurality seats. According to this formula, the PRI needed at least 42.2 percent of the national vote to retain control of the Chamber of Deputies. Third, although the territorial chamber still had 128 members, PR was introduced to the Mexican Senate. The system of election of the territorial chamber became threefold. A fourth of the Senate (thirty-two seats) was to be elected by PR from a nationwide district. From the ninety-six remaining seats (three per state) two-thirds of them (sixty-four seats) were to be assigned to the party that won the plurality of votes in each state. The remaining one-third (thirty-two seats) were to be assigned in each state to the party that finished in second place. The reform had two important effects: on the one hand, it led to significantly decreased territorial malapportionment in the Mexican Senate; on the other hand, it further decreased party overrepresentation in the national legislature.

Regarding reforms that created conditions for free and fair elections, the 1996 reform had three main achievements. First, it explicitly included at the constitutional level a set of democratic principles that involved legislative adjustments for the electoral framework at the state level. The reformed Article 116 established the autonomy of the administrative and judicial institutions responsible for the state and local elections. Furthermore it promoted conditions of equality regarding public electoral financing and access to the media. The members of these administrative bodies that resembled the IFE were appointed by two-thirds of each state congress. Second, at the federal level, the General Council of IFE became a nine-member body, and all these members were appointed by two-thirds of the Chamber of Deputies. In order to maintain the participation of political parties and members of Congress in the discussions of the General Council, legislative counselors and party representatives were allowed in the sessions with voice but no vote. Third, also at the federal level, an electoral court called Tribunal Electoral del Poder Judicial de la Federación (TEPJF) was created as the highest electoral juridical authority in the country. The members of the TEPJF were appointed by two-thirds of the Senate.

Effects of the Reforms on Mexico's Federal System

Contestation

Two congressional federal elections, thirty-one gubernatorial elections, over sixty state congress elections, and more than four thousand local elections were held between 1996 and 2001. This intense electoral calendar resulted in few civil mobilizations and few controversies. Political contestation increased across the three levels of the federal structure, and the reforms created the institutional framework for the 2000 presidential election and the peaceful transition of power from PRI to PAN.

The first test of the 1996 electoral reform was the midterm election of 1997. In 1997, ten states had elections at the state level and eleven at the local level. PAN won two more gubernatorial elections, and Mexico City had its first election for mayor in over fifty years and the fourth election for its local assembly. PRD candidates received enough votes to win the mayoral election and a strong majority of the seats in the assembly. The significant presence of opposition parties at all levels of government can be seen in the number of divided and juxtaposed governments. By 1997 seven states across the nation had experienced a divided government and as a result of the elections in ten states in 1997, six more states had divided governments.[17] The number of juxtaposed governments also rose, and by the end of the transition 53 percent of the Mexican people lived under them (de Remes 2000a).

The most impressive changes occurred in the national institutions. The 1997 congressional elections created the first divided government at the federal level under a PRI president. Although 45 percent of the Mexican population had lived under divided governments at the subnational level, a divided government at the federal level in 1997 was a momentous change. The PRI had 239 seats in the Chamber, but twelve short of the majority. It was unable to prevent the other parties, PRD (125), PAN (121), PVEM (8), and PT (7), from forming a majority opposition front. The existence of a divided government increased the degree of negotiation between parties and between the executive and the legislative branches of government.

In the Senate opposition parties also gained, although the electoral results slightly favored PRI. Of the thirty-two open seats, all of which were PR seats, the PRI gained thirteen, the PAN nine, the PRD eight, the PT one, and the PVEM one. This balance did not change the majority control of the Senate, and the PRI used its dominance in the Senate to stop policy changes promoted by the opposition in the Chamber of Deputies. Simultaneously, the opposition front in the Chamber of Deputies prevented President Zedillo from accomplishing many reforms in the second half of his administration. Although the election of thirty-two senators by PR did not change the ruling majority in the territorial chamber, it affected the degree of party overrepresentation in the Senate. The evolution of overrepresentation in the territorial chamber was striking. In 1988, with little more than 50 percent of the vote, PRI held almost 94 percent of the seats, which resulted in an overrepresentation of 42.8 percent. In 1997, with 38.5 percent of the vote, PRI held 60 percent of the seats with an overrepresentation of 21.6 percent. In ten years PRI's overrepresentation in the Senate decreased by half. The PAN achieved its highest number of seats (thirty-three) and for the first time in its history registered a degree of overrepresentation. The balance for the PRD is also positive, although the results are mixed. The PRD received its highest number of senators (sixteen) while it doubled its percentage of seats from 6.3 to a historical high of 12.5. However, its degree of underrepresentation rose from −10.5 to −13.3 percent.

Multiparty contestation across and within the federal system had reached its highest levels in history. In the period 1996−98, thirty states had an effective number of parties above 2 at their local and state levels, the bipartisan threshold, and ten states were above the multiparty threshold of 2.5. One of every three Mexicans lived under non-PRI governors. Moreover, governors elected from opposition parties or multiparty alliances governed a territory that accounted for over 50 percent of the national GDP (see Table 8.5). The presidential candidates for PAN and the PRD were both acting elected officials at the subnational level: Gobernor Vicente Fox of Guanajuato and Mayor Cuauhtémoc Cárdenas of Mexico City. The PRI nominated Francisco Labastida, the Secretary of Government of the Zedillo administration and former governor of Sinaloa (1986–92), through an open, nationwide primary—the first in Mexico's modern history.

The elections of 2000 took place under the highest standards of fairness registered in a Mexican federal campaign to date. The 1996 electoral reform established a system to promote a fair distribution of public money among the national parties and established a mechanism to define the maximum spending per campaign. Finally, because of a cumulative effort from previous reforms, a nonpartisan institution within IFE enforced such financial regulations. The IFE also monitored the airtime given to each party or alliance from 19 January to 29 June in nationwide radio morning shows and the main television evening news, and PRI's dominance of the media lessened significantly.[18]

Fox's victory in the 2000 election was the result of the contestation that had developed at the state and local levels for over a decade and represented the culmination of these changes at the national level. With 42.5 percent of the 37.6 million votes cast, Vicente Fox became the nation's president, ending Mexico's democratic transition. In addition, for the first time in Mexico's modern history no party had a majority in either chamber of Congress, replicating changes that had already occurred in many state legislatures. In the landmark simultaneous presidential and legislative elections of 2000, PRI gained more seats in the Chamber of Deputies and in the Senate than PAN or any other single party.

These outcomes in the 2000 elections created a new democratic game across the republican and federal structures. For the first time, divided government with no split congress occurred at the national level, and multiple veto points arose that were controlled by different political players. In order to approve legislation and the federal budget, the ruling party PAN required the support of the PRD or the PRI. In order to modify the constitution, the ruling party required the support of PRI. The parties in the opposition can modify any law without the approval of the PAN but would face the president's veto. Moreover, the opposition does not have enough votes to amend the constitution without support from PAN.

Regarding the federalist structure, President Fox faces another challenge. In 2002 members of his party are governors in nine states, while the PRD governs five states and Mexico City, and the PRI governs seventeen of the thirty-one states. At the local level, the PAN governs around 40 percent of the population, with the PRI in close second. What are the implications of this multiparty federal and republican structure for Mexico's democratic consolidation?

Federalism and the Consolidation of Democracy in Mexico

Although federal features created positive dynamics for Mexico's transition, federalism is not a single-edged sword. Several authors in this book have described how federal features can play a positive role in the transition to democracy and an obstructive role in the democratic consolidation. The case of Brazil is the seminal example of such a situation as Alfred Stepan, and David Samuels and Scott Mainwaring forcefully argue in this volume. How will democratic consolidation fare in Mexico's federal system?

Earlier in this volume, Alfred Stepan argues that in a federal system a number of constitutionally embedded practices and decision-making formulas that go against the general democratic principle of "one person, one vote" interact with paraconstitutional patterns of political behavior "to impede systematically a potential majority's capacity to alter the status quo or to facilitate the capacity of the majority to create politywide decisions they deem necessary for the quality of democracy and efficacious policy making." Stepan analyzes four variables in order to describe their "demos-constraining" potential. In this part I will analyze the Mexican case using two of Stepan's variables: (1) the degree of overrepresentation in the territorial chamber, (2) the "policy scope" of the territorial chamber, (3) the degree to which policy making is constitutionally allocated to supermajorities or to subunits of the federation, and (4) the degree to which the party system is politywide in its orientation and incentive systems. I will argue that Mexico's political system, although federal, is largely "demos enabling" on these measures. While granting considerable powers and representation to the states, it is less malapportioned institutionally than any of its federal counterparts in the Western Hemisphere, grants fewer powers to the "territorial" upper chamber of the national legislature, and is dominated by politywide political parties. Some of these features are embedded in the country's orig-

Table 8.6

A Continuum of the Degree of Overrepresentation in the Territorial Chambers of the World's Long-Standing Federal Democracies and Mexico

	Malapportionment in Upper Houses	Ratio of Best Represented to Worst Represented Federal Subunit (on Basis of Population)		Percentage of Seats of Best Represented Decile	
Belgium	NA	Austria	1.5/1	Belgium	10.8
Austria	0.030	Belgium	2/1	Austria	11.9
India	0.075	Mexico (2000)	8/1	Mexico (2000)	14.8
Germany	0.244	Spain	10/1	India	15.4
Mexico (2000)	0.247	India	11/1	Spain	23.7
Mexico (1997)	0.257	Germany	13/1	Germany	24.0
Spain	0.285	Australia	13/1	Australia	28.7
Canada	NA	Mexico (1997)	19/1	Mexico (1997)	28.9
Australia	0.296	Canada	21/1	Mexico (1977)	31.3
Mexico (1977)	0.317	Mexico (1977)	31/1	Canada	33.4
United States	0.364	United States	66/1	United States	39.7
Brazil	0.404	Argentina	85/1	Brazil	41.3
Argentina	0.485	Brazil	144/1	Argentina	44.8

Sources: Data for Mexico calculated by the author with inputs from the Mexican Senate at www.senado.gob.mx. Instituto Federal Electoral (IFE) at www.wife.org.mx. Population data from Mexico's National Institute of Statistics, Geography and Information at www.inegi.gob.mx. Data for malapportionment in the upper chambers for countries other than Mexico obtained from Samuels and Snyder (2001, 662). All other data from Stepan (2001).

inal constitution. For example, the Mexican constitution does not grant the Senate law-making powers over the national budget, depriving it of an important prerogative available to its counterparts in other federal countries in the hemisphere.[19] Others, however, evolved as a result of the push and pull of conflict and negotiations between government and opposition during Mexico's decades-long transition from authoritarianism. If federalism shaped Mexico's political transition, it, in turn, was also shaped by the transition, and the changes introduced heightened the demos-enabling features of the federal system. I will analyze the two variables identified by Stepan that were most shaped by the transition process: the degree of overrepresentation in the territorial chamber and the degree to which the party system is politywide in its orientation and incentive systems.

The Degree of Overrepresentation in the Territorial Chamber

State overrepresentation in the upper chamber can be problematic for democratic practice as a "win-set" of senators representing the minority of the population can join together to prevent significant modifications to the status quo. In this volume Stepan stresses this idea through a proposition: "the greater the overrepresentation of the less populous states (and thus the underrepresentation of the more populous states) the greater the demos-constraining potential of the senate."

Stepan proposes three indicators to measure overrepresentation: (1) the malapportionment index, (2) a ratio of best represented to worst represented federal subunit on basis of population, and (3) the percentage of seats of the best represented decile. The malapportionment index of the Mexican Senate has consistently decreased since 1977. In 2000, as shown in Table 8.6, this index placed Mexico significantly below nonconsolidated federal regimes like Brazil and Argentina. Moreover, its degree is even lower than long-standing federal democracies like Spain, Australia, and the United States. This is the first indicator of the comparatively low demos-constraining potential of the Mexican Senate.

Regarding the ratio of best represented to the worst represented federal subunit in the Senate, the results are also closer to the "demos-enabling" end of the continuum. In 1977 a vote in the least populated state in Mexico, Baja California Sur, was worth thirty-one votes of the most populated state, Estado de México. This 31 / 1 ratio, registered at the beginning of the transition, was already considerably lower than the situation of the United States in 1990, where a vote for the Senate in

Wyoming was worth sixty-six votes for the same election in California. Moreover, Mexico was already in 1977 less demos constraining than Brazil (144/1) and Argentina (85/1) are today (see Table 8.6).

Moreover, after the sixth electoral reform of the transition in 1996, Mexico's ratio decreased even more due to the introduction of PR national senators. After the 2000 election, the state with the highest degree of overrepresentation was Yucatán, with five senators and 1,658,210 inhabitants. Simultaneously, the state with the highest degree of underrepresentation, Estado de México, had only three senators and 13,096,686 inhabitants. Thus, one vote in Yucatán is worth eight votes in the Estado de México. This ratio is even lower than Spain's (10/1), Germany's (13/1) or Australia's (13/1), countries that have a system of election that acknowledges asymmetric representation between territorial subunits regarding population.

Although the current status of the ratio in Mexico is less demos constraining than most federal systems, this ratio is not the result of a constitutionally embedded allocation of seats between subunits but of the interaction between the PR system and the national lists proposed by each party, which is vulnerable to change in the next election. Still, the distribution of the population among states will prevent Mexico from achieving the high levels of malapportionment of Brazil, Argentina, or the United States.

Finally, overrepresentation in the territorial chamber can be measured by the percentage of seats of the best represented population decile. The starting point for Mexico in this variable is also considerably better than the current situation of the biggest federal countries in the continent. Mexico's best represented decile in 1977 had 31.3 percent of the Senate seats. Unlike in Brazil, Argentina, and the United States, overrepresented states, with only 10 percent of the national population, could not prevent constitutional reforms in Mexico (see Table 8.6). The outcome of this tendency was that the best represented decile of the country had only 14.8 percent of the seats in the Senate, whereas Spain's had 23.7 percent and Brazil's 44.8 percent.

From the previous analysis it is possible to arrive at two conclusions. First, it is demonstrable through the data in Table 8.6 that the process of the Mexican transition itself changed some of the structures in Mexico's federalism, in this case to make them less demos constraining. Second, in all three cases, Brazil, Argentina, and the United States are the most demos-constraining long-standing federal democracies and, in all three cases, Mexico's federal system is among the least demos constraining in the world.

The Degree to Which the Party System is Politywide in
Its Orientation and Incentive Systems

The second variable I will use to analyze the possible impact of Mexico's federalism on its democratic consolidation is the degree to which the party system is politywide in its orientation and incentive systems. This variable is addressed in Stepan's fourth proposition: the more political parties are disciplined parties whose incentive systems, especially concerning nominations, privileges politywide interests over provincial and local interests, the more politywide parties can mitigate the inherent demos-limiting characteristics of federalism. As we will see, the Mexican electoral framework has a set of structural incentives, which were created or reinforced throughout the transition, that have resulted in a party system that is much more disciplined and politywide oriented than both Brazil and, arguably, the United States.

In Mexico national party committees have a high influence in the designation of PR and majority candidates across the nation. Primaries are recent phenomena, and even in those cases national party committees may have a strong influence in determining the primary's procedure and validating the final results. Consequently, disciplined and politywide parties characterize Mexico's party system. National committees play a significant role in the nomination of most PR and plurality candidates. A low degree of party discipline in previous elected roles will therefore affect the probability of a politician being promoted again as candidate. The expansion of PR seats throughout the transition and the introduction of a nationwide district in the Senate also strengthened the hand of the national party leaderships. Moreover, the inability of elected politicians to run for reelection reduces the power of incumbency. Likewise, under the current electoral framework, public financial resources are available through the party and finance at least half of any campaign. Such a legal framework diminishes the financial power of an incumbent. Finally, once an elected official leaves office, most future public jobs will be party related.

In addition, since Mexico's first electoral reform in 1977 the legal framework favored politywide parties over regional parties. The Mexican framework established that a party needed to gain simultaneously 2 percent of the national vote and enough votes to pass a regional threshold.[20] All in all, the electoral legal framework created strong incentives for local political societies, as we have argued earlier in this chapter, to form regional branches of national parties rather than regional parties.

Once politywide parties were in place and their national leaders became principal agents of democratic negotiation they had no incentives throughout the twenty-three-year-long transition to modify the electoral framework to promote regional parties. These politywide institutions accomplish fairly well the two theoretical objectives of a party: they are organized electoral machines, and they solve problems of collective action within the legislative branch of government and across the three levels that compose the federal structure. By doing so they have reduced significant demos-constraining characteristics associated with federalism.

Conclusion

I have argued that federal features were influential institutions in the promotion of Mexico's democratic transition. The opening of new electoral spaces at the subnational level allowed opposition parties to enter into competition with the PRI and activated Mexico's federal system. As subnational opposition politicians gained power in the states, they mobilized their supporters in order to push for the respect of electoral laws and for additional electoral reforms. When these pressures reached the national arena, the legislative and executive branches of the national government negotiated and approved legal and institutional reforms that created better conditions for contested elections at the local and state levels. Local political elites took advantage of this opportunity by competing and often winning subnational elections. This phenomenon, along with the introduction of a PR system of election for local, state, and federal assemblies, increased the degree of multiparty representation through different branches of government at different levels of the federalist structure. Simultaneously, as spaces for political contestation in Mexico's federal system promoted democracy, democratic multiparty participation across the three levels of government transformed what was previously a purely legal framework into a functioning federal system. As the opposition claimed a greater share of electoral offices, more legislative work required the opposition's support, and the number of divided and juxtaposed governments increased, which forced the ruling party to negotiate with the opposition over many policies, including further electoral reforms.

Moreover, Mexico's transition did not result in the fragmentation of the political society into multiple regional parties, as might be anticipated in a federal system. In Mexico, regional actors participated within politywide parties, so the process of the transition mitigated potentially "demos-constraining" outcomes associated with a federally driven transition. It is fair to argue, therefore, that Mexico's federalism will not hinder the process of consolidation as has been the case in Brazil and Argentina. If this thesis proves to be right, Mexico will be among the first cases of "Third Wave" democracies in which federalism plays a positive institutional role for both democratic transition and democratic consolidation.

NOTES

This chapter was made possible thanks to the continuous support of Alfred Stepan and Edward Gibson. Both were generous with their time, reading different versions of the chapter, asking multiple questions, and pushing me when writing was difficult. Their passion for political science is inspiring and most appreciated. I especially thank Teri Caraway for her superb editing work, professionalism, and well-spirited patience.

The research for this chapter was supported by CONACYT, Secretaría de Energía, Secretaría de Educación Pública, Facultad de Derecho, UNAM, and Gobierno del Estado de Oaxaca.

1. The bibliography on the Mexican transition is young and growing by the day. The most comprehensive book about the constitutional and legal political reforms promoted in Mexico between 1977 and 1996 is Becerra, Salazar, and Woldenberg (2000). A valuable overview of the electoral reform of 1989–90 and of its immediate results in the federal election of 1991 is Nuñez (1993). For an institutional analysis of the House of Representatives and state congress in Mexico, see Lujambio (2000). Alain de Remes (2000a, b) has produced two studies of the continuous development of political competition at the local level. For a study of the historical evolution of the National Action Party (PAN) see Loaeza (1999). For an historical account of the role of the PRI in the democratic transition see González Compeán and Lomeli (2000).

2. Although the states may not contravene the articles of the national constitution, they did not have to follow all the mechanisms used in federal-level elections until the electoral reform of 1996. Therefore, electoral wrongdoings that were addressed in federal legislation were not always followed promptly or to the same degree at the state and local levels.

3. This provides a sharp contrast to the Brazilian case. See the chapter by Samuels and Mainwaring in this volume. See also Alfred Stepan's contribution to this volume (chap. 2) for a theoretical discussion of "demos-constraining" potentials in federal systems.

4. The party system in 1977 formally included four national organizations, and only PAN was in the opposition. The other three parties—the PRI, the Socialist Popular Party (PPS), and the Authentic Party of the Mexican Revolution (PARM)—were all proregime.

5. In a plurality system of election (also known as "first past the post") the candidate supported by the largest number of voters wins, and all other voters remain unrepresented. Under this electoral system, the winning party tends to be overrepresented in the legislative assembly. In a PR system both majorities and minorities are represented since votes are translated proportionally into seats. Under the PR system, the political parties usually establish a list of candidates prior to the

election. In the Mexican electoral system, the federal congress, state congresses, and city councils evolved from a full plurality system to a mixed system of plurality and PR seats.

6. By 1982 eighteen of the thirty-one states had used their legal prerogatives to include PR seats in their local city councils. Lujambio reports that this included cities with between 25,000 and 200,000 inhabitants.

7. The PR seats replaced the "party deputies," a flexible number of seats assigned to each minority party in proportion to their vote share in the election. "Party deputies" had never exceeded 42 seats since their introduction in 1963.

8. In this chapter I use the effective number of parties on the basis of vote shares for the mayoral elections to analyze political competitiveness at the local level and on the basis of seat shares for state congresses to analyze competitiveness at the state level. Both numbers are indicators in their own right but cannot be comparable against each other because they measure different electoral elements. One measures votes, the other voting outcomes.

9. For an analysis of the effects of the 1977 electoral reform in the Chamber of Deputies, see Becerra, Salazar, and Woldenberg (2000).

10. The increased presence of businessmen in the state and national upper ranks of PAN was called *Neopanismo.* Loaeza (1999) argues that this phenomenon had two important consequences. First, businessmen abandoned traditional mechanisms of extra-party political participation and instead became involved in electoral politics aimed at challenging the status quo. Second, PAN became more inclusive, increased its national scope, lightened its Catholic discourse, and started to promote civil mobilization across regions. Both of these consequences provoked the defection of traditional PAN members between 1984 and 1994.

11. A veto player is an individual or collective actor whose agreement is required for a change in policy. Although veto players may result in the government's inability to govern, it should be acknowledged that the absence of veto players might produce even worse policy results for a country's citizens. The introduction of veto players in an authoritarian regime is an essential step toward democratization. On the negative effects of veto players, see Tsebelis (1995).

12. The Frente Democrático Nacional (FDN), which had served as a vehicle for the 1988 presidential candidacy of Cuauhtémoc Cárdenas was dissolved soon thereafter. In 1989 the Partido Socialista Mexicano (PMS) joined several national and regional former FDN politicians, headed by Cárdenas, to found the Partido de la Revolución Democrática (PRD). PRD became the third largest party in Mexico and a central actor in further cycles of the democratic process.

13. In 1989, for the first time in its history, the PRI lost a gubernatorial election. It was defeated by the PAN in the northern state of Baja California.

14. Elections for governor were held in the northern states of Nuevo León and Sonora, the central states of Guanajuato, San Luis Potosí, Colima, and Querétaro, and the southern states of Campeche and Chiapas. In six states PRI victories were not challenged.

15. The percentage of party overrepresentation in the Senate is the percentage of seats a party gained minus the percentage of votes received by that party (% seats − % vote).

16. The famous statement can be found on the front page of *Excelsior,* 31 January 1996.

17. Before 1997, Baja California (1989–92 and 1992–95), Michoacán (1989–92), Guanajuato

(1991–94 and 1994–97), Baja California Sur (1993–96), Chihuahua (1995–98), Aguascalientes (1995–98), and México (1996–99) had divided governments. In 1997 six more states had divided governments: Coahuila (1997–99), Morelos (1997–2000), Colima (1997–2000), Guanajuato (1997–2000), Querétaro (1997–2000), and Sonora (1997–2000). See Lujambio, (2000, 68).

18. For these data see Becerra, Salazar, and Woldenberg (2000).

19. The Mexican constitution claims that the federal budget is not a law, and this fiction deprives the Senate of jurisdiction over federal budgets. Consequently, senators in Mexico have been living the irony of sharing the responsibility of establishing the nation's taxes, through the federal income law, while being unable to speak or vote on the way such income should be spent. In spite of a number of changes made in the policy scope of the Senate during the long transition process, this critical feature was left unchanged.

20. The latter was simply calculated as the quotient of the number of national votes divided by the number of PR seats. In Brazil, the state threshold was a "quotient" calculated by the division of the number of votes in a state by the number of PR seats in that state. A regional party in Brazil could obtain federal representation through PR winning a minority of votes in its state and without winning a single vote in any other state.

BIBLIOGRAPHY

Becerra, Ricardo, Pedro Salazar, and José Woldenberg. 2000. *La Mecánica del Cambio Político en México*. México D.F.: Cal y Arena.

Cornelius, Wayne. 2000. Blind Spots in Democratization: Sub-national Politics as a Constraint on Mexico's Transition. *Democratization* 7 (3): 117–32.

de Remes, Alain. 2000a. *Juxtaposition in Mexican Municipal Electoral Contests: The Silent Cohabitation*. México D.F.: CIDE.

———. 2000b. *Municipal Electoral Processes in Latin America and Mexico*. México D.F.: CIDE.

González Compeán, Miguel, and Leonardo Lomelí. 2000. *El Partido de la Revolución: Institución y Conflicto, 1928-1999*. México D.F.: Fondo de Cultura Económica.

INEGI. 1996. *Conteo de Población y Vivienda 1995*. México D.F.: INEGI.

———. 2000. *XII Censo General de Población y Vivienda, 2000. Resultados Preliminares*. México D.F.: INEGI.

Laakso, Markku, and Rein Taagepera. 1979. Effective Number of Parties: A Measure with Application to West Europe. *Comparative Political Studies* 12 (April): 3–27.

Loaeza, Soledad. 1999. *El Partido Acción Nacional: La Larga Marcha, 1939-1994*. México D.F.: Fondo de Cultura Económica.

Lujambio, Alonso. 2000. *El Poder Compartido*. México D.F.: Oceano.

Nuñez, Arturo. 1993. *La Reforma Electoral de 1989-1990*. México D.F.: Fondo de Cultura Económica.

Samuels, David, and Richard Snyder. 2001. The Value of a Vote: Malapportionment in Comparative Perspective. *British Journal of Political Science* 31 (4): 651–71.

Snyder, Richard. 2001. *Politics after Neoliberalism: Reregulation in Mexico*. Cambridge: Cambridge University Press.

Stepan, Alfred. 2001. Toward a New Comparative Politics of Federalism, (Multi) Nationalism, and Democracy: Beyond Rikerian Federalism. In *Arguing Comparative Politics*. Oxford: Oxford University Press.

Tsebelis, George. 1995. Decision Making in Political Systems: Veto Players in Presidentialism, Parliamentarism, Multicameralism and Multipartyism. *British Journal of Political Science* 25(3): 289–325.

Weldon, Jeffrey. 1997. The Political Sources of Presidencialismo in Mexico. In *Presidentialism and Democracy in Latin America*, edited by S. Mainwaring and M. S. Shugart. New York: Cambridge University Press.

CHAPTER 9

Do Federal Institutions Matter?

Rules and Political Practices in Regional Resource
Allocation in Mexico

—ALBERTO DIAZ-CAYEROS

Institutions and Political Practices

Do federal institutions matter? This question has become the focus of lively debate decades after William Riker answered it with a resounding "no." In Riker's account, federalism comes about as an institutional solution to the problem of enlarging governments (1964, 2). Despite its origin, Riker argued that the policy impact of federalism was rather limited (1964, 1975).[1] Although he based his argument on scant empirical evidence, the assertion that federalism did not affect policy outcomes remained uncontested for many years. Recently, however, a number of scholars have disputed Riker's claims about the irrelevance of federalism. Stepan (chap. 2), for example, forcefully argues that the institutions of federalism often preserve a structurally induced status quo bias, even against the preferences of powerful political actors. Formal models of federalism have also suggested both the stabilizing and de-

297

stabilizing roles of federal arrangements, and each has important policy implications (Bednar 2001; Dixit and Londregan 1998; Weingast 1995; Weingast and Figuereido 1998).

The rational choice literature on institutions has produced a deeper understanding of the role of institutions in producing stability in what would otherwise be chaotic social choice problems. In particular, formal political institutions are often viewed as instruments designed by politicians in order to narrow the social choice issue space, thereby inducing stable policy outcomes (Shepsle 1979; Shepsle and Weingast 1987).[2] Federalism received far less attention than other institutional aspects of the political system, perhaps because of the shadow cast by William Riker, one of the founders of the rational choice approach. Riker believed that the degree of centralization or decentralization of a federal system (and its policy effects in general) depended on the workings of the party system. Political parties, not federal institutions, had policy significance.

Political parties are political devices that constrain social choice spaces, presumably bringing about stability in outcomes. Parties can create political practices that change the outcome that would have been generated by formal rules and procedures (i.e., institutions). In this sense, parties can become a substitute for formal institutions in solving social choice issues. The Rikerian hypothesis about the "(in)significance" of federalism can be reformulated in the following terms: political practices, including but not limited to the workings of the party system, determine the degree of centralization of federal regimes, which implies that although federal institutional arrangements might be similar in two countries, binding constraints are created by political practices, as expressed in party competition, political bargaining, and internal procedures within political parties.

Willis, Garman, and Haggard (1999) have recently advanced our understanding of federalism in precisely this direction, suggesting that the control of party nominations is the most crucial explanatory variable of the degree of decentralization found in federal (and even unitary) systems in Latin America.[3] In order to think about federal arrangements meaningfully, our theoretical frameworks should therefore combine an institutional approach (the rules and procedures in the federal constitution and other legal provisions that constrain political choice) with political practices (the strategic maneuvering of political parties and bargaining among politicians). An analysis of individual legislators acting alone in the world of legislative rules, committees, agenda formation, and veto powers is insufficient.

On the empirical front, during the last few years scholars have found that federalism has an impact on fiscal transfers, macroeconomic performance, and corruption. For instance, Gibson, Faletti, and Calvo (this volume) provide empirical evidence suggesting that malapportionment in federal systems gives disproportionate shares of financial resources to rural states, at least in the federal systems of Brazil and Argentina. Erik Wibbels has found that federal systems make coordination in macroeconomic adjustment processes more difficult. Daniel Treisman has found that federal regimes are more corrupt than central ones. Nevertheless, Jonathan Rodden found that, controlling for variables related to tax authority and the party system, federalism had no independent effect on the size of government (Rodden undated; Treisman 2000; Wibbels 2000). Although the verdict is still open as to the policy significance of federalism in large N, cross-sectional analyses, specific country case studies are necessary in order to assess the mechanisms through which federalism may or may not have some policy significance.

This chapter uses the case of Mexico to explore the relative importance of the federal institutional framework in an environment of fast-changing political processes. It claims that understanding the outcomes of fiscal federalism in Mexico requires going beyond the formal institutional framework to probe the workings of the Mexican party system. The chapter seeks to explain the allocation of various federal funds across states in Mexico. In particular, it examines whether two key political actors, governors and senators, play a role in the federal allocation of transfers to the states. The analysis shows that the bargaining power of governors and senators is severely limited, but that such limitation arises not from the institutional rules, but from the political practices. The upper chamber, which is meant to represent state interests, has in practice become a space for party, rather than regional representation. Governors have not influenced the allocation of resources to their states because they have been subservient to the party that had determined, until quite recently, their chances for career advancement. The new configuration of party competition that has emerged in Mexico since 1997, with the loss of the Partido Revolucionario Institucional (PRI) majority in the lower chamber and its defeat in the 2000 presidential election, might change the role of governors and senators in the very near future. The implication of the analysis here is that such changes will modify the allocation of financial transfers in the Mexican federation, without any institutional change to the federal organization.

The chapter provides specific empirical tests for the determinants of the allocation of various federal transfers. In particular, the allocation of federal transfers for education and social infrastructure has been primarily driven by a partisan logic of competition and a coalitional imperative to reward smaller units in the federal pact. Competitive states have received larger transfers. In the case of education funds, for example, party competition was more important than number of schools, teachers, or school-aged children as an allocation criterion. This is attributable to the role that teachers have traditionally played in Mexico in the mobilization of votes during electoral processes in favor of the party that ruled the country for seven decades, until 2000. On the other hand, small states seem to have benefited disproportionately from federal transfers because they belonged to a coalition of traditional PRI political players. The larger and more modern political units in the federation have increasingly abandoned the PRI since the 1980s in favor of other party alternatives. Although the analysis does not find an explicit bias in the system of transfers that punishes states that elect opposition governments (Diaz-Cayeros, Magaloni, and Weingast 2002), it does systematically find that smaller states, where the PRI was strongest, received more funds in per capita terms, controlling for other factors.

The next section presents a brief discussion of the institutional context of federalism in Mexico, including the institutional arrangements of fiscal federalism. It discusses the role of states envisaged in the constitution, and within it, the role of governors and the Senate. Since fiscal federalism and the system of transfers is not a constitutional provision, the section ends with a discussion of the provisions contained in the Fiscal Coordination Law for the allocation of transfers across states. The following section analyzes through regression models the allocation of federal resources across Mexican states. The analysis is carried out for the various funds that constitute the backbone of Mexican fiscal federalism, as expressed in the decentralized budgetary items 28 and 33. The last section concludes and suggests a substantive and methodological agenda for further research.

The Institutions of Federalism in Mexico

The Federal Constitution and the States

Can states in a federation be trusted? The Mexican constitution clearly establishes that they cannot. The Mexican federal pact reflects a deeply embedded distrust of state power. The federal content in the document does not reflect an aspiration to bring about, for example, equality of conditions among constituent units, nor does it provide for specific benefits federalism is supposed to bring about for citizens. Federalism is primarily about limiting the power of the states. Although Article 40 of the constitution states that Mexico is a representative, democratic, federal republic composed of free and sovereign states with respect to their internal affairs, and Article 124 gives residual authority to states over anything that is not explicitly granted to the federal government in the constitution, all other provisions contained in the document limit state authority.[4]

Much of this distrust of states is rooted in an historical process of consolidation of national authority. Consonant with Riker's two principles of federalism, the federal arrangement was the only way to keep the country together in the face of the threat of the northern neighbor and the secessionist tendencies of several states (most notably successful Texas, but also unsuccessful Yucatán, for example). At the same time, however, a highly centralized system was established, once the country was pacified in the later part of the otherwise very unstable nineteenth century.

This distrust of states is expressed mainly in the realm of taxation. The constitution contains provisions that limit state authority to tax by granting exclusive rights to both the federal and the municipal governments. The exclusivity for the federal government was a long process, culminating in the 1940s with the exclusive authority being granted to the federal government over several important taxes, although Congress never approved a bill proposed in the 1940s to provide for explicit exclusive tax assignment to the federal government. The exclusivity of municipalities in the property tax is a more recent development, finding its expression in the 1983 reform of Article 115.[5]

Although Article 31 Paragraph IV only provides that Mexicans must contribute to the public expenditures of the federation, states, and municipalities on a proportional and equitable basis, Article 73 establishes explicitly the tax authority of the federal Congress. In practice this means that the federal government has no limitation whatsoever on the taxes it can levy (Paragraph VII of the article states that the federal government can establish the taxes necessary to cover its budget). States, on the other hand, have very specific limitations on several fiscal sources.

The most important limitation emerged in the vigorous fiscal debates of the nineteenth century that dealt with taxes on internal trade (the so-called *alcabala*), which are explicitly forbidden in Articles 116 and 117, although states have often violated these provisions whenever they had the power to do so. The second major limita-

tion is related to taxing natural resources, which are exclusively under federal jurisdiction (Articles 27 and 73). The third limitation is the recent establishment of exclusive authority for municipalities over several areas, including property taxes, with
the 1983 reform of Article 115.

Centralized authority throughout the twentieth century has been enhanced in
Mexico through increasing the authority of the federal Congress in areas as diverse
as the control over natural resources, regulation of financial institutions, and the exclusive right to impose taxes on foreign trade and the production of specific goods
(tobacco, alcohol, beer, electricity, matches, fuel, forest products). All of these reforms were carried out through modifying Article 73, which has been changed thirty-
six times.

In Article 73 the federal government through Congress is allowed to (1) impose
taxes as needed to cover its budget, (2) prevent states from restricting interstate trade,
(3) legislate in oil, mining, cinemas, betting, financial services, electric and nuclear
power, and labor, (4) coordinate states and municipalities on issues of public safety,
(5) distribute education responsibilities "conveniently" between federation, states,
and municipalities for the education function, seeking to unify standards, (6) issue
laws on matters of concurrence between levels of government on population and
environment, and (7) establish taxes on foreign trade, natural resources, credit and
insurance institutions, concessioned services and excises on electricity, tobacco, gas,
matches, alcohol, forestry, and beer.

It is important to note that this authority is not vested in the executive but in Congress. The Mexican executive is, in fact, comparatively weak from an institutional
standpoint. During the era of PRI hegemony, the overwhelming presidential power
was only possible because PRI controlled both chambers and the presidency, and the
political incentives of the system were such that congresspersons and senators were
willing to abide with presidential priorities and policies (Weldon 1996).[6]

On the other hand, the constitution grants exclusive authority to the municipalities over (Article 115): drinking water and sewage, public lighting, cleaning, markets, graveyards, slaughterhouses, streets, parks and gardens, public safety, and, in
the realm of taxation, the property tax. The provision implies that public good provision at the local level is a municipal responsibility, especially public works that are
politically important such as the provision of drinking water (and its user charges
and fees). The inclusion of such detail in Article 115 is a peculiarity of the Mexican
federal arrangement, since municipal authority is no longer a matter decided according to the "internal regime" of each state.

States are explicitly forbidden from taxing the transit of persons or goods in their territory, forbidding or taxing directly or indirectly the entrance or exit of any foreign or national good, taxing consumption through anything resembling internal customs, keeping any tax law implying a difference in taxation due to the origin of a good, contracting foreign debt (Art. 117), taxing production, storage, or sale of tobacco, and taxing imports or exports (Art. 118). These prohibitions are particularly relevant since the Supreme Court does not play an active role in judicial interpretation. The federal government has therefore taken these provisions as the fundamental argument against state sales taxes and exemptions that could easily become "a tax law implying a difference in taxation due to the origin of a good." Such rationale is behind the whole evolution of the System of Fiscal Coordination and the existence of a national value-added tax, discussed below.

Although the constitution does not include any specific provision on the system of federal financial transfers, revenue sharing is explicitly considered in the document at three points. In Article 73, when discussing excises, the constitution specifies that a secondary law will determine the proportion that states will receive from those revenues, and in the case of electricity commands that state congresses shall establish revenue sharing for municipalities on (federal) electricity taxes. Article 115, which gives states the exclusive authority over the property tax, also establishes that municipalities should receive federal revenue shares according to conditions approved by local congresses. Hence, the provisions for revenue sharing again reinforce the notion that municipalities are key players in Mexican fiscal federalism, although the particular distribution of resources across municipalities within a state is regarded as a state matter. But perhaps more importantly, the constitution allows for revenue sharing to be decided in secondary law, which explains the relative ease with which changes to the revenue-sharing arrangements and the introduction of various new decentralized federal transfer funds have been created in recent years.

Governors and Senators

The constitution provides for the direct election of the two main political actors in the federal arrangement—governors and the members of the Senate. The federal constitution provides little insight on the attributes of governors, since their power and authority is considered a matter of a state's internal affairs. However, it does establish in Article 116 that state executive power is vested in the governor, which excludes parliamentary systems in the states. Article 116 also provides for the direct election of both the state executive and the local legislators, and it prohibits reelection (notwithstanding controversial cases of reelection in Guanajuato during the 1950s and Yucatán in the late 1990s). Since the early 1930s, there has been almost no change in the institutional arrangement that constrains governors. However, the role of governors has changed dramatically during the last decade, which suggests that although state constitutions differ in the design of executive-legislative relations, the changing role and behavior of governors in Mexico is not related to institutional changes but to political practices in the party system.

Two changes are particularly important. First, gubernatorial elections have become highly contestable, which weakened PRI presidential authority over its fellow governors. The party nomination is no longer equivalent to electoral success. Second, the presence of governors from parties different from that of the president (PAN and PRD before 2000), and divided governments at the state level have also challenged the PRI's hegemony and altered relations between the executive and the legislature.

Individual politicians might seek to become governors of their states for a variety of reasons, including a desire to continue a legacy, to represent some local bases of support, or to construct national political alliances. Diaz-Cayeros and Langston (undated) suggest that the value of becoming a governor in Mexico depended historically upon (a) the intrinsic prestige of the office, (b) the opportunities for future career advancement, (c) control of patronage and corruption, (d) opportunities for private business, (e) leadership of a local or national team, and (f) the relative safety or risk involved in keeping such office.[7] Within this framework, the greatest constraints a governor faced in office during the time of hegemonic PRI rule were related to governance at the local level, which depended on bases of support and local coalitions constructed by the incumbent governor, the accountability of governors for political stability in their states, the real threat of removal (since the president controlled the Senate), and the dependence of state governments on federal transfers.

These constraints still exist today, but the great decentralization of financial resources and increasing challenges posed by the juxtaposition of municipal and state governments (de Remes 2000), coupled with the presence of divided governments (Lujambio 2000), has made governors more prominent political figures. There is little doubt that the overall value of the office has increased. Although opportunities for corruption, patronage, and doing private business have been sharply reduced by the contestability of elections, governors have become centerpieces of political groups. Their opportunities for future career advancement are better than ever: every single serious contender to become president in the 2000 elections was or had recently been a governor (Fox in Guanajuato, Cárdenas in the Federal District, Labastida in Sinaloa).[8]

Diaz-Cayeros and Langston note that the "easiest" post through which to reach a governorship during the time of PRI dominance was a Senate seat, followed by a Chamber of Deputies seat, and then a bureaucratic post or a job in a federal agency. This finding is significant, since the Senate, in spite of the centralized nature of the PRI regime, could have a link to local politics which federal bureaucratic posts do not necessarily have.[9] A Senate seat was the best career choice to achieve a governor seat. Diaz-Cayeros (1997) shows that over half of the governors from 1935 to 1970, the period during which PRI hegemony was strongest, had once held a Senate seat. Since there were sixty-four Senate seats there was a fair chance for a local politician to reach the highest executive office at the state level through the Senate. During the heyday of PRI hegemony, politicians in Mexico established the role of the Senate primarily as a mechanism for the circulation of local elites into high office, particularly the governorship, rather than an arena for the discussion and enactment of the federal bargain.

One would expect that the processes of decentralization and democratization witnessed during the last years in Mexico should lead to the strengthening of the Senate. The upper chamber representing the states belonging to the federal pact presumably would be strengthened in order to keep an incongruent and symmetrical bicameralism (Lijphart 1984).[10] That is, the composition of the Senate should be different from that of the Chamber of Deputies, and their formal constitutional powers should be symmetric if politicians wanted an upper chamber that would provide a counterweight to the executive and the Chamber of Deputies. Instead, the institutional changes to the Senate during recent years have produced increasingly more congruence between the upper and the lower chambers, while the formal constitutional powers of the Senate have not been increased.[11]

Senators have traditionally been responsive to whoever controlled the nomination procedures to become governor in their states. If the sitting governor was powerful, senators became his agents; if the president determined nominations, senators responded to his preferences. During the nineteenth century, as a consequence of the indirect election method for the Senate, the domination of local strongmen, who were usually also the governors over the local congresses, and the relative decentralization of financial and tax authority, senators were agents of the governors. In the aftermath of the Mexican Revolution this pattern continued, notwithstanding the direct election of senators, because future local careers depended on being on good terms with the sitting governor. During the years of PRI hegemony, Senate seats instead became the main stepping-stone into a governor seat. To capture the party's nomination to a governorship, aspiring candidates had to either become agents of the governor in the case of strong states, or show loyalty and discipline to the president.[12] Senators were also powerful allies of the president in disciplining local politicians by declaring the "dissolution of powers" in states in turmoil. Moreover, the Senate was used to block legislation from the lower chamber, such as the reintroduction of the immediate reelection by the Chamber of Deputies in 1965, which was never passed.[13] This alliance with the federal executive was possible to the extent that a governor nomination depended to a large degree on the will of the president.

In theory, the Mexican Senate would have been the space for the representation of states within the federal institutional arrangement. Such an idea underlies the equal representation of each state, and the Federal District, in that body. In practice, senators have expressed partisan, rather than regional interests, which is a consequence of the no-reelection rule, the concurrent election of senators and the president, the nomination procedure for PRI candidates to governorships, the lack of authority of the Senate over the federal budget, and the electoral rules that have increased the district magnitude for the Senate (Diaz-Cayeros 1998). Although the Senate should be the arena for the discussion of federalism, it has mostly been a space for the political circulation of elites.

Fiscal Transfers and Tax Authority

To finish this overview of the institutions of federalism in Mexico, one must discuss the rules governing federal transfers and fiscal authority of the states. As previously mentioned, the Mexican constitution does not establish the workings of the federal transfer system and an explicit tax assignment as in other countries. A secondary law, the Ley de Coordinación Fiscal (LCF), is the cornerstone of Mexican fiscal federalism. The most important element in the Mexican federal transfer system was, until December 1997, revenue sharing. In 1998 a substantive change was made to the LCF, with the incorporation of federal transfers to states and municipalities, both ear-marked and not, within the new federal budgetary Item 33.[14]

Federal conditional transfers have existed in Mexico at least since the creation of federal budgetary Item 26 in the late 1970s, which was designed to provide match-ing grants for states and municipalities to finance local public works. The evolution of conditional transfers at the time, however, was highly contingent on the priori-ties reflected in federal investment projects and not on a set of rules for the provi-sion of transfers to subnational governments. Funds in Item 26 became extremely important during the Salinas administration (1988–94), since they became the cor-nerstone of the poverty alleviation strategy of the *Solidaridad* program. But even in this clear programmatic structure, *Solidaridad* funds remained highly discretionary and were often criticized for being managed for electoral purposes.[15] These funds were later transformed (during the Zedillo administration [1994–2000]) into the so-called Municipal Social Infrastructure Fund, with their allocation determined by a very complex poverty formula. This transfer was later incorporated into one of the funds in Item 33. Most of the Item 33 transfers relate to expenditures originally un-dertaken by the federal government that have now been converted to conditional transfers. Among these new transfers, the most important relates not to poverty al-leviation and social infrastructure, but to the payroll of teachers, which was decen-tralized to the states through an agreement reached in 1993.

Table 9.1 provides a breakdown of the funds in budgetary Item 33 allocated to the states and municipalities in the 2000 budget. The most important of the funds for states is the education transfer (FAEB), followed by funds for health (FASSA) and public safety. Municipalities receive two funds that are almost equally important, the Fondo para la Infraestructura Social Municipal (FISM) and the unconditional Fund to Strengthen Municipalities (FORTAMUN). The evidence suggests that although the allocation of specific funds might be unequal, the aggregation of all funds fol-lows a relatively equal per capita distribution (Courchene and Diaz-Cayeros 2001). The focus in the analysis of the next section is on each specific fund, however, since the purpose of this chapter is to test for the weight of political practices on the al-location of transfers.

The current system of federal transfers has resulted in a huge vertical imbalance. Not only do states and municipalities collect little revenue, but they are highly de-pendent on federal revenue sharing. There is, however, a wide variation in the de-pendency of states on federal revenue shares. On average, 82 percent of state net rev-

Table 9.1
Funds Transferred in the Mexican Federal System in Budgetary Items 28 and 33

Name of Fund	Purpose	Comment
Fondo de Aportaciones para la Educación Básica (FAEB)	Education expenditures to cover teacher salaries and the costs of previously federal schools.	Transfers were initiated in 1993, although made part of Item 33 until 1998.
Fondo de Aportaciones de Salud (FASSA)	Health expenditures to cover expenses of decentralized health clinics, doctors, and nurses.	States gradually became part of health decentralization after 1992.
Fondo de Infraestructura Social (FIS)	Public works, allocated to municipalities directly by the federal government and a fraction to states.	Poverty formula for allocation was established after 1996.
Fondo de Fortalecimiento Municipal (FORTAMUN)	Municipal priorities, not conditioned.	Allocated in per capita terms as a concession to the PAN in order to approve the 1998 budget.
Fondo de Aportaciones Múltiples (FAM)	School breakfasts and small social programs for children.	Previously centralized funds for DIF.
Fondo de Aportaciones Sociales (FAS)	Technical education and adult literacy programs.	
Fondo de Aportaciones para la Seguridad Pública (FASP)	Resources to jointly fight crime between states and the federal government.	Created in 1999.
Fondo de Infraestructura Educativa (FIED)	Resources for school construction and maintenance.	
Fondo de Fomento Municipal (FFM)	Municipal nonconditioned general revenue sharing.	Driven by a formula including previous allocations and tax effort.
Fondo General de Participaciones (FGP)	General revenue sharing.	20 percent must be transferred to municipalities.
Participaciones sobre Impuestos Especiales de Productos y Servicios (IEPS)	Revenue sharing on excises of beer, tobacco, and alcohol.	Specific formulas for each product.
Incentivos Económicos	Revenue sharing transferred for administrative collaboration in the collection of federal taxes.	Extended to all activities in the value-added tax and the income tax in 2000.
Fondo de Fortalecimiento de los Estados	Funds for states with high debt burden or high educational effort.	Created for 2000 as a preemptive measure to ensure approval of the budget.

enues depend on federal revenue sharing. The median vertical imbalance is slightly higher than that, at 85.6 percent. The distribution of vertical imbalance is also highly skewed. Dependency is higher than 80 percent for twenty-five states. In this sense, the only states that exhibit relatively strong local finances are Hidalgo, Chihuahua, Oaxaca, Quintana Roo, Yucatán, Veracruz, and the Federal District (Courchene and Diaz-Cayeros 2001).

In this "fiscal pact with the devil" (Careaga and Weingast 2000), states in Mexico gave up their local sources of revenue in exchange for unconditional transfers from an exclusively federal tax pool. A slow process of abdication on tax authority by states occurred in Mexico during the course of the twentieth century, reaching the peak of centralization with the creation of the SNCF in 1980 (Diaz-Cayeros 1995). A central feature in the Mexican arrangement, according to Diaz-Cayeros, was that it became sustainable to the extent that all governors and politicians at the SNG level belonged to the same political party and depended for their career advancement and electoral success on the federal government (Diaz-Cayeros 1997). Once multiparty competition set in, this arrangement was no longer a political equilibrium, which explains the increased demand for devolution of authority to states and municipalities witnessed in the last decade.

Political Determinants of the Allocation of Federal Funds

This section tests some hypotheses related to the allocation of federal funds among states in Mexico. In particular, it addresses whether unconditional transfers in budgetary Item 28 and conditional transfers in Item 33 are allocated according to a partisan political logic, rather than simply following the institutional provisions contained in the LCF. In this way we can also assess the relative weight of political practices versus the economic and social criteria contained in the LCF. Where governors, parties, and the system of representation have little role, political variables should not significantly influence resource allocation. Having shown that the key institutional actors (governors and senators) have primarily been motivated by the incentives induced by the hegemonic party system, this section shows that fiscal federalism in Mexico has not been driven by rules but by political practices.

The section tests whether allocations are biased: (1) in favor of states where the ruling party at the federal level, the PRI, was electorally strong, (2) against states governed by an opposition party, either the PAN or the PRD, (3) in favor of states that are more contestable (given a higher competitiveness, as measured by the number of effective parties), and (4) toward small states, with a greater overrepresentation in the Senate.[16] An additional issue, which although deeply political is often couched in terms of economic efficiency, is to test whether allocations of federal transfers reinforce or compensate political units collecting fewer financial resources from their own tax sources. Those political effects are assessed by controlling for economic variables such as the level of development, the pervasiveness of poverty, and indicators of the specific variables to which a particular fund is supposed to respond, such as the number of teachers and doctors for education and health, respectively.

The political variables are operationalized through the percentage of PRI vote in the last federal election (VPRI97), a dummy variable for states with a governor from the PAN or the PRD (GOBOPO), the Laakso-Tagepera index (H) for the effective number of parties, and the overrepresentation in the Senate (MALAPSEN). Per capita own revenue collected at the local level (INGEST or INGMUNP, depending on whether the estimate deals with state or municipal funds) is used in order to control for the strength of local finances and, implicitly, the incentive effects generated by transfers. The economic control variables are the per capita GDP of each state in 1997 (GDPPC97), a poverty index (the Foster-Greer-Thorbecke index with a poverty line set at two minimum wages, FGT22), and the number of students, teachers, schools, doctors, and health clinics, all in per capita terms.

The dependent variables of the estimations are the per capita allocations of funds to each state, according to the 1999 budget, in each of the items considered in Table 9.1. Data were obtained from the federal budget and the finance ministry, as reported by Courchene and Diaz-Cayeros (2001).[17] All estimations are OLS corrected for heteroskedasticity. The use of estimates for only one year, in spite of the radical political transformations witnessed in Mexico since 1997, is adequate given that the distribution of those funds across states has only changed marginally since then.[18]

The first estimation, provided in Table 9.2, shows the determinants of the per capita allocation of education funds by state (FAEB), which is the most important fund within budgetary Item 33. This estimate suggests that funds are provided to states following an economic logic of sending more resources to the richer states, and not a compensatory logic of providing for more basic education funds to poorer states. The allocations do seem to compensate for weak state finances, in the sense of sending more resources to states with less of their own revenue, which is consonant with the constitutional provision of the federal government being responsible

Table 9.2
Determinants of FAEB per Capita Allocation, 1999 (heteroskedastic consistent errors, t statistics in parentheses)

	(1)	(2)	(3)	(4)
Enrollment	−6.21^a	−2.09		
	(1.99)	(1.28)		
Teachers	127.02^a		−2.33	
	(1.98)		(0.06)	
Schools	76.88		51.72	
	(0.70)		(0.73)	
GDP		0.11^b	0.13^b	0.13^b
		(3.29)	(3.66)	(3.85)
Poverty		548.75	224.66	462.88
		(1.26)	(0.39)	(0.99)
State revenue		−1.07^b	−0.66	−0.74^a
		(2.13)	(1.48)	(2.01)
Competitiveness		254.52^a	315.24^b	319.75^b
		(1.80)	(2.35)	(2.38)
Opposition		43.73	47.66	46.57
		(0.50)	(0.51)	(0.53)
Malapportionment		6,821.10^b	6,078.49^b	6,364.11^b
		(6.45)	(5.65)	(6.90)
PRI vote		1,291.60	1,513.76	1,489.22
		(1.37)	(1.42)	(1.46)
Constant	1,180.03	136.61	−787.58	−732.51
	(1.62)	(0.15)	(0.99)	(0.97)
F	4.65	24.04	11.77	18.09
R^2	0.28	0.78	0.77	0.76

^{a}Significant at the 90% level.
^{b}Significant at the 95% level.

for creating relatively even education levels across the territory. States with weak local finances will invest little in education, which provides a rationale for a federal allocation of funds to supplement state expenditure. However, a different interpretation of this negative coefficient is that states that collect more revenue and that spend more of their own funds on education are not rewarded for their effort, while other states behave opportunistically, making little effort of their own, since they benefit from federal transfers.

The positive sign of the per capita GDP variable is somewhat surprising. The federal government commands resources in a disproportionate manner from the rich regions, which suggests redistribution in favor of the poorer states. In the realm of tax collection and revenue-sharing agreements, as long as there is an agency problem, a model provided by Diaz-Cayeros (1997) suggests that redistribution cannot be the rule. But from a public policy perspective one would expect a negative sign in the GDP variable, so overall transfers are redistributive even if the per capita allocations of revenue shares are biased toward rich regions, controlling for population and other variables. This seems not to be the case for education transfers, which suggests that a bargaining effect for richer states is playing a role in these funds, although this result merits further research.

The most important results for the purpose of this paper, however, concern political variables, namely, a highly significant and positive effect of the number of parties, malapportionment in the Senate, and the PRI vote. The coefficients suggest that the federal government has sent more education funds, ceteris paribus, to highly competitive states, where the margin of victory (or defeat) for the PRI is small.[19] This is complemented by the finding that malapportionment turns out to be a very strong predictor of funds going disproportionately to smaller states. There is no evidence indicating that an opposition governor is punished with fewer education funds. However, there seems to be an indication that PRI supporters are rewarded with more resources (in terms of the VPRI97 variable), although the coefficient is not statistically significant.

The first estimate in Table 9.2 does not control for some educational variables, which should play a role in the allocation of education funds, according to the LCF. In particular, funds should be somewhat related to school enrollment (MATRIC), the per capita number of teachers (MAEST), and schools (ESCUE). Surprisingly, these variables, which are included in the law as criteria for the allocation of education funds, fail to be statistically significant. The political variables remain significant, and their coefficients relatively unchanged.

The irrelevance of education variables, coupled with the political findings and the positive sign of the per capita GDP control, suggest that education funds in Mexico are allocated according to the bargaining power of the teachers' union (SNTE), a perception of contestability in the electoral arena where teachers might be important vote promoters for the PRI, and a disproportionate share to small states that might be captured through the Senate seats by members of the SNTE.

The result for the education funds is particularly striking when contrasted with the next most important fund within Item 33, the health fund (FASSA). Table 9.3 shows that, among the political variables, only malapportionment seems to have a

Table 9.3
Determinants of FASSA per Capita Allocation, 1999 (heteroskedastic
consistent errors, t statistics in parentheses)

	(2)		(1)
Doctors	12.02[a]	9.19[b]	
	(4.78)	(2.11)	
Medical units	37.81[a]	37.58[b]	
	(3.29)	(2.06)	
GDP		0.02[b]	0.04[b]
		(2.31)	(3.37)
Poverty		52.16	−71.94
		(0.33)	(0.39)
State revenue		−0.05	−0.22
		(0.48)	(0.51)
Competitiveness		33.43	49.86
		(0.85)	(1.10)
Opposition		3.90	5.61
		(0.23)	(0.18)
Malapportionment		195.08	1,216.83[b]
		(0.44)	(2.73)
PRI vote		−109.78	199.59
		(0.55)	(0.56)
Constant	−34.67	−108.81	−89.50
	(1.40)	(0.57)	(0.34)
F	39.19	9.57	4.69
R^2	0.70	0.78	0.59

[a]Significant at the 99% level.
[b]Significant at the 95% level.

significant effect in the allocation of those funds. The GDP variable is also significant and again shows a positive sign. However, malapportionment ceases to be significant once the relevant criteria contained in the LCF for the allocation of health
funds are introduced. The numbers of doctors and health clinics for every ten thousand inhabitants turn out to be the most important explanatory variables for the allocation of these funds, as the institutional framework would imply.

Table 9.4 carries out the same exercise for all the other funds contained in Item
33. The first fund, FIS, contains both a state and a municipal component. FIS seems
to be allocated primarily based on a political logic of sending more resources to
places with little electoral competitiveness, where a PRI governor is in office, and
where the PRI gets less percentage vote, always controlling for economic variables

Table 9.4
Determinants of Other Item 33 Funds per Capita Allocation, 1999 (heteroskedastic consistent errors, t statistics in parentheses)

	FIS (1)	FORTAMUN (2)	FAM (3)	FAS (4)	FASP (5)	FIED (6)
gdppc97	0.00	0.00	0.01^a	0.00	0.01	0.01^a
	(1.75)	(1.47)	(2.70)	(0.09)	(1.48)	(2.98)
fgt22	118.20^a	-25.72^a	45.23	13.02	-138.02	32.21
	(11.02)	(2.51)	(1.42)	(0.63)	(1.12)	(1.16)
ingest/ ingmun	-0.01	-0.03^a	-0.06^a	-0.03^b	-0.02	-0.02
	(1.15)	(2.74)	(2.08)	(1.87)	(0.24)	(1.05)
H	-8.69^b	0.77	14.46	9.54	54.01^b	4.92
	(1.90)	(0.30)	(1.32)	(1.06)	(1.96)	(0.72)
Gobopo	-3.54^a	1.17	0.70	1.37	23.70	-0.67
	(2.04)	(0.70)	(0.14)	(0.42)	(0.98)	(0.19)
Malapsen	-17.07	1.97	472.78^a	252.79^a	633.62^a	219.99^a
	(0.68)	(0.09)	(5.15)	(3.64)	(4.41)	(3.85)
vpri97	-40.37^a	13.96	69.68	55.46	299.67	14.21
	(2.11)	(1.06)	(1.16)	(1.51)	(1.20)	(0.38)
_cons	36.90^b	151.07^a	-39.13	-26.52	-221.65	-12.61
	(1.74)	(14.64)	(0.73)	(0.72)	(1.31)	(0.36)
F	23.60	1.59	11.38	7.74	4.54	5.88
R^2	0.90	0.41	0.73	0.58	0.54	0.68

[a]Significant at the 95% level.
[b]Significant at the 90% level.

(the relevant one in this case—as it should be according to the LCF—is the poverty index, FGT22).

Social Infrastructure Funds are primarily geared toward public works in municipalities. According to Diaz-Cayeros, Magaloni, and Weingast (2002) one important component of the PRI dominance was the punishment of political jurisdictions that might be tempted to vote for the opposition. In their explanation, PRI hegemony was in equilibrium so long as the threat of punishment remained credible.[20] These results are consonant with such a view. The LCF contained an "equality" provision, which allocated 0.5 percent of the funds to each state equally, regardless of poverty or size. This means that there was bias in favor of small states. However, this bias is captured by the political configuration of the states, rather than by the malapportionment variable.

The malapportionment variable is significant, however, in all other funds, except for FORTAMUN, even when they do not have an explicit "equality" provision. This suggests that something quite fundamental is going on that is not captured by the 0.5 percent equal share to all states in FISM. The political logic of Mexican federalism biases resources in favor of small states.

Among the other funds of Item 33 there are two more that merit special attention. On the one hand, FORTAMUN is allocated on the basis of population, so that it is almost equal in per capita terms among states (differences being due to the population estimates used). No political variable is significant in FORTAMUN, which provides greater confidence of the reliability of the other political results. However, FORTAMUN was deeply political in a different sense: the creation of this fund was the condition that the Partido Acción Nacional (PAN) imposed in order to approve the 1998 federal budget. The estimate of FORTAMUN reveals that a per capita allocation tends to favor states with less poverty and stronger local finances, which happen to be states where the PAN is strongest.

The public safety fund (FASP) shows that there are more funds allocated to states that are electorally more competitive, which suggests more money is being sent to places where the outrage over crime and insecurity might be more readily translated into electoral punishment of the PRI.

To test for whether these allocations are politically biased even in the case of funds driven in their allocation by very strict formulas, Table 9.5 provides estimates for revenue-sharing funds, according to the specific fund and the level of government receiving it. The malapportionment variable is significant only in the case of Municipal Revenue Sharing (FFM), whereas poverty is an important determinant of excise revenue sharing (IEPS), which is highly linked to a derivation principle. Aside from that, the most important fund, the Fondo General de Participaciones, is distributed on an equal per capita principle.

The overall lesson from this study of the allocation of federal resources in the Mexican states is twofold: on the one hand, political practices as expressed in the party system are far more important determinants of the allocation of funds than the institutional rules of federalism. On the other hand, the allocation of funds is deeply politicized, in the sense that political actors have successfully biased shares in their favor. In the case of education, the bias is extreme, and the allocations have no relationship with the underlying public policy rationale.

Table 9.5
Determinants of Item 28 Funds per Capita Allocation, 1999 (heteroskedastic consistent
errors, t statistics in parentheses)

	FFM (1)	FGP20 (2)	IEPS (3)	incent (4)	FGP80 (5)
Gdppc97	0.00	0.01	0.00	0.01	0.02
	(0.60)	(0.37)	(0.68)	(1.32)	(0.17)
Fgt22	60.38	−390.35	−116.80^a	−65.62	−1,323.38
	(0.33)	(1.13)	(5.21)	(1.68)	(1.16)
Ingest/					
ingmun	−0.20	−0.07	0.03	0.04	0.32
	(1.70)	(0.28)	(1.31)	(1.03)	(0.51)
H	41.45	−80.90	0.73	14.77	−289.40
	(1.56)	(0.62)	(0.09)	(1.42)	(0.52)
Gobopo	19.19	−3.82	2.57	8.03	−25.61
	(0.97)	(0.12)	(0.63)	(1.33)	(0.16)
Malapsen	1,283.61^a	564.02	45.26	130.47	2,388.87
	(3.15)	(1.03)	(0.67)	(1.33)	(1.04)
Vpri97	83.62	386.02	31.59	122.17^b	1,579.94
	(0.52)	(1.10)	(0.82)	(1.79)	(1.22)
_cons	−94.83	399.59	32.47	−85.11	1,389.81
	(0.84)	(0.86)	(0.90)	(1.62)	(0.69)
F	3.35	1.83	6.46	2.92	1.91
R^2	0.49	0.25	0.66	0.47	0.25

[a]Significant at the 95% level.
[b]Significant at the 90% level.

Research Agenda and Some Further Issues

Great strides have been made in the transformation of Mexican federalism. Education expenditure has been decentralized, funds to construct infrastructure are no longer discretionally allocated by the president, and revenue sharing has been increased. Funds for regional development probably witnessed the greatest transformation. The highly discretional and politically manipulated Solidaridad program became the Fondo de Infraestructura Social (FIS), and Item 33 stipulated that the financing of local public works would use poverty criteria and public service needs. The change in the design of transfers in Mexico is a remarkable example of how politicians can accept less discretional designs.

However, the pretense of having a system of transfers with no political effects, as the analysis of the last section reveals, is misguided. The transformation was made

possible through allocations that still reflect the balance of political forces. The creation of additional funds, such as the FORTAMUN, allocated on an equal per capita
basis, are not just technical decisions but have a strong underlying political logic: the
new fund favored urban municipalities, where the PAN tended to concentrate its
electoral victories. In fact, transfer design in Mexico must be understood as the product of skillful bipartisan negotiations involving the ruling party, the PRI, and the
PAN, which has traditionally advanced an agenda for greater decentralization and
municipal autonomy.

The FIS, notwithstanding the changes in formulas, still provided an "equity" criteria of distributing 0.5 percent of the funds to each state regardless of size, in contrast to what a poverty fund should do. But this provision was extremely important
for its acceptability to the key political players. Hence the bias in the Mexican system
toward smaller political units can be understood as a reflection of the bargaining
power of states, which, although not economically powerful, had been a central
component of the PRI ruling coalition.

On the other hand, the contrast between the relatively technical decentralization
of resources in health and the highly politicized process in education bears witness
to the difficulty faced by a national government committed to decentralization. It
was unable to create a reasonably equitable per capita transfer of education funds,
which constitute the largest component of Item 33 due to the strength of the national teachers union, its links to the PRI, and the union's "colonization" of the Ministry of Education (Secretaría de Educación Pública).

The analysis of the previous section also raises some methodological issues that
should be addressed in the future. The first is the difficulty of carrying out a statistical estimation with a small N. Federal systems are composed by a set number of units.
For example, although there might be ways to increase this N by conducting a pooled
cross-section time series analysis, the fact remains that funds of an incremental nature have a strong inertia based on the initial assignment, so this is not a reasonable
way to obtain better estimates. The econometrics might look better, but there is no
theoretical reason to believe that the politics underlying them is based on better insights. The estimates we have with a small N are, however, extremely susceptible to
specification bias if there is a crucial excluded variable or multicollinearity problems.
The issues raised by estimation with small N are well known in the OECD literature.
Some of their more descriptive techniques might be useful in the further analysis of
federal systems, using graphical analysis and nonparametric statistics. Municipal-level

analysis, which in Mexico would increase the N to 2,417, might prove insightful if applied to the funds where a municipal political logic might be present.

Perhaps a more substantive issue relates to the measurement of malapportionment. The hypotheses using malapportionment as an independent variable, particularly in a Senate with an equal number of members by state, cannot be distinguished from other alternative "size" hypotheses that would not have the political meaning of malapportionment. On the one hand, an underlying assumption is that some political actors benefit from malapportionment and make efforts to keep those benefits. On the other hand, there is a certain naiveté in measuring malapportionment as an index of the power of an individual legislator without considering the conditions of party discipline or the committee structure in the legislature. In order to have better malapportionment measures we should perhaps produce power indexes more in line with Riker's empirical research on federalism in the United States (which used the Shapley-Shubick power index taking partisan affiliation into account when calculating the probability of an individual legislator being pivotal). A distinction should also be made between malapportionment as a political tool for politicians and as a constitutional design meant to protect minorities.

NOTES

1. Also see Stepan's account of Riker's position in this volume (chap. 2).

2. The structure-induced equilibrium literature has placed particular emphasis on bicameralism as an institutional device that allows, when coupled with veto procedures, for the existence of stable choices (cores) in multidimensional issue spaces; see Hammond and Miller (1987). Within this institutional framework, the federal arrangement is crucial, because it allows for the ideal points of members of the upper chamber to be different from those of the lower chamber. So long as the relevant constituent units of the federal pact (states or provinces) are distinct from the units in the lower chamber, legislators can achieve both feasible and even efficient legislative outcomes. If the ideal policy positions of legislators in the upper and lower chambers are identical, then the existence of dual chambers has no stability-enhancing potential, since social choice problems would be present identically in both chambers. If legislators differ, a core is more likely to exist and to be small, which by definition is efficient in the Pareto sense. It is also stable to the extent that there are no incentives to produce policy or legislation outside of it. For an alternative formulation of the same insight see Tsebelis and Money (1997).

3. This does not mean that other aspects of federalism, such as the ideological commitment to a specific federal contract, or the exit provisions in a federal pact that provide bargaining power to

the constituent units, are unimportant. But they are not responsible for the decentralized outcome of policy choice.

4. *Constitución Política de los Estados Unidos Mexicanos* (1999) (http: // www.juridicas.unam.mx / cnsinfo / fed00.htm).

5. This provision means that the fiscal condition of the municipality is determined not within each state constitution, as it used to be before 1983, but at the federal level, making municipalities key players in the federal arrangement.

6. In social choice terms, this means that in all of these areas the relevant locus of decision making would have been a bicameral core with a presidential veto, since both the upper and lower chambers have authority over federal taxation and revenue. Instead, given the incentives in the party system, the Senate played no role as a regional representation of interests, while presidential initiatives were usually simply rubberstamped by the Chamber of Deputies and the Senate. The weakness of legislators is largely a result of the no-reelection clause and the centralized control of nominations by the PRI (see below).

7. Conventional wisdom indicates that the most powerful and meaningful political posts in Mexico were those in the federal executive branch. More specifically, cabinet and subcabinet posts and a few other jobs in the public sector such as directing PEMEX or IMSS are often viewed as the goal of any ambitious politician. Office in the federal legislature was viewed as instrumental in pursuing such a career; while the thousands of midlevel federal bureaucratic posts (*puestos de confianza*) were considered an essential resource for the construction of *camarillas* (teams of politicians that seek to advance collectively to higher office; see Langston 1995). Within the highly centralized federal system produced by the hegemonic party system, governors were considered less prominent political actors, often viewed as mere administrative agents of the president in the states.

8. In the time of PRI hegemony, a governorship used to be a terminal post. After holding a governorship, local politicians usually retired to engage in business opportunities generated by their previous job.

9. Although a federal post could be "local" in terms of the way bureaucracies have *delegaciones* in the states.

10. Since 1986 three different electoral rules have determined the composition of the Senate, and transitional rules have created both three- and six-year term senators. In a little more than ten years, there have been almost as many changes in the Senate as those observed during the unstable first half of the nineteenth century, when every time the regime alternated between federal and central, the Senate rules also changed. The 1986 reform established a staggered renewal of the Senate by halves every three years. The 1993 reform returned to the full renewal of the chamber every six years concurrent with the presidential term and doubled the size of the Senate, establishing a trinomial formula. The fourth seat in each state would go to the candidate at the top of the "first minority" loser formula. The 1996 reform retained the size of the chamber and the first minority senator but returned to a binomial formula, establishing instead that one-fourth of the upper house would be elected out of a nationwide list by a pure PR principle.

11. Such conditions would render the ideal points of senators closer to those of deputies, hence reducing the probability of bicameralism producing stable social choice.

12. Given the contestability of gubernatorial elections, this disciplining effect is being diminished, so one should observe a Senate increasingly less responsive to the president.

13. The socialist opposition deputy Lombardo Toledano submitted the proposal for reelection, which had been amended by the PRI deputies limiting the reelection to only one term.

14. The current system took shape in 1980 with the establishment of the federal value-added tax (IVA). When the current system was established, the states surrendered their share of a federal sales tax, as well as multiple excise taxes on consumption and production that had been accumulating over the years, in exchange for various funds of revenue sharing from federal taxes. Far and away the largest of these transfers is the Fondo General de Participaciones (FGP).

15. For the most prominent critiques of *Solidaridad* see Dresser (1991), Weldon and Molinar (1994), and Bruhn (1996).

16. Unreported tests were also carried out in terms of the electoral calendars of state and municipal elections, and the profile of state executives, but they failed to provide meaningful results.

17. Allocations of federal public investment (Inversión Pública Federal) and some other federal programs such as the agriculture support program (Procampo) or the poverty fund (Progresa) are not considered in this analysis but should be incorporated into future research.

18. The only exception is the Fondo de Infraestructura Social, where a fraction that was distributed as an equal lump sum per state has been eliminated in the 2002 budget.

19. The correlation between the number of parties variable and the margin of victory is very high, so those two hypotheses are, in fact, undistinguishable.

20. Their analysis claims that the relevant political unit for understanding the Mexican system is the locality. If the municipal level of analysis is best for studying these funds, the equation for FIS could be a fallacy of composition. Results by Mogollón (2002) in the states of Guanajuato, Tlaxcala, and Puebla suggest that this might be the case. They find that political variables are significant, depending on the particular circumstances of each state.

BIBLIOGRAPHY

Bednar, Jenna. 2001. Shirking and Stability in Federal Unions. University of Michigan, unpublished manuscript.

Bruhn, Kathleen. 1996. Social Spending and Political Support: The "Lessons" of the National Solidarity Program in Mexico. *Comparative Politics* 28 (2): 151–78.

Careaga, Maite, and Barry R. Weingast. 2000. The Fiscal Pact with the Devil: A Positive Approach to Fiscal Federalism, Revenue Sharing and Good Governance. Stanford University, typescript.

Courchene, Thomas, and Alberto Diaz-Cayeros. 2001. Transfers and the Nature of the Mexican Federation. In *Achievements and Challenges of Fiscal Decentralization: Lessons from Mexico*, edited by Marcelo M. Giugale and Steven B. Webb. Washington, D.C.: World Bank.

de Remes, Alain. 2000. *Juxtaposition in Mexican Municipal Electoral Contests: The Silent Cohabitation*. México D.F.: CIDE.

Diaz-Cayeros, Alberto. 1995. *Desarrollo Económico e Inequidad Regional: Hacia un Nuevo Pacto Federal en México*. México D.F.: CIDAC / Miguel Angel Porrúa / Fundación Naumann.

———. 1997. Political Responses to Regional Inequality: Taxation and Distribution in Mexico. Ph.D. dissertation, Duke University.

———. 1998. Federalism and Endogenous Institutional Change in the Mexican Senate. Paper presented at the Latin American Studies Association meeting, Chicago, September.

Diaz-Cayeros, Alberto, and Joy Langston. N.d. What Does It Take to Be a Governor? Unpublished manuscript.

Diaz-Cayeros, Alberto, Beatriz Magaloni, and Barry R. Weingast. 2002. Democratization and the Economy in Mexico: Equilibrium (PRI) Hegemony and Its Demise. Unpublished manuscript.

Dixit, Avinash, and John Londregan. 1998. Fiscal Federalism and Redistributive Politics. *Journal of Public Economics* 68 (2): 153–80.

Dresser, Denise. 1991. *Neopopulist Solutions to Neoliberal Problems: Mexico's National Solidarity Program*. Current Issues Brief No. 4. La Jolla, Calif.: Center for U.S.-Mexico Studies, University of California, San Diego.

Hammond, Thomas, and Gary Miller. 1987. The Core of the Constitution. *American Political Science Review* 81 (4): 1155–74.

Langston, Joy. 1995. Sobrevivir y Prosperar: Una Búsqueda de las Causas de las Facciones Políticas Intrarrégimen en México. *Política y Gobierno* 2 (2): 243–78.

Lijphart, Arend. 1984. *Electoral Systems and Party Systems. A Study of Twenty-Seven Democracies 1945–1990*. Oxford: Oxford University Press.

Lujambio, Alonso. 2000. *El Poder Compartido*. México D.F.: Oceano.

Mogollón, Olivia. 2002. De la Discreción a las Fórmulas: Meacanismo de Distribución de Recursos Decentralizados para Alvido a la Pobreza. M.A. thesis, Instituto Tecnológico Autónomo de Mexico.

Riker, William H. 1964. *Federalism: Origin, Operation, Significance*. Boston: Little Brown.

———. 1975. Federalism. In *Handbook of Political Science*, edited by F. Greenstein and N. W. Polsby. Reading, Mass.: Addison-Wesley.

Rodden, Jonathan. N.d. Reviving Leviathan: Fiscal Federalism and the Growth of Government, typescript.

Shepsle, Kenneth. 1979. Institutional Arrangements and Equilibrium in Multidimensional Voting Models. *American Journal of Political Science* 23:27–59.

Shepsle, Kenneth, and Barry R. Weingast. 1987. The Institutional Foundations of Committee Power. *American Political Science Review* 81 (1): 85–104.

Treisman, Daniel. 2000. Decentralization and Inflation: Commitment, Collective Action or Continuity? *American Political Science Review* 94 (4): 837–58.

Tsebelis, George, and Jeannette Money. 1997. *Bicameralism*. Cambridge: Cambridge University Press.

Weingast, Barry R. 1995. The Economic Role of Political Institutions: Market-Preserving Federalism and Economic Development. *Journal of Law, Economics, and Organization* 11 (1): 1–31.

Weingast, Barry R., and Rui de Figueiredo. 1998. *Self-enforcing Federalism: Solving the Two Funda-*

mental Dilemmas. Working Paper 1.67. Berkeley: Center for German and European Studies, University of California.

Weldon, Jeffrey. 1996. The Political Sources of Presidencialismo in Mexico. In *Presidentialism and Democracy in Latin America,* edited by S. Mainwaring and M. S. Shugart. Cambridge: Cambridge University Press.

Weldon, Jeffrey, and Juan Molinar. 1994. Electoral Determinants of National Solidarity. In *Transforming State-Society Relations in Mexico. The National Solidarity Strategy,* edited by W. Cornelius, A. Craig, and J. A. Fox. La Jolla, Calif.: Center for U.S.-Mexican Studies, University of California, San Diego.

Wibbels, Erik. 2000. Federalism and the Politics of Macroeconomic Policy and Performance. *American Journal of Political Science* 44 (4): 687–702.

Willis, Eliza, Christopher Garman, and Stephan Haggard. 1999. The Politics of Decentralization in Latin America. *Latin American Research Review* 34 (1): 7–56.

CHAPTER 10

Electorally Generated Veto Players in Unitary and Federal Systems

—ALFRED STEPAN

My task in this chapter is to reflect on some of the contributions this volume makes to our understanding of modern federal systems, particularly as they function in Latin America. I organize my contribution around the key issue of "veto players." This chapter builds upon distinctions that Arend Lijphart (1984) has made between "majoritarian" and "consensus" democracies, that I make between "demos-enabling" and "demos-constraining" polities (see Stepan in this volume), that Juan Linz and I (Linz and Stepan 2000) have made between "inequality-reducing" and "inequality-inducing" federal systems, as well as the recent work of George Tsebelis (Tsebelis 1995, 2002) on "veto players."

I will use Tsebelis's approach to veto players in an attempt to test, refine, and integrate social science findings about antimajoritarian devices and the relative ease or difficulty with which small groups, in different institutional settings, can create "winsets" that can block major policy changes such as the creation of statewide comprehensive welfare systems.[1] Tsebelis defines a veto player as "an individual or collective actor whose agreement is required for a policy decision."[2] Using spatial modeling and empirical arguments, Tsebelis makes a convincing case that the more institutional veto players there are in a political system, whether unitary or federal, parliamentary or presidential, the more difficult it is to construct a win-set to alter the political status quo.

With this in mind, my aim in this chapter is to examine the *variations* in the potential number of *electorally generated* institutional veto players that different democratic countries can have. Note that I introduce the phrase "electorally generated institutional veto players" to distinguish them from institutional veto players like supreme courts or autonomous central banks, which are important but are not electorally generated.[3] I will demonstrate, on the basis of what I believe is a theoretically and politically reasonable extension of Tsebelis's definition of institutional veto players, that federal systems can have from one to four such players. What is interesting is that, until recently, all of the Latin American federations (Brazil, Argentina, Mexico, and Venezuela) were at the high end of the electorally generated institutional veto player continuum, with three or four potential institutional veto players. Moreover, I will attempt to document that Argentina and Brazil are the only democracies in the world to have four "robust" electorally generated institutional veto players.

If this is right, Latin American federations are distinctive among the world's democracies. These findings have strong theoretical and policy-making implications. Institutions (and politics) matter.

In the first section I make the case for modifying the definition of institutional veto players. I will then demonstrate who the electorally generated veto players are within each OECD advanced economy democracy, unitary or federal. This will show why Argentina and Brazil are unique.

In the second section, I will use the concept of political party veto players, or what Tsebelis calls "partisan," as opposed to "institutional," veto players. I will demonstrate that, under some circumstances, partisan veto players can affect the number of "politically effective federal institutional veto players," changing them from four to one, and back again to four, quite rapidly.[4] Evidence from Argentina will demonstrate this. I will also show, on the other hand, why in post-1985 democratic Brazil comparable shifts in the number of politically effective institutional veto players have been, and will be in the foreseeable future, much less than Argentina's. In contrast to Argentina, no single partisan veto player has had majority control over all the institutional veto players in Brazil because of the nature of its party system. Thus politics (and institutions) matter.

My third point concerns the "demos-constraining" or "demos-enabling" aspects of veto players. Federal political systems, because they are constitutionally embedded, require supermajorities to change their constitutional structures and so are relatively inflexible. However, I show that under democratizing conditions (and even at times in democratic conditions), institutional veto players can become more malapportioned and thus more "demos constraining" than before, whereas others can become less malapportioned and thus less "demos constraining." The Brazilian Senate is a good example of the first, whereas the Mexican Senate is a good example of the second.

Fourth, the emergence of more meaningful, electoral-based, federal institutions, in a context where they have previously been relatively absent, can create new "political opportunity structures," which may facilitate new forms of "resource mobilization" and even create new veto players.[5] Whether this leads to state dissolution (as it did in the former Soviet Union, Yugoslavia, and Czechoslovakia, where the newly empowered constituent members of the federation destroyed the state), or to democratic transition (as occurred in Brazil and Mexico, where newly activated federal political arenas and their veto players constrained the nondemocratic regime and contributed to progressive democratization), or to the emergence of "semiloyal" partisan veto players in the face of ineffective traditional democratic partisan veto players (as in Venezuela) depends to a great extent on certain key contextual political variables, which I identify and analyze.

The Potential for Four "Robust" Executive and Legislative Institutional Veto Players: The Uniqueness of Argentina and Brazil among the World's Democracies

In his analysis Tsebelis identifies three potential institutional veto players in democratic systems. These are, first, the lower chamber, and second, the upper chamber (if it has an absolute veto over some laws). His third institutional veto player is a directly elected president in systems with strong, even if not absolute, veto powers, such as exists in the United States, or to a lesser extent in the semipresidential French Fifth Republic.[6] (In parliamentary systems the prime minister depends on his or her supporters in parliament to promote or block legislation, and thus is not counted, according to the "absorption rule," as an independent institutional veto player.)[7]

The comparative analysis of federalism is strengthened if the possibility of a fourth, quite different, institutional veto player is considered. The constituent members of a federation (states, cantons, or provinces) represent the fourth potential veto player. According to the constitution of some federations, for example, laws cannot be passed without the approval of a majority of the constituent members of the federation. The clearest example of such a country is Switzerland. In Switzerland, even if a proposed law is approved by a large majority of both houses, by the country's collective presidency, and by a majority of voters in a national referendum, that law (if 100,000 citizens sign a petition asking for a referendum) cannot go into effect unless it is also approved in the referendum by a majority of the cantons.[8] Thus, the Swiss cantons clearly meet Tsebelis's definition of an absolute veto player.

Implicitly, Tsebelis relaxes the requirement for an absolute veto power in his definition of an institutional veto player because he includes as institutional veto players directly elected presidents; these have strong but not absolute veto powers because presidential vetoes are subject to supermajority overrides. This implicit exception may make his analysis formally less elegant, but it makes good political sense.[9] In a similar vein, I would like to relax another requirement: Tsebelis talks of the necessity of veto players to "agree" to policy changes. I would like to use the phrase "agree and comply" to changes. If we assume that the compliance of constituent members of a federation is necessary for the success of a central government's policy change, then, if powerful members do not comply, they are in fact institutional veto players. In Argentina, for example, coordinated macroeconomic policies are impossible if the provinces unilaterally issue bonds that are quasi money. As long as this situation obtains, the central government cannot make any "credible commitments," or pass any effective legislation, about macroeconomic policies. In such a situation it makes sense to consider such provinces institutional veto players.

I would like to make one further comment about the definition (and therefore the counting procedures) I use here, and this concerns whether the institutional veto players are "robust" or not. Two countries may both have four potential institutional veto players. However, if in one country all four of the veto capacities are quite broad in scope, while in the other country one or more veto capacities are more restricted in scope, I will count only the first polity as a "robust" four veto player country.

With this analytic framework in place two conclusions will soon become clear. First, unitary states with parliamentary democracies can have, at a maximum, two institutional veto players. They cannot have three, much less four, institutional veto players, because two of the potential veto players do not exist, namely, a chief executive with a veto and constituent members of the federation with veto powers. Second, federal states, on the other hand, can have one, two, three, or four veto players. I now examine the variations in institutional veto players from one to four in unitary and federal systems.

Single Electorally Generated Institutional
Veto Player Countries: Unitary and Federal

If a country is a unitary state, has a unicameral legislature, and is parliamentary, that country is in the least "demos-constraining" position because it has the potential for only one electorally generated institutional veto player—the unicameral parliament. Denmark, Finland, Sweden, Norway, Luxembourg, Greece, and New Zealand are such countries.

The United Kingdom for most decisions is still a single-institutional veto player country. Even though the United Kingdom is bicameral, the upper house does not have an absolute veto. The devolutionary process that has created the Scottish, Welsh, and Northern Irish assemblies may eventually create a two veto player system for those issues most vital to devolution. However, since it is a process of "devolution," and not full-blown constitutionally embedded "federalism," the House of Commons in London can still, under exceptional conditions, by a simple majority unilaterally impose direct rule as they did in Northern Ireland in 2002. Although it may be constitutionally possible to take back powers, in the case of Scotland it may already be politically unfeasible.

For our purposes it should also be stressed that a federal state that is parliamentary and has an upper chamber with a delaying but almost never an absolute veto over legislation has only one institution that is a veto player. Austria is such a country (Obinger 2003).

Two Electorally Generated Institutional
Veto Player Countries: Unitary and Federal

A semipresidential system in a unitary state like the French Fifth Republic is a one-player system when the president controls both houses. However, in cohabitation periods, when political parties in opposition to the president control one or more houses, the French Fifth Republic has two institutional veto players.

A federal state that has two veto players is one that is parliamentary with two chambers, has an upper chamber with an absolute veto over some but not all legislation, and is constitutionally symmetrical with a tradition of the central legislature establishing a "common framework" for all significant social and economic legislation. Germany therefore has two institutional veto players for the approximately 60 percent of the legislation that requires the assent of the upper house, while for the remaining 40 percent of legislation, Germany has only one institutional veto player.[10]

Linz and I argue elsewhere that among the eight developed OECD federal democracies, only three are politically multinational, and all three have chosen "asymmetrical federalism." These countries are Spain, Belgium, and Canada. All are also two institutional veto player countries. One institutional veto player in all three is the lower house of parliament. The other veto player is one or more of the constituent members of the federation. India, except for not being a developed economy, is also in this set. In order to help "hold together" these four fragile multinational states, constitution makers in all four countries have constitutionally embedded somewhat different rights or prerogatives to the different constituent members of the federation.[11] These prerogatives normally grow out of cultural and linguistic demands or historic agreements that directly relate to the different cultural groups that compose the multinational state, such as special linguistic and educational rights for French-speaking Quebec. On anything relating to these special rights the constituent units are veto players. None of the four countries is presidential, so the president as veto player does not exist. Also none of the four countries has upper houses where the exercise of an absolute veto, except in the defense of a constitutionally embedded right of a member unit, is accepted as politically possible.

The Belgium Senate has no absolute veto, but Spain and Canada need a nonbinding comment from their respective upper houses.[12] Spain, for issues that do not affect the prerogatives of the constituent members of the federation, often has the potential for only one institutional veto player, the lower chamber of the federal parliament. For normal issues that concern the prerogatives of any of Spain's asymmetrical federal autonomies, Spain has two institutional veto players. But in the highly exceptional situations involving federal interventions in the autonomy of the member units (called the *autonomías*), the assent of the upper chamber is required, and in these cases Spain has the potential for three institutional veto players.[13] However, Juan Linz says Article 155 has never been applied. Furthermore, he believes this article would be applied only in a constitutional crisis, such as the federal deposition of the government and occupation of the Basque country, or even more remotely, Catalonia. Such a constitutional crisis would probably result in the breakdown of Spanish federalism.[14] In this sense, although Spain has the theoretical potential of being a three veto player country, it seems correct to argue that, barring a constitutional crisis, Spain is a one or two veto player country.

A word is also necessary about Canada. On paper the Canadian Senate has an absolute veto. However, most analysts of Canadian politics in essence argue that the Canadian Senate lacks the legitimacy or nerve to be an institutional veto player. All of its members are nominated by the prime minister. Once appointed, senators do not have to retire until they are seventy-five years old. Many observers estimate that in a democracy such as Canada, if senators with no democratic origins in elections tried to exercise their theoretical potential to be a constitutionally normal veto player, the Senate would risk being abolished.[15]

Countries with up to Three Electorally Generated Institutional Veto Players

The only democracies in the world having more than two electorally generated institutional veto players at the moment are all federal systems.[16] A federal state that is parliamentary (or has a quasi-parliamentary collective executive), that has upper and lower houses both with an absolute veto, and whose full constituent units (states, cantons, or provinces) have significant prerogatives or blocking power over some types of major social legislation or economic policy, such as a referendum requiring their majority support, has the institutional potential for up to three veto players. There are only two such countries, Switzerland and Australia.

In Switzerland, as was mentioned, it takes the signatures of only 100,000 citizens to force a referendum. Referendums that have been used to accept or reject national laws have been used more in "direct democracy" Switzerland than in any other democracy in the world. Owing either to the exercise of such vetoes, or because legislators fear the exercise of such a veto, the referendum veto point has contributed to Switzerland's having one of the least developed and least comprehensive welfare systems among the OECD developed-economy countries.[17]

Even though Australia has more potential institutional veto players (three) than

Switzerland, its political evolution has tended in the direction of lesser powers for the constituent states of the federation. Australia's institutional veto players are, first, the lower house and, second, its upper federal chamber, which has the constitutional right to an absolute veto and is still a major political fact of life in Australia. Very importantly, among democratic countries, Australia, after Switzerland, is the second most frequent user of referendums to block or approve legislation. The approval of a majority of states—in this case four of the six—is required when there is a referendum over a controversial change in the status quo; so Australian states are veto players.[18]

Four Electorally Generated Institutional Veto Player Countries

The only democracies with the capacity for four institutional veto players are necessarily presidential, federal, and bicameral (where both houses have absolute veto powers). The only countries potentially fitting these criteria are the federal systems of Latin America and the United States.[19] Of these, only Argentina and Brazil have four "robust" veto players, in the sense that the veto powers are, in fact, quite broad in scope.

In Mexico, as Ochoa-Reza and Diaz-Cayeros elegantly and clearly establish in this volume, two of the potential four institutional veto players are weak to nonexistent. The Mexican Senate has veto powers, but it cannot veto the federal budget (as the Senate can in the United States, Brazil, and Argentina). Also, although the Mexican states have some constitutionally embedded prerogatives, they are nowhere near as many, nor as powerful, as those in the United States, Brazil, or Argentina.[20] Diaz-Cayeros asks in his chapter, "Can states in a federation be trusted?" He then goes on to argue that "the Mexican constitution clearly establishes that they cannot. The Mexican federal pact reflects a deeply embedded distrust of state power. . . . Federalism [in Mexico] is primarily about limiting the power of the states."[21] We can thus say that Mexico has a relatively weak three-player veto system, the states do not count as veto players, and the Senate is not a very robust veto player.

And how does the U.S. federal system compare? In the United States the states certainly have important prerogatives and veto powers in the areas of taxing authority, criminal law, state and local police, and in welfare policies (the latter policies being those that, in federations such as Austria, Germany, Spain, or Belgium, would be centrally and not subunit governed) (Linz and Stepan 2000). However, on macroeconomic policies, such as the issuing of quasi money or bonds that the central government ends up honoring, the U.S. states have highly constrained powers. The federal government of the United States is credibly committed to not bailing out bankrupt states or municipalities that cannot service their debts (Weingast 1995).

In sharp contrast, in Argentina the twenty-three provinces making up the federation, especially when they are in opposition to the president, issue many bonds that are equivalent to quasi money and that the central government often ends up honoring. It thus makes analytic and political sense to say that in Argentina the provinces exercise much greater veto power over macroeconomic policies than the different states do in the United States. Indeed, in recent years this has meant that provinces in Argentina have had veto power over the most vital policies in the country.[22]

The chapter in this volume by Samuels and Mainwaring shows that a strongly analogous position obtained in Brazil until President Cardoso began to control partially the individual states' bank debts, which were imperiling the federal government's capacity to coordinate and control fiscal policy.[23] Cardoso, by using his great political skills and by spending over US$120 billion dollars of central government funds to clean up the states' debts, managed to contain, but not eliminate, the problem by the end of his second presidential term. Will his successors have his political and financial resources to do the same?

In comparative terms, therefore, Argentina and Brazil had and still have the institutional potential to have robust four-player veto systems, whereas the United States in comparison has a less robust four-player veto system.

We are now ready for a classification of the number of electorally generated veto players in the eleven long-standing federal democracies, fifteen long-standing OECD unitary state democracies, plus for illustrative purposes newly democratized Mexico and the now weakly federal and only partially democratic Venezuela (see Table 10.1).

An Excursus on Inequality and Veto Players in the Universe of the Twenty-three Advanced OECD Democracies: Recasting the Traditional Argument about Welfare States and Federalism

Let me conclude this discussion on the number of institutional veto players with a question. If the United States, the world's only superpower and one of the world's wealthiest economies, is the only democratic advanced economy in the world with

Table 10.1
Classification of Electorally Generated Institutional Veto Players (selected countries)

	State Structure				
Four Institutional Veto Player Democracies	Robust federal; presidential, bicameral with both houses having extensive veto powers, and some member states having de facto veto over fiscal policy implementation (Argentina and Brazil).			Less robust federal, presidential, bicameral with both houses having extensive veto powers, member states have some veto power over welfare policies but not over fiscal policy implementation (U.S.).	
Three Institutional Veto Player Democracies	Robust federal; parliamentary or collective generated by the parliament, upper chamber has veto, frequent referendums in which a law passed by both houses can be vetoed unless a majority of the cantons or member states approve the law (Switzerland and Australia).			Less robust federal; presidential, bicameral in which both houses have veto powers but Senate cannot veto the budget, member states do not have either the de jure capacity to veto laws by referendum or the de facto veto capacity over fiscal policy implementation (Mexico).	
Two Institutional Veto Player Democracies	Federal; parliamentary, bicameral, with upper chamber veto, and the member states exercise veto power only through the upper chamber (Germany).	Federal; presidential, unicameral, with weak member-state veto capacity (Venezuela post-2000).	Asymmetrical federal; parliamentary, bicameral with weak upper chamber veto power, but regions have some constitutionally embedded veto powers (Belgium, Spain, Canada).	Unitary state; bicameral but upper chamber has weak veto, semipresidential system when the president does not command a legislative majority (France during "cohabitation").	Unitary state; parliamentary, bicameral where upper chamber has some veto capacity (Italy, Japan, Netherlands).
One Institutional Veto Player Democracies	Federal; parliamentary, bicameral where upper chamber and member states have no veto (Austria).	Unitary state; bicameral but upper chamber has weak veto, semipresidential system when the president controls a majority in both houses (France during "non-cohabitation").		Unitary state; parliamentary, bicameral but upper chamber lacks veto (U.K., Ireland, Sweden, Norway).	Unitary state; parliamentary, unicameral (Finland, Greece, Luxembourg, Portugal, New Zealand, Denmark, Iceland).

Sources: Lijphart (1999, 189, 212); Tsebelis and Money (1997); and my assessment.

four veto players, what is the problem with four veto players? One problem is inequality.

There are only eight democratic, advanced economy OECD federal states in the world: Austria, Australia, Belgium, Canada, Germany, Spain, Switzerland, and the United States. If we combine the fifteen OECD unitary states and the eight OECD federal states, we get the entire universe of the twenty-three advanced economy democracies in the OECD.

Let us examine the relationship between veto players and inequality within this universe by looking at four widely used measures of inequality from three respected sources. The most widely used measure of inequality is the Gini index of inequality regularly produced by the World Bank. Within the OECD the Luxembourg Income Study run by three distinguished social scientists, Anthony B. Atkinson, Lee Rainwater, and Timothy M. Smeeding, has produced data on two important additional measures of poverty and inequality: the percentage of the total population over age sixty living in poverty or near poverty after all government transfers, and the percentage of children of "lone" mothers who are living in poverty after all government transfers. A fourth indicator of inequality was recently constructed by the World Health Organization (WHO), based on the "fairness of financial contribution," which measures how much citizens in the poorest and wealthiest deciles receive from the health system in comparison to how much they put into it in direct and indirect tax contributions.[24] Table 10.2 shows that, on *each* of these four variables, the United States has the worst level of inequality of any of the eight advanced economy OECD federal democracies. Furthermore, within the twenty-three-country universe of OECD unitary and federal states, the United States, the only OECD advanced economy with four electorally generated veto players, has the worst inequality on two variables and the second worst on the other two variables for, by far, the overall worst ranking in the universe (see Table 10.2).

Our confidence in the proposition that the greater the number of institutional veto players, the more difficult it is to redress poverty and inequality via a politywide welfare system, is increased when we examine the data on countries with three institutional players. As Table 10.2 also demonstrates, on the World Bank's Gini index the three veto player countries, Switzerland and/or Australia, are the second and third worst of the eight federal systems on the Gini index and "poverty over 60" variables, the second worst and tied for the third worst on the WHO variable, and the second and fourth worst on the child poverty variable. No country, federal or uni-

Table 10.2

Inequality in Federal and Unitary States: Advanced OECD Democracies *(federal states in bold)*

Scale, Rank, or Rate	Gini Index of Inequality (1993)	Child Poverty Rate in "Single Mother" Households after All Government Transfers	Percentage of Population over 60 Years Old Living with Poor or Near Poor Income	WHO Ranking of Fairness of Financial Contribution to Health System
Worst	New Zealand (0.439)	**United States (59.5)**	**United States (20.7)**	Portugal (59.0)
	United States (0.408)	**Australia (56.2)**	**Australia (18.7)**	**United States (54.5)**
	U.K. (0.361)	**Canada (50.2)**	**Switzerland (15.7)**	Italy (46.0)
	Ireland (0.359)	Ireland (40.5)	Norway (15.6)	Greece (41.0)
	Australia (0.356)	Netherlands (39.5)	Italy (15.5)	**Switzerland (39.0)**
	Portugal (0.356)	**Switzerland (25.6)**	**Austria (14.2)**	**Australia (27.5)**
	Switzerland (0.331)	France (22.6)	Luxembourg (11.7)	**Spain (27.5)**
	Greece (0.327)	U.K. (18.7)	**Canada (11.5)**	France (27.5)
	France (0.327)	Norway (18.4)	Finland (9.8)	New Zealand (24.0)
	Netherlands (0.326)	Italy (13.9)	Ireland (9.0)	Netherlands (21.0)
	Spain (0.325)	**Belgium (10.0)**	**Belgium (8.9)**	**Canada (18.0)**
	Canada (0.315)	Luxembourg (10.0)	**Germany (8.5)**	**Austria (13.5)**
	Germany (0.300)	Finland (7.5)	France (7.2)	Iceland (13.5)
	Italy (0.273)	Denmark (7.3)	U.K. (6.7)	Sweden (13.5)
	Luxembourg (0.269)	Sweden (5.2)	Sweden (6.5)	Finland (9.5)
	Norway (0.258)	**West Germany (4.2)**	Netherlands (2.5)	Japan (9.5)
	Finland (0.256)			Norway (9.5)
	Belgium (0.250)			U.K. (9.5)
	Sweden (0.250)			**Germany (6.5)**

Best			
Japan (0.249)			Ireland (6.5)
Denmark (0.247)			**Belgium (4.0)**
Austria (0.231)			Denmark (4.0)
			Luxembourg (2.0)
No. Cases	$N = 22$	$N = 16$	$N = 16$	$N = 23$
Rank	U.S. rank = 21/22	U.S. rank = 16/16	U.S. rank = 16/16	U.S. rank = 22/23

Note: There are twenty-three "advanced economies" in the OECD. Mexico and Turkey are in the OECD but are not included in this table because they are not "advanced economies."

On the Gini index (0.000) represents perfect equality—every citizen would have exactly the same income—and (1.000) represents absolute inequality: i.e., one citizen would have all the income in the country. For data on the Gini index see World Bank (2000, 67–68).

In most advanced industrial democracies, two groups of citizens are children in "single mother" households. The indicator of inequality I will use is the country's percentage of such children below the poverty threshold after all government transfers. The Luxembourg Income Study (LIS) defines poverty as the percentage of children living in households with adjustable, disposable income that is less than 50 percent of medium adjusted disposable income for all persons. Income includes all transfers and tax benefits. The LIS contains a smaller set of countries than the World Bank study.

Another group of highly dependent citizens is the over age sixty population. Part of the over sixty group's net income comes from savings from their previous market-related earnings. However, to a significant extent, government-structured social security schemes and a variety of special services for the elderly will determine the percentage of the population who live in poverty. For these data see Atkinson, Rainwater, and Smeeding (1995, 104). Although the data for Belgium are for 1988 and that country did not fully become a federation until 1993, Belgium is written in bold given the federalization process it has gone through since the 1970s.

The World Health Organization attempted to measure the "fairness of financial contribution" to a country's health system in terms of how much citizens in the poorest and wealthiest deciles gave to and received from the country's public health system. The ranking goes from 1 (the best) to 191 (the worst). For the complete ranking see the WHO (2000), Annex Table 7, p. 188.

Sources: For Gini index data, see World Bank (2000); for "single mother households," see Rainwater (1997); for "over 60 population" data, see Atkinson et al. (1995); for WHO data, see World Health Organization (2000).

tary, besides four veto player United States, has such a combined overall bad ranking on these four variables as three veto player Switzerland and Australia.

Further support for the proposition that a high number of veto players is correlated with weak welfare states and high levels of inequality comes from the pioneering and revisionist book on welfare states in advanced economies by Evelyne Huber and John D. Stephens (2001). In their book Huber and Stephens explore eighteen variables to see what correlates most and least with comprehensive welfare states. A key finding is that along with the expected importance of incumbency by a left cabinet or a Christian Democratic cabinet, constitutional structures are unexpectedly (from the perspective of the traditional literature on welfare states) the most powerful predictors in their model. What they code as "constitutional structures: veto points created by constitutional provisions" is very close to what I refer to as institutional veto players. No country with the constitutional structures that would give them more than two institutional veto players has a well-developed and comprehensive welfare system. They state that "our analyses showed very clearly that power dispersion through political institutions is a serious obstacle to constructing generous welfare states. The availability of multiple veto points makes it possible for a variety of special interest groups to mobilize and torpedo major pieces of legislation."[25]

To the extent that macropolitical institutions are discussed in the standard welfare state literature of the advanced economies, there is often the blanket assertion that federalism hurts the development of comprehensive welfare systems. For example, Francis Castles, one of the leading specialists on the analysis of comparative welfare states, asserts that "one may point to the federalism-social policy linkage as one of the very few areas of unanimity in the literature, with writers from all the main competing explanatory paradigms arguing that federal institutions are inimical to high levels of social spending" (Castles 1982). Indeed, a famous article by Aaron Wildavsky (1985) is simply entitled "Federalism Means Inequality."

Surprisingly, Tsebelis, despite having laid the framework for a comparative analysis of the number of veto points, fails to carry out a full empirical analysis of the implications of this framework and simply asserts that "federal countries have *ceteris paribus* more veto players than unitary ones. As a result, federal countries will exhibit higher levels of policy stability" (2002, 136). The above statement by Tsebelis is misleading in two important respects. First, as Table 10.1 shows, if we look at the entire universe of OECD federal democracies, one country (Austria) has one electorally generated veto player, four countries (Germany, Spain, Belgium, Canada) have two electorally generated veto players, two countries (Switzerland and Australia) have three electorally generated veto players, and one country (the United States) has four electorally generated veto players. Thus five of the eight countries in our OECD federal universe subset have only one or two electorally generated veto players. The important analytical point to stress is that federal systems exhibit greater variation than do unitary states in the number of the electorally generated institutional veto players. Unitary states inhabit the world of one to two electorally generated veto players. Federal states can exist in the entire range from one to four veto players, but five of the eight actually have two or one.

The second misleading aspect of the Tsebelis quotation just cited is the strong implication that, in contrast to unitary systems, in *all* federal systems, it is difficult to change the status quo. However, Tables 10.1 and 10.2 together clearly demonstrate that if we assume that the construction of a comprehensive welfare state means a change in the status quo, federal countries with three and four veto players indeed appear to have found it difficult to change the status quo. However, federal countries with only one or two veto players, such as Germany and Austria, have not found it difficult to change the staus quo and indeed are in fact similar in our inequality and welfare indicators to unitary states.

The results of my arguments and data suggest that the debate about inequality, welfare states, and federalism should be recast by stressing, and testing, four findings that emerge from my analysis. First, if we restrict ourselves to the universe of all the federal and unitary OECD advanced democracies, it remains true that on our four indicators of inequality the unitary states have far less inequality than do federal states (see Table 10.3).

However, the second and more important point is that virtually all of the variation between federal states and unitary states is produced by three of the eight systems: the United States, Switzerland, and Australia. These three polities are, of course, the only countries in the entire OECD universe that have three or four electorally generated veto players. Thus, the statement "advanced democracies with three and four veto players have worse inequality than advanced democracies with one and two veto players" is much more powerful than the true but analytically misleading statement that is found in most of the welfare state literature that "federalism, by itself, is welfare state inhibiting" (see Table 10.4).

Third, the greatest variation within the OECD universe is between the federal subset with three and four veto players versus the federal subset with one and two veto players. Thus, the most important variation for further study of inequality is

Table 10.3
Veto Players and Inequality: OECD Federal and Unitary States

	Average Gini Index	Average Post Govt. Child Poverty Rate	Average Percentage of Population over 60 Years Old Living in Poverty	Average WHO Ranking
Total set	0.309	24.3	11.4	21.2
Three and four veto player countries[a]	0.365	47.1	18.4	40.3
One and two veto player countries	0.300	19.1	9.8	18.3
Unitary subset within the one and two veto player countries	0.306	18.4	9.4	19.7
Federal subset within the one and two veto player countries	0.284	21.5	10.8	13.9

Note: The higher the value, the worse the level of inequality.
[a]These countries are the United States, Australia, and Switzerland.
Sources: Same as Table 10.2.

Table 10.4
Aggregate Inequality in OECD Advanced Democracies: Federal and Unitary States

	Average Gini Index (World Bank)	Average Poverty Rate of Children of "Single Mothers" after All Government Transfers	Average Percentage of Population over 60 Years Old Living in Poverty	Average WHO Ranking of Fairness of Financial Contribution to Health System
Federal States[a]	0.314	38.5	14.8	23.8
Unitary States	0.291	17.6	9.3	19.7

[a]These countries are the United States, Australia, Switzerland, Germany, Belgium, Canada, Austria, and Spain. The Luxembourg Income Study did not produce data for all the twenty-three advanced economy members of the OECD. In column 2 the missing federal states are Spain and Austria. In column 3 the missing federal state is Spain. In column 4 there are no missing countries.
Sources: Same as Table 10.2.

Table 10.5
Veto Players and Inequality: OECD Advanced Democracies

	Average Gini Index (World Bank)	Average Poverty Rate of Children of "Single Mothers" after All Government Transfers	Average Percentage of Population over 60 Years Old Living in Poverty	Average WHO Ranking of Fairness of Financial Contribution to Health System
Three and Four Veto Player Countries[a]	0.365	47.1	18.4	40.3
One and Two Veto Player Countries	0.300	19.1	9.8	18.3

[a]These countries are the United States, Australia and Switzerland.
Sources: Same as Table 10.2.

Table 10.6
Veto Players and Inequality: OECD Federal Democracies

	Average Gini Index (World Bank)	Average Poverty Rate of Children of "Single Mothers" after All Government Transfers	Average Percentage of Population over 60 Years Old Living in Poverty	Average WHO Ranking of Fairness of Financial Contribution to Health System
Federal Subset within the Three and Four Veto Player Countries[a]	0.365	47.1	18.4	40.3
Federal Subset within the One and Two Veto Player Countries[b]	0.284	21.5	10.8	13.9

[a]These countries are the United States, Australia, and Switzerland.
[b]These countries are Germany, Belgium, Canada, Austria, and Spain. In column 2 the missing federal states are Spain and Austria. In column 3 the missing federal state is Spain.
Sources: Same as Table 10.2.

not between federal and unitary states, but between states with three and four veto players versus states with one and two veto players (see Tables 10.5 and 10.6).

Fourth, the most widely used and accepted measure of inequality is the Gini index. If we restrict ourselves to this variable alone, we arrive at the surprising finding that within the subset of states with one or two veto players, the federal subset has a better Gini index (0.284) than the unitary state subset (0.306).[26]

The major research question that emerges from my analysis so far is what if anything has produced OECD countries with three or four veto players? More specifically, how did the United States, Switzerland, and Australia generate these "inequality-inducing federal systems" while a country like Germany has produced an "inequality-reducing federal system"? As Charles Tilly and many historical institutionalists might ask, can we find the mechanisms that over time produced, and continue to reproduce, these inequalities? My opening chapter in this volume suggests that the bargains struck in the formation of the three "coming together" federal systems, and their subsequent path-dependent effects, are one of the most fruitful places to start such an inquiry. My hypothesis is that the "veto player" and the "coming together" institutional explanations of inequality are not competing, but complementary, explanations. However, an important task of institutional analysis is to explain the origins of institutions, and especially the motives of the actors, and the contingent contexts, within which the institutions under study were created. I believe the origins of the inequality-inducing mechanisms found in the United States, Switzerland, and Australia (upper chambers with absolute veto power and extreme malapportionment, federal and state constitutions with strong "states' rights" features, and constitutionally embedded referendum procedures) will be much more likely to be found by tracing processes created by the "coming together" movements than by a reliance on "veto players" as such, because these " institutional veto players" were almost certainly a product of the "coming together" processes.

The case of Australia will present a particularly important test case for theories of the effects of "veto players," "coming together federalism," and "welfare states" concerning inequality because in most respects Australia scores higher on the key variables (persistently high percentage of social democratic vote, high union density, low spread in wages among unionized workers due to commitments to solidarity) that the welfare state literature sees as being positively correlated to the emergence of a comprehensive and strong welfare state and consequent low levels of inequality.

It is beyond the scope of this chapter to document fully the inequality-producing mechanisms associated with the three classic coming together federations (Switzerland, United States, and Australia), but Linz and Stepan in their work in progress on federalism will devote a chapter to this task.

Finally, as an agenda for future research for Latin American federalism, scholars must conduct more research to ascertain why Brazil and Argentina, even though they were not classic coming together federations (see Gibson and Falleti in this volume), produced, over time, federal systems with the most robust electorally generated veto players in the world.[27]

How Changing Political Contexts and "Partisan" Veto Players Can Alter Radically the Number of Politically Effective Institutional Veto Players

As I observe in note 4, Tsebelis distinguishes between, and analyzes, "institutional" and "partisan" (political party) veto players. When we add partisan political party players to our consideration, we see their potential to alter radically the number of politically effective institutional veto players.

In 1983 President Raúl Alfonsín of Argentina, heavily supported by the Radical Party's urban middle-class supporters, carried Buenos Aires and became the first elected president of Argentina after redemocratization. Despite his popular election, and his stewardship of Latin America's first ever legally based trials of a previous military junta for human rights abuses, Alfonsín lost control of the federal Chamber of Deputies in the midterm election in October 1987. At this point, Argentina's four potential institutional veto players became four actual institutional veto players, three of which were used systematically against Alfonsín, who therefore could not pass legislation or control the governors. In June 1989, faced with opposition from three veto players and politically unable to coordinate an effective macroeconomic federal policy to combat Argentina's unprecedented "hyperinflation," a humiliated President Alfonsín left office six months early, handing over the presidency to President-elect Menem and his Peronist party allies (see Fig. 10.1).

Less than a year later, under Menem, Argentina's four potential institutional veto players had become reduced to one actual veto player. One partisan veto player, the Peronist Party and their dependent allies, controlled all four institutional veto players (see Fig. 10.2).

How and why did this happen? Because the political party context, greatly facilitated by some highly unusual institutional characteristics of Argentina's federal system, changed radically. Edward L. Gibson and his colleagues have created the fascinating and important concept of "low-maintenance constituencies," which helps us

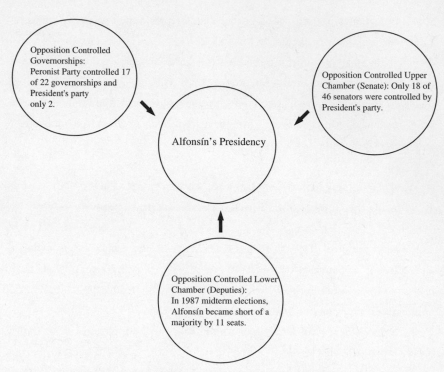

Fig. 10.1. How Four Potential Federal Veto Players Were Four Actual Veto Players: The Alfonsín Presidency after the Midterm Elections in 1987 and before His Early Resignation in 1989. *Source:* Alcántara Sáez (1988).

solve this puzzle.[28] Among Latin America's four federal systems, Argentina has not only the most malapportioned upper chamber, but the most malapportioned lower chamber as well.[29] The federal units that are most overrepresented in the federation are situated in the sparsely settled, relatively poor provinces in the periphery. With only 30 percent of the population, these nineteen provinces nonetheless hold 45 percent of the seats in the federal lower chamber, and 83 percent of those in the Senate. In these poor peripheral units, side-payments produce the most votes for the least cost and, due to massive malapportionment, the most seats for the fewest votes. Thus, the opportunity exists for a "low-maintenance constituency." As Gibson et al. have shown, Peronists used the above opportunity to their advantage. Starting in 1949, Perón, who was correctly confident he could control the conservative provincial machines by the adroit use of patronage, deliberately compounded malapportionment. Institutions are important in their own right, but malapportionment in Argentina is a clear example of the crystallization of a particular, self-conscious set of actor goals. The Peronists have never lost the art of building these "low-maintenance constituencies."

By contrast, owing to its historic urban and middle-class base and organizational style, the Radical Party, unlike the Peronist Party, has been much less able to use malapportionment in its favor. This has made a Radical Party president, since the 1950s, much more vulnerable than most Argentine presidencies to the effective opposition of partisan and institutional veto players with artificial majorities produced by malapportionment. In fact, since Perón first left office in 1955, none of the four democratically elected Radical Party presidents of Argentina (Frondizi, Illía, Alfonsín, or de la Rua) has completed his term of office.[30]

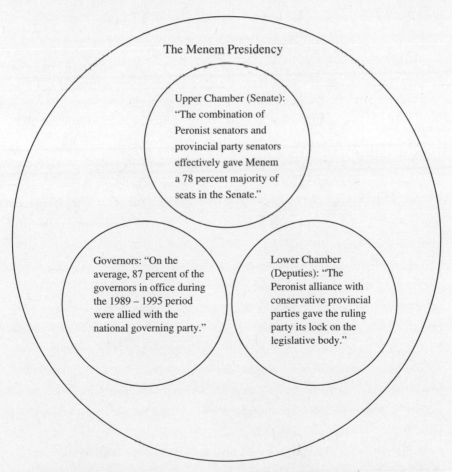

The Menem Presidency

Upper Chamber (Senate): "The combination of Peronist senators and provincial party senators effectively gave Menem a 78 percent majority of seats in the Senate."

Governors: "On the average, 87 percent of the governors in office during the 1989 – 1995 period were allied with the national governing party."

Lower Chamber (Deputies): "The Peronist alliance with conservative provincial parties gave the ruling party its lock on the legislative body."

Fig. 10.2. How Four Potential Federal Veto Players Became Only One Actual Veto Player: President Menem's 1989–95 Term. *Source:* All quotes are from the pioneering article by Gibson and Calvo (2000).

Argentina shows how a system that has effectively only one partisan political veto player (the Peronist Party) and one institutional veto player (President Menem, from the Peronist Party) can return to a system in which all four potential institutional veto players are actualized. After the midterm elections of 1999, President de la Rua, whose base, like Alfonsín's, was in the Radical Party (but who was a less effective politician), once again found himself in a political situation extremely similar to that depicted in Figure 10.1. Controlling the presidency, but completely unable to control the regional governors' production of quasi money or to build a political coalition in either the upper or lower house to address the country's financial crisis, de la Rua, like Alfonsín, resigned the presidency early.

Turning now to Brazil, we see that since civilians reassumed the presidency in 1985 the country has never been anywhere near a position like that shown in Figure 10.1 (a president with a predictable low-cost majority in both federal chambers and among governors). Furthermore, Brazil is unlikely to approximate such a position for the foreseeable future. Why? Because the nature of Brazil's political party system makes it extremely unlikely that any one political party could ever simultaneously have majority control over the lower chamber, upper chamber, the governors, and the presidency, as happened under Menem in Argentina.

Brazil often has a directly elected president (e.g., Collar, Cardoso, or "Lula") whose core party actually holds only between 3 and 18 percent of the seats in either federal chamber.[31] Also, since redemocratization, Brazil has had a Laakso / Taagepera index of effective number of political parties with seats in the federal legislature substantially higher than the index in Argentina.[32] This, plus the fact that many of the Brazilian parties are electorally more volatile than, and not as disciplined as, their Argentine counterparts, makes the task of constructing congruent majorities among the four potential veto players much more difficult in Brazil than in Argentina.[33] Barry Ames has calculated the average number of institutional and partisan veto players in Latin America via two different counting methods ("partial absorption" and "absorption"). In both calculations, consistent with the analysis advanced here, Brazil has the highest number of partisan and institutional veto players in Latin America, while Argentina, because of its fewer and more disciplined political parties, often has fewer (Ames 2001, 12–18).

Politically Induced Changes in the Structures of Institutional Veto Players

Federal political structures are seen correctly as relatively inflexible. They are normally constitutionally embedded and thus need supermajorities to change. How-

Table 10.7

Politically Induced Changes in Federal Structures: Malapportionment in the Brazilian and
Mexican Senates before and after Democratic Transitions

Before Transition		After Transition		
Country	Mal. Index	Country	Mal. Index	Net Change
Austria	0.0301	Austria	0.0301	
India	0.0747	India	0.0747	
Germany	0.2440	Germany	0.2440	
Spain	0.2853	**Mexico (2000)**	**0.2470**	**−0.070**
Australia	0.2962	Spain	0.2853	
Mexico (1977)	**0.3170**	Australia	0.2962	
Brazil (1974)	**0.3350**	Switzerland	0.3448	
Switzerland	0.3448	United States	0.3642	
United States	0.3642	**Brazil (1990)**	**0.4060**	**+0.071**
Argentina	0.4852	Argentina	0.4852	

Note: The date 1977 is chosen for Mexico because the first of the six comprehensive electoral reforms that contributed to the democratic transition was passed in 1977; see Ochoa-Reza in this volume. The date 1974 was chosen for Brazil because the inauguration of Geisel in 1974 is normally considered the start of the *abertura*. See Stepan (1988, 30–44). The years 2000 for Mexico and 1990 for Brazil are the years of the inauguration of the first, postauthoritarian, democratically elected presidents.

ever, political factors can change federal political structures. Snyder and Samuels as well as others in this volume have put the question of malapportionment squarely on the comparative politics agenda.[34] Now one of the important research tasks is to document how, when, and why some apportionment changes make federal structures more "demos constraining" and some less "demos constraining." In this respect, during their transitions to democracy, Brazil and Mexico went in opposite directions vis-à-vis an important institutional veto player, the federal Senate (see Table 10.7).

How did these changes occur?

Brazil was the only one of the "bureaucratic-authoritarian" regimes in the Southern Cone (Chile, Argentina, Uruguay, and Brazil) to attempt to rule (1964–85) via manipulating the Congress but nonetheless leaving it open. Once the actual political opening began (1974–85), the task of managing Congress became more important, and more difficult, for the military and their civilian allies. The result was increased malapportionment. In 1978 the military regime created the state of Mato Grosso do Sul and in 1982 another, Rondônia, out of relatively underpopulated and underdeveloped areas in the North and Center-West. Federal subsidies and a strong military presence made these states more predictably progovernment than those in the more developed South, where civil society organizations, trade unions, and opposition parties were becoming increasingly strong. In the South the military managed to eliminate an entire state by fusing the states of Guanabara and Rio de Janeiro into a single state called Rio de Janeiro.

As a result of the creation of small states in the North, twelve new federal deputy and six new federal senator posts were created. Owing to the fusion by the military of two states in the South, the developed—and increasingly opposition—states eventually lost three senators.[35]

Representation in the Constituent Assembly of 1986–88 to a great extent followed the new militarily crafted edicts. With their 52 percent of seats in the constituent assembly, the states from the North, Northeast, and Center-West voted, almost as a block, to admit a further three new, thinly populated states from their regions: Tocatins, Roraima, and Amapá.[36] In the federal elections of 1990 this block of states, with 43 percent of the population of Brazil, controlled 74 percent of the seats in the federal Senate. Thus, Brazil, which started its democratic transition with a malapportionment index better than that of Switzerland and the United States, ended the transition with a malapportionment index worse than any democratic federal senate in the world, with the sole exception of Argentina's. A major institutional veto player had become even more "demos constraining" in its composition.

The Mexican story is more original in its motivations, to the extent that we understand them.[37] As Ochoa-Reza demonstrates in his chapter in this volume, the ruling party PRI was the only party to support all the major electoral reforms that eventually contributed to its defeat. Obviously, party leaders (possibly pushed by the new transnational context created by the "Third Wave" and NAFTA membership) did this in the hopes of shifting PRI's rule from hegemonic to democratic foundations. PRI leaders always thought they had a reasonably good chance to win in freer elections. Most importantly, presidents who came to rule in questionable electoral circumstances immediately attempted to get "forward legitimation" by initiating, and successfully implementing, cleaner and fairer procedures for the *next* election.

One of the most important reforms was the 1996 electoral reform, the sixth and last of the transition. One of the purposes of this reform for PRI leaders was to increase the number of parties, especially small parties, that could get into the Senate and that could possibly help PRI put back together the constitution-changing majorities they once had. To achieve this aim, PRI decided to have thirty-two seats in the Senate elected from a national, closed-list, PR system. The effect of this law was to decrease malapportionment. The thirty-two seats elected through PR were mostly assigned by the parties to politicians with national reputations, most of who came from the most populous and politically and economically relevant states. After this 1996 law was implemented for the 1997 elections, the Mexican Senate, which had been quite close to Brazil in its malapportionment score at the start of its transition in 1977, became better apportioned than Australia and Spain and just behind Germany. A major institutional veto player had become less "demos constraining" in its composition.

Activation of Federal Institutions and "Political Opportunity Structures" for New Partisan Veto Players to Destroy the State and Build or Erode Democracies

The activation of federalist structures in a context where they had previously been latent rapidly creates "political opportunity structures" and new forms of "resource mobilization" possibilities. Such a new context can facilitate the emergence of new social movements and even new institutional and partisan veto players that can remake the state itself.[38] There is no remotely similar phenomenon in unitary states.

Whether such new federal structures contribute to rapid state termination (as in the former Soviet Union and Yugoslavia), the erosion of a nondemocratic regime and the eventual emergence of a democracy (as in Mexico and Brazil), or polarization and partial democratic breakdown (as in Venezuela) depends on many factors; but here I will pay special attention to how new veto players are created by the activation of federalist structures and to how they and the old veto players interact and with what consequence.

State Disintegration

Communist Europe had nine states. Six were unitary—Poland, Hungary, Romania, Bulgaria, Albania, and East Germany. Three were federal—the Soviet Union, Yugoslavia, and Czechoslovakia. The six unitary states are now five, East Germany having voted to accede to West Germany. In contrast, the three federal states are now twenty-three independent states. Why this disintegration of communist federal states?

If a country is only latently federal, in the sense that its constitution proclaims it as federal, but elections are not competitive and politics is effectively run by a centralized party or by a centralized military, the turn to a more electorally competitive environment opens up numerous new political arenas and offices. The most powerful of these offices are normally the chief executives of the constituent members of the federation. Ideally, particularly in a multinational state, the first important competitive elections should be to produce a government at the center because this will help focus the election on some politywide issues and encourage the formation of politywide parties.

However, in the Soviet Union the first, and in Yugoslavia the only, competitive elections for executive positions took place at the regional level. Since the regional elections in these multinational states increasingly revolved around regional and cultural-political autonomy, *no significant politywide parties emerged.* In the vast majority of what became the twenty-three new states, the dominant political movement in the first election in fact received almost all of its vote from its home federal unit, and almost no votes from anywhere else. In sharp contrast, in Spain, which is also multinational, the first competitive elections to form a government in the founding elections were politywide. Because of the statewide stakes involved, four politywide parties conducted a statewide campaign around politywide themes, winning 319 of the 350 seats. In multinational India, the Congress Party competed in, and did well in, every state in the founding elections.

However, in Yugoslavia, as the once moribund federal institutions increasingly came to life, the federal units, which on paper had always been politically more autonomous and powerful than in any democratic federal system, now became actual institutional veto players. The three communist federations were all variants on this theme. None of the partisan veto players, old or new, was a politywide party. The Communist Party to the extent that it existed often did so by joining the separatist discourse. "Multiple and complementary political identities," which might have been possible before the first elections, came under attack by nationalist leaders, who preferred to create their own ethnic states rather than continuing to be a part of a multinational federation.

Let us briefly look at some telling details of the Yugoslav case. In 1974 a collective executive was created by the 1974 constitution. The collective executive at the time of the first elections consisted of the six national republics that together composed the state of Yugoslavia—Serbia, Croatia, Slovenia, Macedonia, Montenegro,

and Bosnia. Unanimity was required for most major decisions. In this new competitive electoral political context, especially given the role of unanimity decision rules,
each republic met the conditions of being an institutional veto player. Furthermore,
the core political party or movement behind the leaders that emerged from the elections in most of the ethnic republics met the conditions of being a partisan veto
player. In the absence of any politywide party with a strong base in each of the republics, and many institutional and partisan veto players who increasingly exercised
their veto against any fiscal or military claims on their "sovereignty," the Yugoslav
state disintegrated.[39]

Some policy analysts and social scientists conclude that the reason for the collapse
of the communist federations was that they were multinational and "asymmetrical"
(in the sense that different constituent members had potentially different rights and
obligations). They were indeed. However, virtually all of the world's long-standing
multinational federal democracies—Spain, Belgium, Canada, and India—are also
asymmetrical. A crucial difference is the presence of politywide partisan veto players in Spain, Belgium, Canada, and India and their absence in the former Yugoslavia
and the former Soviet Union.

Democratic Transition

In the "Third Wave" of democratization federalism played an especially significant
role in terminating long-standing, nondemocratic regimes in four countries.[40] For
two of these countries—Yugoslavia and the Soviet Union—I have reviewed how federalism terminated the state (and in the process helped spawn many new autocra-
cies). In two other countries—Brazil and Mexico—federalism helped make the democratic transitions. Why were these two Latin American cases so different?

In Brazil the "political opportunity structures" that an activated federalism
opened up were created by the 1982 elections. From 1965 to 1982 the military, despite leaving the malapportioned congress open, had forbidden direct elections for
state governorships or for the mayors of state capitals. In sharp contrast to Yugoslavia or the Soviet Union, in Brazil when direct elections were held in 1982 for
state governorships there was a powerful politywide democratic opposition party,
the PMDB, which campaigned on politywide issues (democratization) as well as local issues. The PMDB won 44 percent of the total vote cast in Brazil and won governorships in nine of the twenty-two states.

The major proregime party, the PDS, won 41.5 percent of the votes cast and won governorships in twelve of the twenty-two states. The only governorship not won by one of the two major politywide parties was won by the PDT in Rio de Janeiro. However, the PDT was not a Yugoslavian-type, single-state party whose leader's political ambitions were confined to that state. The PDT won 23 percent of the vote in Rio Grande do Sul. The PDT, far from being a secessionist party, was actually the party vehicle for the politywide political ambitions of Leonel Brizola, the former governor of Rio Grande do Sul, who shifted his base to Rio de Janeiro to better his chance of presidential election.

Notwithstanding Brazil's weak parties, which I discussed in the previous section, it still makes analytic and political sense therefore to say that in 1982 every single governorship in Brazil was won by a politywide party.

More significantly, the "political opportunity structures" opened up by direct elections for the all-important federal office of governor strengthened democratization greatly. Three of the most powerful industrial, financial, and political states in Brazil, São Paulo, Rio de Janeiro, and Minas Gerais, all with powerful militarized state militias, fell into the hands of not just opposition governors, but oppositional governors who were potential presidential candidates, namely, Tancredo Neves of Minas Gerais, Leonel Brizola of Rio de Janeiro, and Franco Montoro of São Paulo. The next big push for democratization came in the massive 1984 *diretas já* ("direct election now!") campaign. The biggest of these rallies were always mobilized and protected by opposition governors. The governors increasingly became institutional and partisan veto players in what was once a single (the military) veto player game. The first civilian president to be selected at the end of the military regime was Governor Tancredo Neves.[41]

Unlike Brazil, the three major political parties in Mexico are ruled from the center with the party's national leadership playing a pivotal role in nominations and campaign finance.

However, the Mexican case, as Ochoa-Reza documents in this volume, is analogous to Brazil's concerning federalism's positive contribution to democratic transition. But, even more than in Brazil, Mexico's democratic opposition was based on a bottom-up process of gaining control in federal political arenas when "political opportunity structures" became available. The first opportunity structure to open was due to the election law of 1977, which established PR for local council seats in towns with over 300,000 inhabitants and PR for state congress seats. Ochoa's data are dramatic. In 1976, the year before the law was passed, eight of the nine states with elections had a Laakso / Taagepera index of 1.0; that is, they were one-party states. In 1981 eight of eight were over 1.35. By 1997, three years before the victory of an opposition president and the completion of the democratic transition, eight of the eight elections were over 2.0, that is, they were all at least two-party states.

By the early 1990s democratic opposition forces were sufficiently rooted in regional politics that they launched major mobilizations over the rules of the game for gubernatorial elections. A series of these gubernatorial struggles helped to open more arenas to contestation. This in turn broadened the demands for greater democracy per se. After such mobilizations, Vicente Fox in 1995 won an important governorship that helped him greatly in his eventual successful campaign for the presidency.

The democratic opposition forces fought for, and won, more and more opportunities to hold office in Mexico's federal structures. Indeed, *before* Fox won the presidency, politywide, highly disciplined opposition parties governed federal units that controlled about half the country's GNP, held over half the seats in state congresses, and by the seats they controlled in the upper and lower federal houses were already partisan veto players with the capacity to block any last-minute constitutional changes that might have stalled democratization. With the possible exception of Brazil, no other "Third Wave" democratizing country, before it won control of the central executive, had already conquered so many politically influential spaces in the political system. Federalism, and politywide parties, had a lot to do with this outcome in Mexico and Brazil.

Partial Democratic Breakdown

In 1989 Venezuela shifted from de jure to de facto federalism. As in the Soviet Union and Yugoslavia at roughly the same time, many arenas of regional power thus became open to political contestation. In the case of Venezuela, approximately twenty governorships and three hundred mayoral offices became obtainable by direct election for the first time.

Michael Penfold-Becerra's fascinating and disturbing chapter in this volume is the first work to document how some aspects of federalism contributed to a worsening of the overall political situation in Venezuela. Venezuela by late 2002 was a case of intense polarization and "partial democratic breakdown."

Analytically, a radical expansion of leadership spaces obviously creates "political opportunity structures" and new resource mobilization possibilities. The new federal structures in Venezuela undeniably did precisely this. But a question still remains: was it overdetermined that the political opposition, especially the democratically "semi-loyal" forces, should benefit from these political opportunity structures?[42] Or were there major lost opportunities for AD and COPEI, the traditional democratic political parties that had almost continuously governed Venezuela since redemocratization began in 1958, to use these new federal offices to reinvigorate themselves with new leadership? I incline to the latter position.

There has been much talk since the rise of Chávez to the presidency of how the "collapse" of the traditional democratic parties contributed to this result. However, we need to note that in the October 1998 gubernatorial elections, eleven of the seventeen incumbents who were reelected were from AD and COPEI. In fact, these two traditional parties provided the largest share of the votes in thirteen of the twenty-three gubernatorial contests.[43] Thus, a decade after federalism started, and only two months before their supposed "collapse" when Chávez won the December 1998 presidential election, AD and COPEI still had substantial political resources.

At the time of the rise of Chávez to the presidency, there was also much talk of a crisis of democratic belief in Venezuela. However, on the basis of survey data, a more nuanced judgment is warranted. In 1995 the *Latinobarometro* did a survey of public opinion in Argentina, Brazil, Chile, Mexico, Paraguay, Peru, Uruguay, and Venezuela. The comparative data show that Venezuelan public opinion was slightly more supportive of democracy (as a set of procedures) than the Latin American mean and that Venezuela ranked third out of the eight countries polled on this question. However, a battery of questions explored how much confidence (*confianza*) Latin Americans had in the performance of their country's actual institutions. Concerning each one of six key institutions that are particularly important for the quality of democratic governance, Venezuelans expressed the lowest level of confidence of any country in Latin America (see Table 10.8).

Clearly politicians most associated with delivery of services in the past would bear some of the onus for this perceived low quality of government performance. In the case of the AD, the impeachment in 1993 on charges of corruption of Carlos Andrés Pérez, a twice-elected AD presidential candidate, certainly hurt the party. However, for a party that wanted to survive such low governmental trust during a period of new federalization, the availability of new elective offices at the mayoral

Table 10.8

Latinobarometro: 1995 *Attitudes toward Democracy (as a Set of Procedures) and Attitudes toward Actual Performance of Governmental Institutions in Eight Countries*

Respondents Affirming . . .	Venezuela	Latin American Mean	Venezuelan Rank
"Democracy is preferable to authoritarianism"	60%	58%	3/8
"No confidence in the judiciary"	38	25	8/8
"No confidence in the public administration"	43	25	8/8
"No confidence in the police"	44	27	8/8
"No confidence in the national congress"	44	24	8/8
"No confidence in political parties"	54	35	8/8
"No confidence in the government"	42	24	8/8

Source: Latinobarometro: 1995 (1995) Sample size of Venezuela, 1,200. Questions 20, 27D, 27G, 27H, 27I, 27J. Survey directed by Marta Lagos. The eight countries polled were Argentina, Brazil, Chile, Mexico, Paraguay, Peru, Uruguay, and Venezuela.

and gubernatorial level presented major opportunities for the identification, testing, and promotion of new leaders. And as the gubernatorial election results showed, new leaders, from a variety of parties, including AD and COPEI, did indeed emerge. However, exceptionally poor leadership at the top of AD and COPEI resulted in the failure to capitalize on this phenomenon.

The top leaders of AD fought against the emergence of younger leaders at the top of the party, so much so that in 1998 they initially nominated the eighty-year-old secretary general, Alfaro Ucero, as their presidential candidate and thereby created disaffection among their frustrated governors.[44] Similarly with COPEI, in 1995 Rafael Caldera, a COPEI founder who had served as president of Venezuela from 1969 to 1974, blocked, rather than aided, party renewal (and in fact left his party for a new one).

Much of the radical polarization and partial breakdown of democracy in Venezuela occurred not before, but after, Chávez assumed the presidency. Poor political leadership of the traditional parties, rather than federalism per se, facilitated the rapid accrual of extraordinary powers to the democratically elected, but democratically "semiloyal," Chávez. Amazingly, AD and COPEI, with a majority of Venezuelan governorships, agreed to election procedures for a National Constituent Assembly election in which party names were *not* on the ballot. Only the personal names of the candidates, accompanied by a number, were on the ballot.[45] The Chávez allies predictably organized their potential voters by giving them the ballot numbers of the candidates to vote for. The disorganized traditional parties, which by then were largely only regionally based, made no such coordinated national effort. With 56 percent of the total votes Chávez supporters won 93 percent of the seats, and with almost 40 percent of the votes the opposition won almost no seats. With this electoral-based authority Chávez proceeded to write a new constitution for what Guillermo O'Donnell would call a "delegative democracy."[46]

Chávez's supporters, facing no partisan veto players in the Constituent Assembly, proceeded to eliminate, as Michael Coppedge shows, most of the checks and balances of a liberal democracy and even some of the institutional veto players (Coppedge 2003). The new constitution was written in three months. The Constituent Assembly eliminated the Senate, eliminated the old Supreme Court, appointed new members for a revised court, and through their special commission purged hundreds of judges from the lower courts. The Constituent Assembly also appointed a new electoral council, appointed a new comptroller general, and designated a nonelected National Legislative Committee to act as the interim legislature. Chávez also began to undermine the powers of the federal system that had facilitated his rise to power. He not only abolished the Senate but reduced funding for state and local governments and made much of the remaining states' funding subject to his discretion. In this context the constitution was ratified, and a newly elected Congress gave the president great decree powers and more constitutional powers than in any other Latin American democracy.[47]

Some Conclusions

In Latin America, federal systems, unlike in postcommunist Europe, did not contribute to state disintegration. In Argentina federalism played no role in the transition to democracy, but the world's worst malapportionment and the fiscal prerogatives of the states greatly complicated democratic consolidation. In Brazil federalism contributed directly to the democratic transition, but the combination of federalism, presidentialism, party fragmentation, the world's second worst malapportionment, and the fiscal prerogatives of the states made the creation of predictable programmatic support quite difficult. Mexico could be the only "third wave" country in the world where federalism helped the transition and may not create obstacles for democratic consolidation. The Senate is not too malapportioned and does not have a veto over the budget, and the states, unlike Brazil or Argentina, do not have the powers to issue de facto money.

Some lessons for Latin America emerge clearly from this book. More attention should be paid, analytically and politically, to malapportionment in general. In particular there is a great need to diminish in Brazil and Argentina the politically distorting malapportionment in both federal chambers but especially in the Senate.

There are also some lessons that emerge from our comparative analysis of the United States and Switzerland. Many citizens of these two countries historically have had a strong normative preference for high levels of policy-making autonomy of the members of the federation and an associated high tolerance—more than in Australia—for economic inequalities. This normative orientation, plus their high number of electorally generated institutional veto players produced by their "coming together" pattern of federation formation, contributed to a higher level of inequality than that found in any other advanced economies among the long-standing democracies in the world.

Welfare state theorists again and again argue that federalism, per se, produces inequality. This position is no longer defensible given the data I have marshaled along with that of Evelyne Huber and John Stephens.

The unexamined irony is that the most praised federal systems in the world are precisely the three classic "coming together" federal systems: the United States, Switzerland, and Australia. Predictably, given the "veto player" and "coming together" explanations advanced in this chapter, these polities have the least comprehensive and least generous welfare states and are thus "inequality inducing." "Inequality-reducing" federal states like Germany are a more interesting federal variant for Latin American federal states to examine once we have established that federalism, per se, does not necessarily produce inequality.

NOTES

1. For the productive application of veto player theory—that they sometimes call constitutional features—to the study of welfare states, see Huber and Stephens (2001, esp. 67–84). For a conceptually and empirically powerful discussion of Brazil's high number of veto players see Ames (2001, esp. 12–18).

2. For this definition see Tsebelis (1995, 293).

3. A close reading of Arend Lijphart's tables on the democracies that have strong judicial review, and democracies that have strong independent central banks, clearly shows that federal democracies tend to have stronger judicial review and more autonomous central banks than do unitary states; see Lijphart (1999), tables 12.2 and 13.1

4. In his 1995 article, Tsebelis restricted his analysis to "institutional" and "partisan" veto players. For the purposes of this chapter, I too will restrict myself to "institutional" and "partisan" veto players. Tsebelis correctly notes, however, that depending on the issue and the context, one also could consider institutions such as "supreme courts" or "autonomous central banks" as veto players. In his article Tsebelis develops the formal argument and advances some empirical data to support the argument that, among other things, the more institutional veto players there are, and the greater the policy distance between institutional and partisan veto players whose assent is required to change the status quo, the more difficult it is to create a win-set to alter the status quo. He also points out that "agreement of institutional veto players is a necessary and sufficient condition for policy change, while agreement of partisan veto players is, *strictly speaking,* neither necessary nor sufficient. Agreement of partisan veto players is not sufficient for policy change because a proposal which is approved by all partners in a government coalition may be defeated in parliament, in which case no law is changed" (Tsebelis 1995, 302).

5. See, for example, the excellent analysis along these lines for the case of the former Soviet Union in Roeder (1991).

6. Tsebelis (1995, 305–8).

7. In the technical literature on counting veto players the prime minister's blocking powers are counted as being "absorbed" within the parliament's veto power. The prime minister's mandate can be revoked by a hostile vote of the majority of the parliament. In that sense, unlike a directly elected president of the U.S. or Brazilian sort, a prime minister does not have a fixed and independent mandate and cannot sustain a long conflict with the majority in the parliament.

8. Before the constitutional amendment in 1977 only fifty thousand signatures were required to force a referendum.

9. For example, in the 1994 Argentine constitution the president has line item ("partial") as well as entire ("package") veto power over legislation, and an override requires a two-thirds majority in each house. In Brazil the president also has partial and package veto powers. The combination of partial and package veto powers, as well as substantial decree and patronage powers, makes presidents with these powers politically influential veto players, even if their veto is not absolute. For an excellent analysis of presidential veto powers see Shugart and Carey (1992), especially tables 8.1 and 8.2.

10. See the well-documented work by Wilfred Swenden (2000), esp. chap. 6. Also see Leonardy (1999).

11. For my distinction between the "coming together" federalism of previously highly autonomous political units as in the United States, Switzerland, and Australia, and the "holding together" federalism where unitary states, as in Spain and Belgium, choose to become federal in order to hold together their multinational polities, see my other chapter in this volume.

12. See Swenden (2000).

13. Article 155 of the Spanish constitution precludes such intervention without the absolute majority approval of the upper house, so in this respect the upper chamber is an institutional veto player. For federalism in Spain more generally, the best study is Linz (1985). For "asymmetrical federalism" in Spain, see Requejo (2001).

14. Personal communication from Juan Linz.

15. Personal communication by a leading specialist on Canadian federalism, Richard Simeon, Toronto, 7 November, 2002. Also see Tindal (2000).

16. A semipresidential democracy could conceivably have a directly elected president and an upper and lower chamber with absolute veto powers, and thus three institutional veto players. No such state exists at the moment.

17. See the chapter on the origins and power of Swiss referendums in Schmitt (1996, 87–94). For a comparative perspective on the distinctiveness of the powerful veto point role of referendums in Switzerland see Butler and Ranney (1978), especially the chapter on Switzerland by Jean-François Aubert. On how referendums can make cantons the decisive veto players that often stop social welfare legislation see Obinger (1998) and Immergut (1992).

18. For the frequent use of the referendum in Australia see the chapter on Australia by Don Aitkin in Butler and Ranney (1978, 39–66). Swendon (2000) is particularly good in putting the prerogatives of the Australian federal upper house in comparative perspective.

19. Nigeria, if its democracy survives, could join this list. Venezuela in its 1999 constitution abolished the federal Senate and thus does not have the institutional potential for four veto players. Also, after 1999 the states have no effective veto capacity, so Venezuela now is actually only a two electorally generated veto player country.

20. For example, the states in Mexico have little autonomous borrowing capacity, and state debt is low. A Mexican government study estimates that as a percentage of GDP state debt represents 20.6 percent in Brazil, 11.2 percent in Argentina, and only 1.7 percent in Mexico. See Inda (2002).

21. See Diaz-Cayeros in this volume.

22. During the 2001–2 financial crisis, one of the reasons why Argentina and the IMF could not arrive at an agreement was that no president or finance minister of Argentina could make a credible commitment that the provinces would no longer issue bonds and that the center would not under any circumstances bail them out. Half of the 4.2 billion pesos in bonds in circulation in Argentina had their origin in the provinces (the other half were national government bonds to cancel debts with the provinces). See the newspaper *Clarín* (2 April 2002), as well as de la Torre et al. (2002).

23. See Samuels and Mainwaring in this volume. Other works that provide great detail on quasi-autonomous state borrowing are Abrucio (1998), Makler (2000), and Dillinger (1997).

24. For much more detail on these variables and in particular how U.S. federalism helps induce this inequality, see Linz and Stepan (2000).

25. Huber and Stephens (2001); see p. 82 for the quote; for the regressions on social security benefits of the eighteen variables, see their table 3.2.

26. This is based on my analysis of the raw data that went into compiling Table 10.4. The federal ranking by WHO is also better than the unitary state ranking, but unitary states do better in both the Luxembourg Study indicators. Thus, within the universe of democracies with one or two veto players, the distinction between unitary and federal states is not very determinative concerning inequality.

27. The chapter by Gibson and Falleti provides an important step in this direction. The authors

reject the "coming together" scenario advanced by Riker for the Argentine case and provide theory and historical evidence to explain how weak provinces designed and used federal institutions to counter the hegemonic power of rival provinces.

28. See Gibson and Calvo (2000, 34), and the chapter in this volume by Gibson, Calvo, and Falleti.

29. See Snyder and Samuels in this volume, table 4.1.

30. Sadly the last democratically elected Radical Party president of Argentina to complete his term of office was Marcello T. de Alvear in 1928.

31. Quadros, elected in 1960, like Collar, who was elected in 1989, was an antiparty politician. "Lula" in 2002 won the presidential election by more than nineteen million votes over Serra, and he and his PT party are strong party loyalists. However, the PT holds only three of Brazil's twenty-seven governorships and less than 20 percent of the seats in either federal chamber.

32. For example, the mean number of parties, based on number of lower chamber seats, was 8.7 in 1990 in Brazil, compared to 2.8 in 1993 in Argentina; see the introduction by Scott Mainwaring and Timothy R. Scully in Mainwaring and Scully (1995, 30).

33. Mainwaring and Scully also calculated the Pederson index of electoral volatility, which measures the net change in the seat (or vote) shares of all parties from one election to the next. Argentina from 1983 to 1993 had a Pederson index average of 12.7, whereas Brazil from 1982 to 1990 had a Pederson index of 40.9 (ibid., 6–8). On the Brazilian political party system, see the massively documented work of Scott Mainwaring (1999); in table 5.3 of this book, he documents that 51.7 percent of all deputies in the 1991–94 period in Brazil changed their party.

34. In addition to their chapter in this volume, see also Samuels and Snyder (2001).

35. See Stepan (2000). For the military regime's manipulation of the electoral system (manipulation that often backfired), see Fleischer (1994).

36. For this struggle at the constituent assembly, see the well-documented and richly detailed study by Backes (1998).

37. Memoirs of key PRI leaders or interviews with them, especially of the last PRI president of Mexico, would be helpful in illuminating this point.

38. For a brief history and bibliography of the concept "political opportunity structures," which originated with Charles Tilly, see Tarrow (1999, esp. 18–20). Also see McAdam et al. (1996).

39. For data on the absence of politywide parties, see Linz and Stepan (2001). On how the first competitive federal elections aggravated "stateness" problems in the Soviet Union, see chapter 19 of Linz and Stepan (1996). For a comparative work that is particularly good on Yugoslavia, see Bunce (1999). Carol Skalnik Leff (1999) is particularly helpful for Czechoslovakia.

40. In Spain the creation of federalism certainly helped make democratic consolidation possible, but it should be remembered that Spain's democratic transition began, and was well advanced, while Spain was still a unitary state.

41. For more detail on the role of opposition governors in the Brazilian democratization see Stepan (1988, chap. 5).

42. For the concepts of "disloyal" and "semiloyal" oppositions, see Linz (1978). In terms of democratic theory and the Linz / Stepan work on democratic breakdown, Chávez came on the Vene-

zuelan national political scene as a leader of a *golpista* "disloyal opposition" and later became a democratically elected president, some of whose speeches and actions were only "semiloyal" to democratic institutions.

43. See Penfold-Becerra in this volume (Table 6.3).

44. See Penfold-Becerra in this volume and his excellent analysis of these leadership-produced party splits in AD and COPEI.

45. Personal communication from Penfold-Becerra.

46. See O'Donnell's classic article (O'Donnell 1994).

47. The above paragraph is based on Michael Coppedge's important article (Coppedge 2003).

BIBLIOGRAPHY

Latinobarometro. 1995. *Latinobarometro 1995*. Santiago: MORI.

World Bank. 2000. *World Development Indicators: 2000*. Washington, D.C.: World Bank.

World Health Organization. 2000. *World Health Report: 2000*. Geneva: World Health Organization.

Clarín. 2002. Empezo la Puja con el FMI por los Bonos de las Provincias. *Clarín*. Buenos Aires.

Abrucio, Fernando Luis. 1998. *Os Barões da Federação: Os Governadores e a Redemocratização Brasileira*. São Paulo: Editora Hucitec.

Alcántara Sáez, Manuel. 1988. *Elecciones y Consolidación Democrática en Argentina*. San José, Costa Rica: Cuadernos de CAPEL.

Ames, Barry. 2001. *The Deadlock of Democracy in Brazil: Interests, Identities, and Institutions in Comparative Politics*. Ann Arbor: University of Michigan Press.

Atkinson, Anthony, Lee Rainwater, and Timothy Smeeding. 1995. *Income Distribution in OECD Countries: Evidence from the Luxembourg Income Study*. Paris: OECD.

Backes, Ana Luiza. 1998. Democracia e Sobre-Representação de Regiões: O Papel do Senado. Master's thesis, Universidade de Brasília.

Bunce, Valerie. 1999. *Subversive Institutions: The Design and the Destruction of Socialism and the State*. Cambridge: Cambridge University Press.

Butler, David, and Austin Ranney, eds. 1978. *Referendums: A Comparative Study of Practice and Theory*. Washington, D.C., American Enterprise Institute for Public Policy Research.

Castles, F. G. 1982. *Comparative Public Policy: Patterns of Post-war Transformation*. Cheltenham: Edward Elgar.

Coppedge, Michael. 2003. Explaining Democratic Deterioration in Venezuela through Nested Inference. In *Advances and Setbacks in the Third Wave of Democratization in Latin America*, edited by F. Hagopian and S. Mainwaring. Cambridge: Cambridge University Press.

de la Torre, A., et al. 2002. Beyond the Bipolar View: The Rise and Fall of Argentina's Currency Board. Working paper, National Bureau of Economic Research, Washington, D.C., October.

Dillinger, William. 1997. *Brazil's State Debt Crisis: Lessons Learned*. World Bank Departmental Working Paper 17430, No. 14, September. Washington, D.C.: World Bank.

Fleischer, David. 1994. Manipulações Casuísticas do Sistema Eleitoral durante o Período Militar, ou Como Usualmente o Feitiço Se Voltava contra o Feiticeiro. In *21 Años de Regime Militar: Balanços e Perspectivas,* edited by G. Soares and M. C. D'Araújo, 154–97. Rio de Janeiro: Fundação Getúlio Vargas.

Gibson, Edward, and Ernesto Calvo. 2000. Federalism and Low-Maintenance Constituencies: Territorial Dimensions of Economic Reform in Argentina. *Studies in Comparative International Development* 35 (3): 32–55.

Huber, Evelyne, and John D. Stephens. 2001. *Development and Crisis of the Welfare State: Parties and Politics in Global Markets.* Chicago: University of Chicago Press.

Immergut, Ellen M. 1992. The Rules of the Game: The Logic of Health Policy Making in France, Switzerland, and Sweden. In *Structuring Politics: Historical Institutionalism in Comparative Analysis,* edited by S. Steinmo, K. Thelen, and F. Longstreth, 57–89. Cambridge: Cambridge University Press.

Inda, R. 2002. *Nuevo Esquema de Financiamiento para Gobiernos Estatales.* Mexico City: Mexican Secretary of Treasury and Public Credit.

Leonardy, Uwe. 1999. The Institutional Structures of German Federalism. In *Recasting German Federalism: The Legacies of Unification,* edited by C. Jeffery. London: Pinter.

Lijphart, Arend. 1984. *Democracies: Patterns of Majoritarian and Consensus Government in Twenty-one Countries.* New Haven: Yale University Press.

———. 1999. *Patterns of Democracy: Government Forms and Performance in Thirty-six Countries.* New Haven: Yale University Press.

Linz, Juan J. 1978. *The Breakdown of Democratic Regimes: Crisis, Breakdown, and Reequilibration.* Baltimore: Johns Hopkins University Press.

———. 1985. De la Crisis de un Estado Unitario al Estado de las Autonomías. In *La España de las Autonomías,* edited by F. Fernández Rodríguez, 527–672. Madrid: Instituto de Estudios de Administración Local.

Linz, Juan J., and Alfred Stepan. 1996. *Problems of Democratic Transition and Consolidation: Southern Europe, South America, and Post-Communist Europe.* Baltimore: Johns Hopkins University Press.

———. 2000. Inequality Inducing and Inequality Reducing Federalism: With Special Reference to the "Classic Outlier"—the USA. Paper presented at the World Congress of the International Political Science Association, Quebec City.

———. 2001. Political Identities and Electoral Sequences: Spain, the Soviet Union and Yugoslavia. In A. Stepan, *Arguing Comparative Politics,* 200–212. Oxford: Oxford University Press.

Mainwaring, Scott. 1999. *Rethinking Party Systems in the Third Wave of Democratization: The Case of Brazil.* Stanford: Stanford University Press.

Mainwaring, Scott, and Timothy R. Scully, eds. 1995. *Building Democratic Institutions: Party Systems in Latin America.* Stanford: Stanford University Press.

Makler, Harry M. 2000. Bank Transformation and Privatization in Brazil: Financial Federalism and Some Lessons about Bank Privatization. *Quarterly Review of Economics and Finance* 40 (April): 45–69.

McAdam, D., et al. 1996. *Comparative Perspectives on Social Movements: Political Opportunities, Mobilizing Structures, and Cultural Framing.* Cambridge: Cambridge University Press.

Obinger, Herbert. 1998. Federalism, Direct Democracy, and Welfare State Development in Switzerland. *Journal of Public Policy* 18 (3): 241–63.

———. 2003. From Habsburg to Haider: Federalism and Social Policy in Austria. In *Federalism and Social Policy,* edited by S. Leibfried and H. Obinger. Washington, D.C.: Brookings Institution.

O'Donnell, Guillermo. 1994. Delegative Democracy. *Journal of Democracy* 5 (1): 55–69.

Rainwater, Lee. 1997. Inequality and Poverty in Comparative Perspective. Estudio/working paper 110. Institute Juan March, Madrid.

Requejo, Ferran. 2001. Political Liberalism in Multinational States: The Legitimacy of Plural and Asymmetrical Federalism. In *Multinational Democracies,* edited by A.-G. Gagnon and J. Tully, 110–32. Cambridge: Cambridge University Press.

Roeder, P. G. 1991. Soviet Federalism and Ethnic Mobilization. *World Politics* 43 (January): 196–232.

Samuels, David, and Richard Snyder. 2001. The Value of a Vote: Malapportionment in Comparative Perspective. *British Journal of Political Science* 31 (4): 651–72.

Schmitt, Nicolas. 1996. *Federalism: The Swiss Experience.* Pretoria: HSAC Publishers.

Shugart, M. S., and J. M. Carey. 1992. *Presidents and Assemblies: Constitutional Design and Electoral Dynamics.* Cambridge: Cambridge University Press.

Skalnik Leff, Carol. 1999. Democratization and Disintegration in Multinational States: The Breakup of the Communist Federations. *World Politics* 51 (2): 205–35.

Stepan, Alfred. 1988. *Rethinking Military Politics: Brazil and the Southern Cone.* Princeton: Princeton University Press.

———. 2000. Brazil's Decentralized Federalism: Bringing Government Closer to the Citizens? *Dædalus* 129 (2): 145–69.

Swenden, Wilfred. 2000. Federalism and Second Chambers: Regional Representation in Parliamentary Federalism. D.Phil. thesis, Oxford University.

Tarrow, Sidney. 1999. *Power in Movement: Social Movements, Collective Action, and Politics.* Cambridge: Cambridge University Press.

Tindal, C. R. 2000. *A Citizen's Guide to Government.* Toronto: McGraw-Hill Ryerson.

Tsebelis, George. 1995. Decision Making in Political Systems: Veto Players in Presidentialism, Parliamentarism, Multicameralism and Multipartyism. *British Journal of Political Science* 25:289–325.

———. 2002. *Veto Players: How Political Institutions Work.* Princeton: Princeton University Press.

Tsebelis, G., and J. Money. 1997. *Bicameralism.* New York: Cambridge University Press.

Weingast, Barry R. 1995. The Economic Role of Political Institutions: Market-Preserving Federalism and Economic Development. *Journal of Law, Economics, and Organization* 11 (April): 1–31.

Wildavsky, Aaron. 1985. Federalism Means Inequality. *Society* 22 (2): 42–50.

Contributors

Ernesto F. Calvo is an assistant professor of political science at the University of Houston. He has published articles on comparative political economy, territorial politics, and methodologies of ecological inference in *American Journal of Political Science, Electoral Studies, Studies in Comparative International Development,* and *Desarrollo Económico.* He is also co-editor, with Luis Abal Medina, of *El Federalismo Electoral Argentino* (Universidad de Buenos Aires, 2001).

Alberto Diaz-Cayeros is assistant professor at Stanford University and adjunct professor at the Instituto Tecnológico Autónomo de México. He has published articles and a book on Mexican federalism, regional politics, and the political economy of development.

Tulia G. Falleti is an assistant professor of political science at the University of Pennsylvania and was a postdoctoral fellow at the Kellogg International Institute for International Studies and an I. W. Killiam Postdoctoral Fellow at the University of British Columbia. She is the author of "Governing Governors: Coalitions and Sequences of Decentralization in Colombia, Argentina, and Mexico" (Ph.D. diss., Northwestern University) as well as articles on subnational politics in Latin America.

Edward L. Gibson is associate professor of political science and Charles Deering McCormick Professor of Teaching Excellence at Northwestern University. He is the author of *Class and Conservative Parties: Argentina in Comparative Perspective* (Johns Hopkins University Press, 1996) and several articles on party politics, federalism, and territorial politics.

Scott Mainwaring is Eugene Conley Professor of Political Science at the University of Notre Dame. He served as Director of the Kellogg Institute for International Studies from 1997 to 2002. His books include *The Third Wave of Democratization in Latin America: Advances and Setbacks* (Cambridge University Press, forthcoming, co-edited), *Democratic Accountability in Latin America* (Oxford University Press, forthcoming, co-edited), *Christian Democracy in Latin America* (Stanford University Press, forthcoming, co-edited), *Rethinking Party Systems in the Third Wave of Democratization: The Case of Brazil* (Stanford University Press, 1999).

Enrique Ochoa-Reza is a Ph.D. candidate in political science at Columbia University. He received his B.A. in Economics from the Instituto Tecnológico Autónomo de México and has a law degree from the Universidad Nacional Autónoma de México. He is completing his dissertation on the impact of federalism on income inequality, focusing on Mexico in comparative perspective.

Michael Penfold-Becerra holds a Ph.D in political science from Columbia University (1999). He is the author of *The Venezuelan Cost: Policy Options to Enhance Competitiveness* (Corporación Andina de Fomento, 2002) and is the co-editor of a volume on *Decentralization and Intergovernmental Relations in Latin America* (Nueva Sociedad, 2002). He has taught at Columbia College, Universidad de los Andes in Bogotá, and the Instituto de Estudios Superiores de Administración in Caracas.

David J. Samuels is associate professor of political science at the University of Minnesota. He is the author of *Ambition, Federalism, and Legislative Politics in Brazil* (Cambridge University Press, 2003).

Richard Snyder is associate professor of political science at Brown University. He is the author of *Politics after Neoliberalism: Reregulation in Mexico* (Cambridge University Press, 2001) and of numerous articles on comparative political economy and regime change.

Alfred Stepan is Wallace S. Sayre Professor of Government at Columbia University and was formerly Gladstone Professor of Government at All Souls College, Oxford University. He is a fellow of the American Academy of Arts and Sciences and of the British Academy. Among other books, he is the author of *Arguing Comparative Politics* (Oxford University Press, 2001) and co-author, with Juan J. Linz, of *Problems of Democratic Transition and Consolidation: Eastern Europe, Southern Europe, and Latin America* (Johns Hopkins University Press, 1996).

Index

Figures and tables are represented by the italicized letters *f* and *t* following the page number; notes are represented by *n* followed by the note number.